INTERNATIONAL ENERGY AGENCY

SECURITY OF GAS SUPPLY IN OPEN MARKETS

POWER AT A TURNING POINT

INTERNATIONAL ENERGY AGENCY
9, rue de la Fédération,
75739 Paris, cedex 15, France

ORGANISATION FOR ECONOMIC CO-OPERATION AND DEVELOPMENT

The International Energy Agency (IEA) is an autonomous body which was established in November 1974 within the framework of the Organisation for Economic Co-operation and Development (OECD) to implement an international energy programme.

It carries out a comprehensive programme of energy co-operation among twenty-six* of the OECD's thirty Member countries. The basic aims of the IEA are:

• to maintain and improve systems for coping with oil supply disruptions;

• to promote rational energy policies in a global context through co-operative relations with non-member countries, industry and international organisations;

• to operate a permanent information system on the international oil market;

• to improve the world's energy supply and demand structure by developing alternative energy sources and increasing the efficiency of energy use;

• to assist in the integration of environmental and energy policies.

IEA Member countries: Australia, Austria, Belgium, Canada, the Czech Republic, Denmark, Finland, France, Germany, Greece, Hungary, Ireland, Italy, Japan, the Republic of Korea, Luxembourg, the Netherlands, New Zealand, Norway, Portugal, Spain, Sweden, Switzerland, Turkey, the United Kingdom, the United States. The European Commission also takes part in the work of the IEA.

Pursuant to Article 1 of the Convention signed in Paris on 14th December 1960, and which came into force on 30th September 1961, the Organisation for Economic Co-operation and Development (OECD) shall promote policies designed:

• to achieve the highest sustainable economic growth and employment and a rising standard of living in Member countries, while maintaining financial stability, and thus to contribute to the development of the world economy;

• to contribute to sound economic expansion in Member as well as non-member countries in the process of economic development; and

• to contribute to the expansion of world trade on a multilateral, non-discriminatory basis in accordance with international obligations.

The original Member countries of the OECD are Austria, Belgium, Canada, Denmark, France, Germany, Greece, Iceland, Ireland, Italy, Luxembourg, the Netherlands, Norway, Portugal, Spain, Sweden, Switzerland, Turkey, the United Kingdom and the United States. The following countries became Members subsequently through accession at the dates indicated hereafter: Japan (28th April 1964), Finland (28th January 1969), Australia (7th June 1971), New Zealand (29th May 1973), Mexico (18th May 1994), the Czech Republic (21st December 1995), Hungary (7th May 1996), Poland (22nd November 1996), the Republic of Korea (12th December 1996) and Slovakia (28th September 2000). The Commission of the European Communities takes part in the work of the OECD (Article 13 of the OECD Convention).

FOREWORD

This study *Security of Gas Supply in Open Markets: LNG and Power at a Turning Point* is the successor of *The IEA Natural Gas Security Study* published in 1995. Since the 1995 publication, the gas industry in IEA countries has seen many impressive developments: *i)* progress in the opening to competition of gas and electricity markets, *ii)* the tremendous increase of gas-fired power generation worldwide as a new driver of gas demand, and *iii)* cost reductions in the LNG chain allowing more flexible LNG trade.

While proven worldwide gas reserves have increased faster than gas demand, OECD countries increasingly need to import gas, as the discovery of additional gas reserves in OECD countries has not kept pace with the depletion of gas reserves and the increase in gas demand. This growing import dependence calls for a greater awareness of gas policies in supplier countries and along ever longer pipelines. Given these new dynamics, it is time for a new look at the issue of gas security.

Based on input from the various stakeholders, official information from member governments as well as publicly available information, this study presents a comprehensive overview of the recent status of the gas industry in IEA countries. It analyses the most recent developments of security of gas supply in the three OECD regions in the context of open markets and in view of the new demand and supply trends. Annexes included in a CD-Rom present the views of the main stakeholders (governments, regulators, industry, customers and other organisations).

The study makes policy recommendations on security of gas supply for IEA policy makers and seeks to identify the regional and global challenges that governments and market players will face in the next 30 years. In open gas markets, supply and demand can usually be balanced by the market. The challenge for security of supply is to make sure that the market can always achieve this balance and that adequate investment all along the gas chain can be mobilised in a timely way.

With market opening, the role of governments has changed but is still very important: instead of managing the sector, they have to set objectives to minimise and mitigate the implications of increasing import dependence and to define the right framework to enable the markets to deliver reliable gas supplies from the production/import point to the final customer. In particular, governments have the responsibility for defining clear policies on security of gas supply and the responsibilities of each player.

This book is published under my authority as Executive Director of the International Energy Agency.

Claude Mandil,
Executive Director

ACKNOWLEDGEMENTS

The main authors of this book are Sylvie Cornot-Gandolphe, Principal Gas Expert, and Ralf Dickel, Head of the Energy Diversification Division. Anouk Honoré analysed and summarised the contributions of the IEA governments. The work was done under the supervision of Noé van Hulst, Director of the Office for Long-Term Cooperation and Policy Analysis of the International Energy Agency.

The book also benefited from the input by several IEA colleagues: Jun Arima, Fatih Birol, Jean-Yves Garnier, Klaus-Dietmar Jacoby, Emmanuel Bergasse, Mabrouka Bouziane, François Cattier, Dunia Chalabi, Doug Cooke, Laura Cozzi, Meredydd Evans, Peter Fraser, Rebecca Gaghen, Dagmar Graczyk, Kristine Kuolt, Dong-Wook Lee, Jeffrey Logan, Isabel Murray, Anne Neumann, Mieke Reece, Julia Reinaud, Olga Sorokina and Christof van Agt. Kathleen Gray, Jenny Gell and Virginia Prystay gave valuable assistance in producing and editing the book and the annexes.

Pierre Lefèvre, Fiona Davies and Loretta Ravera of the Publication Information Office provided essential support in producing this book. The special appreciation of the authors goes to Bertrand Sadin for his creative contribution in preparing all figures, the CD-Rom and the cover of the book. In addition, special thanks go to Muriel Custodio for her dedication in making this publication possible.

Representatives of the member governments carefully read the manuscript and amended it through useful suggestions and comments; in particular, the representatives of the US Department of Energy and the UK Department of Trade and Industry took great care and effort in checking the respective parts on the US and UK. The authors would like to extend their thanks to all IEA member governments for their written contributions to the book and their valuable comments.

The book benefited greatly from the contacts and constructive discussions with the following representatives of companies and associations, who contributed useful facts, data and insights into the gas industry and feedback on earlier drafts of the manuscript: Olivier Appert (Institut

Français du Pétrole), Sergei V. Balashov (OAO Gazprom), Peter Botschek (Cefic), Georges Bouchard (Gaz de France), Stéphane Caudron (Statoil), Marie-Françoise Chabrelie (Cedigaz), Peter Claes (IFIEC Europe), Wilfried Czernie (Ruhrgas), Sebastian Eyre (EnergyWatch), Simon Griew (National Grid Transco), Bruno Gruson (Total), Ali Hached (Sonatrach), Mark Hives (ExxonMobil International), Jess Bernt Jensen (GASTRA), Koji Kosugi (TEPCO), George Kowalski (UNECE), Pierre Lepesan (Gaz de France), Juho Lipponen (Eurelectric), Margot Loudon (Eurogas), Colin Lyle (Centrica), Philippe Mannoni (Gas Transmission Europe), Michael Mollner (Eurogas), Ahmed Mazighi (Sonatrach), Werner Nowak (Ruhrgas), Knud Petersen (Shell Gas & Power), Keiichi Ogi (Tokyo Gas), Brian Raggett (OGP), Howard Rogers (BP Gas Power & Renewables), John Ryan (APEC Energy Working Group), Philippe Sauquet (Total), René Snijder (Gasunie), Erik Sørensen (Energy Charter Secretariat), Helen Stack (Centrica), Roberta Stucchi (ENI Gas and Power) and Doug Wood (BP).

The final responsibility for the study lies with the authors.

TABLE OF CONTENTS

LIST OF TABLES IN TEXT

LIST OF FIGURES IN TEXT

PART C. ANNEXES (CD-Rom)

Annex 1. Views of IEA Governments on security of gas supply

- Introduction
- Australia
- Austria
- Belgium
- Canada
- Czech Republic
- Denmark
- Finland
- France
- Germany
- Greece
- Hungary
- Ireland
- Italy
- Japan
- Korea
- Luxembourg
- The Netherlands
- New Zealand
- Norway
- Portugal
- Spain
- Sweden
- Switzerland
- Turkey
- The United Kingdom
- The United States

Annex 2. Outcome of the Workshop with gas regulators on *Security of gas supply in liberalised markets*, Paris, 27 June 2003

- Background
- Programme and welcome
- Highlights

Annex 3. Views of gas operators on security of gas supply

- Introduction
- BP (United Kingdom)
- Centrica (United Kingdom)
- DONG Transmission/GASTRA A/S (Denmark)
- ENI (Italy)
- Eurogas
- Gasunie (The Netherlands)
- Gas Transmission Europe (GTE)
- Gaz de France (France)
- OAO Gazprom (Russian Federation)
- Ruhrgas (Germany)
- Shell Gas & Power (The Netherlands/United Kingdom)
- Sonatrach (Algeria)
- Statoil (Norway)
- Tokyo Gas (Japan)
- Total (France)
- Transco (United Kingdom)

Annex 4. Views of large gas customers/associations of gas customers on security of gas supply

- The European Chemical Industry Council (Cefic)
- Energywatch
- EURELECTRIC
- IFIEC Europe
- TEPCO

Annex 5. Views of other international and regional organisations/associations on security of gas supply

- APEC Energy Working Group
- Energy Charter Treaty
- The International Association of Oil and Gas Producers
- UN Economic Commission for Europe – Gas Centre

SECURITY OF GAS SUPPLY IN OPEN MARKETS: MAJOR ISSUES

⟨ In open gas markets, supply and demand can usually be balanced by the market. The challenge of security of supply is to make sure that the market can always clear supply and demand. Open markets allow customer choice. Eligible customers can choose their suppliers and eventually their own level of reliability of supply, but they are responsible for that choice. Open markets will not always result in lower prices for customers, but they will result in an efficient allocation of resources, capacity and investment. Compared to markets for commodities, the design of gas markets requires special consideration as gas delivery is capacity-bound and therefore supply is restricted in the short term, and because part of gas demand is price-inelastic, especially the household sector, which is even temperature-dependent. Therefore prices may be volatile, when capacity limits are close, and there is a risk that supply and demand do not meet for low-probability events, whatever their cause. ⟩

Governments in open gas markets play a different, but important role to ensure secure and reliable gas deliveries from the production/import point to the final customer. Instead of managing the sector, they have to set clear policy objectives all along the gas chain to manage the geopolitical implications of increasing import dependence and impacts on the environment, and to ensure the working of markets to deliver reliable gas supplies. At the time of state-owned gas companies, or private companies with exclusive concession rights, governments played an important role in the management of the sector but delegated responsibility for security of supply to these entities and made all customers pay for it. These companies were responsible for security of gas supply across the whole gas market. In open markets, governments have to define the right framework for the market players so that markets can deliver reliable gas supplies, and they have to make sure that market players follow the rules. Governments have the responsibility of creating a framework for security and for defining the responsibilities of each player. However, low-probability events (like supply interruptions and extreme temperatures) may not necessarily be valued by the market itself. Governments therefore should set objectives for reliability of gas supply, especially to ensure gas deliveries to household customers at extreme low temperatures. They should also foster demand-side response as one of the important policies to ensure security of supply. The opening of the gas (and electricity) market results in the development of hubs and market centres which prove a useful instrument to optimise the use of the capacity of the gas system, to bring gas to its highest value use and foster market transparency.

Governments may be concerned that market outcomes – like volatile prices, or high prices – may lead some industries to relocate to regions with lower gas/electricity prices. Governments may take unsatisfactory market outcomes as an impulse to rethink the framework and implement its modification to mitigate market outcomes in line with their policy. However, dealing with the day-to-day operation of the market is hardly the role of governments. While some of the arguments to ensure security of gas supply are similar to oil, the arguments for establishing stocks and a coordinated stock draw do not apply to gas. Strategic gas storage is much more expensive than oil storage and requires additional substantial investment into a spare transport infrastructure. Other instruments like interruptible contracts or fuel switching may be less expensive than strategic gas storage, if storage is possible at all. As the market is not yet global and disruptions only have local impact, a global response is not possible. It is therefore best to leave the design of the response mechanism to individual countries and their market players, taking into account the effect of the development of larger regional gas markets.

The global gas supply and demand balance is at a turning point. From 1971 to 2000 worldwide gas consumption more than doubled from 895 mtoe to 2,085 mtoe. *World Energy Outlook 2002 (WEO 2002)* projects another doubling to 4,203 mtoe by year 2030. Gas consumption for power generation was about a quarter of total gas consumption, or 207 mtoe, in 1971; a bit more than a third in 2000, 725 mtoe; and is expected to come close to half of total gas consumption, or 2,032 mtoe in 2030, so gas consumption for power generation almost triples every 30 years.

For OECD countries the trends in gas consumption look similar: from 1971 to 2000 gas consumption almost doubled from 653 to 1,143 mtoe and is projected to almost double again to 2,012 mtoe by 2030. Gas consumption for power generation was 117 mtoe in 1971, or about one-sixth of total gas consumption, increasing to 328 mtoe in 2000, or a bit more than a quarter of total gas consumption, and is projected to reach 958 mtoe in 2030 – almost half of gas consumption in OECD countries. So in OECD countries the trend towards increased use of gas in power generation is even more pronounced, due to increasing saturation in the residential, commercial and industrial sectors.

The import dependence of OECD countries is projected to increase from a total of 274 bcm/a or a share of about 20% of total gas consumption in 2000, to a total of 1091 bcm/a, or more than 40% of gas consumption. The major part of increase in gas imports is explained by the projected increase in gas used in power plants.

Gas has developed into the fuel of choice for the residential and commercial sectors, but also for process and small applications in the industry sector, wherever gas can be economically supplied. While gas can be replaced for each individual customer mainly by oil products, which define price limits for individual customers, many IEA countries have no large-scale alternative to gas on a country-wide scale. The use of gas is not only linked to a long-lasting investment decision on the customers' side, but also to large investment in the gas infrastructure, which would become obsolete in case of a substantial shortage of gas.

With domestic gas reserves of IEA countries on the decline, imports are going to cover an increasing part of gas demand in most IEA countries. This raises the issue of import levels from different non-OECD countries versus the ability of the market to handle a gas shortfall. It also raises the issue of the implications of uneven reform in countries along the gas chain.

The increase in gas use for power (and the dominance of gas as a fuel for new power generation since the beginning of the 1990s in many IEA countries) is driven by the high technical and economic efficiency of new gas turbines and CCGTs, as well as by the environmental advantages of gas compared to other fossil fuels. Projections show that there is likely to be a substantial increase in gas use in power generation in OECD countries, which, on balance, will have to be imported from non-OECD countries. The result will be a strong increase in import dependence in most OECD countries/regions and a strong increase in cross-border trade of gas by pipeline and as LNG.

For volume and diversification reasons, gas for export from an increasing number of resource-owning countries will mainly be developed as LNG. The LNG industry has now entered an era of unprecedented growth. New large markets are emerging, cost reductions along the LNG chain allow new projects which were uneconomic 20 years ago, and increased inter-regional trading adds flexibility and security to the global gas sector.

Larger regional markets are emerging with the opening of gas markets (in addition to the already strongly interlinked North American market), e.g., in the EU. With more flexible LNG trade, more trade develops between LNG buying countries, like Japan and Korea, and also in the Atlantic basin between parts of the EU and the US. The creation of larger markets offers more possibilities for underutilised capacity/volumes to find their way to other regions, with higher gas value, thereby creating higher liquid volumes on which to draw in case of shortage or extreme temperatures. Creating a larger (regional) marketplace may require extra investment into interconnection infrastructures, which so far have been built on the basis of national markets. This may require governments to define common standards (e.g., technical norms, gas quality, LNG specification and safety norms for LNG tankers), to foster inter-operability, and to arrange for the right framework to remove obstacles to cross-border investment and trade.

Increased links between open gas and power markets offer the chance for more efficient use of both systems. However, the reliability of each system must also be ensured in view of the interlinks between them. The increased use of gas in power generation combined with the parallel opening of both sectors creates operational and market links between the sectors. However, it must be observed that while the link is creating greater flexibility for the use of gas and for the production of electricity, both systems are capacity-bound. Experience shows the need to set reliability objectives, which take into account the interdependencies of the systems. The projected high dependence of power generation on imported gas might create a domino effect on the power sector in cases of gas supply shortages, if not anticipated.

The willingness of non-IEA gas-rich countries to develop their gas resources for export is key to the further development of gas markets in IEA countries that increasingly depend on such exports. This will require a stable balance of interests between gas importing and gas exporting countries. The import volumes of all OECD regions are increasing substantially and even the UK and US are becoming substantial net importers of gas. About 10% of world proved gas reserves are in OECD countries, whereas non-OECD gas reserves are highly concentrated. More than 50% are in three countries: almost 30% are in Russia, 15% in Iran, 9% in Qatar. While the investment decisions for exploration and production, transportation and other gas infrastructure, as well as on the use of gas, is best left to private investors, the decision on the depletion of natural resources is in most countries vested in the government of the resource-owning country. To optimise the use of their resources, they have to decide on the development path for their reserves, on domestic and export use, as well as on maximising the remuneration for the export of a finite resource. While maximising the rent income for a finite resource is a sensible objective for an exporting country, IEA gas importing countries will try to subject such rent transfers to competitive forces by promoting diversification of supply sources, routes and the use of other fuels. >

While IEA countries are interested in reliable gas supplies at competitive prices, governments of resource-owning countries will look for secured access for their gas to IEA markets and for a reliable income from selling their resources. Long-term contracts have been a useful instrument to create a stable balance between gas exporters and importers. With more open markets new, additional instruments develop, such as selling into a liquid market, as well as more flexible LNG deals, but long-term contracts will remain an important instrument, although with increasing flexibility as markets mature. While having a bankable gas market or a creditworthy gas buyer is a major precondition for viable investment in gas production and export infrastructure, a clear framework for foreign investors and a neutral conflict resolution mechanism would help to mobilise financing for new export capacity at favourable conditions. A suitable way to address how to create a fair and stable balance between gas producing and consuming countries is to foster more dialogue between them.

Governments have to ensure that investment for all parts of the gas chain can be mobilised in a timely way and in competition with other capital use. The increase in gas demand requires the alignment of timely investment in all parts of the gas chain, from exploration and production to transporting the gas to the market, as well as investment into the distribution and gas consuming infrastructure, especially gas-fired power. While governments cannot and should not play a role in managing geological, technical or commercial risks, they should help to reduce sovereign and regulatory risks. This is particularly important in creating clear and stable frameworks for investment, especially in cross-border infrastructure, where there is the risk of abuse of market position. They should also help with the adoption of clear and streamlined siting rules, while minimising regulatory risk by creating a stable and predictable regulatory framework, which would allow investors free commercial disposal of their property and, where regulated, a risk-adjusted rate of return competitive with other investment opportunities.

The choice of instruments to hedge long-term risks should be left to market players. Both the industry from all parts of the gas chain and the resource-owning countries have an interest in being able to hedge their decisions dedicating investment or gas resources on a long-term basis. A variety of instruments linked to the development and maturity of reforms in each gas market/region has evolved to hedge the risks stemming from the long-term nature of the gas business:

■ Long-term sales contracts associated with long-term transportation contracts;

■ Vertical integration along the gas chain;

■ Access to liquid markets (by investing into LNG regasification terminals and import pipelines) and to financial instruments derived from liquid gas markets.

Governments of IEA countries should leave the choice of instruments to the market players concerned; they should not favour or disfavour any of these instruments, as long as they do not negatively impact competition.

In spite of generic and global developments the status of market opening and the challenges of security of gas supply are specific for each IEA region and in some cases even for single countries:

North America: open gas markets introduced in the 1980s were able to mobilise private investment in time for expansion of the infrastructure and the development of reserves. These markets led to the development of liquid hubs and gas exchanges and to a more efficient use of the gas infrastructure. So far gas supply and demand have been balanced by markets. Upstream, the role of governments was restricted to rule setting and in the case of Canada, also encompassed rent taking – however, with some restrictions on E&P in US federal/state owned land, offshore and in arctic areas. The decline in production due to the depletion of North American gas reserves combined with the massive increase in gas use in CCGTs with only limited fuel-switching capacity, resulted recently in rising gas prices so that some industrial gas users considered moving to other regions. This situation signalled the need to increase LNG imports substantially to satisfy the projected use of gas in power generation. After the requirements were dropped for third-party access (TPA) in LNG terminals, many new projects emerged. While the chances of obtaining diversified LNG supplies are good, the expected large share of LNG supply may raise the question whether interruptions of LNG supplies can be compensated by the market.

Europe: there is a marked difference between the UK gas market and the continental gas market. While the UK was a frontrunner in opening the gas market, the opening in the continental part of the EU happened more recently with the two EU Gas Directives and their implementation in EU member states. The opening of the gas market in the UK resulted in the establishment of the National Balancing Point (NBP), a liquid (notional) market place where gas is traded on a daily basis. It assisted the massive use of gas for power generation in the 1990s and, in parallel, a remarkable increase in gas production from the UK continental shelf (UKCS). However, lacking large new finds in frontier areas and with the UKCS becoming a mature gas province, within a short time span the UK will change from being a net gas exporter to a massive net importer. Long-term contracts are still predominant in the UK, though now they are increasingly linked with the price at the NBP and in some cases also use the NBP as the delivery point. The UK is well underway to attract the additional supplies and the necessary investment to adapt its infrastructure, although with some specific challenges caused by the differing quality of the gas to be imported. Another challenge to be addressed is the link between gas and power, as a large increase in imported gas will go to gas-fired power plants.

In continental Europe, the implementation of the two EU Gas Directives is underway with some decisive changes to become binding as of 1 July 2004. Several of the challenges for reliable gas supplies set before the gas sector by the Directives still lie ahead, such as finding the right allocation between the responsibility for reliable gas supplies and the effects of unbundling; finding the right incentives for the enlargement of the transport, import and storage infrastructure by allowing for a rate of return which is competitive in a global context. Creating more regulatory stability by giving the industry the time to adapt to and to fulfil the requirements stemming from the Directives currently in force is now of paramount importance.

In view of the increasing import dependence from only a few gas exporting countries, long-term contracts will remain an important instrument to ensure gas supplies. In the continental gas market, some hubs are developing, although they still do not have a deep liquidity. However, beyond the challenge of creating open gas markets in each EU member state, the challenge remains to create a single gas market for the EU, which requires rules, standards and technical regulations as uniform as possible. The infrastructure, which was built on a national basis driven by large import projects, must be adapted to allow for more EU-wide gas trade and liquidity. As in North America, the projected strong increase of gas in power generation, which will, on balance, be based on imported gas, raises challenges of increased gas import shares from non-IEA countries and their impact on the gas and power sector. The pace of supplier and transit gas sector reform has important implications for the quality and reliability of security of gas supply to European end-use customers.

The EU is to a large extent dependent on Algerian and Russian gas imports, which are projected to increase substantially. Both countries have a long-standing record as reliable suppliers, fulfilling their contractual obligations. However, in 1980, Algeria cut off supplies to its US and European customers to make them accept unilateral changes in contract terms. While the interruption was only temporary for Europe, it led to the collapse of Algerian LNG trade with the US. There is some concern about the long-term future of gas imports from Algeria and Russia: neither of these countries has yet a clear gas upstream nor transport regulation. In addition, gas production and export are managed by companies which, in addition to their commercial role, exercise sovereign rights of the state in the gas sector. Another concern is that the transit of Russian gas to the EU is highly concentrated in Ukraine, a country which is struggling to find an appropriate regulatory framework for its gas sector. Increased diversification of suppliers and supply routes, and provision of market flexibility (back-up supply and/or demand management), will remain crucial issues for the EU.

OECD Pacific: the gas industries of the OECD countries in the Pacific region differ very much from each other: Japan and South Korea are almost entirely dependent on LNG supplies, Australia is becoming a large LNG exporter and New Zealand is so far self-sufficient. While Japan and South Korea were the driving force of the growth in the LNG trade, market reforms in both countries has led to more uncertainty about future gas demand growth. This has led the LNG importing companies to seek more volumes and pricing flexibility in their LNG contracts. Increased competition among LNG suppliers, as well as cost reductions in the LNG chain, allow producers to accept more flexible LNG terms. Security of supply in the region has always been ensured through diversification of supplies and infrastructure. The recently increased flexibility of LNG trade allowed importing companies to swap LNG cargoes, e.g., to exchange cargoes to meet peak gas demand. It allowed Japanese and Korean buyers to successfully manage the seven-month shut-down of the Indonesian liquefaction plant at Arun in 2001.

Policy-makers now have to define the objectives and the framework for the global role of gas for decades to come. Decisions for major expansions and replacement of gas and electricity infrastructure have to be taken soon. These decisions stem largely from a need to enlarge and replace power generating capacity (built in the aftermath of the 1973/74 and 1979/80 oil price crisis) with a view to minimising environmental effects and GHG emissions. Due to declining domestic gas reserves in IEA countries and the increased use of gas for commercial purposes, but also for GHG mitigation reasons, the overall dependence on imported gas will increase. That raises the question of a stable balance between the interests of gas exporting and importing countries, the issue of diversification of gas supply and the potential of the gas market to cover any interruption of gas supply, or that of the electricity market to mobilise back-up capacity to compensate for any shortfall in gas supplies.

RECOMMENDATIONS

In open markets, supply and demand are balanced by the market. Therefore, IEA governments should rely as much as possible on competitive markets and ensure their working. However, because of the limits of what open and competitive markets can deliver with regard to low-probability events, and in view of the high transaction costs for small customers, and markets being subject to sovereign decisions of resource-owning and transit countries, the following measures should be considered by IEA governments:

WORKING OF THE MARKETS

- Ensuring that markets can work in an unimpeded way;

- Defining clear policies on security of gas supply, objectives and responsibilities of different players for security of supply, in particular for low-probability events. According to the national features and circumstances, governments may define minimum requirements, but should leave the mix of instruments to the market;

- Ensuring national regulatory frameworks conducive to business, comprising: clarity on which regulation applies, regulatory stability, lean regulation, providing a competitive rate of return in regulated business, leaving implementation as much as possible to industry, with the government only monitoring the fulfilment of objectives. Streamlining and coordinating non-economic regulatory procedures;

- Promoting international harmonisation of regulatory standards, e.g. within the framework of the Energy Charter Treaty (ECT) or the World Trade Organisation (WTO);

- Minimising commercial restrictions on the use of investment (e.g., third-party access requirements) to stimulate new investment. TPA should not apply to new investment which can be contested, such as LNG regasification terminals, import pipelines and storage. If TPA is necessary for new investment, an open season procedure is appropriate;

- Monitoring investment performance and making the status public. If the market fails to generate the necessary investment on its own, governments should act, i.e., provide additional market incentives;

- Monitoring the link between gas and electricity with regard to synergies, but also systemic stress, for reliable supplies of both gas and electricity;

- Fostering demand-side response. The opening of the household sector to competition should be in line with its demand-side response possibility.

IMPORT DEPENDENCE

- Fostering diversification of supply (including routes and modes of imports of natural gas and LNG whenever possible): no single import-related risk – country or infrastructure – should exceed the possible compensation by the market and the range of instruments market players have developed;

- Fostering a dialogue of IEA member countries with producing and transit countries. This dialogue can be reinforced by international mechanisms such as the ECT and the WTO which can promote convergence of market principles and practices along the entire gas chain mitigating risks for investors and consumers alike;

- Removing obstacles to cross-border gas trade: confirm the international framework for long-term contracts and for upstream/downstream integration all along the gas chain. Supporting the investment climate in those countries where access to resources is possible;

- Being prepared to suspend restrictions on exploration and production, where possible, to compensate for serious supply disruptions and having an emergency plan ready to deal with the effects of serious supply disruptions.

GAS TO POWER

Countries where the volume of imported gas represents a major part of the gas input into power generation should mitigate the impacts of gas supply disruptions on the power sector:

- Ensuring dual-firing capacity plus minimum standards for reserve of back-up fuel (even if the fuel is distillates; if necessary, allowing temporary exemption from environmental restrictions);

- Promoting back-up power generating capacity based on fuels other than imported gas (e.g., coal, nuclear, heavy fuel oil), to be able to bridge a long-lasting interruption of a large gas supply source (e.g., by mothballing old coal-fired power plants or allowing, if necessary, for an exemption from GHG restrictions).

LNG

- Streamlining siting procedures for regasification terminals;

- Fostering uniformity and compatibility of shipping standards and LNG quality;

- Considering creating an international forum on safety and other technical standards.

GENERIC

- Ensuring adequate staffing in national governments and international organisations to be able to handle the policy discussion on gas, independent of regulatory agencies;

- Using the IEA as the coordinator and facilitator for IEA governments to exchange views and best practices on security of gas supply.

EXECUTIVE SUMMARY

The starting point of this study is that in open gas markets, gas supply and demand can increasingly be balanced by the market. Security of gas supply can be defined as the capability to manage, for a given time, external market influences which cannot be balanced by the market itself.

Compared with other commodities, gas is special: *i)* it is capacity-bound to highly capital-intensive transportation and distribution infrastructure, and *ii)* there is little demand-side response, especially in the household sector. The challenge therefore is to design the market: *i) in the short run* to successfully allocate gas volumes available within the capacity restrictions to its highest market value and *ii) in the medium to longer run* to mobilise the gas resources and incentivise the infrastructure investment necessary to develop and bring them to the marketplace in time to meet demand.

The key issues therefore are to ensure that markets will, to a maximum extent, provide secure and reliable gas supply all the way to the final customer and deliver timely signals and competitive incentives for investment to guarantee secure supplies in the future.

PART A – GLOBAL/GENERIC DEVELOPMENTS

A changed role for governments and contracts in open gas markets

Reliability and security of gas supply: role of markets and governments

In open markets, supply and demand can be balanced by the market according to the preferences of market participants. Open markets ensure that gas goes to its highest value use. They provide a variety of instruments to mitigate external market influences. However, open markets raise new issues.

With market reforms, no one single entity is responsible for security of gas supply across the *whole* gas market; each company is responsible for its own customers only, and for its part of the gas chain (except for integrated companies).

Open markets will not by themselves value investment in insurance assets to ensure secure supplies to the end-consumer under low-probability/high-impact events, for instance, extreme weather conditions or a large non-technical disruption of supplies. As these events have a very low probability of occurring, market players will not invest in insurance assets against such events if there is no incentive for them to do so.

Therefore, while open markets provide consumers with choice and more efficiency, market reform also changes the well-established business environment that has supported security of supply, and raises new issues that policy-makers must address. Where possible, market mechanisms should be the basis of security decisions. Nevertheless, governments do have a role to play:

■ In providing a market framework and its implementation that ensure gas markets can work properly;

■ In setting a framework in which risks can be managed and costs reduced, in particular, through securing an international framework for investment and trade, and facilitating interconnection and exchanges among neighbouring countries;

■ In determining acceptable reliability levels, especially where small customers and safety are concerned;

■ In providing a clear policy for dealing with emergency situations.

The emergence of spot trading

Open markets may come with volatile or high prices. These high or volatile prices will give all market participants the signals that the system may be close to its limits so that market participants on the demand and on the supply side can act accordingly – both short and long term – thereby improving security of supply. On the other hand, volatile prices may lead to speculative behaviour instead of investment, and high prices may lead to the outsourcing of gas-intensive industries. This must be expected in a global economy, but may cost jobs, creating social and political problems. Governments may be concerned about market outcomes and may take them as an impulse to rethink the framework and implement its modification to mitigate market outcomes in line with their policy. However, dealing with the day-to-day operation of the market is hardly the role of governments.

With the development of more open markets and liquid and deep marketplaces, investors will increasingly base their decision on their assessment of future market development, as seen in North America and the UK. However, in export projects based on the dedication of large gas reserves and the development of large transportation infrastructure, most investors will look for a long-term hedge of their investment risk by using elements of vertical integration or by using the feature of long-term contracts, adapting them to the new market realities.

The evolving contractual framework

For each link along the chain – from exploration and production to the final user who pays for the gas itself or the service created by the gas – long-term contracts may play a useful role and have been applied to hedge long-term risks where the instruments of liquid and open markets were not applicable or useful.

Long-term contracts between suppliers and importers have been the basis of the development of cross-border trade in Europe. Experience in open markets shows that long-term contracts do not disappear with market liberalisation, but will continue to be a fundamental part of the gas supply mix. Even if long-term contracts remain a major part of future gas supplies, their structure and pricing clauses are likely to undergo substantial changes. Already, changes in structure and pricing of new continental European and Asian long-term gas supply contracts can be observed as a reaction to market reform and a portfolio approach by buyers: *i)* shorter terms for new contracts (between 8 to 15 years in Europe and 15 to 20 years in Asia instead of the more traditional 20-25 years); *ii)* smaller volumes (for new contracts or renewals of LNG contracts): 0.5 to 3 bcm/a; these are favoured by the increasing share of gas in power generation and the multiplication of regasification plants; *iii)* greater flexibility in reviewed contractual terms (more flexibility in ToP and swing); *iv)* new price indices (electricity pool prices and spot gas prices).

However, for new greenfield LNG projects there is still a trend to have a major part of the output capacity sold under long-term contracts of 20 to 25 years as an anchor for the project. Whereas long-term contracts allow the financing of large new gas supply sources, spot contracts, which are emerging in Europe, allow a short- and medium-term balancing of supply and demand. Therefore, they offer more efficient use of existing infrastructure and thereby better flexibility and security. They are seen as complementary: spot trading for efficient short-term balancing and long-term contracts for securing long-term supply and large-scale investments.

For forty years, in gas contracts both in the UK and continental Europe, as well as in Asia, netback pricing based on the replacement value was used in long-term contracts. This concept allowed gas to compete with alternative fuels on the buyers' markets, while covering the costs of bringing the gas to the market place – actually to the burner tip – left the remainder for the producers/the resource owner. This fostered competitiveness (in the sectors targeted by the price formula) and gave the resource owner the maximum value for a predictable sales volume.

The pricing issue is more complicated when gas is sold for power generation, where competition occurs ultimately at the busbar. The problem is the difference in the long-run marginal cost and the short-run marginal cost merit order. The benefit of a gas-fired CCGT is not only its higher electric efficiency but also the much lower specific investment costs. This raises the question of how to split the investment premium, which, according to the netback philosophy, would mainly go to the gas seller. The move away from oil-linked price clauses in long-term contracts to contracts with gas-linked pricing poses a substantial challenge to gas sellers, reflecting the major changes in the marketplace.

Market reforms fragment demand, at a time when European supplies from non-OECD countries are becoming more concentrated. Suppliers from non-OECD countries so far retain monopoly structures for their gas export sales.

One reaction of non-EU suppliers to regulatory changes and a perceived high regulatory and market risk is to move downstream, in order to ensure their market outlets and hedge their income.

The new pattern of natural gas supply/demand in OECD countries: impact of the power sector

The global gas industry is in many aspects at a turning point

The gas industry worldwide and in OECD countries is now at a turning point in many aspects, demand, market, trade and supply: *i)* gas demand is changing with a new demand wave triggered by gas to power, *ii)* the gas sectors are opened up to more competition with a new market design, and increased interlink between the gas market and the electricity market, *iii)* the global gas trade is shifting to more LNG trade allowing more flexibility and the mobilisation of more reserves, and *iv)* most IEA countries (except Australia, Canada and Norway) are now becoming import dependent.

The role of gas to cover the increase in electricity demand will differ from country to country, but will certainly be supported by the policy to mitigate GHG emissions by the power sector. The prospects of using more gas for power generation to satisfy the increased demand for power will require additional import of gas. As OECD domestic production is not expected to cover the projected growth, on balance, the increased volumes required by the power sector will be imported gas. Overall, there is no lack of proven gas reserves worldwide and an impressive number of new supply projects – mainly LNG but also some pipeline projects – show the willingness of reserve owners and investors to supply the needs of the markets. However, the interface for imported gas for power generation will need to be addressed.

Impact on security of gas supply of the growing use of gas for power generation

The impressive increase in gas for power generation in the last ten years has been driven by technological development, by the steady increase in efficiency of gas turbines and combined cycles, while specific costs of installed capacity decreased. The combination of gas as a clean and easy to handle fuel with the high efficiency of the new gas turbines and CCGTs makes gas the fuel of choice for power generation to minimise local pollution and GHG emissions. In addition, because of the low economies of scale of gas-fired power, new capacity can easily be adapted to the development of demand and be deployed close to consumption without loss of economic efficiency. Gas-fired power fits well into competitive gas and electricity markets. >

The increase in gas-fired power generation capacity in many OECD countries created a new link between their gas and electricity markets. The use of substantial gas volumes in the power sector brings in a new dimension of price elasticity of gas demand, both short term and long term, based on the alternatives to gas for power generation offered by the electricity system in its totality. On the other hand, as the gas and the electricity systems become more closely interlinked the reliability of the two systems has to be assessed in combination.

Gas use for power generation has become the driver for a second wave of gas demand, as the traditional gas market segments are approaching saturation in many OECD countries. The increased use of gas for power generation has strong implications for both the long-term external security of supply and the short-term reliability of the power and gas systems, because when gas enters the electricity sector, it is the last fuel in the merit order, just before oil products in peaking plants. Governments may also be concerned about the impact thereof on future gas prices as well as the issue of the volatility of gas prices. The increased interdependence between the gas and electricity systems must be addressed.

The rising use of gas in the power sector raises the question of the competitiveness of natural gas against other power alternatives, and what effect this has on gas prices. The increasing use of CCGT plants in the generating systems may affect short-term gas prices, since they can run as multi-fired plants, but would then require lighter oil distillates. This alters the economics of dual-firing (compared to the past, when most dual-firing was based on dual-fired boilers able to burn heavy fuel oil), since lighter distillates, such as gasoil, are more expensive than heavy fuel oil, and shift the balance of back-up fuels away from an almost exclusive use of heavy fuel oil to more and more light distillates. A major risk associated with gas-fired generation in CCGTs in competitive markets is the price volatility of natural gas. Electricity prices are going to be affected by gas price volatility.

Basing large-scale power production to a greater extent on imported gas is a new feature, driven not only by environmental concerns but also by electricity market reforms. This raises the issue of reliability of electricity supply in case of a gas supply disruption, and the question of possible back-up fuels for gas in power plants. >

<The impact of a gas supply disruption on electricity security will depend on the flexibility developed in both systems. Although 50% of power capacity based on gas is multi-fired, the alternative fuel will be oil distillate, which is much more expensive than fuel oil. CCGT operators do not always have enough economic incentives to store the alternative back-up fuel (even for short periods). In addition, environmental legislation may restrict the use of any alternative fuel and seriously limit fuel-switching possibilities. >

The increased use of gas in power generation does not create security of supply problems at present. However, it indicates a need for governments to monitor future developments, in particular in countries or regions where the growing use of gas in power generation is based on increased gas imports. Concerns over security of supply do not justify restricting the use of gas in power generation, however, as long as there is a reasonable portfolio.

Impact of new technological developments on security of gas supply

Technological developments have helped to shape every aspect of gas market demand, supply and trade, and thereby have an impact on security of gas supply. The development of even more efficient gas turbines in the 1980s and 1990s allowed the spectacular growth of gas demand in the power sector. On the supply side, 3D and 4D seismic and large computers to evaluate seismic data, along with the introduction of horizontal drilling substantially improved the finding and recovery rates of gas deposits. Cost reductions in the LNG chain are transforming regional markets into a wide global market. Offshore pipelines can now be built at water depths of 2,000 metres, allowing trade between countries which was previously technically impossible.

The larger-scale use of gas in cars, e.g., in fuel cells, remains a challenge, as costs need to be brought down to a level competitive with cars based on the traditional combustion engine.

The more imminent technological developments, which are aimed primarily at reducing costs, will increase security of supply by enabling access to resources and enlarging the size of gas markets due to the higher economic reach of gas transportation. Major cost reductions in gas transportation are still expected, in particular for high-pressure long-distance pipelines and LNG. This should foster a remarkable development of cross-border gas trade needed to satisfy the increase in demand in OECD countries.

The role of LNG in security of gas supply

< Tremendous cost reductions have been experienced in all parts of the LNG chain in recent years. The fall in tanker prices over the last decade led to a much wider economic reach of LNG transportation. The dramatic cost reductions for LNG liquefaction trains, especially for expansion trains, but also for new trains such as the Trinidad and Tobago project, made LNG projects viable even if only part of the capacity is secured by long-term sales. This created an amount of contractually free LNG export capacity, necessary to provide flexibility of LNG supply. The recent re-opening of two US east-coast terminals and the numerous proposed projects to build new terminals in the US and Mexico provide an attractive market outlet, able to absorb all volumes within the capacity of the terminals. >

As most of so far undeveloped gas reserves are located far away from OECD markets, it is clear that LNG will play a key role to bring this gas to the market, when distance or natural and political obstacles make pipeline transport impossible.

< The growing supply of LNG, accompanied by the increased flexibility in LNG trade, which can physically be directed to the highest value market, are adding to the security of gas supply. Contractual arrangements are also more flexible. Spot and flexible LNG purchases are increasingly used to cover part of peak gas demand. Even though a global gas or global LNG

market may still be a long way off, LNG is already linking different markets together, by allowing shifting volumes between regions, benefiting from differences in their supply and demand balance. Indirectly this adds to the market flexibility of formerly non-connected marketplaces. Some recent events, like the shutdown of the Indonesian liquefaction plant in Arun due to violent attacks and the accident in Algeria's Skikda, have demonstrated the increase in security of gas supply due to the growing flexibility of LNG trade. >

The LNG trade is changing and adapting to new market conditions. There is growing recognition on the part of both producers and consumers of the increasing role of short-term and spot sales. These sales play a niche function to sell spare build-up capacity on the producing side, and to complement long-term purchases for buyers. While long-term contracts will remain dominant in the foreseeable future, spot sales (which mean short-term deals or the sale of one cargo) are expected to take a growing share. However, most experts agree that this development will not lead to large-scale trading as happens in the oil market, with an extensive paper as well as physical market. There is an overall consensus that LNG spot trade may amount to 15-30% of global LNG trade.

A more flexible approach to and a wider range of pricing is emerging in the LNG industry. Suppliers are adopting different pricing policies according to the buyers' market. For instance, Qatar, which sells in the three main LNG markets, has pegged its LNG sales to crude oil prices in Japan, to Henry Hub spot prices in the US, to NBP spot prices in the UK, and to fuel oil prices in continental Europe.

Competition between suppliers is fierce as more and more countries are seeking to monetise their gas resources. Due to lower specific costs, project sponsors are absorbing greater risks but also have the potential for higher rewards. Greenfield projects and expansion trains are moving forward without all volumes sold under long-term contracts. The vertical risk-sharing of long-term contracts – still widely used for greenfield projects – is increasingly complemented by vertical integration and by risk taking in liquid markets. In particular, greater integration through equity sharing by various parties along the chain, e.g., upstream equity investment by the buyer and downstream equity by the seller, evolves as an instrument to improve security of supply.

However, these positive developments for security of supply, including long-term access to more gas resources and extra options to provide additional gas volumes for low-probability events, also bring more import dependence. The development of the LNG trade and industry raises several issues, linked with the location of LNG sources, the financing required to expand production/liquefaction and trade, and the safety of LNG in general.

PART B – REGIONAL ISSUES

Security challenges differ between OECD regions

While all IEA countries have embarked on gas market reform, the basic features of the gas industry vary strongly between IEA members, as do the starting conditions and the status of gas market reform. The existence of domestic gas resources, the development of supply and demand, the depth and liquiditiy of marketplaces, the role of gas in the power sector and the interlink between the gas and the power sector differ from one country to another. Similarly, what can be covered by the market mechanism in the short run as well as in the long run differs between the various IEA regions and has a corresponding impact in shaping the security of supply issue.

Security of gas supply in North America

In North America, the market plays a primary role to secure supply through supply and demand response to price changes. Due to the large resource base and the possibility of a large, well-interconnected marketplace to react in the short and long term to any curtailment of supply, it can be expected that prices will be able to balance supply and demand in North America, both in the short and the long term. In particular, it can be expected that the capacity of the US/North American market will be sufficient to meet the demand of sectors with inelastic demand.

However, the market outcome may not be satisfactory, due to high prices and high price volatility and their impact on gas-intensive industry and household customers' bills. Demand destruction (e.g., the relocation of gas-intensive industries to countries with low-cost gas resources) may be an unwelcome market outcome.

⟨The North American market is at a turning point, from a self-sufficient market to a partly import-dependent market. In this new environment, access to secure and diversified long-term supply both from domestic and external sources is essential for future security of gas supply. LNG can play an important role, bringing access to world gas resources and the ability to react quickly to changing market conditions. ⟩

Governments might reconsider the access to domestic resources not open for exploration and production so far, while giving due consideration to environmental concerns, and continue to facilitate the building of new LNG receiving terminals by removing regulatory and local barriers. To the extent that the North American market becomes dependent on a significant share of LNG imports, the question of external security of supply should be addressed.

⟨Demand-side response will become an important component of future security of supply, which will allow curving peak gas demand and alleviate tight gas supply situations. Increasing fuel-switching capacity in power and industrial sectors in particular will serve to buffer short-term pressures on the supply/demand balance. ⟩

As the supply structure is changing, new investment will be required in transportation and storage infrastructure to meet the future needs of the market. The possibility of relying on long-term contracts and the allowance of appropriate rates of return are two important instruments to foster the building of new pipelines and storage.

Another challenge is the increasing share of gas in power generation, especially when linked to a reduced capability to switch at short term to other fuels. A long-term issue is to what extent investment in other large-scale power production capacity (like coal or nuclear) is restricted due to regulations which make it very difficult, if not impossible, to choose a fuel other than gas. While wind and other "green power" may be promoted by some states, their contribution to the overall electricity mix is projected to remain low in the foreseeable future.

Security of gas supply in OECD Europe

The European gas market is undergoing substantial changes. These changes are driven by major trends: the increase in the use of gas for power generation driven both by market reform and concerns about GHG emissions; the Gas Directive 2003/55/EC accelerating market opening and the unbundling of functions; new actors on the demand side; increasing imports from non-OECD countries; and the shift in the EU eastern border. Profound changes are taking place in the political structure of Europe with the enlargement from 15 to 25 member countries in May 2004 and discussions for further enlargement to the south-east.

Increasing demand will spur the need to build new pipelines and LNG terminals, and increase storage capacity and interconnectivity of the gas grids. Supply and transportation flexibility will decrease as imports have to come from more remote areas and exporters seek to make best use of their assets. This will be partly compensated by increased LNG supplies, which offer more and more flexibility and additional *ad hoc* supplies if the price is competitive with that of other LNG importing regions.

Challenges for security of supply in OECD Europe come not only from a national dimension – which is key – but also from a regional and global dimension. For any EU country, the dimension of a single European market is increasingly important for security of supply as cross-border gas trade develops. A clear understanding of the roles of governments, regulators and companies of the European countries and of the European Commission is essential. With the development of a more flexible LNG market the dimension of global competition with other LNG importers for LNG supplies and investment into the LNG chain is becoming relevant.

The key external challenge of the European market is how to reconcile the objective of competition with the need for many European countries to secure future supplies at competitive conditions in a timely manner from non-OECD Europe. The continental European gas industry is characterised by: *i)* a capital-intensive supply infrastructure and customers who are bound by substantial long-term investment to using gas, and *ii)* a linkage of that infrastructure to remote production facilities, involving long lead-times for investments and considerable reliance on producing countries (increasingly from non-OECD regions), with only a few players involved. The European Commission's recognition of the importance of long-term contracts for gas supply acknowledges that situation. On the buying side, a credible commitment by the buyer is essential. The buyer has to be given sufficient room to develop the capabilities and the financial strength to aggregate demand, and to purchase and deliver gas to the market in time. A major element is to provide the incentives to invest and the instrument to hedge long-term investment into the transportation infrastructure, such as the possibility of long-term transportation contracts. While much can be left to unregulated competition, where regulation is necessary, it should provide for an internationally competitive rate of return.

Two major internal aspects of market reforms for security of supply are the unbundling of activities – which in turn leads to the unbundling of responsibilities for security of supply – and the lack of clear market signals and incentives for investments in assets for low-probability/high-impact events. Governments thus retain a key role and the overarching responsibility for security of supply, even if the management of security of supply shifts away from governments and incumbent companies to all market players.

Algeria and Russia are major exporters to the OECD European market. After the accident at the Skikda LNG plant in January 2004, which completely destroyed three liquefaction trains, the Algerian oil and gas company, Sonatrach, has been able to meet its contractual commitments by boosting exports by pipeline and from its second LNG plant.

Russia plays an important role for current and future European supply. It is expected that Russian gas exports to Europe will continue to rise. Russia is also considering targeting new markets in Asia (pipeline gas and LNG) as well as entering the Atlantic LNG business. Growing domestic and export sales will call for higher investment in all links in the gas supply chain over the coming decades. Most of the capital will be needed for upstream developments to replace declining production from the maturing Western Siberian super-giant fields that have been the backbone of the Russian gas industry for decades. But a failure to implement much-needed market reforms in Russia, including raising domestic prices to cost recovering levels and giving third parties effective, non-discriminatory access to Gazprom's monopoly national transmission system, could impede the development of new reserves and the financing of new projects as this would limit the opportunities for independents to develop their own reserves.

Especially important is the challenge of creating a competitive industry structure in the gas sector and addressing the dominant role of Gazprom. The emergence of independent gas producers is a first step to create more competition, but more will be needed in view of the enormous investment challenges ahead. A problem inherited from the Soviet Union – compounded by geography – is the interlink of the gas pipeline systems of the Central Asian countries to the Russian pipeline system as a main link to reach the European market. The issue raised is how to best mobilise the substantial gas reserves of countries like Turkmenistan to contribute to secure gas supplies to the EU.

It is in the interest of the EU's future gas supplies that Russia succeed in mobilising the investment for additional gas export projects. In the long run, the best basis for security of gas supply and security of revenue will be the successful transition to a market economy and a gas industry open to competition in Russia and the transit states, and the successful creation of open gas and electricity markets in the EU. All decisions along the gas chain would then be more uniformly driven by competition and markets. In the meantime the dialogue between the EU and Russia remains vital in furthering a joint understanding of the upcoming investment challenges needed to maintain secure gas deliveries in the future. It will also be important to reinforce proven instruments for gas exports, like long-term contracts and joint ventures, while adapting them to the new realities of opened markets in the EU and to the changes stemming from the further reform needed for the gas sector in Russia.

Security of gas supply in the United Kingdom

The UK gas market is the largest in Europe. Demand has grown rapidly over the past decade, driven by the increasing use of domestic associated gas in the power sector. In addition, the power market has opened up and close links between the gas and power markets have developed in recent years. The UK gas market is different from that of continental Europe. It has become a fully liquid open market where supply and demand can be balanced by price. For the last twenty years or so, it has been self-sufficient and even a net exporter through the Bacton-Zeebrugge Interconnector. The issue of reliable gas supplies was confined to the internal dimension of security, i.e., ensuring sufficient investment in gas infrastructure. The supply situation is now changing, with a rapid depletion of domestic resources and decline of production after 30 years of exploitation resulting in the need for steeply increasing imports. Several new projects to import gas by pipeline and LNG are being launched, attracted by the liquid UK market. The switch from net exporter to large importer and the changes in the marketplace raise new issues for security of supply for the UK: *i)* increasing import dependence to match a still growing demand; *ii)* availability of peak gas supply; *iii)* facility concentration; *iv)* interoperability of different qualities of gas; *v)* investments in transmission and insurance assets in an open gas market; and *vi)* gas and electricity interface.

The present system of competitive markets and transportation regulation improves reliability of supply by allocating available volumes by the market. However this will not necessarily guarantee reliability of gas supply for low-probability/high-impact events. As long as the UK was completely supplied by many fields from the UKCS under the governance of the UK market, the probability and consequences of a longer-lasting loss of a source were low. This is set to change, as the UK will import gas under some large projects, also from non-OECD countries. The UK has installed comprehensive, transparent monitoring of key developments of the reliability of gas supply situation, which should allow any upcoming concern to be addressed in a timely manner. With growing import volumes this monitoring would have to include the implications of the new large import projects for security of gas supply.

Security of gas supply in OECD Pacific

The gas industries of the four OECD countries in the Pacific region are extremely varied: Japan and South Korea are almost entirely dependent on LNG supplies, whereas Australia is becoming a large LNG exporter and New Zealand is so far self-sufficient. The level of market opening differs greatly too, with Japan and Korea in the relatively early stages of gas market reform, while Australia has been applying TPA to its grid since 1998. So far the issue has not been relevant in New Zealand, as most of the country's supply comes from one single field, transported and delivered under long-term contracts.

It is therefore not surprising that security of supply issues differ greatly from country to country. In Japan and South Korea, security of supply issues are linked with import dependence, the possible conflict between the opening of the markets and the need to rely on long-term import contracts. The internal dimension of security of supply is linked with investment into new gas infrastructure, the issue of facility concentration and investment in insurance assets for low-probability events. The interface between the electricity and gas sectors is not yet a relevant issue as the share of gas in the power sector is limited and neither sector has yet opened to competition in the two countries.

Although Japan and South Korea are almost completely dependent on outside supplies, their experience shows that this situation can be addressed successfully with policies to diversify supplies, and cooperation with exporting countries and between LNG buyers.

Japan is an illustration of that policy. Japan, as one of the largest economies in the world, has managed to cope well with its very high dependence on LNG (and oil) imports by adopting specific policy measures to address this situation. Japan has always maintained a highly diversified portfolio of supplies: LNG comes from eight countries and ten LNG plants. Suppliers include both Asia Pacific and Middle East producers. Over time, Japan has developed and maintained strong economic and political ties with the countries from which it imports gas always with a view to the interests of the supplying countries. Japan has also developed financial links with its LNG suppliers, by investing in liquefaction plants dedicated to export to Japan.

PART C – ANNEXES

In open gas markets security of gas supply is a subject for which responsibility is shared between all players involved, although they have different roles to play. This study tried to include the views of the main players by organising conferences and workshops on subjects pertinent to the various aspects of security of gas supply. In addition, it provided the opportunity to include the views of the players by different means, such as questionnaires, written contributions and proceedings of a workshop. The views of governments, regulators, gas industry, large consumers and international organisations are given in annexes included in a CD-Rom.

PART A

GLOBAL/GENERIC DEVELOPMENTS

OBJECTIVE AND SCOPE

This study *Security of gas supply in open markets* is the successor of *The IEA natural gas security study* published in 1995. Since the 1995 publication, the gas industry in IEA countries has seen many impressive developments which call for a new look at the security issue: *i)* progress in the opening of gas and electricity markets, *ii)* the tremendous increase of gas-fired power generation worldwide as a new driver of gas demand, and *iii)* cost reductions in the LNG chain allowing more flexible LNG trade, more players on the supply and demand side creating closer links between the regional markets. While proven worldwide gas reserves increase faster than gas demand, OECD countries increasingly need to import gas, as finding of additional gas reserves in OECD countries do not keep pace with the depletion of gas reserves and the increase in gas demand. Even the US and UK are about to become substantial net importers of gas from non-OECD countries.

The impacts of gas market reforms on flexibility as an important element of security of gas supply were analysed in the IEA publication *Flexibility in natural gas supply and demand*, published in 2002, which is a main building block of the present study.

The main motivation for IEA to revisit the issue of gas security is – as expressed in the title – to assess the impact of opening of gas markets (and in parallel electricity markets) on security of gas supplies. Market reform in most IEA countries was still in its inception phase when the 1995 study was written. The judgment was rather cautious: "Liberalisation and competition are increasingly affecting gas markets throughout the IEA. The implications for security depend both on the form of liberalisation and the characteristics of the gas market into which is it introduced, although it is difficult to find instances where liberalisation and competition have jeopardised security of supply. Nonetheless the evidence from particular markets where competition has been introduced does not suggest that competition need be incompatible with secure gas supplies. In general there is evidence of positive impacts on some elements of security such as development of production, transmission and storage capacity".

Even though gas market reform in North America and the UK were already advanced in the mid-1990s, major developments only occurred thereafter, such as the emergence of a main marketplace like the NBP in the UK, and important regulatory changes in the US. Now with almost ten additional years of real life experience with the opening of gas (and electricity) markets in North America, Australia and the UK and first experiences emerging also in other EU countries, it seems possible to be more affirmative regarding the role of markets. The experience since 1995 suggests that the markets for gas on a national, regional and even global level will play an even more prominent role. As stated in the publication on flexibility, "The opening of the gas sector has created a situation in which parts of supply and demand are balanced by the price mechanism. It also led to the development of flexibility services, which are traded in a competitive environment and are therefore valued by the market. Yet, customers with no fuel-switching capabilities and whose demand is price inelastic still need secure, uninterrupted supply."

The objective of this study is to look at security of gas supply in open markets (which are almost in OECD countries) and especially to review the role of markets in ensuring reliable and secure gas supply. Based on input by the various stakeholders, official information by member governments as well as publicly available information, the study presents a comprehensive overview of the recent status of the gas industry in IEA countries. It gives the analysis of the IEA secretariat on the most recent developments of security of gas supply in the three OECD regions under the framework of open markets and in view of the new demand and supply trends. In particular, it discusses whether markets will value by themselves security of gas supply and deliver timely signals for investment to guarantee secure supplies. As security challenges vary in the three OECD regions, due to their different characteristics in terms of gas reserves, production and imports, demand size and maturity of the market, the study analyses the issues related to each region.

The nature of external security of supply threats from gas suppliers from non-OECD can vary largely. Incidents experienced so far were: interference into export or transit of gas, based on political motivations or due to a lack of clear regulations, threats by illegal political groups, or incidents due to a lack of technical and commercial state-of-the-art performance. While it would be of great interest to identify such elements and ways for non-OECD Governments to address and mitigate such risks, they are not the subject of this IEA publication. Even if IEA member countries can try to influence non-OECD gas exporting countries to mitigate and minimise the risk of supply disruption, these threats are outside the control of IEA member countries. While past experience indicates a low probability of such events, there were serious examples of supply interruptions and in view of their potentially high impacts they are relevant for policy makers in IEA countries. This book therefore concentrates on ways to address the impacts of low-probability/high-impact events, like supply disruptions and extreme weather conditions, and not on ways to try to reduce their likelihood which is outside the control of IEA Governments. It gives policy recommendations on security of gas supply for IEA policy-makers and presents the regional and global challenges that governments and market players will face in the next 30 years. >

This study responds to the requests of the IEA Ministers at the 2001 and 2003 IEA Ministerial meetings to strengthen IEA's activities on energy security and gas issues. With market opening, more stakeholders play a role. Therefore the views of the different stakeholders were gathered during the past two years by organising conferences and meetings on the different aspects of security of gas supply:

- IEA regulatory forum *Competition in energy markets: implications for public service and security of supply goals in the electricity and gas industries*, organised with the French Ministry of Economics, Finances and Industry, Paris, 7-8 February, 2002;

- IEA workshop on *Cross-border gas trade issues*, Paris, 26-27 March, 2002, and related regional workshops on south-eastern Europe and South America;

- IEA workshop and high-level meeting with IEA member governments and industry on *Security of gas supply*, Paris, 21 June 2002 and 23 October 2002;

- IEA workshop with gas regulators on *Security of gas supply in liberalised markets*, Paris, 27 June, 2003.

Through its consultation with IEA Governments, industry, regulators, consumers and other international organisations, the Agency has gathered information and viewpoints of these stakeholders. The views of the IEA Governments and other stakeholders are presented in the annex of this study in a CD-Rom.

IEA is going to continue do deal with security of gas supply by bringing together IEA Governments and other stakeholders to exchange views and best practices on security of gas supply in open markets.

2

A CHANGED ROLE FOR GOVERNMENTS AND CONTRACTS IN OPEN GAS MARKETS

While import dependence of OECD countries raises concerns about the external dimension of security of supply, the opening of the gas and electricity sectors to competition adds an internal dimension. It raises the questions of whether the market itself will value security of supply and deliver timely signals and competitive incentives for investment to guarantee secure and reliable gas supply all the way to the final customer. Compared with other commodities, gas is special: *i)* it is capacity-bound to highly capital-intensive transportation and distribution infrastructure, and *ii)* there is little demand-side response, especially in the household sector. In the absence of demand response by a large market segment, the market itself may not value security of supply. Therefore there is a need to delineate what can be left to the market, what should be defined by governments and what should be ensured by long-term instruments like contracts.

This Chapter first highlights the range of specific characteristics of gas and the varying implications for reliability and security of supply, the role of governments and commercial actors. Then, it describes the development of hubs, spot and futures markets, analyses the impact of spot trading on security of supply, and discusses whether spot gas prices are sufficient market signals for investment. The final part reviews the role played by contracts all along the gas chain and discusses their adaptation to the new market environment.

RELIABILITY AND SECURITY OF GAS SUPPLY: ROLE OF MARKETS AND GOVERNMENTS

Reliability and security of gas supply

For most commodities, security of supply is not an issue, as supply and demand are balanced by the price mechanism. If supply is tight, prices will direct supply to the highest value use and if the high price is due to a scarcity rent beyond production and marketing costs, it will attract more entrants to the market on the supply side reducing the scarcity rent. Security of supply is an issue for basic goods which are necessary for maintaining a reasonable standard of living and which cannot be easily substituted.

Another issue is reliability of supply, i.e., that supply which has been committed will in fact be delivered. This is an issue for the type of goods and services which cannot be easily stored or substituted to bridge a failure in delivery, and where a default in delivery has serious consequences for the customer. A striking example is certainly failure of power supply, but also gas for household customers.

Why gas is special

There are several features which distinguish gas from other commodities:

Natural properties of gas

Gas needs large-scale investment into a fixed infrastructure which cannot be used for other purposes. Gas is a natural finite resource, which is found in deposits varying from small fields of several million cm to a few billion cm, like in North America, to fields of 1,000 bcm and more, like Groningen in the Netherlands, Troll in Norway and a limited number of other identified super giant fields, all of which are outside IEA countries. Gas may come in association with oil or condensates and its components vary from field to field. Contrary to solid minerals or coal, single gas deposits need a uniform management under a single operator due to their uniform pressure regime. Depending on geology, production of gas may have an atomistic structure, such as in the US with more than 9,000 producers, or may have an oligopolistic structure, where (potential) production from one large field could cover a large share of market supply (Groningen in the Netherlands).

Governance elements linked to gas

Laying pipelines requires using public or private ground along a defined route. Endorsement by public authorities is required, either as owners of the ground, as in the case of municipalities, or to enforce – if necessary – ceding of ground rights all along the route of a pipeline. The rights to gas as a finite resource are – except for the US – vested in the state. Exploration and production are subject to sovereign decisions by governments, defining the development and eventually the depletion rates of large reservoirs as well as the rent taking regime for gas. For gas exports, in particular, sovereign decisions of the government of the resource-owning state will matter.

Special economic features of gas

Gas pipelines have strict capacity limits defined by pipeline diameter and the pressure at the inlet and outlet points. Any capacity change requires additional, substantial investment like looping the pipeline (laying a parallel pipeline for part of the distance) or adding extra compression. The transportation capacity of pipelines has substantial economies of scale.

Gas distribution will always be a natural monopoly which can only be contested for very special customers. Gas transportation may or may not be a natural monopoly: pipeline-to-pipeline competition exists, e.g., in North America and in Germany.

Gas by pipeline is delivered through a long fixed chain of capacity-bound investment, where any part of the chain may prove to be a weak link for the rest of the chain. LNG supplies, because of lower economies of scale and because of easy re-routing of tankers offer more flexibility.

Short-term and long-term reliability of gas supply

Reliability of gas supply depends on providing sufficient capacity and adequate gas volumes to supply gas to the final customer. Both are defined by past investment decisions. For reliability of supply, not only do possible supply disruptions have to be bridged, but varying demand also has to be met. Demand may vary as a function of external parameters, like temperature, which are beyond the control of customers. A failure to deliver gas on a cold winter day would have serious consequences for most households which mainly use gas for heating and may have only very limited alternatives. While household customers expect gas to be as reliable as the main alternative – oil, reliability of gas supply to households has a "public good" character, as it is delivered via a distribution grid, and there is no possibility of discrimination between customers. A failure in gas supply may also have serious consequences for industrial purposes, when gas is used as process gas, e.g., for the production of sheet glass. In the given example, gas is perfect for providing the constant and uniform heat required, but any interruption may destroy not only the glass output but may damage the whole plant.

Governments may have to define objectives, and eventually even standards, for reliability of supply. These are usually defined in terms of extreme weather conditions, supply disruptions and facility failures to be covered.

Some customers may be in a position to accept interruptible gas supply or may even make their off-take dependent on price. For them the level of reliability is a question of price linked to the alternatives available; their gas demand is price elastic. They implicitly or explicitly value reliability of supply. However, for other important segments of the gas market, reliability of supply is vital because their gas demand is price inelastic. To ensure a high level of reliability to these customers, the gas supplier has to invest in insurance instruments, like storage or extra supply capacity to cope with low-probability events (i.e., extreme weather conditions or supply disruptions). Gas companies have developed a specific mix of tools and mechanisms, often in cooperation with national governments, to ensure reliable and secure gas supply. Traditional instruments include: diversification of supply sources and routes, interconnection of national grids, long-term contracts, storage facilities, flexibility instruments (supply flexibility; interruptible contracts, etc.) and back-up and cooperation agreements. Relying on curtailment of supplies to interruptible customers or buying extra gas at the price requested by the market, can be used as an instrument in deep and liquid open gas markets to avoid investment into extra capacity which may never be used.

At the wholesale level, the inelastic demand for reliable gas (aggregated by distribution companies or retailers) meets the more price elastic demand by industrial users and power generators. The wholesale level in open markets offers the possibility to provide extra supplies by buying gas in spot markets or redirecting supply away from interruptible customers to meet the inelastic demand. Trade can be organised on a shorter-term basis, i.e., relying on finding a seller or buyer when needed, as compared to agreeing deliveries under longer-term contracts. This way decisions can be fine-tuned close to the time when the gas is needed. However, companies responsible for reliable supplies are limited by the depth and liquidity of the marketplace. Otherwise they will have to rely on more long-term contractual arrangements or other instruments.

At the retail level, gas distribution will usually be a regulated monopoly and include supervision of the adequacy of the grid, in particular for defined extreme weather conditions. Ensuring sufficient supply under these defined conditions will be left to the gas retailer. However, distribution companies may have to act as suppliers of last resort.

For long-term reliability of supply, as supply and demand develop additional investment into increased capacity and supply will be needed as well as investments into additional insurance assets. While market prices for gas and transport capacity give location and time signals of scarcity, investment in insurance assets against low-probability/high-impact events may not be valued by the market. In such cases, as well as when investment into infrastructure is made by a regulated monopoly, it is up to the government/regulator to allow for a rate of return which is competitive with other alternatives. Part of government actions is to reduce (perceived) regulatory and other policy uncertainties.

Another issue is that projects for the expansion of gas production and supply have to compete for financing, decided by the rate of return on investment. Competition for financing would normally result in the best allocation of capital, i.e., investing in an enlargement of parts of the gas chain where it is most needed vs. investment into other parts of the economy. However, political and regulatory risks – even if only perceived by the investors – may hamper new investment. These risks can include risks stemming from acts of either governments or monopolies of non-OECD countries.

A major issue is how signs of capacity constraints will be translated into timely investment to remove those constraints and what signals will be needed for an expansion of infrastructure and supply. From the moment new capacity comes on-stream the scarcity might disappear, and with it the scarcity price, so that the investment may be obsolete the moment the capacity is put into operation. Investors may prefer to rely on fundamentals, like a robust increase in demand for the time horizon of the commitment of the new investment.

The internal and external dimensions of security of gas supply

So far, security of gas supply was mainly viewed as an insurance against interruption of external supplies. While this definition is still valid, the concept of security of gas supply needs to be revisited in view of the changes taking place in global and IEA gas markets. The new concept involves recognition that security of supply no longer stops at the border but extends to the final customer. Security of supply has also two equally important constituent parts: physical availability and price.

Security of supply is best seen in terms of risk management, i.e., reducing to an acceptable level the risks and consequences of disruptions. Five main categories of risks can be distinguished:

■ Technical risks, i.e., system failure due to weather, etc;

■ Political risks, i.e., interruption of external supplies;

■ Regulatory risks, i.e., failure of deliveries due to flawed regulation;

■ Economic risks, i.e., when gas producing countries are not willing to develop reserves for export at prevailing prices and conditions; lack of investment; and

■ Environmental risks, i.e., unacceptable level of greenhouse gas emissions.

The time horizon of the different risks differs considerably. Short-term risks refer to supply interruptions due to technical failures, accidents, political intervention, or extreme weather conditions. Long-term risks generally cover economic and political risks. They refer to the lack of investment – or insufficient investment in the development of production and transportation facilities for new supplies – or to politically driven interruption of supplies.

As gas is network energy and as gas projects have a long lead-time, risk relates not only to the commodity or sources of supply (which are abundant, although access may be an issue) but also to the adequacy of the linking infrastructure and the timing of investment. With market reforms and unbundling of the transportation and supply functions, the link between investment decisions on infrastructure and the development of new resources may weaken.

In open markets, unbundling raises new challenges for reliability and security of supply. In the past, in most countries, governments delegated responsibility for reliability of supply to one single actor, either a *de facto* monopoly state-owned gas company, or a private company with exclusive concession rights. This entity was responsible for reliability of gas supply across the whole gas market. In open gas markets, a single national company can no longer be assigned the responsibility for security of supply of the whole gas market. It will have to be a shared responsibility to ensure that within the gas chain all issues have been assigned and responsibilities are performed.

The unbundling of gas companies implies unbundling the responsibility for reliability along the gas chain, which raises the issue of how to ensure consistency of compliance with reliability standards by all players from the production site to the burner tip. Instead of handling reliability within an integrated company, reliability now has to be passed on from one company to the next along the gas chain under contractual arrangements.

The internal challenge, as described above, is to ensure reliable gas supply long enough into the future, by mobilising investment for the development of the gas infrastructure and production capacity in time to ensure future reliable supplies. Gas as a natural resource is under the sovereignty of governments, and its supply may not only be subject to resource rent optimisation but also to non-economic political influence. When it comes to the resources of their own country, governments often have a clear policy on depletion and rent-taking, while investment and depletion decisions are left to commercial operators. For very large fields, like Groningen and Troll, governments tend to maintain a strong influence on the management of the field, e.g., by state participation.

As OECD countries become more import dependent, gas supply becomes subject to decisions made by non-OECD countries. To ensure short-term reliability, defined threats of external disruptions of gas supplies (for whatever reason) should be manageable by the domestic gas system: through market reaction and instruments developed to cope with disruptions. But governments must be increasingly alert to collective vulnerabilities inherent in an internationally integrating market.

So far exporting countries have demonstrated their interest and capacity to bridge any shortfall in deliveries by their own means, like Indonesia providing additional LNG from its second LNG plant during the shutdown of Arun, or Algeria boosting deliveries from Arzew and from the Maghreb and Transmed pipelines after the Skikda accident. Beyond their interest in the continued cash flow, they are anxious to maintain their standing as reliable suppliers, fulfilling their contracts. However, security of supply risks for gas from non-OECD countries remain beyond the risks which are accepted as normal business standards in OECD countries. These risks especially include political interference into commercial transactions, impacts of political instability and a lack of enforceability of contractual and other legal provision.

Definition of security of gas supply

Security of gas supply is the capability to manage, for a given time, external market influences which cannot be balanced by the market itself.

In open markets, supply and demand can be balanced by the market according to the preferences of market participants. Open markets ensure that gas goes to its highest value use. They provide a variety of instruments to mitigate external market influences in line with the preferences of market participants.

Security of supply has always been a question of how to handle external supply disruptions. In open markets, ensuring reliable gas supply all the way to final customers according to their preferences raises other issues.

For most small customers, individual demand reaction is limited and, for household customers in particular, demand itself varies strongly depending on the temperature. Customers linked to a distribution grid with a 'public good' character cannot individually value reliability of supply.

In the short term, security of supply covers the adequacy of supply and capacity to avoid unforeseen interruptions of customers. In the long term, it includes the capacity to mobilise investment to develop supply and infrastructure as well as the insurance assets to ensure reliable supply.

Security of supply is best seen in terms of risk management, i.e., reducing to an acceptable level the risks and consequences of disruptions. Management of risk is a central activity for the gas industry and its customers. Where possible, market mechanisms should be the basis of security decisions. Nevertheless, governments do have a role to play:

- In providing a market framework and its implementation that ensure gas markets can work properly;

- In setting a framework in which risks can be managed and costs reduced, in particular through securing an international framework for investment and trade, and facilitating interconnection and exchanges among neighbouring countries;

- In determining acceptable reliability levels, especially where small customers and safety are concerned;

- In providing a clear policy for dealing with emergency situations.

Role of open markets for reliability and security of supply

Open gas markets are powerful "tools" for providing efficiency and ensuring that gas goes to its highest value. In the short term, they allow supply and demand to be balanced by the price mechanism. In deep and liquid markets, like the US and UK, suppliers/consumers will always be able to sell/buy gas on the spot market, providing they accept the market price. As there are a larger number of players, responsibility for reliability of supply can be more effectively arranged in open markets.

With the opening of gas markets, the role of the customer has changed. Eligible consumers, like power generators, industrial users and, in some markets, residential and commercial users have the possibility to choose their supplier and to buy (eventually regulated) transportation services and (negotiated or regulated) storage services. This choice extends to the level of security of supply the consumer desires/requires. Eligible customers have to assume responsibility for reliability of supply themselves by having back-up solutions to deal with interruptions or to contract for a certain level of security of supply from their supplier and pay for it accordingly.

The opening of the gas and electricity sectors to competition raises the questions of whether the market itself will value security of gas supply and deliver timely signals for investment to guarantee secure supplies. Since companies are only responsible to their shareholders and customers, they will not provide extra investment for reliability of supply if they are not ensured a competitive payback on this investment. And the government will be held responsible for security of supply by voters/small customers even if it is the companies that have the contractual obligation to deliver gas. Hence the importance of making sure the market works and making it clear what markets can or cannot deliver.

Reliability of supply, where it goes beyond what can be delivered by markets, has two main aspects:

■ Short-term, i.e., continuity and reliability of gas supply, under rare and extreme conditions;

■ Long-term, i.e., concerns about timely investment into supply and infrastructure capacity to ensure reliability in the future. In addition there are the internal and external dimensions of security of supply.

Both short-term and long-term gas supply aspects require attention to:

■ The availability of gas volumes to meet firm demands;

■ The availability of transportation and distribution capacity to move these volumes of gas to the end consumer;

■ Insurance assets in case of low-probability/high-impact events.

Availability of gas

In the short term, markets will play a key role for better allocation of supply/demand. Short-term deep and liquid markets will contribute to security of supply by matching supply and demand. The development of liquid spot gas markets adds instruments to provide reliability of supply to cover interruptions of gas supplies and to cover extreme weather conditions.

When gas is supplied from domestic small fields (US for instance), the market is a powerful instrument to send signals when new supplies are required. The price will increase and producers will drill more wells, increasing gas supply with a certain time lag.

When gas is imported, markets can also send a signal to mobilise additional short-term imports, for instance, reversing the flow of the UK Interconnector from exporting to importing mode, or importing spot cargoes of LNG. In the short-term, the limit lies within the additional spare exporting capacities. In the case of tight supplies, the risk is that prices will skyrocket.

For long-term adequate supply, the role of markets will be limited. In the case of domestic supply, geology and resource management policy and market fundamentals will define the limits of future domestic production. In the case of imported gas from large fields, especially if located outside OECD countries, the price signals sent by open markets will not automatically translate into additional supply from non-OECD countries. Therefore the external dimension of security of supply still needs to be addressed in open markets. It even requires increased attention given the growing dependence of most IEA member countries on imports from non-OECD countries. Import dependence is not a threat in itself. However, consuming countries will increasingly have to import gas supplies that are not geographically diversified and are sometimes located in unstable political areas.

In the case of new LNG imports, market signals may help to confirm market fundamentals. LNG suppliers appear to be ready to take the market risk of deep and liquid markets, such as the markets in the US and UK.

Transportation

Open gas markets allow for the development of a transportation market, where shippers buy different transportation services (firm, interruptible, short and long term). In many countries, because of the absence of pipeline-to-pipeline competition, and the monopoly character of transportation, these services are regulated and tariffs are fixed by regulatory authorities under principles/concepts defined by governments.

In the short term, transportation capacity is given and cannot be expanded by further investment (even if the market signals a bottleneck by high entry fees, like at St Fergus in the UK). Means to allocate scarce capacity must be used.

In the long term, the question is to have clear market signals for future investments. When access to transport is regulated, the major instrument to incentivise investment in new transportation is the allowed rate of return. For national pipelines, if the rate of return is sufficient compared to other investments, private investors will develop the grid in a timely and appropriate manner. To invest the substantial funds needed in infrastructure, regulatory certainty and stability is needed.

The unbundling of gas supply and transportation activities creates additional uncertainty, as it makes it more difficult for transporters to assess where future supply will come from. Investment in capacity may no longer correspond to what is necessary to transport new supplies, as shippers do not necessarily reveal their long-term needs.

Insurance assets

Open markets will not by themselves value investment in insurance assets to secure supplies to the end-consumer under low-probability/high-impact events, for instance extreme weather conditions or a large non-technical disruption of supplies. As these events have a very low probability of occurring, market players will not invest in insurance assets against such events if there is no incentive to do so.

A fundamental question is whether consumers can correctly ascertain the actual level of supply interruption risk associated with different sources of supply. Market participants can generally assess medium- and high-probability events, such as severe winters, because there is a historical record for such events with respect to their frequency and severity. Low-probability events are particularly difficult to assess because there might never have been a past occurrence of such an event. The full ramifications of such low-probability events on gas supplies are therefore unclear. For certain segments, especially for small customers, there is the "free rider" problem: they cannot individually choose the level of security of supply they require.

While open markets provide consumers with choice and more efficiency, market reform also changes the well-established business environment that has supported security of supply and raises new issues that policy-makers must address.

Role of governments

Policy-makers have the responsibility of creating a clear framework for security of gas supply and defining the responsibilities of each player.

a) Governments should define the *objectives* for security of gas supply, including both supplies and infrastructure. Objectives may include ensuring:

- Security of gas supply for household customers, commercial and small industrial users (who cannot switch to alternative fuels);

- That demand in the most severe winter day or period on record (historical over a certain time span) is met;

- Covering a certain time span of interruption of a major supplier – internal or external;

- A specific resilience against failure of a major element of the infrastructure for a specified number of days at a specified time of year (suppliers and networks operators);

- That suppliers hedge prices for all residential gas users for a specific period of time;

- Security of gas supply of the combined electricity/gas system because of the interlink between gas and electricity (obligations for gas-fired power generators, if any, should link to electricity security framework); and

- Adequate security of gas supply for the overall economy in view of the potential damage of insufficient gas supplies on the economy (as natural gas consumption offers an economic advantage compared with the consumption of alternative fuels).

Some customers do not have the possibility to switch to alternative fuels at short notice and the damage of supply disruption may be high.

However, in the future, the market might give these customers additional incentives for a more flexible demand-side reaction than at present. It is the responsibility of policy-makers to organise the special protection required for these customers. In particular, they need to judge the balance between the cost and damage caused by any interruption of supply to small customers and the cost of the extra investment necessary to avoid it.

Governments may need to set out national/individual standards in line with their objectives for the adequate provision of both supplies and infrastructure. Diversification of external sources will help the domestic market to cope with any external disruption, as any single interruption is more likely to be compensated by supply and demand flexibility. Sufficient domestically available flexibility instruments, like storage, flexibility in supply, fuel-switching capacity and demand-side response may also help to bridge any shortage of an external supply source.

The combination of instruments to bridge external disruption may best be handled by each market individually taking into account the existence of domestic supply, dependence on imported gas, the role of gas in the energy mix, the share of non-interruptible demand, the availability of supply and demand reactions, and insurance assets and their costs. Given the high costs of insurance assets for gas and their dependence on market specifics, governments must be clear in their requirements for market players to provide an optimal combination of instruments to meet those expectations. Individual countries may also have different disruption risk comfort levels depending on the characteristics of their energy/gas markets.

b) Governments should clearly define and allocate the respective roles and responsibilities of the different market players to ensure that objectives are fulfilled. However, governments should leave market players the choice of instruments/means to provide the required level of security of gas supply.

Suppliers and producers have the responsibility to ensure there is sufficient gas both in terms of production capacity and volume. This includes the responsibility for sufficient supplies for extreme low-probability events (although certainly other tools will also be used jointly in such event). The responsibility to ensure sufficient transportation capacity lies with Transmission System Operators (TSOs) and shippers. Each TSO has to provide transportation capacity to meet its contractual obligations and, where applicable, nationally agreed safety/resilience standards. To enable TSOs to do this, shippers have a prime responsibility for signalling their future capacity requirements by revealing their real demands for capacity to meet their customers' needs under both average conditions and low-probability events. This second condition is certainly more difficult in open markets as it is not certain that shippers take into account their customers' needs in the case of low-probability events. Finally it is the responsibility of TSOs to maintain system integrity.[1]

c) Governments should monitor investment performance within their jurisdiction to ensure that companies provide adequate levels of security of gas supply. They should rely on market instruments as far as possible to overcome eventual bottlenecks, such as investment incentives, instead of interventions. The monitoring of the fulfilment of objectives and responsibilities might be delegated to the regulators. Policy-makers must also remain alert to deficiencies in investment performance all along the gas chain.

d) If the market fails to generate the necessary investment unaided, governments should act, i.e., provide additional incentives, to ensure that timely investment in supplies and infrastructure is made to meet future demand.

One of the main concerns is financing new projects. Governments can help by putting in place stable rules and avoiding over-taxation. Government should ensure that authorisation procedures are streamlined, without compromising democracy.

e) Governments should monitor gas and electricity demand jointly when gas has a major share of the electricity mix. With the parallel opening to competition of the gas and electricity markets, combined with the increasing use of gas in the power sector, the security of gas and electricity supplies become intertwined. Where both sectors have been reformed and liquid and deep marketplaces have developed, arbitrage can help to solve supply problems because it serves to move the gas and electricity to the highest value use of those fuels, which minimises the economic losses

---

1   GTE (2003f), Eurogas (2002).

resulting from physical supply shortages. Moreover, if there is over-capacity in power generation, this may add more flexibility and switching possibilities to the gas sector. However, in exceptional circumstances, such as extreme cold weather, peak demand in both the gas and electricity sectors may coincide, creating further stress on both systems.

f) Governments should also play a role in encouraging cross-border trade by:

■   Putting a stable market framework in place in their own country;

■   Promoting international harmonisation of regulatory standards, e.g., within the framework of the ECT or the WTO;

■   Helping to create a favourable political climate, e.g., by fostering more dialogue between gas producing, transiting and consuming countries;

■   By sharing experience on market reforms with producing/transiting countries; by encouraging and eventually backing FDI in production/transport/transit.

One major challenge is to create a favourable framework for the investment necessary to develop the gas resources and bring them to the market. The main contribution on the part of IEA governments is to create a clear market and investment framework, which will define the revenue of the export projects. Gas exporting countries can help to mitigate investment risks and thereby provide lower cost financing by creating a clear investment framework on their side, and by accepting international arbitration for dispute settlement, for example as provided for in the Energy Charter Treaty. Mitigating investment risks is easier for LNG projects in view of the flexibility to deliver to a variety of consumers.

g) Governments should use the IEA as a facilitator for member governments, regulators and industries of IEA countries to exchange views and best practices on security of gas supply.

h) Governments should ensure adequate staffing in national governments and international organisations to be able to handle the policy discussion on gas, independent of regulatory agencies.

THE EMERGENCE OF SPOT TRADING

This section reviews the emergence/development of spot trading in OECD countries and its impact on security of supply. Based on the IEA publication *Flexibility in Natural Gas Supply and Demand,* it describes the development of hubs, spot and future markets, and then looks at experiences developed in the US and UK where spot trading dominates, and describes the emerging hubs in continental Europe. It goes on to consider the impact of spot trading on security of supply, and discusses whether spot gas prices are sufficient market signals for investment and how price volatility should be dealt with, in particular for household customers.

Hubs/marketplaces/spot and futures markets

Hubs/marketplaces

With the introduction of third-party access, new trading opportunities are emerging in places where different pipelines owners meet up, as one owner may now use the other's line.[2] At some locations, where several pipelines meet and where storage facilities and consumption centres are both close by, a marketplace for gas can develop – a hub. A hub can be defined as a physical transfer point where several pipelines connect to a facility that redirects properly metered gas volumes from one pipeline to another.

This definition corresponds to local hubs, like Henry Hub, Bacton or Zeebrugge, where gas transfers and transactions are operated at a well identified geographical point. It has been extended to notional hubs, like the NBP (National Balancing Point) in the UK, and the TTF (Title Transfer Facility) in the Netherlands, where gas transfers and transactions are operated, not at a single physical location on a gas grid, but at every entry or exit point of the transport network, respectively the NTS in the UK and the GTS in the Netherlands. This has been made possible by the introduction of "entry-exit" tariff systems in these two countries, which do not distinguish between volumes of gas already present within the network, once the corresponding entry fees have been paid.

---

2   CEC (2000).

Hubs enable the parties to exchange gas at the same point and to trade volumes and transport capacities. For a hub to qualify as a market, the hub operator must provide the following services: interconnections between the pipelines to allow the gas to be interchanged between the systems and, ideally, storage facilities; ease of transportation to and from the hub; and several associated services, such as balancing[3] and recording of title transfers. Short-term balancing of supply and demand is a major function of a market hub. Storage at hubs, particularly when they are close to markets, is a valuable tool for traders. Storage adds flexibility to the marketplace, both in physical terms, via access to gas (at times of peak demand) and in trading terms, by providing physical hedging and the ability to arbitrage.

Trading at marketplace must be liquid enough to allow the determination of the price of gas in accordance with supply and demand. The number of sellers and buyers at a hub is important: it needs to be large enough to create a liquid market, where there is sufficient supply and demand for gas to be traded rapidly and freely. It also needs to be large enough to ensure that one transaction will not alter the market price. The size of the "churn" – the ratio of traded volumes at a hub to actual physical volumes – is generally deemed the yardstick for when a hub becomes a successful pricing reference.

An important prerequisite for successful short-term trading at a hub is the speed at which contracts can be concluded. Standardised contracts expedite trading. An active approach on the part of participating gas operators can also contribute to the success of a hub.

Spot and futures markets[4]

Once trading at a hub develops into a liquid market, spot and futures markets will form and a market price for immediate and future delivery will emerge. Spot markets usually start with over-the-counter (OTC) trades based on standardised agreements for a fixed volume of gas. They are made either bilaterally between the two parties concerned or through a broker. Gas delivery can be for periods of between one day and one year,

---

3   A short-term interruptible arrangement to cover a temporary imbalance between supply and demand.
4   This section is drawn from the IEA publication on *Flexibility in Natural Gas Supply and Demand*, IEA (2002a).

either for prompt (very short-term) or forward (long-term) delivery at a defined location, usually the hub.

Deliveries in the future are dealt with in forward contracts, which are a commitment to deliver or take a specific amount of gas, usually in units of 10,000 million Btu, at a defined time and place for an agreed price. The financial transaction takes place on the day of delivery. Forward contracts are traded over the counter, in customised one-off transactions between a buyer and a seller.

Futures markets emerge in countries that have fully liquid spot markets for immediate and forward delivery. Although they have similar names, "forward" contracts and "futures" contracts are quite different instruments. Gas futures are usually paper trades that track the daily movement of the expected future price until the expiration date of the contract, when gas must be delivered or the differential between the agreed price and the spot price on that day must be settled in cash. Unlike forward deals, which may be traded over the counter and always related to final physical delivery, futures contracts are traded on organised commodity exchanges with standardised terms. Futures contracts – because they are financial hedging instruments – can be traded independently from delivery to the underlying spot gas marketplace. They nevertheless need a spot market as a final reference point.

Derivatives are financial markets that are derived from other markets. The two main types of derivatives are options, which give the holder the right to buy and sell at a certain price in the underlying market, and swaps, which exchange a floating price for a fixed price. They are generally traded OTC in energy markets at the moment.

Futures markets provide an independent and transparent pricing signal for future price development and this can be used as a pricing indicator for other contracts. The future price represents the current market opinion of what the gas will be worth at some time in the future. It is the only indicator (although by no means a correct prediction) of the expected spot price of the commodity in the future. Futures prices also serve as a stimulus to store or release gas from storage.

The other main function of the futures market is to transfer risk. Hedging allows market participants to lock in prices and margins in advance.

Hedging reduces exposure to price risk by shifting it to those with opposite risk profiles or to speculators who are willing to accept the risk in exchange for possible profit. By using futures contracts, anybody who is dependent on gas prices may offset or minimise the risk inherent in a fluctuating gas price. A gas buyer may have an interest in buying gas futures within a certain price limit to hedge the cost of using gas as an input into his productive activity. A seller, perhaps a small independent producing company, may want to hedge its earnings to meet its minimum income requirements such as interest payments on its financing.

US experience

In the US, the 278,000-mile gas pipeline system includes numerous pipeline interconnections. Before the establishment of open access in 1986, little could be gained from using these interconnections. Open access to transport and storage has completely modified the picture. It is now possible for everyone to move gas between pipeline systems and between pipeline and storage systems. This has engendered hubs as natural transfer and trading points of gas. The North American natural gas market includes 37 market centres (28 in the United States and 9 in Canada), with transparent spot markets. The largest market centre is Henry Hub located in Louisiana, which began operating in 1988. It connects 14 pipelines and has access to three salt storage caverns. It is accessible to major producers from both onshore and offshore Louisiana. Information on prices and other relevant matters is readily available. It has a very high liquidity: its churn ratio is approximately a hundred to one. Henry Hub also serves as the delivery and reference point for the New York Mercantile Exchange (NYMEX) gas futures contract and is the reference for all gas export contracts to Mexico.

Figure 6.4 (Chapter 6) shows Henry Hub prices since 2000. After a long period of stable prices during the 1990s at about $2/million Btu, natural gas prices are now characterised by high volatility and a sustained higher level since the beginning of 2003. Gas futures are currently trading between $4 to 6/million Btu (beginning of December 2003). Volatility in prices is a natural development of these centres. To hedge against price risks, the NYMEX launched the world's first natural gas futures contract in April 1990.

US market centres and hub services

The type of services provided by market centres and hubs varies significantly. The Federal Energy Regulatory Commission's Office of Economic Policy provides a comprehensive list of the available services. The major ones include:

Balancing – A short-term interruptible arrangement to cover a temporary imbalance. This service is often provided in conjunction with "parking" and "loaning".

Electronic Trading – Trading systems that either electronically match buyers with sellers or facilitate direct negotiation for legally-binding transactions. Customers may connect with the hub electronically to enter gas nominations, examine their account position, or access e-mail and bulletin-board services.

Loaning – A short-term advance of gas to a shipper by a market centre that is repaid in kind by the shipper a short time later. Also referred to as "advancing", "drafting", "reverse packing" and "imbalance resolution".

Parking – A short-term transaction in which the hub holds the shipper's gas for redelivery at a later date. Often uses storage facilities, but may also use displacement or variations in line-pack.

Peaking – Short-term, usually less than a day and sometimes hourly, sales of gas to meet unanticipated increases in demand or shortages of gas experienced by the buyer.

Storage – Storage that is longer than "parking", such as seasonal storage. Injection and withdrawal may be separately charged.

Title Transfer – A service in which changes in ownership of a specific gas package are recorded by the market centre. Some gas titles may be transferred several times before the gas leaves the centre. This service is merely an accounting or documentation of title transfers. It may be done electronically and/or by hard copy.

Wheeling – Essentially a transportation service. Transfer of gas from one interconnected pipeline to another through a hub, by displacement, including swaps, or by physical transfer over a market-centre pipeline.

Source: EIA (1997)

Figure 2.1. Major hubs/market centres in North America

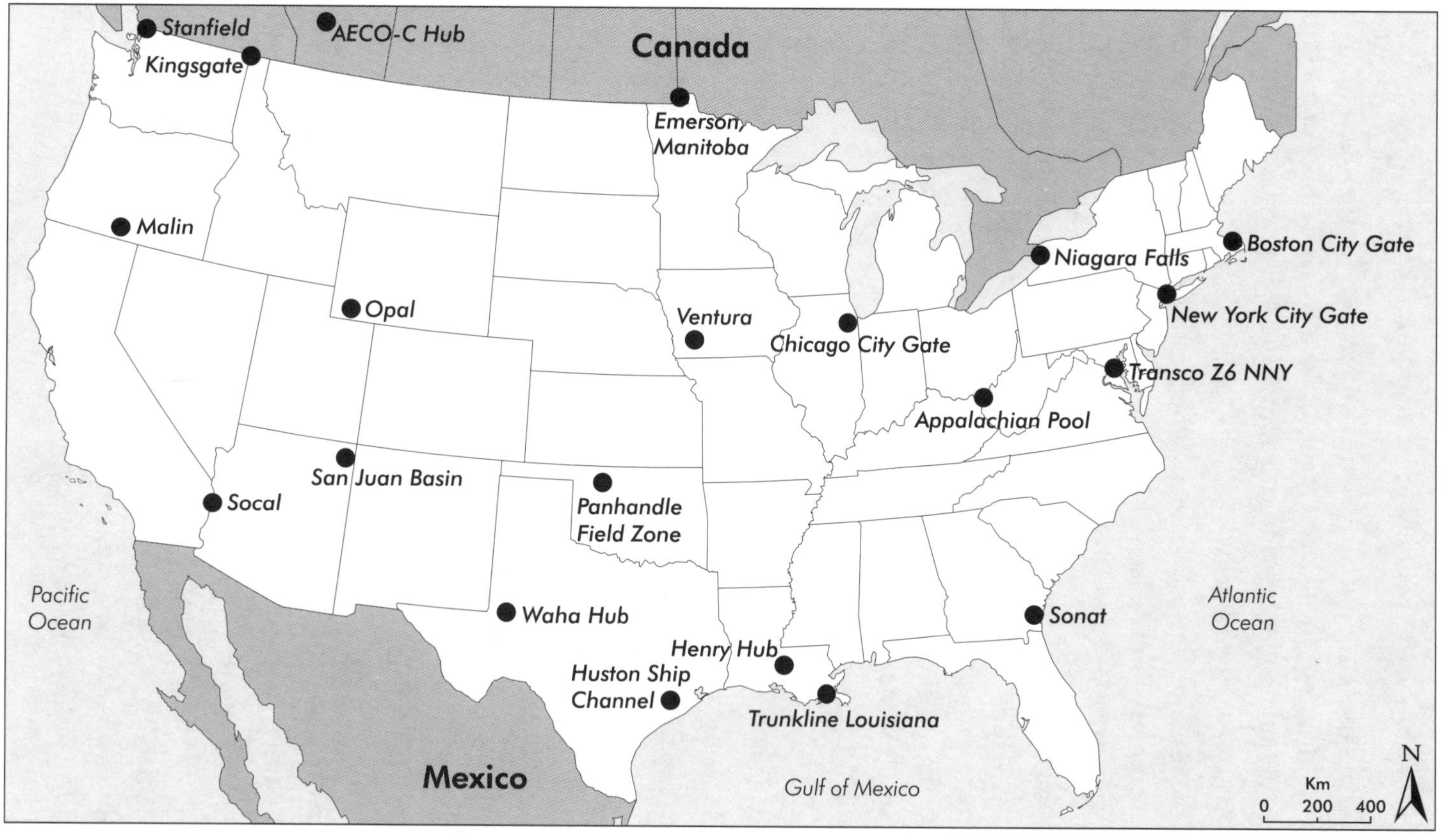

Source: IEA, World Gas Intelligence, Natural Gas Week

Today, natural gas futures traded at the NYMEX have a depth of up to 6 years. Volumes and "open interest" (the number of futures or options natural gas contracts outstanding in the market) have grown rapidly, and the NYMEX gas contract is the fastest growing instrument in the exchange's history. The estimated trading volume, around 20 bcm of gas a day (7300 bcm/a), is ten times the amount of gas delivered in the United States. In October 1992, NYMEX marked another milestone in the energy markets when it launched "options" on natural-gas futures, giving market participants still another instrument to manage their market risk.

In Canada, the "Natural Gas Exchange" (NGX), located in Calgary, provides electronic trading and clearing services to natural-gas buyers and sellers in Canadian markets. The NGX started service in February 1994. In March 2004, NGX was purchased 100% by the TSX Group (the Group's principal activities are to provide electronic, screen-based equity securities market information). Over the past ten years, NGX has grown to serve over 150 customers. In Canada, the regulation of commodity trading is under provincial jurisdiction. The Alberta Securities Commission is NGX's lead regulator.

UK experience

In the UK, when gas-to-gas competition began, conditions were created specifically to allow new entrants to sell gas directly to end-users, i.e. third-party access, a gas-release programme for British Gas and a cap on British Gas market share (see Chapter 8). Nevertheless, even in these favourable conditions, few participants seemed to envisage the development of a spot gas market. The spot market only began to develop when shippers needed to balance their position on the transmission system and started to trade with each other in order to achieve it.

In 1994, the National Balancing Point (NBP) became an informal market for gas trading among UK power generators. Transco's introduction in September 1996 of a tight daily balancing system, backed by penalties, led to NBP using geographical locations – such as Bacton, the main landing point for North Sea gas in England, or its Scottish equivalent, St. Fergus – as the main places for spot gas trading activity. Approximately 15% of the gas at the beach[5] is sold directly to the wholesale spot market.

A similar proportion is sold as one-to-three year contracts, with the remainder being sold on traditional long-term contracts, most of them indexed to oil prices, although in new contracts and renegotiations pegging to the NBP spot price becomes the more common feature.

The NBP is a virtual trading place covering the whole network of Transco, the UK gas transmission company. Due to the short average transport distance and the high number of entry and exit points at relatively short distances, the UK system is like a grid. Gas on which the entry fee has been paid is treated as being at the NBP, in other words, on the marketplace. To take the gas out of the NBP an exit fee has to be paid. The NBP endorses a triple role in the running of the gas business process, under Transco's Network Code:[6]

- As a tool for daily gas balancing: the NBP is the support for the On-the-day Commodity Market (OCM), which provides a screen-based anonymous gas trading market in which the shipper and Transco can post bids and offer to buy and sell gas within the National Balancing Point. Transco uses this market as a means of securing or disposing of gas in order to keep the system in balance;

- As a support for a comprehensive market centre, enabling all authorised shippers and traders to buy and sell gas from each other before it reaches the consumer. They operate in the OCM and on future markets (day-ahead, week-end, end of month, next and following months, next quarter, next year, etc.);

- As a marker for the market-price of gas in Great-Britain, organised by the International Petroleum Exchange (IPE), setting a possible reference for the indexation – partial or integral – of long-term take-or-pay gas contracts.

The NBP has progressively acquired credibility as a reliable market reference. The total volumes of trade amounted to 675 bcm in 2003 (or about 2 bcm a day, i.e., six times the volume of gas consumed in UK). Currently, about 50 traders are active on the NBP. The churn ratio is 15-20

---

5   In the UK, when gas has been brought ashore to a terminal by producers but is not yet in the National
    Transmission System, the gas is called "at the beach".
6   CEER (2003a).

to 1 (Figure 2.2). Trading at NBP decreased in 2001 with the collapse of Enron, a major actor on the NBP, as well as in 2002 with the withdrawal of US energy trading companies from Europe. Trading is now recovering and the market is very liquid. 90% of volumes are traded via OTC, 10% on IPE.

Figure 2.2. Trading at NBP

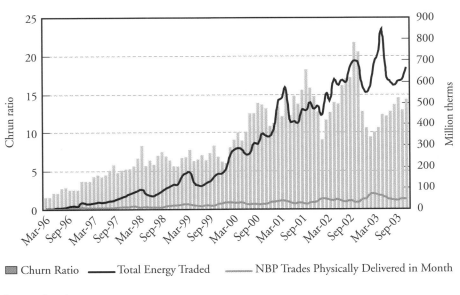

Source: Centrica

The NBP market has acquired sufficient credibility to allow gas operators to depart from the traditional contractual schemes and to utilise the NBP either as an outlet for future gas imports in the UK or as a price reference for long-term transactions. A first example is provided by the 10-year contract signed in 2002 by Statoil and Centrica for 5 bcm/a, with deliveries starting from October 2005. The breakthrough is not that deliveries have to be made at the NBP, but that the contract price is linked to the UK gas market rather than to world oil prices. Later on in 2002, Centrica signed a long-term agreement with Gasunie for the delivery to the UK of a total volume of 80 bcm over a 10-year period, also at conditions linked to the NBP gas prices.

The International Petroleum Exchange (IPE) launched a gas futures contract in January 1997. It is traded electronically on the IPE's automated Energy Trading System. Volumes of trade average more than

2,000 lots per day. The contract results in physical delivery only if position(s) are not closed out prior to expiry. Physical delivery takes place within the UK natural gas grid at the NBP.

The development of gas hubs and trading in continental Europe

Under the impetus of TPA to the grid and evolving competition, spot trading in continental Europe is developing although it is still in its infancy. New gas hubs are emerging in several locations mostly in north-west Europe, to provide physical balancing and trading services with the likely evolution of new commodity spot markets. Trading is developing at Zeebrugge (Belgium), Emden, Bunde (Germany/Netherlands), TTF (Netherlands).

Unlike the UK or US, there is not yet any gas exchange in continental Europe. OTC transactions are the only way to trade. This means that so far no official price exists, although prices at Zeebrugge and Bunde are reported by specialised press agencies (Heren, Platt's, Argus). Trading is still limited at these hubs and they do not offer a solid pricing reference. After the Enron collapse and the withdrawal of US companies from European trading, liquidity had taken a hit, but markets finally started to recover in 2003, due to the entrance of banks and the growth of trading subsidiaries of producers and utilities.

As most transactions on continental Europe are governed by long-term contracts, the availability of uncommitted resources is quite limited, not exceeding 5 to 10% of the demand. Therefore the emergence of liquid markets allowing a large number of actors to trade both in space (local transactions and trades) and in time (futures and options) will remain limited for the coming years.

Zeebrugge hub

The Zeebrugge hub in Belgium is the first gas-trading hub launched in continental Europe by Distrigas in October 1999. It is located at a coastal town where gas pipelines from the United Kingdom (Interconnector) and Norway (Zeepipe) meet. There is also an LNG import terminal and a link into the Belgian national gas transmission network. Zeebrugge is linked by large pipelines to France, the Netherlands, Germany and Luxembourg. These pipelines and terminals are all interlinked, so that gas can physically be moved or exchanged between them. The various facilities at Zeebrugge together have an annual throughput capacity of 40 bcm per year which represents about 10% of west European gas consumption.

The hub is connected to the Dutch H (high calorific value) gas grid. LNG cannot be traded at the Zeebrugge hub at the moment because Algerian LNG is not compatible with the Interconnector gas quality and thus hub quality.

Zeebrugge is operated by Huberator (Fluxys). Huberator has two functions: to manage physical gas flows between the different inlet and outlet points in Zeebrugge and to act as a broker between the partners using the Zeebrugge hub.

The number of customers of Huberator rose during the first half of 2003 from 47 to 54. On average, 41 of those are active on the hub on a daily basis. The liquidity at Zeebrugge has grown in line with Interconnector usage and the market opening in the European Union. In 2002, estimated traded volumes reached 67 bcm. They have increased by 40% in the first half of 2003. But volumes are far lower than those at the NBP, and prices at Zeebrugge are heavily dependent on the UK. This is largely due to the presence of the UK-Belgium Interconnector pipeline, which allows gas to flow from one market to another. Thus the basis difference between the two markets is, in theory, limited to the transportation costs of transporting the gas from one hub to another. Prices diverge only when the Interconnector is out of operation. This means that, excluding periods of Interconnector outage, the IPE's NBP natural gas futures contracts can be used as an effective hedge for Zeebrugge price exposure.

Bunde/Oude Stadenzijl

Trading is developing in the German-Dutch border region (Bunde/Oude Stadenzijl). Bunde is a crossing point for three important pipelines. The first carries Dutch gas from the delivery point at Oude Stadenzijl to the east and south of Germany. The second carries Norwegian gas from the Emden/Dornum landing points to the south of Germany. The third, the Midal system built to compete with the existing pipeline system, links North Sea gas to Russian gas imports. The Etzel, Dornum and Rheden storage facilities are close by and Bunde is also close to the Ruhr, one of

Germany's major industrial areas. This movement in northern Europe is extremely important for future trading. Given its favourable location, Bunde/Oude could well develop into a true European hub.

Trading in the region encompasses two initiatives to create a local hub, Hubco and EuroHub, as well as a recent notional hub, TTF. The total transit volume at Bunde is estimated to be at least 30 bcm, of which 2 bcm is believed to be available for short-term trading. Despite their strategic location, trading at the two local hubs is not developing, limited by transport capacity constraints. Trading at TTF, on the other hand, is developing fast.

HubCo

The North-West European Hub Company (HubCo) was created in November 2001 by the German companies, Ruhrgas, BEB and the Norwegian company Statoil as founding members. The hub is located at Emden, in Germany, adjacent to Bunde Eurohub, with which it is in competition for trade. Hubco started its commercial activities in September 2002 as a hub service company. It offers international gas traders fully integrated hub services for the Bunde/Emden hub. They include the provision of transportation capacity, coordination of transportation between different delivery and redelivery points as well as back-up services for trading transactions. A tailor-made agreement has been designed to trade at the hub "EBT 2002". Furthermore, HubCo handles petroleum tax formalities for its customers in case of import or export via Bunde. In March 2003, German Wingas took a 25% share in Hubco. Currently, Hubco has seven customers.

Eurohub

Created by Gasunie on 27 February 2002, EuroHub is wholly owned by Gastransport Services, the transportation branch of the Dutch company NV Nederlandse Gasunie. It aims to offer a complete range of trading services to the different marketing points on the Dutch high calorific Oude Statenzijl/Bunde/Emden gas network.

Phase I of Eurohub, which started in February 2002, comprised simple title-transfer of gas at the hub. In September 2002, phase II expanded these services to include transportation between various entry points and a 6-hour balancing service. Phase III (beginning 2003) joined all the entry points into one single trading point. There is also a connection between the GTS virtual points and Eurohub. Eurohub, which controls entry and exit capacity at both Emden and at Bunde, is currently used primarily to transfer gas between the two points. By 1 October 2003, the new D-Gas flange had been added as the seventh transfer point. The D-Gas feeder pipeline connects the gas storage caverns at Nuttermoor.

By the end of 2003, EuroHub had 13 customers and extended its activities to a wider trading service, supported by an IT system, communicating with its users via Internet. Estimated traded volumes amounted to 5 bcm in 2002.

Title Transfer Facility (TTF)

On 1 January 2003, GTS introduced an entry/exit tariff system on the Dutch H-gas grid and launched a new service called Title Transfer Facility (TTF), to manage the transfers of gas from one shipper to the other, a service which resulted in the creation of a Dutch NBP for H-gas, applicable to all volumes already present within the GTS grid.

Gas traded on TTF originates from a variety of sources, including Dutch domestic, Norwegian gas arriving at Emden, German and Russian supplies of high and low calorific gas from the Bunde/Oude Statenzijl region on the Dutch/German border, gas at Bocholtz being directed to Italy by German energy company RWE, and Dutch and Norwegian gas en route to France at 'S-Gravenvoeren. Traders can arbitrage between prices from these different locations.

TTF immediately started with relatively high, short-term deal liquidity. There are now ten participants with 5-10 deals a day, trading a volume equivalent to 5% of Dutch gas consumption. TTF is becoming the dominant form of transaction in the Bunde/Oude-Statenzijl/Emden trading region. Its success to some extent reflects that competition for industrial and commercial users is a reality in the Netherlands, and this brings with it the need for a shipper's balancing market. TTF is a much more localised market than NBP, serving medium end-users in the Netherlands with gas from a number of locations.

Baumgarten

Austrian OMV is developing a hub at Baumgarten on the Austrian-Slovakian border. The creation of a liquid hub at Baumgarten was an obligation put by the regulator E-control on OMV and EVN, Wiengas, Linz AG, Begas and OO Ferngas AG before allowing them to merge their industrial business in Econgaz. OMV has accepted a release programme and must auction 250 mcm/a until Baumgarten is established as a sustainable gas trading hub. As the liquidity is limited by the availability of free gas volumes, Econgas auctioned 250 mcm in July 2003 to improve liquidity at Baumgarten. A title tracking service will be offered in 2004 by the hub operator Central European Gas Hub (formerly Gas-Hub-Baumgarten GmbH), 100% owned by OMV Erdgas.

Other possible hubs

It is likely that other hubs will emerge either at junction points where physical infrastructure meets, or at significant points of delivery, such as at the end of large transit pipelines from Africa, Eastern Europe and the North Sea fields. Possible candidates include: Wallbach on the German-Swiss border, Frankfurt (Oder) situated in the far east of Germany on the Polish Border, Lampertheim in the south-west of Germany, near Milan in Italy, and one hub in southern France/northern Spain.

Impact on security of gas supply

Increased short-term security

Spot markets provide a place where market participants can trade their short- and medium-term volume imbalances. The spot price mobilises access to short-term gas resources and allows for demand-side response, curtailing demand when prices increase. They allow for exchanges, swaps and trade between stakeholders, thereby playing a major role in enhancing short-term security of supply.

It should be noted that in the cases of both North America and the UK, this model was developed in markets characterised by over-capacity of domestic supplies. The US and UK cases illustrate that spot markets which are deep enough can always provide gas. They can constitute the supplier of last resort. Spot markets increase efficiency, as gas supplies always go to the highest value market. Future markets also enhance security of supply by offering future delivery and price discovery and the possibility to hedge price risks.

If the spot market is deep and liquid, it can also constitute a credible outlet for new large supply projects. However, these instruments implicitly suppose that there will be secure supplies in the future, i.e. that supply and demand can be matched by a market at a specific time in the future. This might not be the case if substantial supply disruptions occur or if investments into the expansion of production and the transportation system do not keep pace with the growth of demand.

Spot prices and market signals

The role of spot markets for long-term security of supply is less clear. Forward prices are indicators of the price level in the future (although by no means the exact level). They reflect what market participants are willing to lock in. These price signals help consumers, suppliers and producers alike to see when supplies are relatively plentiful or tight. If producers, traders and consumers anticipate that gas supply will – or may – be short within the next few weeks/months, their estimate of the future value of gas will rise. This expectation would in principle drive up the current price of forward contracts, indicating the need for short-term new supply (for instance, reverse flows from the Interconnector or import of spot LNG cargoes). However, in order to have valid price signals, spot and future markets must be liquid, which is not yet the case in continental Europe. Even on the NYMEX and the IPE, the liquidity falls when the term extends. For instance, open interest, i.e., the number of contracts that are still outstanding at a particular time for a particular futures contract, is decreasing sharply over time (Figure 2.3). Therefore prices quoted for more than 3 years ahead in the US, and one or two years ahead in the UK, are certainly representing the view of only a small number of players. The interest of forward prices as a price indicator is therefore limited when time elapses.

There are therefore considerable doubts that forward markets provide appropriate market signals for long-term investment. To be able to provide such signals, markets need to be liquid, prices need to be available on a long-term basis, and they should be robust and sustained. However, spot and forward prices are valid for the short term only.

Figure 2.3. NYMEX natural gas futures – Prices and open interest, as of December 2003

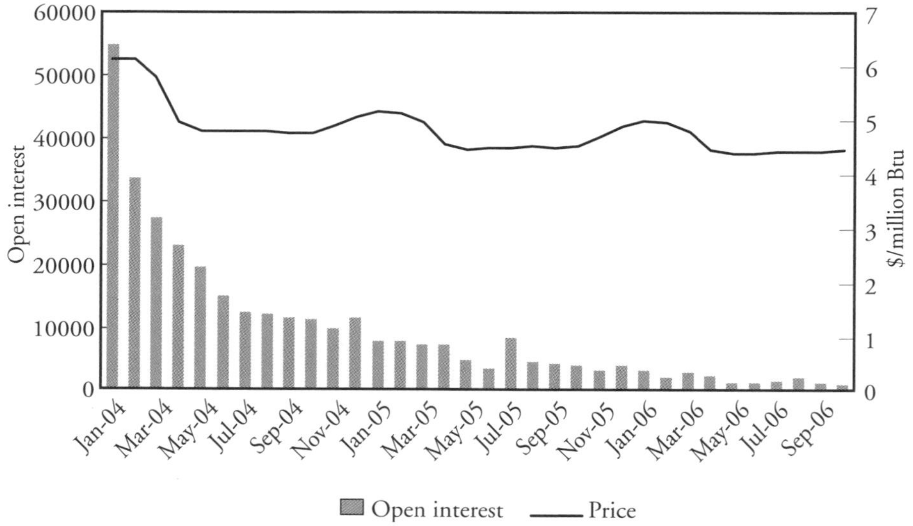

Source: BTU Weekly, 8 December 2003

However, in the US at least, where there are many small fields to be drilled by wildcatters, the drilling rate follows spot prices with a delay of about six months, which may be a reaction to prices and expectations as well as a reaction to the change in cash flow available to drill new wells. These cases, however, do not require large amounts of capital with a long-term amortisation period. Otherwise, investment in production facilities (in particular outside the country), storage and transportation have long lead-times. Ensuring that the market will make enough gas/capacities available for requirements in 4-5 years is a key question, which is even more acute for investment in resilience to supply shocks.

As spot prices are not sufficient to attract long-term investment, most investors simply base their investment decisions on long-term supply/demand analysis. Spot and future prices help them to test their long-term investment decision. Price peaks will reflect the time and location of bottlenecks in a system and signal the need to invest in the expansion of the capacity of the system. However, with volatile markets, price signals will often be ambiguous and intermittent rather than clear and sustained. Excessive and sustained price fluctuations can discourage investment in large, capital-intensive supply projects, as volatile markets are perceived as higher risk.

Volatility and price transparency

Price volatility[7] is inevitable in competitive markets. When the industry operates close to full capacity, small changes in supply and/or demand or relevant news items or sound bites may cause strong market pressures and substantial price increases or decreases. This was illustrated in the US in late 2000 and early 2003, when gas supply/demand imbalance led to a price surge. It is hard to identify and weigh causes of price volatility. In the US, prices have been very volatile in the recent period as supply tightened and neither supply nor demand sectors were able to quickly adjust to unexpected changes in market conditions.

Another issue is price manipulation in some natural gas marketplaces. The falsification of price information by some companies in the US has led to an investigation into the price-gathering methodologies of companies reporting prices and into the validity of gas pricing information given to reporters by market players. Transparency of gas prices – as well as reliability of fundamental data (production, demand and storage) – has also become a major issue in the gas industry.

The US exchanges are under the control of the US Securities and Exchange Commission (SEC). With the emergence of increasingly complicated risk-hedging instruments, there is a rising risk of misuse or lack of control, as was demonstrated by the tremendous pressure on energy merchants in the wake of the spectacular bankruptcy of Enron in December 2001. As a consequence of the failure of Enron, the stocks of some major US energy companies have fallen more than the stock averages over the past two years. Some of them are also under investigation by the SEC and the Federal Energy Regulatory Commission for possible

---

7   Volatility is measured as the relative deviations around an average price value.

trading or accounting irregularities. Serious questions surround the issue of risk-hedging operations and overly "creative" accounting practices. The recent events in US energy markets have brought to the fore the need for mitigating counter-party risk in gas trading and ensuring that trading markets do work fairly and efficiently. Spot and futures markets do offer new flexibility to individual buyers and sellers. But if the system does not send the proper market signals so that the underlying physical flexibility instruments are developed in time to cover variations in supply and demand, the market will remain very volatile. Volatility is unlikely on over-supplied markets, but is a real threat when the market is tight, i.e. the case where new investment is needed to secure supplies.

Dealing with volatility for household customers

In liquid open markets, exposure to price volatility to a great extent is about choices that market participants make. Many customers and producers have access to a broad range of physical and risk management tools to help manage the risk of price volatility. Although these tools do not eliminate risk, they can allow price certainty. Risk management tools include contract purchases of various lengths and terms, and financial instruments such as futures or derivatives. Also physical hedge – storage – can be used and even upstream downstream integration along the gas chain.

For wholesale markets, there are extensive hedging mechanisms to deal with the commodity price, pipeline transportation rates and storage rates, as well as mechanisms to deal with the option to deliver or buy volumes. Hedging with swaps (forward contracts) will lock the position of the company, with no ability to benefit from market price movements. Options allow protecting the sale from adverse movements, while profiting from beneficial price movements, but cost a premium.

Wholesale customers are usually able to understand the market and its development, and can make educated decisions, hedge the price risks and often have alternatives to the use of gas. Retail customers cannot usually deal with price volatility. In the first instance, this is due to the fact that retail customers are not aware of real time price developments, nor do they have the capability to make decisions based on the market development. Above all they do not have the possibility to react to price changes as their demand is inelastic and mostly dependent on external parameters. Furthermore, the transaction costs to follow price development and understand the market are relatively high compared to the relative consumption by households.

< A key question is whether utilities will pass on the price development of the wholesale market to retail customers (in addition to the charges for transmission and distribution), thus exposing them to price volatility. While there may be retailers which offer products which mitigate price volatility, most retail customers use the distribution companies as a default scheme. If distribution companies offer default schemes which link the retail customer to the price volatility of wholesale markets this might result in a large share of retail customers being exposed to price volatility. If household customers are routinely linked to price volatility this will give the distribution companies no incentive to look for any hedging of the inelastic household demand on the wholesale market and rather reinforce volatility. In cases of high volatility and high gas prices passed on to many household customers – especially if via the default scheme – this will build up political pressure, tempting governments to cap prices which would defer investors and aggravate the problem. >

Policy-makers may therefore consider ways to suggest schemes where tariffs linking retail customers to price volatility are subject to a deliberate decision of the retail customer, and where the default scheme is a stable, hedged scheme. The difficulty is to find methods and yardsticks for efficient hedging of price variations. Utilities may run the risk that long-term contracts they conclude may not be judged acceptable by a regulator in the light of real price developments. Compared to passing on the spot prices as a default scheme, any long-term price hedge made by a utility would entail a degree of judgement by the utility. The minimum might be to ensure that the household customer has a choice between a tariff linked to the wholesale price and to a more constant tariff, and that the household customer needs to make a deliberate choice to be linked to the price volatility of the wholesale market. While in the first instance this is an element to reduce price volatility, it has an important impact on investment signals and the possibility to lock in long-term secure demand by the household sector into long-term investment decisions on supply.

THE EVOLVING CONTRACTUAL FRAMEWORK

The context for long-term contracts

Long-term contractual relationships are common in many industries as an instrument to coordinate labour in an economy based on the division of labour, e.g., long-term contracts between car manufacturers and suppliers of tyres. In the gas industry, they have been used successfully for many years to deal with the long-term nature and the high specificity of investment in all parts of the gas chain from exploration and production to the final customer. The rationale behind this is the nature of gas as a natural resource coming from reservoirs whose size can vary from small fields of one bcm to super giant fields with over 10,000 bcm of gas, the high specificity and costs of the investment to transport and distribute gas, as well as the substantial investment that binds consumers to gas once they have made an investment decision. Each of the elements along the chain – from production to the final customer – has to be linked and aligned in a way that allows all participants to hedge their long-term risks of gas supply and earn an adequate return on investment or compensation for a finite resource. Basically such long-term hedges are not necessary when elements of the gas chain are competitive and can be ruled by market forces. Alternatively, two consecutive elements of the chain can be integrated into one company or linked by long-term contracts. The underlying elements keep changing, e.g., there are more reserves looking for a market or more mature provinces; cost reductions in transportation (especially in LNG) in recent times, or the increasing density of grids are leading to more flexible relations between gas suppliers and customers. In addition, demand-side changes are allowing for more demand-side response, and power generation based on gas is becoming an increasingly important part of gas consumption.

All of these developments loosen the specificity of gas-related investment and make it possible to hedge long-term risks by relying on the market, while integration and long-term contracts can still provide a long-term hedge for the gas chain in cases where these developments cannot or do not yet happen.

With the development of liquid gas hubs in the US the need for long-term contracts decreased, as suppliers no longer had to worry about market outlets, provided they were prepared to accept the market price.

A crucial point is the high specificity of gas transportation due to the low energy intensity of gas, i.e., most of the investment is dedicated to a specific project and cannot be redirected to another use, once the investment is made. This applies to pipelines (once they are in the ground they link input at point A to market at point B and if either the input at point A is stopped or the market at point B disappears, the project collapses). With increasing interconnections of the pipeline infrastructure more alternatives emerge, and the specificity with regard to markets or supply sources loosens up.

The specificity of LNG transportation is in principle less pronounced as tankers can be re-routed, so that LNG offers competition both on the supply and on the market side. Nevertheless, for a long time the economics of LNG projects were even tighter than for pipeline projects. The economics of LNG operations had to be protected by long-term contracts with very strict supply and off-take obligations. With the price for tankers dropping in the 1990s, the reach of LNG tankers increased. When the costs of liquefaction also fell, there was less need to protect the economics of a project by very strict take-or-pay (ToP) contracts, opening the way to more flexible supply. This also applied to the extension of contracts based on amortised infrastructure. In parallel, the growing number of receiving terminals created a real choice on the market side.

Technical progress has speeded up the exploitation of gas fields, especially for smaller finds in mature provinces. Horizontal drilling has made it possible to have many equally distributed draining points in a reservoir with one well drilled, leading to more complete and rapid drainage of reservoirs, as can now be seen in the faster depletion rates in North America. However, some reservoirs are very large compared to the size of the market (like the giant fields supplying the European market (Groningen, Troll, Hassi R'Mel, Medvedye, Urengoy and Yamburg) or the North Field in Qatar. The depletion of these fields will be determined by policies relating to present and future effects on the market, and eventually with regard to domestic use vs. export.

Demand, which was driven by using gas as a substitute for oil products, is now increasingly determined by the use of gas in power generation. The link to the power grid introduces more flexibility on the demand side, not only because gas can be substituted in multi-fired power plants, but also because in the short run gas-based power can be replaced by increasing power generation from other plants. >

Given the increased price elasticity at both ends of the chain, long-term supply contracts lose part of their raison d'être and can increasingly be replaced by other instruments. This is less so for transportation between the production areas and main markets, i.e., access to the marketplace, which still needs to be secured by either investing or booking long-term capacity. This is similar for access to LNG terminals. It is necessary to have access to both the market (by securing the inlet via LNG terminal and then on to the main market hubs) and to gas reserves. Access to the market can be secured by free investment, while access to reserves differs according to the governance of the resource-owning country.

Long-term contracts are still useful for export/import where there are no alternatives, or as price/income hedging instruments over a long period. They are also useful in the case of continued specificity, like the Russian gas export infrastructure, or because of the need to find a long-term hedge for a certain share of the market (where the project is large compared to the market).

Contracts along the chain

For each element of the chain – from exploration and production to the final user who pays for the gas itself or the service created by the gas – long-term contracts may play a useful role and have been applied to hedge long-term risks where the instruments of open and liquid markets were not applicable or useful.

Exploration and Production

The right to explore for hydrocarbons and to produce gas is granted by the owner of the resources, which are usually vested in the state, except for the US, and in some special cases in Canada, where it is vested in the owner of the land (which can be the federal or state Government).

The exploration and production phase can be quite short. In North America it often takes only a few days to get permission to drill a well and drilling only takes a few days. Contracts with the landlord are of private nature, and the term should not necessarily be very long, as depletion of the smaller fields may only take a few years. Compensation to the landlord in the US is usually a flat royalty rate.

However in other areas, e.g., the Norwegian North Sea, concessions are granted by the Government to private companies for exploration and production. They typically last some 6 years for the exploration phase and, in case of a commercial find, a production licence of 30 years will be signed with the possibility of prolongation. This reflects the high upfront investment and the character of the fields, which often take 30 years or more until depletion, e.g., gas production under the Ekofisk licence with Phillips (now Phillips-Conoco) as an operator started in 1976 (and oil even earlier). The production licence was repeatedly extended, and now runs until 2029. Given the importance of a field like Ekofisk for the resource owner, the high investment needed for its development and the optimisation of its recovery, it is understandable that both the Norwegian State and the private investors preferred a long-term licence and even long-term prolongations when the issue of reinvestment was up for consideration. At the same time, private investors were interested in having the main part of their gas sales covered by long-term contracts in congruence with the licence terms.

Domestic transportation

Domestic transportation (or transportation within North America) in open markets is often driven by market signals, like the price differential between hubs (known as the basis). Given that there is short-term TPA to free capacity, the existing capacity tends to be almost fully used. Price differentials between hubs, as well as the load factors for the use of existing infrastructure, are providing signals and incentives for private investors to bridge upcoming bottlenecks by building new capacity. However, private investors have tended to secure financing of the new pipeline capacity based on long-term transportation contracts often tendered in the frame of an open season process.[8] In turn, producers of large volumes will need to be sure of access to pipelines to bring the gas to the market. Similar considerations apply for access to LNG terminals in the US. As both

---

8   Open season: A process during which shippers of natural gas can contract with pipeline companies for firm delivery capacity.

Canada and the US have large markets which can absorb variations in volume by market mechanism, cross-border pipelines between the two countries function more as an interconnector linking two markets, rather than as an export pipeline. Both countries are characterised by a significant number of small fields (except for large gas production potential in the Prudhoe Bay and in other Arctic areas). Development decisions (except for the Arctic area) are therefore smaller scale and do not affect the balance of either market. The similarity between the two markets means that for any player it makes little difference which market extra gas is sold in. This also applies to the rent received by private landlords in the US or by the provinces in Canada. In that regard security of supply is already provided by a market mechanism in both countries and an interconnector just creates a larger, better interconnected market, offering increased potential for security of gas supplies.

Cross-border transportation

Gas transportation projects crossing a border into OECD countries other than North America were usually large import projects – pipeline or LNG – with long-term gas sales contracts involving no more than a handful of companies on either side. The transportation infrastructure was based on the revenues of the long-term sales contract, with the price for the gas set at a level that would make it competitive in the buyers' market. However, the seller's revenue was reduced by the costs for the transportation infrastructure. In many cases special transportation companies were set up by the project partners, to organise the construction and operation of the export or import pipelines. The main concept in the exporting and importing spheres tended to be vertical integration, to hedge the risks along the pipeline, and horizontal joint ventures to make use of economies of scale in dimensioning the pipeline (similar driver, but an alternative procedure to the open season pipeline). However, the booking of pipeline capacity was often done under long-term contracts with the pipeline owners. It is unclear how that structure of long-term capacity booking will develop under the new EU Gas Directive's TPA regime.

In contrast with the case between the US and Canada, export projects and their related transportation infrastructure have so far been only slightly driven by market signals, and more by fundamentals. For gas-exporting countries the domestic gas market is either not big enough to absorb an optimal production rate from their large fields (e.g., The Netherlands, Norway, Qatar, Abu Dhabi, Trinidad and Tobago, Oman), or in spite of its substantial potential, is not attractive in view of the low price/high risk income from their administered domestic market (Russia, Indonesia, Malaysia, Nigeria) or both (Algeria). The Interconnector between the UK and the Continent is a notable exception, as it was only partly driven by the economics of gas exports to the Continent, as the idea of linking two gas markets also played an important role. In addition, the Interconnector, which followed an open season approach, is characterised by long-term transportation contracts, whereas only part of the transportation capacity is backed by long-term sales and purchase contracts. While in principle linking the two marketplaces created more potential to have recourse to the market reactions of both markets in case of shortages, it also created price links between the two markets, by which price spikes were transmitted in particular to the smaller but more flexible UK market.

In markets which can rely on domestic gas and are not dominated by large gas fields, like North America, gas is traded at many places, sometimes under long-term contracts, although essentially it is possible to buy and sell at any time and at almost any place. This is similar to the UK, the only difference being that it has basically only one marketplace as a reference point: the NBP. Different players may have different needs for the duration of their gas supplies, but in liquid markets, security of supply can be covered by the marketplace. This would not exclude players from opting for long-term contracts and other hedging instruments, like mergers between gas and electricity companies. As mentioned above, crossing the border from Canada to the US does not create special hindrances: their regulatory frameworks are similar and both marketplaces are closely interlinked. When there is a clear upstream taxation regime which defines off-take for all gas produced, the fiscal income is unaffected whether the gas is exported or consumed domestically.

In continental Europe and in Asia Pacific much of the gas will cross a border so an export contract between two, often essentially different, jurisdictions is implied. Norway's only direct income for its gas comes from exports, while in the case of Russia and Algeria domestic and export pricing is fundamentally different; only Dutch exports have comparable export and domestic values. But in any case, the rent for the producing country is defined at the export point. This was similar for earlier LNG exports to Japan. A country commits parts of its reserves and dedicates them to a special market. At the outset, since these export contracts were based on very large fields in view of emerging markets, long-term contracts were necessary, partly because the size of the projects was clearly beyond the range of market reaction. Long-term contracts were necessary to back and guarantee the payment and construction of the infrastructure between production, transportation in the exporting country, in transit countries and in the buying country and to give the final customer an incentive to invest in gas consuming equipment. To the extent that gas was sold at its replacement value, the risk of interruption was balanced: the exporting country would lose the amount of revenue corresponding to the market value of the gas for the other side. Both sides were tied to the project with a substantial project-specific investment. Reservoir risks were allocated to very large fields, sometimes even to the overall resources of a country, and partly even with an obligation to invest in substitute production from other fields, thereby securing long-term gas supply. A minimum pay clause, aimed to secure the income from gas sales by securing gas market position in the market, forced the buyer to undertake efficient marketing. As it was not possible for the buyer to cover more than a small part of a minimum pay obligation out of his profits, he, in turn, had to back his minimum pay obligation by long-term sales or by predictable access to a market for the gas.

Importation

Gas importers will have to hedge their long-term minimum pay commitment by having reliable long-term marketing possibilities, for instance by an exclusive concession to sell to a certain group of customers, e.g., residential and commercial and small industry at regulated or monitored prices. Sometimes the gas importer will not have an exclusive concession himself but sell under a long-term contract to utilities that do have an exclusive concession. In both cases the importer would provide for the security of supply to cover peak winter demand and to bridge to a certain extent import shortfalls, either under a policy defined by the government or under self-established standards. Demand from this market segment is reasonably predictable, as it depends mainly on demographic, climatic and generic economic developments, so it can serve as a basis for long-term commitments on which to base investment in the gas chain. With the introduction of eligibility for household customers, gas importers will lose the predictability of this long-term part of their sales. It remains to be seen what alternative ways of demand aggregation will develop as a back-up for the long-term minimum pay commitments of long-term contracts.

Final users

Demand by large industrial gas customers may vary with the business cycle, with the competitive position of the individual industrial customer in his own market, and with the development of the competitive position of gas for use by that customer. In order to make gas attractive to industrial customers, importers may try to conclude long-term contracts which at least create a long-term customer relationship, a necessary step. However, in this era of globalisation, industry production may be relocated to other countries if competitiveness requires. Sales to industry can be regarded as stable and predictable only for the medium term. Although gas supply is only one element in any industry's siting decision, for large gas consumers the price is usually one of the decisive factors, along with the political stability of the country. Long-term contracts with industrial customers – if they are not replaced by large customers buying on the wholesale market – will have to accommodate this changing business perspective.

Large-scale sales of imported gas to power plants are a rather new feature, except in OECD Pacific. The demand by a single large gas-fired power plant is easily in the order of one billion cubic meters per year, so that it can be attractive for the exporting company to handle it directly, especially for a new gas exporter (see Chapter 3).

So far household customers had little choice in their supplier. They were supplied under regulated tariffs but also assured of deliveries, independent of temperature and external supply interruptions. In addition, in most countries there is a *Public Service Obligation*, guaranteeing that every customer at a reasonable location will be connected. Households have had little incentive and rather limited possibilities to react to price fluctuations. While part of their demand variation is predictable according to social or climatic patterns, they also create the need to cover low-probability events because the failure to supply households is considered unacceptable in most countries, where utilities have an obligation to supply these customers under defined criteria included in their licence. Making household customers eligible to choose their supplier, in principle under freely-negotiated contract, will raise the questions of who will take responsibility for security of supply, who will pay for it, and how can the reliable development of the demand by the household sector be used to finance the necessary gas infrastructure.

Principles of long-term import contracts

Currently, most gas in continental Europe and OECD Pacific is imported through long-term Take-or-Pay (ToP) contracts. These contracts have played a very important role for the build-up and development of the gas industry. In particular, investment in the gas supply industry has usually been underpinned by the conclusion of long-term contracts between sellers and buyers. These contracts provide for a long-term commitment to deliver a defined volume of gas based on certain reserves and commit the buyer to take certain volumes for his market based on a competitive price for the gas.

De facto the buyer commits a certain share of his market. The minimum pay obligation puts an implicit limit on how much other gas the buyer can buy, unless he develops more demand. The obligation to grant a competitive price will implicitly restrict the seller from selling into the same market via another channel.

Long-term contracts thereby divide the risks associated with large gas projects (commitment of large reserves and of substantial capital) between producers and importers. They typically put the price risk on the seller, and the risk related to marketing the gas on the buyer (ToP obligations).

Long-term ToP contracts are generally considered as "rigid" contracts, mainly because they link sellers and buyers into a bilateral situation for a long period, generally 20 to 25 years, during which both of them have strictly defined obligations. In particular, they include a ToP clause, which requires the buyers to pay for contractually specified quantities of gas, even if delivery is not taken, as well as an obligation to make available defined volumes of gas. ToP clauses are included in most European and Asian contracts. Long-term contracts usually follow a netback approach, i.e., a pricing system which takes as a starting point the value of the gas in the market and deducts all costs reasonably incurred by the marketing company, including profit, to determine the price paid to the exporter. This means that the producer (and in the end the resource owner) takes all the risk and chances of price variation, whereas the buyer earns a margin from the volumes he has undertaken to market. As long as there was no direct market valuation for the gas, the value of the gas was determined by the replacement value principle which looks at the costs to replace gas with other fuels, including differences in investment, operating costs and fuel efficiency. In the past, the main substitutes for gas were fuel oils, in some cases crude oils, so the gas price was pegged to the prices of the next best substitute to gas, gasoil for small customers and for process use, and heavy fuel oil for large industrial/boiler use. The base price allowed the importer to recover the cost for the infrastructure from the import point to the consumer. Over time other substitutes came up, such as coal and electricity. In some countries where gas-on-gas competition exists, such as in the UK, the value of the gas could be derived by a liquid market.

In view of changes in the competitive position of gas, the sharing of risk and reward based on the above principles can only be reflected by volume and pricing conditions for a limited time. Many long-term contracts contain review clauses which allow for price and quantity adjustments usually every three years. These review clauses are designed to adapt the contract to changing market realities and especially to ensure that the price of gas allows the contracted volumes to be marketed. In case of disagreement, the dispute can be brought to a neutral institution for decision, usually under an international arbitration procedure.

In continental Europe, the pioneer gas contract between Gasunie and European buyers had and still has high volume flexibility, high enough to provide the swing required by the market. Long-term contracts concluded later in continental Europe were based on gas which had to use a much longer and more capital-intensive infrastructure. They had much less volume flexibility so that the market swing had to be provided by flexibility instruments of the buyer like storage and interruptible contracts. The volume flexibility still allows for a limited degree of supply price optimisation and also helped to phase in new large supply contracts. In the past there was even less flexibility under LNG contracts, as the economics of the chain were even tighter than for pipeline gas.

Volume flexibility in long-term contracts

The flexibility offered by long-term contracts consists mainly in the difference between the capacity and the off-take/minimum-pay obligation for various time spans; a year for long-term flexibility and a day or an hour for short-term flexibility.

■ Annual flexibility is typically of the order of 10% above or below the annual contractual quantity. The minimum pay-out is mainly a provision to protect the cash flow of the seller. So, contracts usually have a carry-forward provision, which allows gas taken in excess of the minimum pay obligation to be credited against future minimum pay-out obligations. There is also a make-up provision, under which gas not taken may be treated as a prepayment which can be counted against future off-takes above the minimum pay obligation. In addition there may be clauses that adjust the annual volume obligations as a function of exogenous influences like average temperature.

■ Daily flexibility is measured by the difference between daily capacity and the daily off-take obligation. A daily off-take obligation is not necessary to protect the seller's cash flow. But it may be necessary because of technical minimum-flow restrictions or to guarantee the outlet of associated gas. Gas from pure gas fields usually has a very low daily minimum off-take obligation or none, while gas from associated gas fields may have a minimum daily off-take obligation not very much lower than the one-day average annual obligation.

- The "swing" given by a contract results from the relation between the daily and annual obligations. Where the daily availability is considerably higher than the average annual availability the contract allows for a large swing to follow the market. The Dutch contracts provide such a large swing; so did the early UK delivery contracts from the fields in the southern UK Continental Shelf. Both were for short-haul gas. For long-haul gas, daily availability is usually not larger than average annual availability, as a higher daily availability would require investment in capacity without a guaranteed cash flow.

- A new feature was included in some of the long-term UK export contracts for delivery to the Continent via the Interconnector. It is called a "clawback gas" provision. It gives the supplier the right to interrupt the normal contractual flow to take advantage of high UK spot prices. Contrary to the traditional volume-related elements of flexibility this adds a price optimisation element to the flexibility provisions.

Source: ESMAP (1993), European Gas Matters, 30 April 2002.

As can be seen by the permanent adaptation of mainly the pricing, but increasingly also the flexibility conditions to changing market realities in the course of either price review or by modifying the formula in new contracts, the concept of long-term contracts was flexible enough to follow market developments.

The changing role of long-term contracts

In both North America and the UK, the transition from long-term to short-term contracts has been very difficult for the parties involved.[9]

---

9   In the United Kingdom, over-supply and regulatory reforms led to a complete restructuring of long-term ToP contracts as spot sales developed. Contract obligations were very costly to change for the companies involved as there were no re-opener clause. It cost British Gas £2.5 billion to renegotiate its contracts with North Sea producers when gas prices dropped to 9 p/therm, while the cost to British Gas for buying it averaged 19 p/therm. In the US, long-term ToP contracts collapsed in the 1980s for various reasons, including over-supply, lower gas demand than expected, falling fuel oil prices and regulatory changes. FERC Order 436 granted third-party access to pipelines to producers and consumers. Taking advantage of the supply surplus, this access boosted the development of short-term, spot and future contracts and the price level dropped again. Pipeline companies faced severe financial difficulties as a result of the ToP provisions as they were no longer able to take delivery of the contract quantities. To alleviate the obligations of the pipelines, FERC intervened with Order 500 which granted ToP credits to pipelines if they granted TPA to their creditors. Many parties settled their contracts in the following years by including additional price flexibility and dropping ToP obligations.

There was a need to renegotiate long-term take-or-pay obligations, which took a long time and resulted in heavy payments by the purchasing companies. With the UK and US soon to become substantial importers of gas, a renewed trend to use long-term contracts to secure gas supply is re-emerging. Examples are the long-term pipeline supply contracts of Centrica in the UK with Norwegian and Dutch producers, both with relatively high volumes and a 10-year contract term, as well as the long-term commitments by gas producing-countries and some oil majors to supply LNG to the UK and US.

The main discussion on long-term contracts took place in the EU. Since the introduction of the first Gas Directive, there has been a debate in Europe between the European Commission and major gas operators about the role and necessity of long-term contracts. The European Commission has recently fully recognised the importance of long-term contracts for security of supply and the financing of major new gas supply projects. It is reflected in the second Gas Directive and the proposed Directive on security of gas supply.

A recent report commissioned by the European Commission concludes that whatever the changes currently taking place in the gas industry, long-term contracts will continue to underpin gas trade because they fulfil five critical needs:[10]

- Producers use them to help underpin their market position;
- Project sponsors depend upon them to assure off-take and thus justify large investments in production and transportation;
- Project developers and financial institutions need them to provide security both for project finance and for corporate finance;
- Primary buyers rely on them to provide certainty and stability of physical supply, and as a price hedge. Primary buyers typically have consumers who also seek long-term supplies.
- A strong long-term portfolio is a powerful marketing instrument that helps both primary and secondary buyers to sell their gas. The supply security that end-users are seeking is an important factor encouraging primary buyers to maintain long-term supply portfolios.

---

10 *Europan Gas Matters*, 15 November 2003.

The report states that future developments could reduce the need for long-term contracts, or could make primary buyers less willing to sign them. Among the possible factors that could drive the supply market in this direction, the report mentions:

- A trend towards shorter-term purchasing on the part of secondary buyers;
- Further privatisation and progressive retreat of state influence in the sector;
- Possible lower future growth rate if expected continental "dash for gas" fails to materialise;
- Increasing liquidity in the short-term market;
- A rising proportion of the infrastructure being depreciated and thus able to support new gas sources with efficiently lower total capital costs;
- The possible re-emergence of radical innovators such as Enron;
- Increased concentration on both producers' and buyers' side.

The overwhelming consensus in the European gas industry is that long-term and spot contracts will co-exist and that the share of the spot market will remain limited in the total volume of gas traded in Europe. Whereas long-term contracts allow the financing of large new gas supply sources, spot contracts allow a short- and medium-term balancing of supply and demand and therefore offer more efficient use of existing infrastructure and thereby better flexibility and security. They are seen as complementary: spot trading for an efficient short-term balancing and long-term contracts for securing long-term supply and large-scale investments. Buyers are adopting a portfolio approach to gas purchasing combining the more traditional long-term contracts with new or renegotiated more flexible long-term contracts and spot purchases. Both sellers and buyers have the opportunity to profit, either by selling additional supply or by purchasing gas at a lower price than existing contracts in order to ease their minimum pay obligation and to optimise their purchasing costs.

So far spot sales represent a small proportion of gas purchases in both continental Europe and Asia. Belgium's Distrigas bought 25% of its supplies on the spot market in 2002. Spain's Gas Natural, which buys spot LNG cargoes in winter to cover its peak gas demand, bought 4.2 bcm under spot/short-term deals in 2002 representing 33% of its supplies. South Korea, which has the same strategy for its seasonal needs, has never bought more than 10% of its LNG supplies on the spot market. Contrary to the deep and liquid gas markets in the US and UK, spot sales at gas hubs in continental Europe is more a complementary than a crucial feature of the gas market. No supplier has yet undertaken to build a new facility on a speculative basis without a contractual outlet for a substantial part of the production.

Another change in Europe is the emergence of new players. Traditionally, state-owned companies or *de-facto* monopolies accounted for most of the trade and aggregated demand of multiple end-user customers. Since new suppliers are emerging and eligible customers are now able to negotiate directly with suppliers, there are several new companies entering the international trading part of the gas chain. However, only large companies (mostly electricity companies and groupings of local distribution companies) are able to negotiate their supplies directly with exporters. The best examples can be seen on the Italian and Spanish markets, where new customers buying their gas directly include: Enel, Edison, Energia S.P.A. in Italy, and Union Fenosa, Cepsa, Endesa and Iberdrola in Spain.

Balance of power between primary sellers/buyers

The cross-border nature of pipeline and LNG trade makes market liberalisation in Europe more challenging. Long-term contracts between suppliers and European importers have always been signed with European companies that have the scale and the ability to evaluate and aggregate the many small parcels of demand in local markets. In producers' views, the security of gas demand is as important as security of gas supply is for importing countries. In the past 40 years, the "risks of security of demand" were covered by the long-term supply contracts on a take-or-pay basis. Contracts were signed with buyers which were either state-owned companies or franchised utility companies from OECD countries and their ability to market the volumes was not an issue.

Open-market competition fundamentally changes the equilibrium and mechanism for enduring reliability and supply, as well as the responsibilities. Market reforms fragment demand, at a time when European supplies from non-OECD are becoming more concentrated. Suppliers from non-OECD so far retain monopoly structures for their gas export sales.

Since 2001 a new element on the supply side has surfaced with the creation of the Gas Exporting Countries Forum (GECF). Since its creation, participants in the GECF have stressed that this Forum was neither a pressure group nor a cartel and would solely aim at promoting policy discussion and exploring avenues of technical cooperation. Its main purpose is claimed to be an exchange of views on a number of gas issues of interest to gas exporting countries, from technical aspects in the upstream to transportation and marketing issues. The Forum claims to promote policy discussion and to explore avenues of technical cooperation. The first Ministerial meeting of gas exporting countries, which endorsed the creation of GECF, was convened in May 2001 in Tehran, at the invitation of the Iranian Minister of Petroleum. A second meeting was held in Algiers in February 2002 and a third meeting in Doha on 4 February, 2003. A fourth Ministerial is planned in Egypt in 2004.

After 11 countries met at the first meeting, GECF now involves 14 key gas exporting countries (which control three-quarters of global gas reserves and exported 368 bcm in 2002, or 53% of global gas trade, of which 139 bcm as LNG, or 92% of global LNG trade): Algeria, Brunei, Egypt, Indonesia, Iran, Libya, Malaysia, Nigeria, Oman, Qatar, Russia, Trinidad & Tobago, United Arab Emirates and Venezuela. GECF has no headquarters, Secretary General, staff or budget. Current work is coordinated by the host country of the next meeting. The Forum agreed to establish a liaison office at the meeting in Doha.

The number of gas exporting countries involved and their share in global gas exports have raised concerns among consumer countries, in particular the possibility of this Forum trying to influence pricing. It is in IEA interest that no group impedes the working of competition in the evolving global gas market. While there are concerns on the character of GECF, their influence on the short-term balance of supply/demand is limited in view of the lack of a global gas market, the liquidity and depth of the current LNG market and producing countries' adherence to long-term contracts. Delegates to GECF gave assurances at each meeting that the purpose of the

Forum is not to influence prices. Several statements by Energy Ministers, for instance by the Algerian Energy Minister Chahib Khelil, indicated that the GECF has been established primarily to defend producers interests: "To understand the challenges posed by the development of a global gas market and especially the threats for producers and exporters posed by its rapid and unorganised liberalisation". However, commercial issues for gas exports are included among the topics discussed by the Forum.

In the way it has evolved since 2001, the Forum now intends to be a platform for producers voicing concern about the current way market liberalisation is organised. One of the Forum's major arguments was that producing countries had not been consulted in the process of liberalisation and these countries needed to cooperate to prevent any potential negative effects thereof. Their first focus has been to defend very strongly their long-term contracts with importers to allow the financing of multi-billion gas projects and the need for a fair sharing of risks and rewards between producers and importers.

One reaction of non-EU suppliers to regulatory changes and a perceived high regulatory and market risk is to move downstream, in order to ensure their market outlets and hedge their income. The EU Directives and the non-discrimination rules of WTO allow freedom of entry to exporters. Therefore exporters are integrating downstream. An example is the integration of the Algerian state company Sonatrach in Spain. Sonatrach, Spain's major supplier took a 30% share in Spanish refiner Cepsa and French Total's joint gas sales business in Spain in September 2003. The deal represents Sonatrach's first downstream move in the EU gas market. Another example is BP/Sonatrach's planned joint venture that would pool import capacity at the UK NGT LNG terminal at Isle of Grain. Qatar is also integrating downstream in the UK. ExxonMobil, in partnership with Qatar Petroleum, has a project to build a more than 20 bcm/a LNG import facility at Milford Haven in Wales. The two companies are also integrating downstream in Italy. This is an important change compared with the situation eight years ago when the European Commission blocked the joint sale of Algerian In Salah gas by Sonatrach and BP.

It has often been argued that the counterbalance monopsony power that is currently exercised by a few powerful downstream market players in gas purchase may be lost due to unbundling and more competition. Unbundling causes the merchant companies, the traditional engines of aggregation and coordination in the gas system, to lose the use of their network assets as an integral part of their financial strength and hence reduces significantly their ability to absorb the risks associated with major gas purchases. Also, because of the loss of exclusive concessions and the envisaged complete opening, sales development is more difficult to manage, even for the residential and commercial sectors. Although the Gas Directive 2003/55/EC only prescribes legal (not ownership) unbundling of the integrated companies, in several countries such companies are moving to full unbundling.

However, the loss of marketing power by wholesale companies is counterbalanced by the mergers & acquisitions trend observed in the energy (and gas) market. Corporate strategies and the obligation to compete at the European level lead energy companies to merge to reach a critical size. The expansion of business beyond the original boundaries, into other fuels (gas and electricity synergies), and up and down the value chain to spread risks, creates utilities – such as E.on, Suez, RWE, Edison, Eni, EDF – selling gas and electricity all over Europe. The growth of these utilities will lead to a greater concentration in the electricity and gas business in Europe. The result of this concentration on competition is not straightforward. From a security of supply perspective, these companies will play an essential role as they have the size and the balance sheet necessary to develop new highly-capital intensive supply gas projects. The German Government's support for the E.on-Ruhrgas merger was motivated partly by the strengthened financing capability that the merger would give to the new company for investments in Russian and other gas-supply projects.

A key issue for the future development of the European gas industry in an open market is the question of how the market will be able to perform the functions of evaluation and aggregation of demand in a timely fashion, and offer acceptable and reliable revenue and demand for new projects, in terms of an acceptable level and distribution price and volume risk, to justify the huge investments required. The process of identification and aggregation of demand and the interface between aggregator of demand and supplier is becoming even more relevant as a consequence of the shift towards a new customer base. So far, demand has come from residential and industrial customers and has been relatively predictable compared with the power sector, the main target for future growth of the gas market. The dynamics of power sector development provide only a limited certainty about the timing and scale of investments and the competitive situation of gas as a fuel of choice.

Changing features of long-term contracts

With market reform, some significant changes in the structure and pricing of long-term ToP contracts can be observed. Experience in open markets shows that long-term contracts do not disappear with market liberalisation but will continue to be a fundamental part of the gas supply mix. Even if long-term contracts remain a major part of future gas supplies, their volume and pricing clauses are likely to undergo substantial changes.

In the UK, about 85% of gas is delivered at the beach under long-term contracts, as is about half of the wholesale gas in the US. But the 5-to-8-year duration of US contracts and the 2-to-5-year duration of those in the UK are shorter than in continental Europe and contracts have different pricing formulas. Moreover, in the UK, gas is traded repeatedly on the National Balancing Point before it reaches the final customer, and there are numerous trades between producers, suppliers and consumers on price, volume and delivery point. As gas-to-gas competition increases and oil products become less relevant as the immediate competing fuel – especially with the increasing use of gas in the power generation markets – prices in most contracts are partly or totally indexed to changes in spot or futures gas prices. Oil prices nevertheless continue to influence gas prices.

The British experience of the past decade demonstrates that the existence of a competitive market does not itself lead directly to spot gas replacing other escalators in long-term contracts. From the early 1990s the only real demand for (new) long-term supply was from power generators, which escalated against the power pool price. Other customers in the gas market were supplied either directly from the spot market, or under 2-to-5-year contracts which might be indexed to spot price indicators, or by direct transfer from upstream affiliates, again usually indexed to the spot price. To compete with other suppliers, Centrica, which has a 60% share of the UK household market, has moved the majority of its gas purchase contracts away from oil to gas. As each long-term contract indexed to oil comes to an end, it is replaced by one indexed to gas.

Changes in term and volumes flexibility

Changes in structure and pricing of new continental European and Asian long-term gas supply contracts can be observed as a reaction to market reform and a portfolio approach by buyers:

- Shorter terms for new contracts (between 8 to 15 years in Europe and 15 to 20 years in Asia instead of the more traditional 20-25 years);

- Smaller volumes (for new contracts or renewals of LNG contracts): 0.5 to 3 bcm/a; these are favoured by the increasing share of gas in power generation and the multiplication of regasification plants;

- Greater flexibility in reviewed contractual terms (more flexibility in ToP and swing);

- New price indices (electricity pool prices and spot gas prices).

However, for new greenfield LNG projects there is still a trend to have a major part of the output capacity sold under long-term contracts of 20 to 25 years as an anchor for the project.

Looking at recent LNG contracts signed since 2000 (see Table 2.1), there seems to be clear evidence for a trend of shortening duration and smaller volumes. In OECD Pacific, the trend is towards shorter-term duration, a softening of ToP clauses, more spot contracts and a move from cif to fob for long-term contracts. The contracts signed in February 2002 between three Japanese gas utilities, Tokyo Gas, Toho Gas and Osaka Gas, and Malaysian LNG Tiga were the first sign of a change in LNG marketing in Asia. The contracts provide for a portion of the volume to be supplied fob rather than ex-ship and also include a buyer option to reduce contracted volumes. Flexibility may also involve reduction in the ToP minimums or the inclusion of optional cargoes at the buyers' discretion such as Korea's contract with Qatar's Rasgas. However, for new greenfield projects [LNG from Russia, Egypt, Nigeria (fourth train), for instance], contracts for 20 to 25 years are still the norm.

In Europe, several shorter-term contracts have recently been signed, mainly to supply the Spanish market. However some very large (in terms of volume and duration) long-term ToP contracts will remain in force for decades to come. These include contracts between Gazexport and Ruhrgas (prolonged in 1998 until 2030), the Troll contracts, Gasunie and Sonatrach contracts.

Table 2.1. LNG contracts signed since 2000

Buyers	Country	(mtpa)	Contract period
Algeria (Sonatrach)			
Endesa	Spain	0.75	2002-2017
Cepsa	Spain	0.45	
Iberdrola	Spain	0.75	End 2002-2017
Statoil	US (Cove Point)	0.75	Dec. 2003-Dec. 2006
Egypt (Partnerships)			
Union Fenosa	Spain	3.20	2004-2029
Segas	Spain, others	2.40	2004-2029
Gaz de France	France	3.60	End 2005-2025
BG Gas Marketing Limited	US	3.60	2006-2007
BG Gas Marketing Limited	US, Italy	3.60	2008-
Nigeria			
Iberdrola	Spain	0.36	2005-2025
ENI SpA	Italy	1.10	2005-2025
Shell Western LNG	US	1.10	2005-2025
Transgas	Portugal	1.50	2005-2025
Enel	Italy	1.85	?
BG LNG Services	US	2.20	2005-2025
Endesa Generacion SA	Spain, US	0.75	2006-2016
Total Gas & Power Limited	Europe, US	0.90	2007-2027
Shell Western LNG	Spain, US, Mexico	1.40	2007-2027
Enel	Italy	1.85	?
Australia			
Tokyo Gas	Japan	1.073	2004-2029

Table 2.1. LNG contracts signed since 2000 (continued)

Buyers	Country	(mtpa)	Contract period
Toho Gas	Japan	0.297	2004-2029
Osaka Gas	Japan	1.00	2004-2034
Tohoku Electric	Japan	0.40	2005-2020
Kyushu Electric	Japan	0.50	April 2004-
Guangdong LNG Terminal and Trunkline Project JV	China	3.30	End 2005-2030
Kogas	Korea	0.50	End 2003-2010
Shizuoka Gas Co.	Japan	0.135	2005-2029
ChevronTexaco	US	2.00	2008-2028
Kansai Electric Power Co.	Japan	0.50 0.93	2009-2014 2015-2023
Chubu Electric Power Co.	Japan	0.60	2009-2024
Tokyo Electric/Tokyo Gas	Japan	3.00	2006-2023
Shell Western LNG	Various	up to 3.7	2004-2009
Indonesia (Tangguh LNG)			
China National Offshore Oil Co.	China	2.70	2007-2032
Posco/SK Corp	Korea	1.1	2005-2025
Sempra Energy LNG Corp.	US, Mexico	3.7	2007-2022
Malaysia (MLNG Tiga)			
Tohoku Electric Power	Japan	0.90	2005-2025
Tokyo Gas	Japan	0.34	2004-2024
Toho Gas	Japan	0.22	2004-2024
Osaka Gas	Japan	0.12	2004-2024
Osaka Gas	Japan	0.90	2005-2025
Japan Petroleum Exploration	Japan	0.48	2003-2023
Tokyo Gas	Japan	2.60	April 2003- March 2018
Tokyo Electric Power Co. Inc.	Japan	4.80	April 2003- March 2018
Kogas	Korea	2.00	2003-2010
Norway (Snøhvit LNG)			
Gaz de France	France	1.25	2006-2023

Table 2.1. LNG contracts signed since 2000 (continued)

Buyers	Country	(mtpa)	Contract period
El Paso LNG	US	1.30	2006-2023
Iberdrola	Spain	1.10	2006-2023
Russia (Sakhalin Energy)			
Tokyo Gas	Japan	1.10	April 2007-2031
Tokyo Electric Power Co.	Japan	1.20	2007-2029
Kyushu Electric Power Co.	Japan	0.50	2010-2031
Trinidad			
AES Group	Dominican Rep.	0.75	2003-2023
Abu Dhabi (Adgas)			
BP Gas Marketing	Spain	0.75	2002-2005
Oman			
Shell Western LNG	Spain	0.70	2002-2007
Union Fenosa	Spain	1.60	2006-2026
Union Fenosa	Spain	1.33 (in total)	2004-2005
BP	Spain	0.6	2004-2010
Qatar (Qatargas)			
Gas Natural	Spain	1.50	Oct. 2001-2009[a]
Gas Natural	Spain	0.58	July 2002-2007[a]
Gas Natural	Spain	1.5	2005-2025
ExxonMobil	UK/Europe	14	long-term
Conoco Phillips	US	9.2	long-term
Qatar (Rasgas)			
Edison Gas	Italy	4.70	2007-2030
Chinese Petroleum Company	Taiwan	1.68	2008-2028
Endesa Generacion SA	Spain	0.80	2005-2025
ExxonMobil	US	15.60	2008/2009-2033

(a) Extended to 2012 in January 2004.
Source: Cedigaz. Country submissions.

Destination clauses

One recent change in some European gas contracts is the drop of destination clauses. Destination clauses prohibit the reselling of gas by the buyers to a third party outside the national borders. These clauses are not in line with European competition law as they restrict the resale and flow of gas between countries. Nigeria LNG in December 2002 was the first external supplier to remove destination clauses from existing and future contracts with European customers. NLNG has also pledged not to introduce profit-sharing clauses and also confirmed exclusion of "use restrictions" from future contracts, which are clauses preventing the buyer from using gas for any purpose other than what has been agreed.

Russian Gazprom agreed in July 2002 to drop the destination clause from all future contracts. In October 2003, the European Commission announced a settlement between Italy's Eni and Gazprom over destination clauses in their existing sales contracts. Eni will no longer be prevented from reselling outside Italy gas it buys from Gazprom. Equally, Gazprom will be free to sell to other customers in Italy without Eni's consent.

Algeria has also indicated that it would not introduce limitations on future cross-border gas sales with European importers. However, the issue remains for existing contracts and in particular for LNG. Sonatrach recently entered into commercial discussions with its customers to amend existing contracts. The company indicated that destination clauses are still important unless replaced by an alternative that is discussed and agreed by both parties.

Pricing issues

For forty years, in gas contracts both in the UK and continental Europe, as well as in Asia, netback pricing based on the replacement value was used in long-term contracts. This concept allowed gas to compete with alternative fuels on the buyers' markets, while covering the costs of bringing the gas to the market place – actually to the burner tip – left the remainder for the producers/the resource owner. This granted competitiveness (in the sectors targeted by the price formula) and gave the resource owner the maximum value for a predictable sales volume.

With the removal of the European ban on the use of gas in large power plants, gas-to-gas competition developing in the UK, and with pipeline-to-pipeline competition in Germany more gas was sold to the power plants, namely to new CCGTs, which resulted in adjusting the import price formulas by pegging a share of the price to the price of imported coal in German contracts.

With the development of gas-to-gas competition, a credible spot gas market developed in the UK on the NBP, so that the closest competitor for newly imported gas would be spot gas (i.e., on the supply side domestic gas from smaller fields) on the NBP. Pegging the price of an import contract to the spot price is in line with the basic philosophy of a netback contract, but it relates directly to the market value of the gas.

The issue is more complicated when gas is sold for power generation, where competition happens ultimately on the power grid. The problem is the difference in the long-run marginal cost and the short-run marginal cost merit order. The benefit of a gas-fired CCGT is not only its higher electric efficiency but also the much lower specific investment costs. This raises the question on how to split the investment premium, which according to the netback philosophy would mainly go to the gas seller. Selling the gas at a price basically competing with coal although taking into account the different efficiency, results in a very low gas price. If the price is not bound to the use of the gas for power generation this would undermine the overall market. Rolling the investment premium into the gas price, as was done in the deal between the Norwegian GFU and the Dutch Power company SEP, results in marginal costs of power production of the CCGT plant which are clearly not competitive on a marginal cost basis with existing coal-fired power generation. >

The issue of crude oil linkage for gas-fired power generation is illustrated by the Japanese experience. When the precedents for the oil-linkage were first established, Japanese power generation was heavily dependent on sweet light crude oil firing. The decision to tie LNG ToP contracts to a crude oil pricing standard indirectly linked the dispatch of the LNG and oil-fired generating units since both fuels were similarly affected by changes in crude oil prices. This precluded an incentive for fuel-switching possibilities from gas to oil. But oil-firing, which represented 66% of the electricity mix in 1974, had fallen to 11% by 2001. The growth of base-load coal and nuclear generation has not only displaced most of the oil generation, but it has also increasingly forced LNG use into middle/peak load. The high short-run marginal generating cost for gas may lead to a reduced use of gas-fired power generation at times of economic stagnation. This may reduce LNG requirements and create ToP problems.

In continental Europe, with the development of hubs and marketplaces and the increase in liquidity, indexing of long-term contracts may be based on spot gas prices as is already observed for the long-term contracts signed in the UK, which are based on prices at NBP, and for sales in the US based on Henry Hub. So far, the lack of depth of the continental European hubs seems to be the main hindrance to use their prices as a reference in long-term contracts. Moreover, prices at hubs are volatile, and a number of European operators are reluctant to price their long-term contracts against a volatile reference. However, there are ways to eliminate this volatility in contracts (index on average monthly or quarterly prices, for instance). It is likely that the increased liquidity and depth at continental European hubs will have a significant impact on the pricing of long-term contracts. Some changes were already observed from the reviews between buyers and Norwegian producers.

However, these changes lead to increased risks for sellers. There are three differences between the use of a gas market indicator and an oil indicator as a measure of change in energy prices.[11] First, gas prices appear more volatile than oil prices. Second, because of transportation costs, there are no global gas prices and some geographic "place differential" or "basis differential" must be utilised to relate geographically dispersed sales prices to the marker price. This is particularly relevant for the US market where LNG entering at the four existing receiving terminals can be credited with a premium or a discount compared with Henry Hub spot prices. This basis differential is monitored and published by trade press services. However, the local market can easily be overloaded, sharply affecting the historic differential and introducing a new element of risk in the

---

11 Jensen J. (2003b).

transaction. And finally, if the gas is delivered to the same physical market as the gas market quotation, and if the market is sufficiently liquid, the effect is to eliminate most of the buyer's risk – the buyer will always be able to resell gas on the market at the market price used in the contract – thereby transferring all the contract risks to the seller.

Therefore the move away from oil-linked price clauses in long-term contracts to term contracts with gas-linked pricing poses a substantial challenge to gas sellers, which reflects the major changes in the marketplace. It remains to be seen if and how sellers ultimately adapt to this new risk profile to shape the future structure of the gas industry.

3

THE NEW PATTERN OF GAS SUPPLY/DEMAND IN OECD: IMPACT OF THE POWER SECTOR

SUPPLY/DEMAND TRENDS IN THE OECD REGION

The OECD region is the largest energy market in the world, with 5,321 mtoe consumed in 2002, compared with 3,365 mtoe in 1971. Its energy consumption is expected to continue to grow, albeit at a lower rate than experienced in the past three decades, while the rest of the world will see its energy consumption rising more quickly. On balance, the OECD share of world energy demand will decline from 58% in 2000, to 47% by 2030.

Figure 3.1. Energy consumption by fuel in OECD, 1971-2030

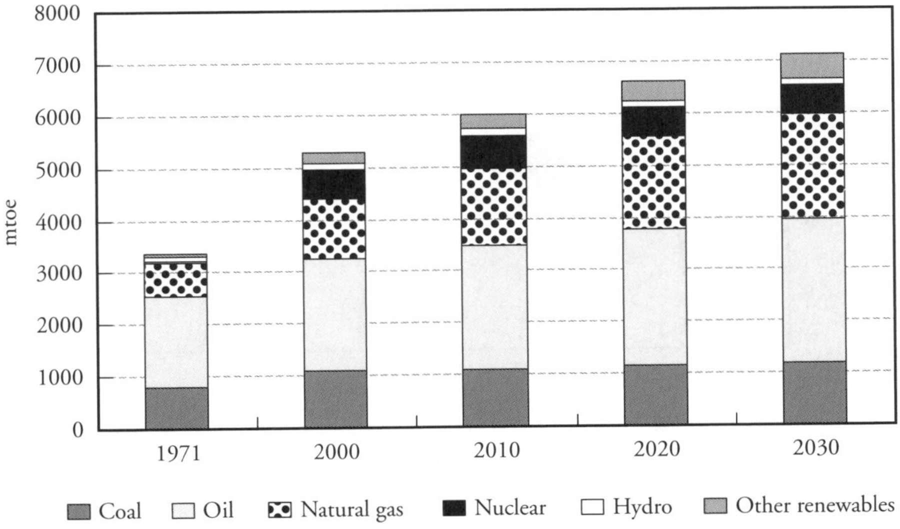

Source: *WEO 2002*

Natural gas accounts for 22% of energy demand in OECD countries. Between 1971 and 2000, gas consumption almost doubled from 653 to

1,143 mtoe. It is expected to increase by 1.9% per year on average between 2000 and 2030 and to reach 2,012 mtoe in 2030, or 28% of energy demand. Natural gas is the fastest growing energy source among fossil fuels, mainly driven by the increased gas demand in the power sector (72% of the total increase). It is expected to become the leading fuel in electricity generation in OECD countries by 2030, with a share of 32% of power generation in 2030, just before coal at 31%.

The development of the gas market in the 1970s and 1980s came in the aftermath of the 1973/74 and 1979/80 oil price shocks, driven by a policy to replace oil consumption with gas. It was concentratred on the residential and commercial sectors and on industry. Use of gas for power generation was predominantly based on domestic gas and even became restricted by regulation, so strong was the fear of scarcity in gas reserves.

Figure 3.2. Gas consumption by sector in OECD, 1971-2030

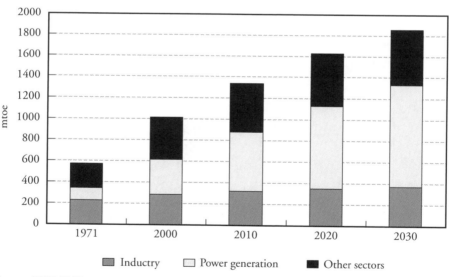

Source: *WEO 2002*

Since the beginning of the 1990s, a new – this time worldwide – wave of gas consumption has been steadily mounting, as gas is increasingly used in power generation. This remarkable increase is expected to continue for the next two to three decades. It is driven by several parallel developments.

One is the steady progress in gas turbine technology, which has substantially improved the competitivness of gas-fired power generation. This development offers new opportunities for gas-fired power generation, driven both by comercial advantages and by better environmental and GHG performance. Opening the electricity and gas markets to competition and revoking the restrictions on the use of gas for power have given gas the opportunity to win increasing shares in the power market.

Gas consumption in the OECD power sector was 117 mtoe in 1971 or about one-sixth of total gas consumption, increasing to 328 mtoe in 2000, or more than a quarter of total gas consumption and is projected to reach 958 mtoe in 2030, almost half of gas consumption in OECD countries. The other gas sectors (residential/commercial and industry) have almost reached saturation point and their gas consumption is expected to grow by only 0.9% per year on average between 2000 and 2030 (+229 mtoe). Future gas growth will therefore depend on the electricity sector.

Gas production in OECD countries amounted to 1,115 bcm in 2002 and represented 80% of OECD supplies. The maturity of geology provinces in most OECD countries means that in the majority of them gas production will at best stagnate and in some countries decrease. An increase in gas imports will thus be needed to cope with increased demand. Global proven gas reserves are abundant: 181 tcm at the beginning of 2003, or 70 years of current gas production, and proven gas reserves increased significantly faster than gas consumption. They are largely sufficient to cover the expected growth in global gas demand in the next 30 years. Gas reserves, however, are mainly found outside OECD countries. Although they are better distributed than oil reserves, they are nevertheless concentrated in two regions, the FSU and the Middle East. Three countries, Russia, Iran and Qatar account for 55% of gas reserves.

The OECD gas market is at a turning point. While OECD gas demand is expected to increase rapidly, OECD gas production is levelling off and will not be able to cover the expansion of the gas markets. Imports from non-OECD regions are therefore expected to surge. The result will be a strong increase in import dependence. This raises the issue of external security of gas supply: how to ensure that resource-owning countries will

Figure 3.3. Natural gas reserves in the world

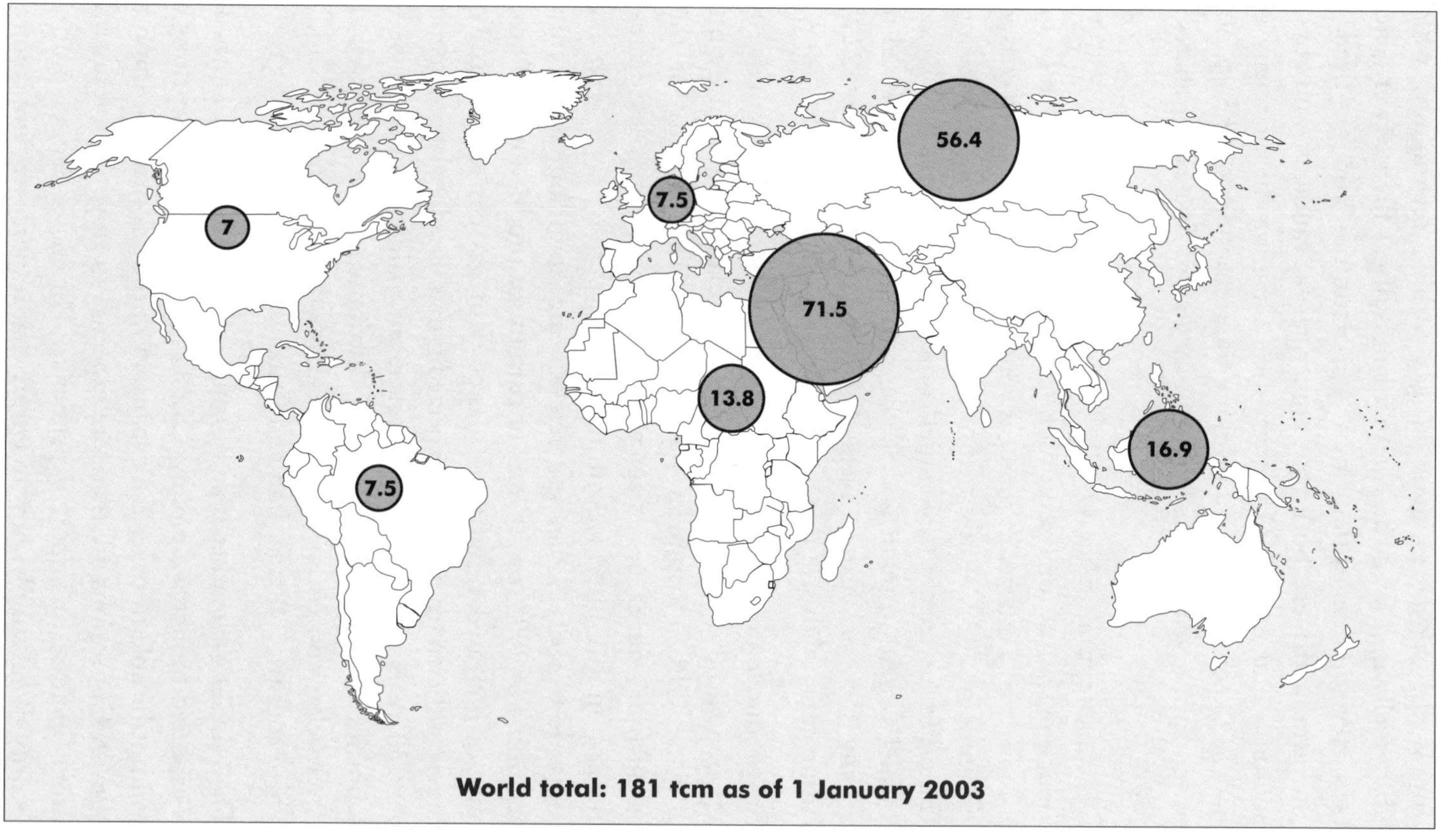

World total: 181 tcm as of 1 January 2003

Source: Cedigaz

make gas avaible for export at competitive conditions. Even for non-OECD countries, gas imports are beginning to play a role, and therefore security of gas supply may also become an issue for non-OECD countries.

These developments in gas markets will require a spectacular increase in global gas trade. Whereas global gas trade represented only 22% of global gas consumption, this share is expected to rise to 40% by 2030. A large increase is expected in LNG trade in particular. Increased LNG inter-regional trading will add flexibility and security to the global gas system.

The import dependence of OECD countries is projected to increase from a total of 274 bcm in 2000, or a share of about 20% of total gas consumption, to a total of 1,091 bcm or 45% of gas consumption by 2030. All OECD regions will become more dependent (on volume) from outside suppliers. For some regions (North America) or countries (UK), this is a major change, as they are moving away from self-sufficiency to net import dependence.

Table 3.1. Natural gas import dependence in OECD regions

	2000		2030	
	bcm*	%**	bcm*	%**
OECD North America	5	1	345	26
OECD Europe	186	36	625	69
OECD Pacific	83	67	121	50
OECD	**274**	**20**	**1091**	**45**

* Net imports in bcm
** Per cent of primary gas supply
Source: *WEO 2002*

So far, competition for external gas supplies with non-OECD countries has not been an issue for OECD countries. However with the development of imports by China and India, in particular, competition for LNG supplies emerges. Given the projected import capacity in China and India (50 bcm overall by 2030), its impact on security of supply in OECD countries is expected to be limited.

Figure 3.4. Global net inter-regional trade and production, 2001-2030

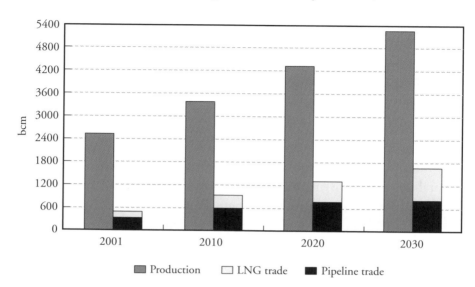

Source: *World Energy Investment Outlook 2003 (WEIO 2003)*[12]

IMPACT ON GAS SECURITY OF THE GROWING USE OF GAS FOR POWER GENERATION

This section reviews the increasing use of gas in power in OECD markets. It raises the issue of the growing part of electricty based on imported gas. It reviews the implications of seasonal changes in gas demand in power generation. It also addresses the issue of the link between gas security and electricity security, as well as the risks of gas prices going above those of gasoil in the short term.

Increased use of gas in the electricity mix in OECD

WEO 2002 projects that OECD will require more than 2,000 GW of new total generating capacity over the period 2001-2030 and will also need to replace more than a third of today's total power generating capacity. Most of the retired capacity will be coal-fired. The retirement of old fossil-fuel plants in the OECD will create opportunities to improve efficiency and to reduce CO_2 emissions. Older and inefficient coal plants are expected to be replaced,

---

12   IEA (2003a).

in most cases, by gas-fired plants or cleaner coal-fired plants. Almost half of the new generating capacity will be gas-fired. It is projected that out of a total capacity in operation of 3,294 GW in 2030, about 35% will be non fossil: nuclear: 8%; hydro including storage: 15%; other renewables and fuel cells: 12%. Fossil fuel-based power generation is projected to be 65%, with oil-fired power generation capacity being reduced in absolute terms to about 5% of capacity. 60% is projected to be gas-fired or coal-fired.

In 2002, gas accounted for 18% of electricity generation in OECD. This share is expected to reach 32% in 2030.

Figure 3.5. Electricity generation by fuel, OECD

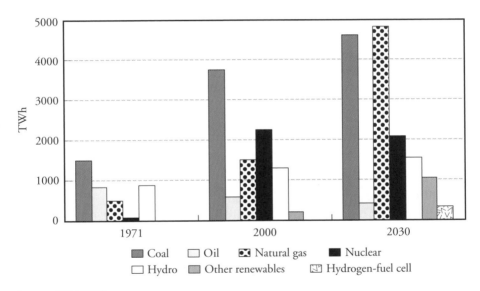

Source: *WEO 2002*

The preference for gas over alternative fuels is explained by a number of economic, technical, environmental and regulatory factors:

■ The major advantages of CCGT plants in comparison with coal-fired steam power plants are lower specific investment costs, higher electric efficiency, and a shorter construction time, modular building and higher flexibility in operation;

■ Open electricity markets also favour CCGT plants. Their lower specific investment, shorter construction time, the possibility of building them in modules, and their low economies of scale make them better adapted to meet demand, with regard to both timing and location, than capital-intensive plants like nuclear or coal plants, which have large economies of scale;

■ CCGT plants have lower specific emissions of pollutants like SO_2, NOx, particulates and mercury than coal-fired power plants; although coal-fired power plants can be built to meet stringent standards for these pollutants. Their superior environmental performance and smaller size mean that CCGTs usually do not encounter siting problems;

■ In addition to the higher electric efficiency of CCGT, gas chemical composition will result in a lower specific CO_2 emission per kWh produced. CCGTs are also a better match for combined heat and power. Faced with the new challenges of open electricity markets and uncertainty about the future rules on GHG emissions, CCGTs are considered to be the best solution.

For all these reasons, most of the global orders for new plants are CCGTs or gas turbines – 65% of the capacity ordered since 1991.

So far, the share of gas in the electricity mix is under 30% in most OECD countries and averages 18% (Table 3.2). There are six exceptions: the UK and the Netherlands, which have a larger share of their electricity mix based on domestic gas. Ireland, Italy and Turkey, which import the predominant part of their gas, have a share close to 40%, although this cannot be considered excessive as these countries have no domestic alternative fuel and no nuclear power generation. Luxembourg, which is almost completely dependent on gas for its electricity generation, is a special case. The small volume of electricity consumption in the country means that it relies on generation from just one CCGT plant.

Overall, gas demand by the power sector in OECD countries is expected to reach 958 mtoe in 2030 compared with 328 mtoe in 2000 (Table 3.3). This increase represents around 72% of the increase in gas demand in OECD.

Although the outlook for gas consumption in the power sector is very promising, there are major uncertainties about the projected rate of growth:

i) Concerns about the development of gas prices;

Table 3.2. Gas-fired electricity generation in OECD countries, 2002 vs. 1990

	1990		2002		2002 vs. 1990
	TWh	% of total generation	TWh	% of total generation	Average annual % change
Australia	16.36	10.6	29.25	13.1	5.0
Austria	7.73	15.7	10.05	16.7	2.2
Belgium	5.41	7.7	17.80	22.0	10.4
Canada	9.70	2.0	34.60	6.1	11.2
Czech Republic	0.60	1.0	3.00	3.9	14.3
Denmark	0.69	2.7	8.99	23.3	23.8
Finland	4.66	8.6	9.93	13.2	6.5
France	3.03	0.7	17.12	3.1	15.5
Germany	40.49	7.4	55.90	9.6	2.7
Greece	0.09	0.3	6.73	13.4	43.0
Hungary	4.47	15.7	10.08	27.9	7.0
Ireland	3.94	27.7	10.43	43.0	8.4
Italy	39.71	18.6	108.72	39.4	8.8
Japan	164.75	19.4	249.65	23.0	3.5
Korea	9.60	9.1	32.30	10.6	10.6
Luxembourg	0.03	4.8	2.48	92.9	43.0
Mexico	13.01	10.6	69.13	32.1	14.9
Netherlands	36.65	50.9	59.00	61.3	4.0
New Zealand	5.69	17.6	10.13	25.6	4.9
Norway	-	-	0.27	0.2	-
Poland	0.14	0.1	1.50	1.1	21.9
Portugal	-	-	9.10	20.0	-
Slovak Republic	1.16	5.0	2.46	7.7	6.5
Spain	1.51	1.0	32.39	13.4	29.1
Sweden	0.40	0.3	0.55	0.4	2.8
Switzerland	0.30	0.5	1.03	1.6	10.7
Turkey	10.19	17.7	52.50	40.6	14.6
UK	5.00	1.6	150.23	39.3	32.8
USA	381.67	12.0	716.34	18.1	5.4

Source: IEA *Electricity Information* 2003

Table 3.3. Increase in OECD gas demand by the power sector (mtoe)

	1971	2000	2010	2030
OECD North America	97	175	300	491
OECD Europe	19	96	182	339
OECD Pacific	8	57	80	128
OECD	**124**	**328**	**562**	**958**

Source: *WEO 2002*

ii) The conditions for (imported) gas for power generation may not be sufficiently attractive;

iii) Policy choices may result in lower growth of electricity consumption by promoting more efficiency in electricity application, or may set objectives which reduce the attractiveness of gas in power generation.

i) Gas-fired power-generation has been the most economic option so far but alternatives like coal-fired and nuclear power generation have historically offered much lower and more stable fuel costs, while gas prices are considered less predictable. To alleviate the latter concerns, in a number of cases gas suppliers and power generators have tried to hedge the price risk, e.g., by merging with gas production companies or by concluding long-term contracts for new power plants with price indexation, designed to provide long-term assurance of price competitiveness. These contracts are particularly important for independent power producers (IPP), often operating a single power plant, at a small margin. Another way is to run gas-fired power plants more as peaking plants, based on a favourable spark spread[13], e.g., at high power prices and relatively low gas prices to recoup the investment and earn a profit during a few hours of high electricity prices.[14] Where gas markets are liquid, power plant operators may resell gas they are committed to take if the spark spread does not favour power production.

---

13 The spark spread is defined as the difference, at a particular location and at a particular point in time, between the fuel cost of generating a MWh of electricity and the price of electricity. It is calculated as the difference between the product of the gas price and the heat rate of a power plant (a measure of thermal efficiency) used to generate the electricity less the spot price of electricity at that location. As a result, a positive spark spread indicates the power generator should buy electricity rather than make it.

14 See *Power generation investment in electricity markets*, IEA (2003d).

ii) If gas supply conditions are not sufficiently supportive, generators may not be ready to embrace the gas option to the extent the growth projections for gas suggest. They may prefer to defer investment decisions, or invest in the prolongation of nuclear, or increase power production based on coal, eventually by increasing the efficiency of coal-fired power. In some countries, a substantial part of a rather sluggish increase in power demand will be satisfied by renewables.

iii) In the *WEO 2002* alternative scenario, electricity demand by OECD is lower due to assumed policies favouring more efficient use of power, resulting in lower overall power consumption and consequently in lower use of gas for power generation as well as a reduction in gas import requirements. Future demand growth will be influenced by political choices (in particular with regard to environmental legislation), the future of nuclear and coal, and the relative competitiveness of gas compared with other fossil fuels. CO_2 price and emission trading will have an influence either. The over-capacity in power generation on the European market led to low wholesale prices across various parts of Europe (mainly in the UK, France and Germany) and has substantially slowed down the construction of new gas-fired power plants and with it the growth of gas consumption in power generation. The situation is changing as electricity prices have started to rise in several EU countries. In North America, current high gas prices may challenge the growth of gas in the power sector and may revive coal and nuclear options. The future of the next wave of CCGTs is uncertain if prices remain at their current level.

Figure 3.6 shows the costs of electricity generation for new coal-fired power plants and gas-fired CCGTs (with selected gas prices). It shows that at gas prices above $5/million Btu, total costs of newly constructed coal-fired plants are more economical than those of new CCGTs. Because of greenhouse concerns, nuclear and clean coal technologies would probably be the most attractive alternative. Investment in new base-load power plants is based on long-term price expectation, not on short-term prices. However, the overall consensus in the US is that supply/demand fundamentals will lead to a sustained level of prices. If relative fuel prices shift dramatically in the long run, electricity generators will be searching for lower-cost alternatives.

Figure 3.6. Nominal busbar costs

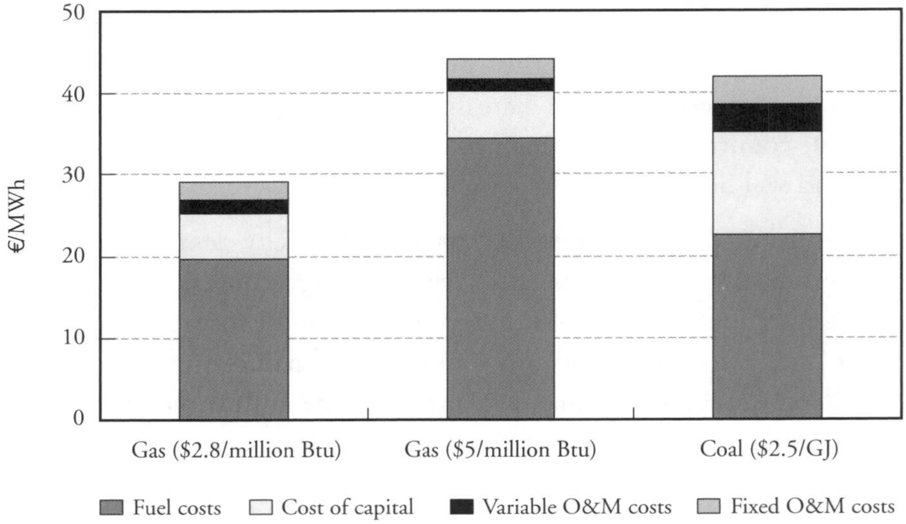

Source: IEA (2003g)

Impact on security of gas supply of the growing use of gas for power generation

The increased use of gas for power generation has strong implications for both the long-term external security of supply and the short-term reliability of the power and gas systems, because when gas enters the electricity sector, it is the last fuel in the merit order, just before oil products in peaking plants.[15] Governments may also be concerned about its impact on future gas prices as well as the issue of the volatility of gas prices. The increased interdependence between the gas and electricity systems must be addressed.

Additional gas-fired power generation based on imported gas

Basing large-scale power production to a greater extent on imported gas is a new feature – except in OECD Pacific – driven not only by environmental concerns but also by electricity market reforms. So far, power production is still predominantly based on domestic resources (coal, lignite, hydro, or domestic gas in the UK and the Netherlands) or quasi-domestic (nuclear) or on imported coal for which a world market exists.

---

15 Bourdaire J-M. (2003).

However, *WEO 2002* projections show that most of the gas increase in power generation will be based on imported gas. In OECD countries, gas to power is expected to increase by 630 Mtoe over the period 2000-2030. During the same period gas imports will increase by 817 Mtoe. For the North American and Pacific markets, the increase is based on LNG imports. This is less true for Europe, where the increase of gas to power will rely on a mix of LNG and pipeline imports. Figure 3.7 shows that for North America the increase in imports and the increase in the use of gas in power generation are very similar, indicating that the increase in consumption outside of the power sector, theoretically, could be covered by North American gas production. For OECD Europe the increase in imports is substantially larger than the increase in use for power generation and even larger than the increase in total gas consumption, a reflection of the stagnation of domestic OECD gas production. For OECD Pacific, the increase in gas imports is less than the increase in consumption in power. However, one must keep in mind that OECD Pacific comprises large gas importers, Japan and Korea, but also Australia, a country which is expected to become a substantial gas exporter not only to Japan and Korea, but also to China and India. Thus, taking Japan and Korea alone, which are practically 100% dependent on gas imports, would show an increase in imports of the same size as the increase in gas consumption.

This raises a number of questions:

i) Will enough gas resource-owning countries be willing to dedicate sufficient reserves for export to be used in power?

ii) Will it be possible to obtain a satisfactory degree of diversification of suppliers (from the point of view of the importing countries)?

iii) Will it be possible to mobilise the investment necessary for the development of these gas reserves and for the export infrastructure? and,

iv) How will the interface for the imported gas for power generation be organised? This will be different for LNG and pipeline gas, for the OECD regions and for various export countries.

i) LNG exporters' response to the growing import needs of the US and UK suggests that countries like Algeria, Qatar, Nigeria, Trinidad and Tobago and other Atlantic suppliers are interested in supplying LNG to

Figure 3.7. Use of gas in power and gas imports, OECD (2030 vs. 2000)

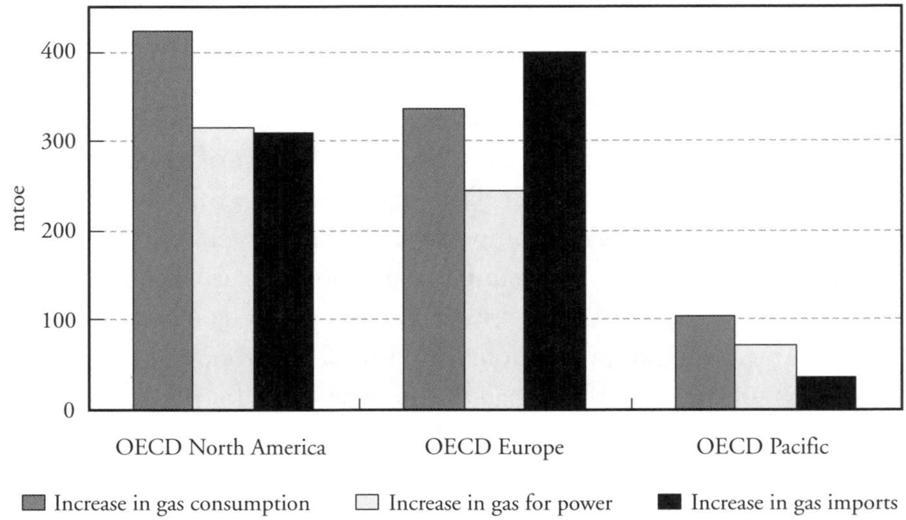

Source: *WEO 2002*

the US and UK. In the UK, there are also several new projects to import gas by pipeline. Similarly, Indonesia, Malaysia, Australia, Russia (Sakhalin) and Qatar and other suppliers show willingness to supply LNG to the Pacific market, including China and India. In all cases the gas will on balance predominantly be used in the power sector. The import gas prices in the UK and US are based on gas-to-gas competition, which will include the demand by the power sector. The main competitor for imported gas in the US will be domestic gas, which – given the maturity of US resources – will probably increase in costs/price. In the UK too, the speed of decline of domestic production will mean that delivering gas to the UK will not present a significant risk for a gas exporter. The fact that gas will mostly be dedicated to power generation is not a specific issue for exporters of gas to these markets. In Japan and Korea, prices are linked to crude oil and LNG has always been imported mainly for power. Both markets are attractive markets for LNG.

The question of which price mechanisms will be applied to gas imported for power is open in continental Europe, which is mainly supplied by pipeline gas. The largest gas resource owner, Russia, which has the potential for substantial domestic use of gas, has not yet shown how it wants to deal with that issue, except for the Sakhalin project dedicated to Asia.

ii) It looks as if the US will have the chance to be well diversified. Substantial capacity from the Atlantic basin will be dedicated to the US and reach the US market when US prices are competitive with the European market. The share of LNG, with its associated geopolitical risks, like passing the Strait of Hormuz or the Suez Canal, seems to stay within the limits of what would probably be covered by the overall US market, albeit with some regional market impacts. A similar picture seems to be emerging for the UK. For Japan and Korea, LNG supplies are already very well diversified. The EU is now well diversified and new gas for power comes mainly from several LNG suppliers for countries bordering the Atlantic market and the Mediterranean countries. For the rest of continental Europe extra gas would probably come by pipeline from Russia, Norway or Central Asia.

iii) Financing of exploration and production is straightforward if international oil companies are involved. This depends on the upstream regime. More and more gas resource-owning countries are trying to come up with upstream governance rules to attract more foreign investors.

Financing of LNG export infrastructure does not seem to impose an undue risk premium, as long as there is a credible buyer for the LNG or access to a liquid marketplace like the US or UK. The remaining risk is concentrated on the sovereign country risk. A positive example is the credit rating of the Oman gas project within the A range. However, in the light of the Iraqi war, the credit rating of several countries in the Gulf region has suffered recently.

A major issue is the building of LNG receiving terminals by importing countries. Here there are two positive developments in the US: the Hackberry decision, which allows the sole use of LNG investment by the investors and the streamlining of the siting procedures by FERC (see below). Similar tendencies are developing in the UK. Since these developments, investors have being queuing up, and there is a long list of proposed projects at various stages of implementation (see Chapter 4).

In Europe, financing of new pipeline infrastructure is mostly concentrated on the former Soviet Union and Algeria. The financing of these projects will still depend on long-term gas contracts, which are difficult to design for volumes allocated to power generation (see Chapter 2).

iv) In the US and UK, the interface between gas and electricity is linked to liquid gas and power markets, and therefore is not an issue. In addition, to the extent that gas is imported as LNG, it is much more flexible than exports of gas by pipeline: LNG can be directed to serve several markets, and the development of capacity can be adjusted to the development of demand. Nor is there any danger of undermining existing marketing by exporting LNG to the US. The main issue seems to be to ensure access to the US/UK markets by building or contracting regasification capacity.

In countries with liquid gas and power markets, it might be that new power generation capacity based on gas will be added as long as the spark spread allows money to be made. The investment into power capacity will follow the scarcity for that market to provide extra power generation capacity (whether it will be used as peak load or base load).

A different issue arises in markets like Spain or Italy, because there is no liquid gas market as yet. On these markets, the growth in power demand is still high (3-4% per year), most of which will be supplied by gas-fired power generation, as well as for more base-load applications. In the absence of a liquid gas market, long-term commitment of new power generation to gas instruments such as long-term contracts or vertical integration seems to be the appropriate alternative. In these markets, one solution may be for exporting countries to be involved downstream, for instance Sonatrach in Spain, where the company is involved in regasification (El Ferrol) and in the marketing of gas through its joint venture with Cepsa and Total. Qatar Petroleum with ExxonMobil also recently acquired stakes in Italy's LNG project in Rovigo.

Germany, and to some extent France, are in a different situation as growth rates of electricity consumption are more moderate and the debate is more focused on the continuation or replacement of existing fuels like nuclear or lignite and hard coal which makes it more difficult to determine the competitive situation of gas for power generation.

How can long-term contracts address the interface between gas and power generation? It is difficult for producing countries to capture the premium of gas in power generation because the premium accrues in the investment phase. The indexation on oil products, which is justified for the other segments of gas consumption, may be inappropriate in the case of power plants. Could other pricing schemes offer better risk/reward sharing? Other indexation schemes have been tested in the past (SEP agreement with the GFU of Norway or Enel agreement with Nigeria LNG) which used indexation on coal prices which are more stable. However, in both cases, the agreements were not a success as the price of electricity collapsed in Europe while at the same time gas prices rose.

One of the major difficulties is to capture the difference in the long-run marginal costs and the short-run marginal costs between a gas-fired power plant and a coal-fired power plant. While the specific investment of a coal-fired power plant is about twice that of a CCGT, the price of coal on an energy content basis is only about half of the gas import price at the German border.[16] Therefore gas will not be able to compete with coal on the basis of marginal costs. As long as there is unused capacity in coal-fired power generation, gas would go to peak load. On the other hand, selling gas at a price competitive with coal on a short-run marginal cost – and receiving the investment premium as a lump sum or as a capacity charge – would undercut the gas import price for other applications/contracts. A minimum-take clause based on a price reflecting the long-run marginal costs of a competing coal-fired power plant may be possible but there would be no incentive to run the plant beyond the minimum pay and little room for the optimisation of the plant in the merit order.

How can the necessary investment be financed, given that there will be no firm demand for gas when used for power generation in an open power market? As indicated by Eurelectric[17], long-term contracts (for electricity sales) are important as they give investors an opportunity to justify their investment decision when seeking to raise the necessary capital.

There will be competition for gas in power with gas-producing countries that may wish to build up an electricity or gas-intensive industry of their own. Why export gas over long distances or as LNG to produce gas-based power, which in turn will serve to keep up the electricity or gas intensity of

---

16   Even after the recent price hike in coal prices (from about $40/t of coal to about $60/t of coal at Rotterdam).
17   Eurelectric (2003).

GDP in the importing country? Companies in gas-rich countries could make use of their competitive advantage by producing aluminium or ammonia and exporting them, instead of exporting their gas.

Apart from the good fit of gas-fired power into open power markets – at least for peak load – there is also the environmental driver of GHG benefits. Decisions for base-load, on the other hand, will be based more on fundamentals like growth in demand and other possible options. The advantage of lower investment into gas-fired CCGTs is offset by the relatively higher investment upstream of the delivery point for the gas. Investment will be necessary in liquefaction plants or pipelines in non-IEA countries as well as in developing their resources. In this regard, IEA countries are trading – *ceteris paribus* – lower GHG emissions against gas-import dependence from non-IEA countries. On the other hand the risk of misallocation of investment is not that large in IEA countries as gas-fired power can still be used as a peaking plant. Uncertainty about long-term GHG mitigation policies may impede long-term investment decisions in the power sector.

Will producing countries claim for the premium from lower CO_2 emissions of gas-fired power plants? How should CO_2 emissions of gas transportation outside of Annex 1 countries (e.g., about 12-15% energy consumption in liquefaction plants, 1 to 2% for compressor stations per 1000 km) be dealt with?

Governments will need to monitor these developments as import dependence increases in OECD countries.

Link between reliability of gas supply and electricity supply

The growing share of imported gas for electricity generation raises the issue of reliability of electricity supply in case of a gas supply disruption and the question of possible back-up fuels for gas in power plants.

The impact of a gas supply disruption on electricity security will depend on the flexibility developed in both systems. In addition to the gas industry's back-stop tools in case of disruption (flexibility from other gas supplies, storage, interruptible customers, spot markets, availability of short-term LNG cargoes), flexibility in the electricity system may also help. This includes the traditional instruments of fuel switching in dual-fired plants as well as using spare capacity from other power plants linked to the grid and in open electricity markets, using the market to balance supply and demand.

Reserve margins are a key element for flexibility in the electricity system. However, in the 1990s generation reserves have declined in most OECD countries.[18]

While the situation varies strongly between different IEA countries, several developments which tie the reliability of the gas supply to the reliability of electricity supply to customers can be observed:

- Change in fuel switching/dual-firing capacity;

- Change in seasonality;

- Price volatility;

- Increased linkage between gas and power.

Fuel switching/Dual-firing capacity

Dual-firing plants are still an essential instrument in case of disruption of gas supply. Table 3.4 and Figure 3.8 show the capacity of single-fired and multi-fired gas power plants in OECD countries.

In 2001, 50% of power capacity based on gas was multi-fired. However, in 1990, 80% of gas plant capacity was multi-fired. In the aftermath of the 1973/74 oil price crisis and (shown on the graph) in the aftermath of the 1979/80 oil price crisis, a large number of oil-fired boiler power plants, mainly in the US, were retrofitted to also run on gas. The new gas-fired generating capacity in the 1990s was predominantly gas turbines and CCGTs which were gas-fired only. Gas-fired boiler plants were only built in exceptional cases, for smaller sizes. New highly efficient CCGT plants with fuel back-up can only run on very clean fuel because of severe technical problems and the risk even of potential damage. Therefore, although GTs and CCGTs can be run as multi-fired plants, the alternative fuel will be oil distillate, which is much more expensive than fuel oil. CCGT operators do not always have enough economic incentives to store the alternative back-up fuel (even for short periods). In addition, environmental legislation may restrict the use of any alternative fuel and

---

18 IEA (2002g).

Table 3.4. Single gas- and multi-fired generation capacity in OECD countries, 2001

| | Single-fired | | Multi-fired | | | | |
| | | | Total | | Solid/ Gas | Liquid/ Gas | Solid/ Liquid/ Gas |
	MW	%	MW	%	%	%	%
Australia	6 944	89.7	800	10.3	0	2.1	8.3
Austria	1 044	22.6	3 579	77.4	26.3	48.5	2.7
Belgium	1 031	14.1	6 299	85.9	1.7	59.3	24.9
Canada	6 003	74.5	2 057	25.5	20.2	5.3	0
Czech Republic	0	-	0	-	-	-	-
Denmark	1 678	48.9	1 756	51.1	7.3	21.8	22.0
Finland	414	9.4	4 001	90.6	5.6	36.0	49.0
France	540	16.5	2 742	83.5	21.3	33.9	28.4
Germany	14 760	45.4	17 745	54.6	7.9	27.0	19.7
Greece	1 112	100	0	-	-	-	-
Hungary	0	-	4 065	100	0	95.2	4.8
Ireland	345	17.7	1 600	82.3	0	82.3	0
Italy	6 646	20.9	25 101	79.1	0	64.4	14.7
Japan	35 504	60.3	23 356	39.7	0	39.7	0
Korea	6 415	47.1	7 216	52.9	0	52.9	0
Luxembourg	65	100	0	-	0	0	0
Mexico	8 708	54.4	7 289	45.6	0	45.6	0
Netherlands	11 392	60.8	7 332	39.2	18.9	20.3	0
New Zealand	1 584	61.3	1 000	38.7	38.7	0	0
Norway	35	100	0	-	-	-	-
Poland	194	100	0	-	-	-	-
Portugal	1 176	62.0	722	38.0	0	38.0	0
Slovak Republic	471	24.4	1 458	75.6	23.9	43.7	8.0
Spain	3 665	54.1	3 115	45.9	0	45.9	0
Sweden	-	0	0	-	-	-	-
Switzerland	325	100	0	-	-	-	-

Table 3.4. Single gas- and multi-fired generation capacity in OECD countries, 2001 (continued)

| | Single-fired | | Multi-fired | | | | |
| | | | Total | | Solid/ Gas | Liquid/ Gas | Solid/ Liquid/ Gas |
	MW	%	MW	%	%	%	%
Turkey	4 850	67.8	2 303	32.2	0	32.2	0
United Kingdom	22 293	96.7	771	3.3	0	3.3	0
United States	135 263	47.5	149 794	52.5	0	52.5	0

Actual US fuel-switching capability may be more limited than the table suggests (see Chapter 6).
Source: IEA

Figure 3.8. Evolution of single and multi-fired gas capacity in OECD

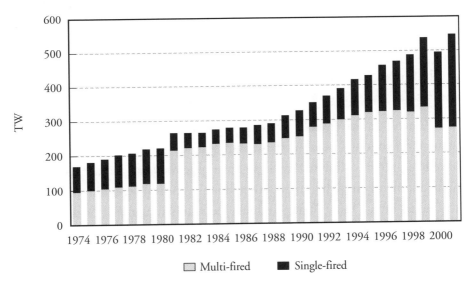

Source: IEA

seriously limit fuel-switching possibilities. With the building of substantial new CCGT capacity since 1999 in the US, some of the dual fired boilers were retired, leading to decreases in absolute dual-fired capacity.

It should be noted that the future development of CHP will tend to be based on single-firing. Although CHP and multi-firing are not mutually exclusive, multi-firing can adversely affect the economics of very small CHP plants.

These trends result in a more inelastic demand for gas during times of high electricity demand.

Impact on seasonality of increased use of gas in peaking power plants

The cost characteristics, i.e., low capital cost of gas-fired power plants and the relatively high fuel costs of gas, favour the use of gas in middle and peak generation, and the use of capital-intensive coal and nuclear plants in base-load. Gas turbines can be built within a short time to make up for tight generating capacity. They can be operated to meet instantaneous power demand increases. This technical advantage has contributed to the dispatch of gas (in gas turbines) in peak load.

The use of gas for middle or peak loads can add to and amplify the seasonality of gas demand. In countries and regions with simultaneous gas and electricity demand peaks, such as most parts of northern Europe, the demand patterns of the power supply industry can compound the peakiness of the gas demand rather than reduce it. It will be the opposite for most parts of the US where electricity consumption peaks in summer and induces a main peak for gas demand by the power industry in summer and a secondary lower peak in winter.

The use of gas in middle or peak loads alters gas supply requirements which will follow a more variable and seasonal trend. If power operators have long-term contracts for their gas supply, they can choose to resell gas on the spot market when their power plant is not in operation or operates at a lower rate. They can also reinject gas into storage. For peaking plants using gas, these plants have extremely low load factors, so gas supply using short-term storage is very attractive. This need is driving some of the US development of short-term storage, particularly salt cavern storage.

Given this gas use at the margin, spot price signals play a fundamental role. When extreme cold or warm air moves into a region, demand for electric power can quickly escalate to meet the increased requirement for heat or air conditioning. In such circumstances, gas-fired "peaking units" will come on-line to supplement the base-load generation. Prices for this peaking generation will often be much higher than the prevailing price before the change in weather.

Impact on prices/price volatility

Risks of gas prices going above gasoil prices

Natural gas has no captive customers since it can always be substituted (sooner or later) by alternative fuels for each customer, however not necessarily on the level of the whole market. In the power sector, gas power plants are in competition with coal, nuclear and renewables; in the industrial sector, fuel oil is the main competitor, and in the residential sector, electricity and heating oil. This is why, when a competitive gas market exists, although oil and gas prices move independently, they will influence each other. Historically, natural gas prices have been lower than crude oil prices in OECD countries, except in Asia/Pacific where LNG prices have always been higher than oil prices (Figure 3.9). The evolution of future prices in *WEO 2002* is based on the assumption that natural gas prices remain below crude oil prices or maintain their relationships with crude oil prices.

Figure 3.9. Evolution of international fossil fuel prices

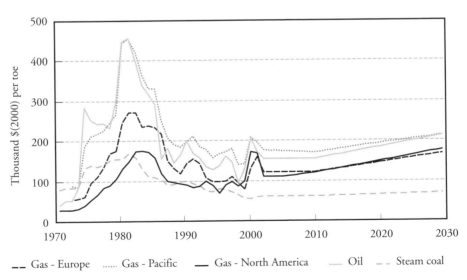

Source: *WEO 2002*

The rising use of gas in the power sector raises the question of the competitiveness of natural gas against other power alternatives and what effect this has on gas prices. The increasing use of CCGT plants in the generating systems may affect short-term gas prices since they can run as multi-fired plants, but would then require lighter oil distillates. This alters the economics of dual-firing (compared to the past when most dual-firing was based on dual-fired boilers able to burn heavy fuel oil) since lighter distillates, such as gasoil, are more expensive than heavy fuel oil, and shift the balance of back-up fuels away from an almost exclusive use of heavy fuel oil to more and more light distillates.

In OECD open gas markets, short-term gas prices may go well above the price of gasoil. The short-term setting of gas prices in competitive markets that use gas in power provides an illustration of this.[19]

Fuel-switching is possible on a short-term basis in dual-fired industrial or power plant boilers or turbines and in dual-fired CCGT plants. Electricity demand plays a more important role because, unlike industrial use, which is based-load (constant over the year), electricity demand has a seasonal and variable demand with gas and petroleum used at the margin, i.e., for mid and peak loads, once all the other means with lower variable costs have been used. So in competitive markets, electricity is at the heart of inter-fuel competition and of gas price-setting mechanisms. This is illustrated by the US market, where the gas price is set on the basis of variable fuel cost (per kWh output) in the power sector. It can either be equal to the price of its marginal competitor or oscillate between different competitors, such as:

- A floor set by coal and a heavy fuel oil ceiling in periods of over-supply;

- A floor set by heavy fuel oil and a heating oil ceiling under normal supply circumstances;

- Above a heating oil floor in periods of scarcity.

When gas is abundant (the "gas bubble" period), gas is the preferred fuel and it substitutes against all switchable petroleum consumers and has to compete with coal on the basis of marginal costs of a kWh produced (i.e., taking into account the higher efficiency and lower operating costs of

---

19 Bourdaire J-M. (2003), Jensen J. (2002).

Figure 3.10. US spot fuel prices for power generation

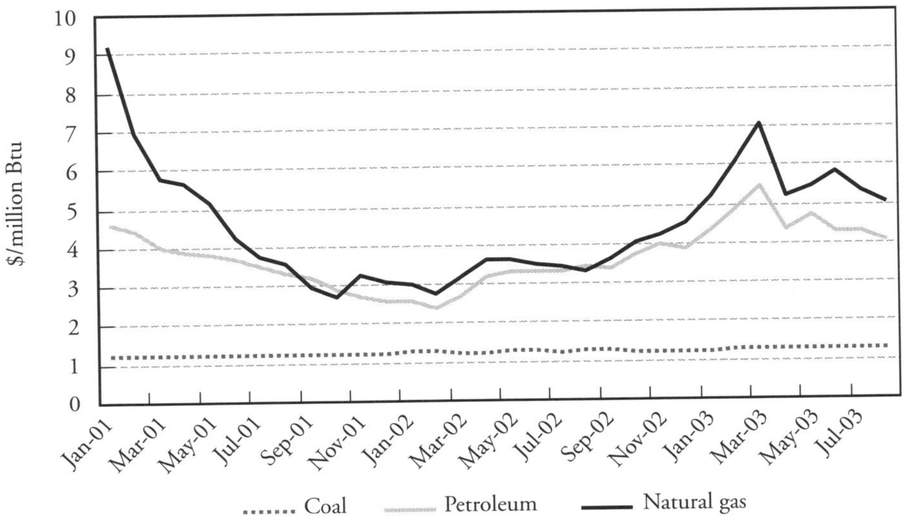

Source: EIA *Electric Power Monthly*, December 2003

natural gas). This happened during the 1990s when gas was priced at around $2/million Btu.

When gas supply is less abundant, and when all dual coal-gas burners are turned to coal, gas is then set at the burner tip of the dual-gasoil boilers against heavy fuel oil costs (3.5%, 1%, 0.7% or 0.3% sulphur content depending on local environment constraints) and other variable costs on a kWh basis. At this level, all dual-fired utilities (classic steam boilers) and industrial boilers will switch to gasoil (residual fuel oil). This happens during most winters in the US north-east region.

When all dual-fired gas/ heavy fuel oil plants have turned to heavy fuel oil, gas price rises to the next marginal fuel, oil distillates used by clean boilers or in CCGTs, as happened in winter 2000/2001, and in winter 2002/2003.

Lastly, when natural gas supply becomes so tight that all interruptible dual-fired capacities are switched to other fuels, gas price can skyrocket. In practice, this will be limited by price elasticity phenomena (reduction of demand – see Chapter 6).

In the long run, as gas is always substitutable, the price of alternative fuels may constitute a ceiling for gas prices. However, with more stringent environmental regulation, the only possible substitute may be oil distillate, and therefore there is a risk that in a tight supply situation gas prices will ultimately stay close to gasoil prices.

This is an issue that governments must address. There are some possible back-stops. The existence of dual-fuel fired plants running on fuels other than distillates may be an immediate instrument to limit a spike price. In general, spare capacity in electricity generation based on fuels other than gas and distillates which can be mobilised in a relevant timeframe should be a price back-stop. Mothballed coal-fired power plants could be used in case of rising gas prices. However, all remedies have a cost. In the case of dual-firing plants, the costs of the back-up fuel stocks may be a barrier, and mothballing coal-fired power plants instead of closing them down is not necessarily a cheap option.

Volatility

A major risk associated with gas-fired generation in CCGTs in competitive markets is the price volatility of natural gas. Electricity prices are going to be affected by gas price volatility. In many regions of the US, gas-fired generators set the clearing price for electricity in wholesale markets. Therefore electricity consumers will feel the impact of changing gas prices. A key feature of competitive markets is the development of price risk management. Electricity generators may choose a variety of financial instruments and contracts to stabilise their fuel costs (see Chapter 2).

Stronger interdependence between gas and power systems

Coincidence of peak gas and electricity demand

The increasing share of gas in the electricity mix leads to concerns about the impacts of simultaneous occurrence of peak demands in both commodities. Periods of peak demand for gas (due to colder than normal weather) will tend to occur at the same time for electricity in cold climates. The occurrence of both peaks may create additional stress on electricity and gas systems. However, the resilience of the gas and of the electricity system is different. An imbalance between supply and demand in the electric grid may lead within minutes to a larger blackout, as was recently demonstrated. The gas system is more resilient to the extent that line-pack is available, but even in the case of imbalance the immediate consequence would be a pressure drop in the system, which would not necessarily result in an immediate collapse of the system. So the gas system can mitigate a significant proportion of the risk of concurrent peaks. ⟩

Arbitrage in open liquid markets

With the increased use of gas for power generation and the opening of the electricity grid to competition, demand for gas for power generation becomes more price elastic in the short-term as the competitive electricity market offers short-term incentives to take gas or not, according to its price. Power producers can resell gas they have purchased under long-term contracts (if contracts permit). They can sell the gas at the current market price and buy electricity from the grid, if that gives a higher yield than using the gas to produce power.

In competitive gas and electricity markets, the operator of a gas-fired power plant can optimise his operations according to the "spark spread". Arbitrage between the electricity and gas markets functions as follows: when the market price of electricity is higher than the price of gas at the power plant, plus variable power production costs and taking into account the thermal efficiency, the power generator will generate electricity from gas. In the opposite case, he will produce from another energy source or buy electricity on the spot market.[20] He may interrupt his own production and sell gas instead of burning it. The market price of spot gas, therefore, is increasingly determined by the spot price of electricity.

While arbitrage is making better use of spare capacity in each system, it may conceivably result in a systemic stress on both systems.

Conclusions

The increased use of gas in power generation does not create security of supply problems at present. However, it indicates a need for governments to monitor future developments, in particular in countries or regions where the growing use of gas in power generation is based on increased gas imports.

---

20 In this case, he also needs to take into account the cost of not using his gas plant.

Concerns over security of supply do not justify restricting the use of gas in power generation, however, as long as there is a reasonable portfolio.

On the other hand the parallel opening of the electricity and gas markets leads to synergies and new flexibility of the gas and electricity sectors by relying on the market reactions of both sectors. However, it may also lead to concurrent stress on both systems.

The preceding discussion identifies a number of rising risks: increase price risk and volatility of prices; import dependence on gas for electricity production; fewer multi-firing plants and therefore less scope for the system to react to a disruption of gas supply without the risk of short-term price spikes. Under such circumstances, it will be important to maintain some flexibility in both systems, such as some back-up capacity based on coal when possible, and to encourage (with market intensives) dual-firing capability and fuel-switching capabilities, inclusive of back-up fuel storage. If such measures were required, they should be duly paid for by all consumers through market mechanisms. This should be based on a cost/benefit analysis as the costs incurred should be proportionate to the actual risk of disruption.

IMPACT OF NEW TECHNOLOGICAL DEVELOPMENTS ON SECURITY OF GAS SUPPLY

Technological developments have helped to shape every aspect of gas market demand, supply and trade, and thereby have an impact on security of gas supply. The development of even more efficient gas turbines in the 1980s and 1990s allowed the spectacular growth of gas demand in the power sector. On the supply side, 3D and 4D seismic and large computers to evaluate seismic data, along with the introduction of horizontal drilling, substantially improved the finding and recovery rates of gas deposits. Cost reductions in the LNG chain are transforming regional markets into a wide global market. Offshore pipelines can now be built at water depths of 2,000 metres, allowing trade between countries which was previously technically impossible.

The larger-scale use of gas in cars, e.g., in fuel cells, remains a challenge, as costs need to be brought down to a level competitive with cars based on the traditional combustion engine.

The more imminent technological developments, which are aimed primarily at reducing costs, will increase security of supply by enabling access to resources and enlarging the size of gas markets due to the higher economic reach of gas transportation. Major cost reductions in transportation of gas are still expected, in particular for high-pressure (HP) long-distance pipelines and LNG. This should foster a remarkable development of cross-border gas trade needed to satisfy the increase in demand in OECD countries.

This section summarises the major technological developments that impact security of gas supply.

Exploration and production

On the production side, advanced technological development tends to increase gas supply. The improvement of exploration techniques such as 3D seismic and better interpretation due to more computing power result in higher success rates in exploration. Production techniques such as horizontal drilling will increase recovery rates of fields close to the market and allow a better exploitation of provinces close to existing gas markets. While horizontal drilling allows for a higher recovery rate, it often leads to a higher depletion rate of reservoirs, resulting in a need to replace producing wells faster. Further development of deep-water technologies offers considerable potential to prove more reserves in the deep-water rim off North America and Europe, notwithstanding certain restrictions of a more regulatory nature.

At present, the production of gas hydrates is uneconomical. In the long run, if gas hydrates become economical to produce, this would significantly expand the gas resource base, with a large potential in OECD countries.

Transportation by pipeline

Developments over the past decade in offshore pipeline technology have contributed to lower unit costs and have facilitated deep-water projects that were previously impossible. The development of a pipe-laying technology capable of laying pipes at a depth of 650 metres represented a breakthrough in the early 1980s and paved the way for the laying of the Enrico Mattei (Transmed) pipeline between Tunisia and Sicily. Offshore pipeline technology also played a big role in the exploitation of North Sea gas resources in the 1970-80s and more recently in the Gulf of Mexico. The J-lay method to install offshore pipelines at great depths has recently allowed the construction of the Blue Stream Project, delivering Russian gas across the Black Sea to Turkey at water depths of more than 2,000 metres.

The most significant positive impact on security of gas supply should come from further decreases of specific transportation costs. Cost reductions can be expected from stronger steels, high-pressure technology, and deepwater pipe-laying:

- For gas transportation by pipeline, the development of higher quality steel (X-80 steel) makes it possible to reduce the wall thickness of pipelines, resulting in lower specific material and pipe-laying costs. Pipe-laying technology is also improving continuously, both offshore and onshore;

- High pressure (HP) technology is expected to play a major role in reducing the unit cost of large-scale, long-distance pipeline projects. HP technology is more economic than conventional technology for an annual throughput capacity of more than 10 bcm, and its competitiveness improves linearly with capacity. Cost savings for a transmission system of 5,000 km with a capacity of 15 to 30 bcm/a are estimated at 10% to 30%;

- Although deep-water pipe-laying, such as the Blue Stream pipeline, opens possible new pipeline routes, only a few additional routes will affect gas supply to IEA member countries.

In the past, progress has been most rapid in offshore pipeline technology. New technologies have been developed, including automatic laying methods, the use of high tensile steels and high pressure transport. Such technologies may also be progressively applied onshore, with a significant impact on the development of an interconnected grid on the intercontinental scale.

Improvement to transport technology is the key factor for further extending and increasing the density of gas grids worldwide. However, cost reductions in pipeline construction usually go hand-in-hand with ever larger volumes to benefit from economies of scale, and these are not so easy to market on the already mature OECD markets.

LNG chain

‹ The LNG chain has seen a very significant reduction of specific costs for liquefaction and LNG tankers, partially due to technological developments, but also due to more competition on the engineering and shipbuilding side. This development will foster flexibility in gas supplies to OECD member countries and more flexible trade between them. ›

Cost reductions in liquefaction are currently focused on increasing economies of scale from larger train sizes. Several plants under construction or in the planning phase, such as Melkoya Island in Norway, Gorgon in Australia and the Gulf of Paria in Venezuela, will have train capacities in excess of 4 mtpa. Capacities on planned new trains in Qatar range from 5 to 7.5 mtpa. These capacities, which could reduce unit construction costs by 25% compared to 3 mtpa trains, should become operational within the next few years. Improvement in fuel efficiency and unit investment costs are expected from larger gas turbines as train size increases. Optimisation of design parameters, improved reliability, closed-loop cooling systems, the exploitation of cold-recovery and the new heat-exchanger designs under development could yield further cost reductions. Savings in engineering costs and more competitive bidding processes will reduce the costs of existing liquefaction plants.

Overall, capital costs of LNG supply chains are expected to continue to fall, but at a slightly lower rate than over the past decade as the scope for learning and exploiting economies of scale diminishes. Total capital requirements have fallen from around $700 per tonne in the mid-1990s to around $500 today. Costs are projected to fall to $420 per tonne by 2010 and $320 per tonne by 2030 assuming a shipping distance of around 4,000 km.

There is a potential for further cost reductions from the use of new equipment and more efficient processes. These trends are illustrated by the economic benefits resulting from the use of new processes, Liquefin, for instance, and Floating Liquefaction Storage and Off-loading (FLSO) units.

Liquefin: The Liquefin process was designed by the Institut Français du Petrole (IFP). The process can be scaled up, thus enabling the capacity of a liquefaction plant to be gradually increased. Investors using Liquefin could begin with a capacity of 4 mtpa, then increase to 6 mtpa on a single train. The advantage would be considerable in terms of reducing the unit costs of LNG produced, thanks to economies of scale and to gradual adapting to market needs. A number of producing countries and potential LNG exporters have expressed their interest, for instance Iran's NIOC has ordered a front-end engineering and design (FEED) on Liquefin. Liquefin provides the means to make 20% savings compared to the cheapest processes available on the market.

FLSO units: In the longer term, FLSO plants, where processing and storage facilities are based on a vessel moored offshore in the vicinity of the producing fields, could provide a flexible use of the liquefaction plant and thereby make it feasible to develop small and remote gas reserves or deep offshore gas. This technology can reduce costs by minimising the cost of offshore platforms and pipelines, eliminating the need for port facilities and reducing the time needed to build the plant. Construction can be carried out in a low-cost location and the vessel transported to the production zone. FLSO plants can also address siting (NIMBY[21]) problems that arise for facilities onshore. Investors may see them as less politically risky in some countries. FLSO plants are under study in Australia, Nigeria and Angola. Recent developments, such as cryogenic flexible pipes for LNG loading/unloading should help to make this option economically feasible in the near future.

The potential for shipping cost reductions is mainly confined to further increasing carrier size. The next generation of LNG carriers, now under development, will have a capacity of 165,000 cm, which would yield modest economies of scale. Carriers of up to 200,000 cm, which could potentially reduce unit costs by 10% compared to the current maximum size of 140,000 cm, are being considered. The main obstacle to increasing the capacity to that size is port capability to receive such tankers (problems of draft).

---

21 NIMBY: Not in my back yard

LNG storage is the largest single cost in the regasification terminal (from 40 to more than 50% of the total direct costs depending on the site). The volume of each LNG tank usually represents twice the tanker size. Therefore, any incentives aimed at decreasing costs should be considered. Even if today most of the onshore LNG tanks are based upon self-supporting tank technology, membrane technology can bring significant cost reductions. In addition to better space optimisation, it offers several other advantages, like safety in case of leakage, particularly for buried storage.

LNG vs. pipelines: The changes in costs also affect the relative attractiveness of the pipeline and LNG options. In determining the most economic transportation method for a given supply route, distance and the volumes transported are the key factors. For short distances, pipelines – where feasible – are usually more economic. LNG is more competitive for long distance routes, since overall costs are less affected by distance. The breakeven distance for a single-train LNG project against a 42-inch onshore pipeline is about 4,000 km and about 2,000 km for an offshore pipeline (Figure 3.11).

Figure 3.11. Pipes/LNG competition for 30 bcm/a capacity

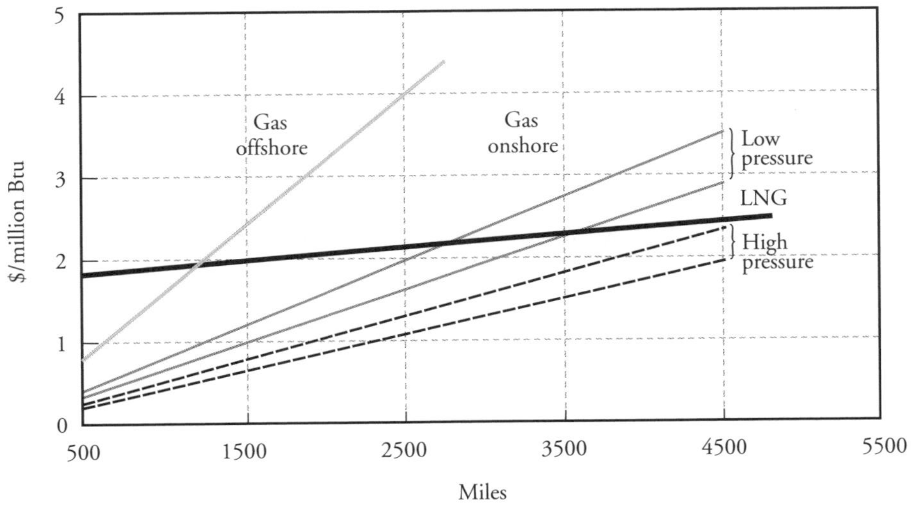

Source: ENI

The breakeven distance has tended to fall over the last decade, as LNG costs have fallen faster than pipeline costs. But technology advances have made possible short-distance offshore pipelines where previously LNG had been the only viable option. For large deliveries (around 30 bcm/a), the transport of gas by HP pipelines appears very much competitive. For long distances, LNG appears competitive for capacity below 10 bcm/a. For Middle East supply to Europe for instance (between 4,500 and 6,000 miles), LNG allows a cost saving of up to 30% with respect to HP pipe technology. Therefore, LNG could be preferred for small fields exploitation on a long distance transportation.

In practice, however, LNG projects seldom compete directly against pipeline projects for the same supply route. The falling costs of LNG transportation allow for a much larger economic reach of LNG and allow for more flexibility in supply, which makes LNG fit well into the development of more competitive markets. It also allows LNG to become more of a supplier of last resort for unexpected demand. Moreover, besides the economics – at full utilisation – of each solution, there are three main elements that influence the specific costs:

- Utilisation/market size;
- Financing conditions;
- Development of level and size of investment.

The development of the three elements has favoured the economics of LNG versus pipeline, shortening the breakeven distance. The new projects on the markets are much smaller than they were in the 1980s. Huge projects, like Troll in Norway or SoyuzGasexport or Yamal delivering Russian gas to Europe with 20 or more bcm/a are increasingly rare today. Projects of 5 bcm/a are more typical. However the levelised cost shown on Figure 3.11 is based on a throughput of 30 bcm/a. At a 5-bcm/a throughput, specific pipeline transportation costs are much higher than indicated by the line representing the cost of a 42-inch onshore pipeline. Financing of LNG is lower risk (e.g., Oman LNG with an A rating by Standard & Poor's). In the case of pipelines, each country border and ethnic enclave crossed adds to the risk premium, which increases the levelised costs. In addition, evolution of investment costs is coming down more favourably for LNG than for pipelines, where cost reductions are mainly linked to an increase in capacity that is difficult to absorb by the market.

For smaller projects to fit into more competitive markets or markets that start with a small bankable demand, LNG should be more attractive than pipeline gas even at much shorter distances (2,000 to 4,000 km).

New transport technologies

LNG and pipelines are not the only options to transport natural gas. New developments (Coselle, Enersea, etc.) are under way, using dedicated gas carriers to transport Compressed Natural Gas (CNG), i.e., gas under high pressure. CNG technology only requires investment into the ship, and compression on the producing side which can be used to feed it into the consumer grid. However, the energy density of pressurised gas is lower than for LNG. The CNG technology may have the potential to challenge LNG transportation for some niche markets, namely for short distances and small markets (such as the Caribbean market, for instance). However, the feasibility and economics of this new technology still need to be tested. Another option currently being explored, with similar aims, consists in transporting natural gas in the form of hydrates.

Consumption

On the consumption side, more demand is coming from the development of highly efficient gas turbines and CCGTs. In principle, the use of gas in power offers more possibility of replacing gas in both the short and the long run. Even in the very short run, security of gas supply is enhanced by the switching possibilities of modern gas turbines, which are able to switch to clean liquid fuels, such as distillates, during operation. While the technical possibility exists, it may be restricted due to regulation or due to lack of back-up fuels (see previous section).

Transformation of gas into tradable products

Gas-to-Liquids (GTL) technology (this technology converts natural gas feedstock into conventional oil products). The development of techniques to monetise gas resources in another way than export, might in theory create more competition for gas resources and thereby curtail security of gas supplies. However, there is so far no indication that GTL would mobilise gas reserves which would otherwise be used for gas export. The outlets for the LNG and GTL chains are completely different, and their markets appear complementary rather than competing. LNG is aimed at gas markets, while GTL is meant for a fuel market. Therefore GTL appears as an alternative way of exploiting gas reserves in remote gas-rich areas where no local market exits or where gas reserves are so plentiful that they cannot all be exported, like in Qatar. Development of GTL might also have the effect of encouraging countries to find and develop additional gas reserves.

Improvement of the catalysts used in the Gas-to-Liquid process – which produces waxes and clean diesel based on the classic Fischer Tropsch synthesis – have continuously brought down specific costs. Three commercial-scale GTL plants in the world have been designed and built under special economic circumstances: Mobil MTG in New Zealand, Mossgas in South Africa and Bintulu in Malaysia. The technology has now reached a decisive turning point. Qatar, in addition to its ambitious LNG export policy, has decided to build six large-scale GTL plants to diversify its gas utilisation. Three contracts were signed at the end of 2003. The $900 million Oryx GTL plant at Ras Laffan, with a capacity of 34,000 bpd due on stream in 2005, is the first of the country's six planned GTL projects. The second "heads-of-agreement" was signed in October 2003 with Royal Dutch/Shell to set up a $5 billion project to produce 140,000 bpd of GTL from 2008. And in December 2003, a third $5 billion contract was signed with ConocoPhillips to process gas into 160,000 bpd of GTL.

Beyond 2010, GTL plants could potentially lead to the development of a large volume of gas reserves. In *WEO 2002*, global GTL demand for gas is projected to increase from 4 bcm in 2000 to 21 bcm in 2010 and 170 bcm in 2030. The rate of increase in GTL production is nonetheless subject to enormous uncertainty, particularly after 2010. These projections are highly dependent on oil-price developments and the successful demonstration of emerging technologies.

The economics of GTL processing are highly dependent on plant construction costs, product types and yields, and the energy efficiency of the plant itself, as well as the market prices of the liquids produced and the cost of the gas feedstock. GTL plants are complex and capital-intensive, requiring large sites and construction lead times of two-and-a-half to three years. They are also very energy-intensive, consuming up to 45% of the gas feedstock. This characteristic raises concerns about CO_2 emissions. On the other hand, GTL plants generally produce a range of middle distillates with good environmental qualities, for which there is a rising demand.

Other efforts to valorise gas reserves comprise transforming gas into methanol and DME. Cost reductions in these processes could lead to competition for gas resources, which would otherwise be available for gas export, thereby negatively affecting security of gas supplies. This would, however, suppose that the cost reductions for such processes clearly outperform the cost reductions in gas transportation, which seems a remote likelihood today. In addition, the market volumes for methanol and DME are limited compared to the size of global gas reserves.

Hydrogen

Hydrogen and fuel cells could also change the demand for gas in the future. Hydrogen can be produced from natural gas and other fossil fuels, but production without CO_2 emissions depends on successful application of renewable energies, carbon sequestration technologies or nuclear-generated electricity. In the electricity sector, the fuel cells that are expected to achieve commercial viability first will involve the reforming of natural gas. In the *WEIO* 2003 reference scenario, about 100 GW of fuel cells are expected to be constructed in OECD countries by 2030 for distributed power generation.

4

THE ROLE OF LNG IN SECURITY OF GAS SUPPLY

The current development of the global LNG industry will have substantial implications for the global gas industry and in particular for security of gas supply. Tremendous cost reductions have been experienced in all parts of the LNG chain in recent years. The fall in tanker prices over the last decade led to a much wider economic reach of LNG transportation. The dramatic cost reductions for LNG liquefaction trains, especially for expansion trains, but also for new trains such as the Trinidad and Tobago project, made LNG projects viable even if only part of the capacity is secured by long-term sales, so that the remainder could be sold on a flexible or spot basis. The recent re-opening of two US east-coast terminals and the numerous proposed projects to build new terminals in the US and Mexico provide a potentially attractive market outlet, able to absorb all volumes within the capacity of the terminals. >

As most of so far undeveloped gas reserves are located far away from OECD markets, it is clear that LNG will play a key role to bring this gas to the market, when distance or natural and political obstacles make pipeline transport impossible.

At the same time, the increasing use of gas in power generation is creating a market able to absorb very substantial new gas volumes, opening the perspective for many gas-reserve-owning countries to monetise their gas reserves via LNG sales. The decreasing costs of the LNG chain, as well as the increasing number of players both on the sellers' and the buyers' side, are helping to overcome the rigidities inherent to LNG in the past. >

The growing supply of LNG, accompanied by the increased flexibility in LNG trade, which can physically be directed to the highest value market, are adding to the security of gas supply. Contractual arrangements are also more flexible. Spot and flexible LNG purchases are increasingly used to cover part of peak gas demand. Even though a global gas or global LNG market may still be a long way off, LNG is already linking different markets together, by allowing shifting volumes between regions, benefiting from differences in their supply and demand balance. Indirectly this adds to the market flexibility of formerly non-connected marketplaces. However, these positive developments for security of supply, including long-term access to more gas resources and extra options to provide additional gas volumes for low-probability events, also bring more import dependence.

A key issue is to make sure that LNG trade can develop without market barriers, by streamlining administrative procedures while ensuring high safety and environmental standards for the whole LNG chain.

This Chapter looks at major trends in LNG trade, the fast growing LNG demand, the development of new supplies and the emergence of new flexible, global commercial trends. It goes on to review the implications of this spectacular development for security of supply. It also discusses possible safety concerns raised by the recent accident at the Skikda liquefaction plant in Algeria, the first serious accident in the hitherto impeccable safety record of the LNG industry since the beginning of international LNG trade.

INTERNATIONAL LNG TRADE

LNG flows have doubled in the past decade and reached 150 bcm in 2002, corresponding to around 3 mbpd, with twelve importing and twelve exporting countries. LNG now represents 22% of the world's total cross-border gas trade, and 6% of total world consumption of natural gas. At the beginning of 2004, there were 15 operating LNG export terminals, 43 operating LNG import terminals and 154 LNG tankers. The LNG business is growing fast:

- 8 export terminals are being expanded;
- 5 new export terminals are being built;
- 8 new import terminals are being built in the OECD region;
- 54 new LNG ships are on order;
- Around 30 new LNG supply projects are planned;
- Spot trading has become a reality and represents 8% of global LNG trade.

LNG trade is projected to experience strong growth in the coming years, by rising to 360 bcm by 2010, 560 bcm in 2020 and 840 bcm by 2030 (*WEIO 2003*).

Figure 4.1. International LNG trade, evolution and outlook

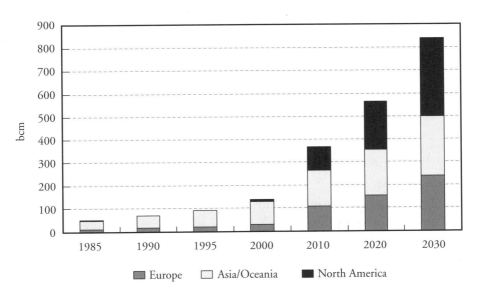

Source: Cedigaz, *WEIO 2003*

The international gas trade between countries and continents has so far largely been dominated by pipeline gas, accounting for 78% of cross-border gas trade. However, the supply of natural gas markets via gas pipelines faces some technical, economic, even political limits, while cost reductions promote more LNG trade:

■ Geography: the different locations of gas reserves and gas markets are often beyond the technical and economic reach of gas pipelines, and political difficulties can be encountered in potential transit countries;

■ Some of the major traditional gas-exporting OECD countries via pipeline (Canada, the Netherlands, Norway) will approach their peak capacity of production/exports in the next ten to twenty years. Europe will continue to be well placed to import increasing volumes of pipeline gas from non-OECD countries, first of all from its existing suppliers, Russia and Algeria, but also from new suppliers, Libya, and possibly Central Asia and the Middle East. Imports of LNG along the Atlantic coast and in the Mediterranean basin offer the opportunity of a major supplementary supply and of additional diversification.

■ For geographical reasons, any additional imports to North America can only be in the form of LNG (directly or indirectly via gas imports from Mexico). Similarly, LNG is the main source of gas for Japan and Korea, although some ambitious pipeline projects are under discussion.

■ New gas importing countries (India, China), which have only limited access to the main domestic pipeline gas networks, seek supplies adapted to their fast growing needs often concentrated in coastal regions. LNG, a maritime option with excellent modularity and progressiveness in project capacity, meets this requirement.

■ Additional LNG receiving terminals can partially compensate for lack of network integration, and allow isolated regions to be connected.

■ For all gas importing countries diversification of supply sources is a primary concern, which can be met by LNG, with its increasing number of suppliers. Another advantage of LNG is that it can in principle be redirected to other markets or sourced from other suppliers.

■ LNG is currently liquefied in the country of gas production and is therefore only subject to the country risk of the producing country, unlike pipelines which can accumulate country risks all along the transit route.

■ The opening of the power market to gas-fired power creates a large new outlet for gas. Some regions, like the Middle East, had no access to European and US gas markets during their build-up/development phase because of high transportation costs, so the lowered costs of LNG, now give them the chance to participate in the second gas expansion wave triggered by gas in the power sector and to monetise their gas reserves.

■ Gas-fired power plants, often on coastal or nearby sites, offer an attractive market for new LNG projects: several dozen projects combining LNG receiving terminals and gas-fired power plants are currently on design boards throughout the world.

■ The opening of electricity and gas markets is causing a change in traditional industrial structures, the diversification of contractual forms, and the multiplying of players and trading flows. This favours the growth of independent LNG import terminals (in Spain and Italy, for instance).

■ Finally, LNG is much more flexible than pipeline gas, which allows cost optimisation and arbitrage opportunities.

REGIONAL TRENDS OF LNG DEMAND

So far LNG markets have been regional. In 2002, Asian importing countries imported 69%, Europe 26% and North America 5% of world trade. Among producing regions, 50% came from the Asia/Pacific region, 23% from Africa, 22% from the Middle East and 5% from the Americas. However, this regional characterisation is softening with the development of a genuine Atlantic basin market and eventually a Pacific basin market.

LNG demand in the Asia/Pacific basin

Asian markets, mostly Japan and Korea, currently dominate the Pacific basin. There are, however, numerous proposed regasification projects on the US west coast and Mexico, which may extend LNG trade in the Pacific basin.

The Asian market has been the entire focus and the driving force of the LNG market until recently. It imported 104 bcm in 2002, with Japanese gas and electricity companies buying three-quarters of the regional total. Between 1985 and 2002, Asia accounted for about 70% of the increase in world LNG demand, and LNG has played a major role in diversifying sources of energy and in mitigating air pollution.

Japan was the first Asian country to import LNG and is currently the world's biggest importer, taking 73 bcm in 2002 (80 bcm in 2003) from eight supplying countries. South Korea started to import LNG in 1986 and is now the world's second largest importer, taking 24 bcm in 2002. Japan has one new terminal under development, as does Korea. Taiwan began importing in 1990, and India, the latest new emerging LNG importer in the region, started its LNG imports in January 2004 at the Dahej terminal. Next to come is China with the Guangdong project, whose first phase is expected to become operational in 2006. An LNG terminal is also under discussion in New Zealand. Overall, the Asian market will continue to be a large market for LNG, with just under half of the world's LNG import capacity. By 2030, the region is expected to import 260 bcm (*WEIO 2003*), compared with 104 bcm in 2002.

China and India are entering the LNG scene, representing possible competitors for IEA as LNG importers, mainly for the Pacific basin. However, in view of the limited volumes projected to be imported as LNG in the next decades, and in view of large untapped gas reserves which could supply the OECD Pacific region, the influence of additional demand competition by China and India on security of gas supply of IEA countries in the OECD Pacific region seems limited.

LNG imports in China and India

China's natural gas industry, which is at an early stage of development, is poised for rapid expansion. The government is committed to a rapid increase in the share of natural gas in the country's energy mix. This policy is driven by concerns about the environmental impact of heavy dependence on coal and the energy-security implications of rapidly rising oil imports. While there are significant gas reserves in China, mainly in the Tarim basin in the West of the country, China is also looking for imports, as pipeline gas from Siberia and as LNG. China has several proposed LNG terminals, either planned or under development.

Chinese companies have started construction of two LNG import terminals, and are holding discussions on others. The first terminal is located in Guangdong and will start importing 3.3 mtpa of LNG from Australia by 2006. A second terminal in Fujian Province, with 2.6 mtpa capacity, will bring LNG from the Tangguh project in Indonesia starting in 2007. Both terminals are scheduled to expand with follow-on phases. Other terminals along China's eastern seaboard, including Zhejiang, Jiangsu, Shandong, Tianjin and Shanghai, could follow quickly depending on developments. Potential suppliers include Russia (Sakhalin), Malaysia, Oman, Indonesia, Australia, Iran, Yemen, and Qatar.

WEIO 2003 projects that 31 bcm of regasification capacity will be built in China by 2030. The pace of development of gas infrastructure will ultimately depend on policy reforms to clarify the investment and operating environment and proactive government measures to boost the competitiveness of gas against cheap local coal. Important challenges remain for both the government and industry, including, in particular, the lack of a legal and policy framework to encourage and steer investment in the gas sector; and the lack of knowledge over how to best develop natural gas technology and markets.[22]

India is also emerging as a new LNG importer. At the beginning of 2004, Qatar's RasGas has started to supply LNG to the Indian company Petronet after the completion of a 5-mtpa terminal at Dahej. Its capacity could be doubled later.

India has a dozen proposed import terminal projects, but at present only three or four look likely to materialise. Only Shell continues to pursue new LNG projects, despite problems with financing, due to pricing of the gas in India, worries about consumer creditworthiness and a lack of transmission and distribution infrastructure. The 5-mtpa Dabhol terminal initiated by Enron was almost completed when the construction was halted in 2001. It is likely to be completed once a buyer is found for Enron's share of the project.

By 2030, it is expected that India will hold a regasification capacity of 23 bcm. The prospects for a rapid increase in LNG imports will depend critically on power- and fertiliser-sector reforms. These sectors will be the main consumers of gas, but they both sell their output at subsidised prices. The government intends to reduce subsidies, however, no definite time plan has been announced for bringing tariffs to cost-recovery levels.

The dire financial health of many state power companies is likely to represent a major constraint in financing new LNG regasification plants. Three major challenges remain for the development of the Indian gas market: *i)* lack of sufficient transmission infrastructure, *ii)* lack of a coherent legal and regulatory framework for the sector; and *iii)* questions about the affordability of gas.

---

22 IEA (2002i).

LNG in Asia is at a transition point, with significant changes ahead in Japan, South Korea and Taiwan, as well as in the new emerging LNG markets. The market was shaken by the Asian financial crisis in 1997-1998, when Japanese and Korean buyers found themselves stuck with volumes contracted well above their requirements. Demand uncertainty has also increased as a result of market liberalisation. In Korea, Kogas has not been allowed to sign long-term contracts. This brought home the need to reduce the length of contracts and increase their flexibility.

In this new environment, the traditional market model – based on long-term contracts indexed to oil with a security of supply premium – is now under revision as a result of changing market conditions. When renewing existing contracts, Asian LNG purchasers are seeking periods of 15 to 20 years rather than 20 to 25, more flexible off-take volumes and purchases on a fob basis[23] instead of the cif[24] basis in previous contracts. The contracts signed in February 2002 between Japan and Malaysia were the first signal of a change in LNG marketing in Asia. Seasonal flexibility/requirements are being addressed through medium-term supply contracts with seasonal weighting and complemented by spot cargoes.

LNG pricing in the new emerging LNG markets, India and China, is a challenge, as they cannot afford the same level of prices as Japanese or Korean customers. The bidding process in China was a new procedure and has set a new benchmark. Prices for China are lower than supplies to other Asian buyers and the indexation formula is also quite different (see below). This will have repercussions in the forthcoming negotiations for renewals of contracts with Japanese buyers. 25 mtpa of contracted supply are up for renegotiation between 2009 and 2011. To the already large volume of liquefaction capacity in Asia/Pacific, additional projects (MLNG Tiga, Tangguh, Sakhalin II) combined with moderate demand growth and slow contract build-up have the potential to create short- to medium-term over-supply. However, Asia remains an important market in which producers can negotiate long-term contracts.

---

23 Free-on-board (fob): Under a fob contract, the seller provides the LNG at the exporting terminal and the buyer takes responsibility for shipping and freight insurance.
24 Cost, insurance and freight (cif): A cif price means that the cost of transportation, insurance and freight to a given destination are all included in the price. The seller is usually responsible for arranging transportation.

LNG demand in the Atlantic basin

LNG trade in the Atlantic basin (Europe and North America) is expected to quadruple over the next 10 years, going from 47 bcm in 2002 to around 210 bcm in 2010. It is commonly projected that LNG imports into Europe will grow from the current level of 9% of total gas consumption to 25% by 2010/20, and into North America from 2% in 2003 to 15% by 2020/25.

The US will be the key for LNG market growth. LNG imports doubled in 2003 to 14.6 bcm. Under the impetus of gas demand growth and assuming a sustained level of gas prices (they amounted to $6/million Btu at the beginning of 2004), LNG imports are expected to increase sharply. US EIA Annual Energy Outlook 2004[25] foresees an increase of 15.8% per year between 2002 and 2025 to 136 bcm. This is a major change with previous official outlooks. All four regasification terminals are now re-opened, with a current importing capacity of 29 bcm/a. In addition, four new projects have been approved and more than 30 proposed LNG regasification projects have been announced. Total capacity of the projects amounts to 33 bcf/d (340 bcm/a).

Part of the LNG deliveries from Algeria and from Trinidad and Tobago to the US are received under long-term contracts. Spot cargoes have been imported from Qatar, Nigeria, Australia, Oman, Indonesia and Abu Dhabi. The spot LNG sales market is very active in the US, with 12.6 bcm or 86% of total LNG supplies received under spot or short-term sales in 2003. Over the long term, LNG is likely to be an attractive option for increasing gas supplies to the US as costs of LNG compare favourably with costs of most new domestic supplies.

Contracted supplies from Norway, Qatar, Nigeria, Trinidad and Tobago, Australia, Algeria, Egypt and Indonesia already exceed 50 mtpa (although not all contracts are firm – see Chapter 6). In particular, US companies are negotiating major long-term supplies with Qatar. ExxonMobil signed an agreement with Qatar Petroleum to supply around 15.6 mtpa to the US for 25 years (Rasgas III). Deliveries are expected to start in 2008-09. Conoco Phillips has also signed a Memorandum of Understanding with Qatar for

---

25 EIA (2003a).

long-term supply of 15 mtpa of LNG to the US market (Qatargas III). While the companies contracted the gas on a long-term basis, they will sell into the US market under short or spot sales conditions.

On the other side of the Atlantic, the European LNG market is also very dynamic. Europe imported 42 bcm of LNG in 2002, representing 9% of European gas consumption, although the share is much higher for some Mediterranean importers. In Spain, for example, LNG accounts for 58% of gas supplies. In Europe, LNG competes with pipeline gas, and both compete with other fuels. European buyers choose LNG either to diversify their gas portfolio or to supply areas far from the main gas grid or to optimise their grid. The major suppliers have been Mediterranean countries: Algeria and, to a lesser extent, Libya. Since 1999 and 2000, additional LNG supplies have come from Nigeria and Trinidad and Tobago.

LNG is likely to vary in importance in different regions of Europe, due to economics of transportation related to geographical positions. LNG will have a competitive advantage along the Atlantic side on the Iberian Peninsula, in parts of France and the UK, whereas for the rest of Europe pipeline gas will have an economic advantage. With some 50 bcm/a of new LNG supply projects currently identified, LNG will not be able to replace the need for more pipeline gas into Europe, but it may make an important contribution to the growth of the European gas market, in particular in Mediterranean countries and the UK. The share of LNG will be influenced to an extent by the gas policies of Norway and Russia.

Continuing increases in demand and the reforms of European gas and power markets are leading to new opportunities for LNG, especially for the Mediterranean countries. Despite strong competition from pipeline suppliers, LNG deliveries to Europe are expected to rise steeply, reaching 240 bcm in 2030, approximately six times as much as in 2002 (*WEIO 2003*). The current existing capacity of the 11 operating terminals is 56 bcm/a. This is going to expand to 100-120 bcm/a by 2010. New LNG receiving terminals are planned in France, Italy, Spain and the UK, which is going to resume importing LNG. In Turkey, oversupply meant that the new Egegaz terminal at Izmir is lying idle, built without supply or off-take agreements in a country already well supplied with pipeline gas.

Much of the growth in the European LNG trade depends on UK imports. There are ambitious projects to import LNG and build large regasification terminals (see Chapter 8), facilitated by a favourable regulatory regime for new import terminals, which exempts the investor from the TPA obligation on a case-by-case basis. The EU Gas Directive 2003/55/EC provides for regulated third-party access to LNG terminals, but foresees exemption under certain conditions.

LNG is playing a major role in the liberalisation process, as many new entrants have chosen to build their own LNG terminals and to import gas directly. New players, principally electricity companies, are entering the LNG business, for instance: Union Fenosa, Iberdrola, Cepsa, and Edison, and major oil companies are integrating downstream in regasification plants: Total, BP, Shell and ExxonMobil.

As competition in their markets increases, European LNG buyers have begun seeking contracts that are more flexible than the traditional 20-25 year ToP contracts pegged to oil prices. LNG spot sales have rapidly increased since 1997. Spot and short-term sales in Europe amounted to 5.9 bcm in 2002, most of them for the Spanish market. Shorter-term contracts are also being signed with suppliers.

Trans-Atlantic LNG arbitrage

A Trans-Atlantic LNG market is emerging, with spot trading and physical arbitrage between European and US markets. This arbitrage benefits from price differentials between the two markets.

To benefit from growing LNG markets, companies at the rims of the basin are trying to develop their presence in LNG projects on both sides of the Atlantic while optimising the use of their assets by using these arbitrage opportunities. **Tractebel**, for instance, owns US Cabot LNG (now Tractebel LNG North America) and Belgian Distrigas LNG assets. Its Everett terminal has a prime location, close to customers and downstream from historic pipeline bottlenecks to transport gas from the Gulf of Mexico to the north-east. Tractebel is also partner of the Trinidad Atlantic LNG project and is developing a regasification terminal in the Bahamas (Bahamas LNG at Freeport). **BG**, another "Atlantic arbitrager", has also acquired producing LNG assets in the Atlantic basin: in Egypt, Nigeria,

Figure 4.2. Trans-Atlantic LNG arbitrage

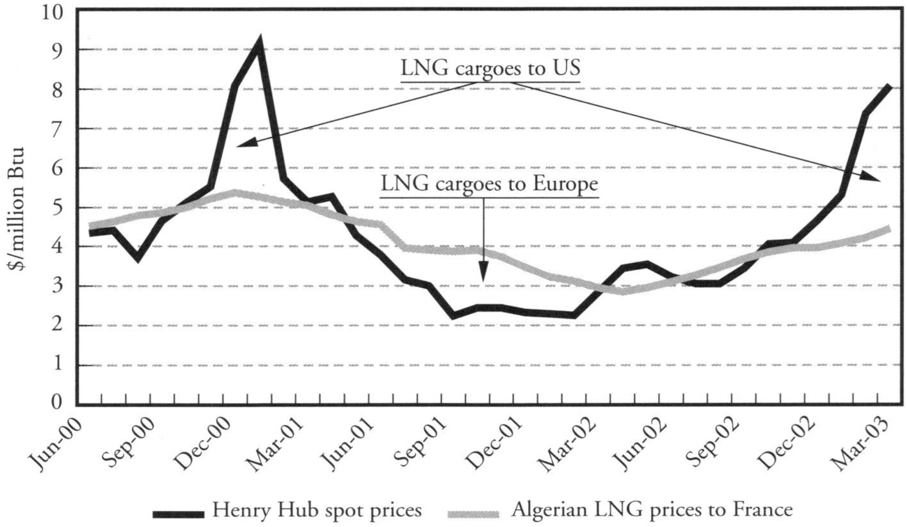

Source: World Gas Intelligence, IEA

Equatorial Guinea and Trinidad, owns the Lake Charles terminal in the US, and has recently acquired rights in Elba Island. It is also involved in the Italian regasification terminal at Brindisi and is developing a new terminal project in the US (Keyspan LNG, Providence, RI).

The Spanish company **Repsol** has also developed an LNG strategy based on synergies in the Atlantic Basin. The company is an equity partner in the Trinidad & Tobago project and a shareholder of Spain's Gas Natural. This has allowed the company to develop swap agreements[26] involving exchanges of Trinidad and Algerian LNG. **Gaz de France** and **Statoil** are the two other companies developing Atlantic arbitrager positions. Gaz de France re-routed 12 Algerian LNG cargoes to the US in 2003 through its joint-venture with Sonatrach Med LNG & Gas to benefit from price differentials between the US and European markets. Statoil, which is developing the LNG Snøhvit project with customers on both sides of the Atlantic, has bought a long-term one-third entry capacity at the Cove Point terminal in the US.

---

26 A swap is usually an exchange of volumes not driven by price considerations, but by transportation optimisation. Swaps make it possible to avoid cross-shipping, and therefore lead to substantial reductions in transportation distance and costs.

Market price mechanisms, however, differ on each side of the Atlantic. In the US, pricing is dominated by NYMEX based on the Henry Hub with regional differentials according to transportation costs. In Europe, pricing is dominated by long-term oil-linked contracts. Spot markets are still in their early stages. This is also a major difference between the Atlantic and Pacific markets. Anyone selling into the US and UK must accept spot gas prices (Henry Hub and NBP), whereas in both continental Europe and Asia, prices are still linked with oil prices. So the US, and to some extent the UK once it begins to import LNG, can take in any volume of LNG if the price is right, whereas in continental Europe and the Asian market, LNG has to be sold at a price competitive with its import alternatives.

Regional trading has so far been limited by the infrastructure, not so much of import regasification terminals (the re-opening of two LNG terminals in the US has largely reduced this constraint), but more on the supply side.

The global scale of the future LNG market is demonstrated by the following recent examples: In 2003, the shutdown of 17 nuclear power plants in Japan dried up the available supplies for spot LNG trading in the Pacific, with an impact even on the Atlantic basin.

MAJOR LNG PRODUCERS

Global LNG production is growing fast. At the beginning of 2004, there were 15 LNG production sites in the world, with 66 liquefaction trains (see Table 4.1) and a potential capacity of 133.5 mtpa (180 bcm/a). The Air Products and Chemicals Inc (APCI) liquefaction technique was used on 55 of these trains (83%). Capacity increased during 2002/03 by 13.2 mtpa as major new facilities came on stream in Malaysia, Trinidad and Tobago and Nigeria. By January 2004, other plant expansions were close to completion in Australia and Qatar. In January 2004, however, the first serious accident in the LNG industry in the 40 years since the start of commercial LNG operations destroyed three trains at Algeria's Skikda LNG plant.

Table 4.1. LNG liquefaction capacity at the end of January 2004

	Start-up date	Number of trains	Nominal capacity (mtpa)	Present capacity (mtpa)
North America		2	1.1	1.5
United States		2	*1.1*	*1.5*
Kenai	1969	2	1.1	1.5
Latin America		3	9.6	9.9
Trinidad and Tobago		3	*9.6*	*9.9*
Atlantic LNG (1st train)	1999	1	3	3.3
Atlantic LNG (2d train)	2002	1	3.3	3.3
Atlantic LNG (3rd train)	2003	1	3.3	3.3
Africa		24	34.1	30.4
Algeria		18	*22.5*	*20.3*
Arzew GL4Z	1964	3	1.1	1.1
Arzew GL1Z	1978	6	7.8	7.8
Arzew GL2Z	1981	6	7.8	8.4
Skikda GL1K I & II [a]	1972/81	3	5.8	3
Libya		3	*2.6*	*0.6*
Marsa El Braga	1970	3	2.6	0.6
Nigeria		3	*9*	*9.5*
Nigeria LNG (1st & 2nd trains)	1999	2	5.9	6.6
Nigeria LNG expansion (3rd train)	2002	1	3.1	2.9
Middle East		10	25.2	28
Abu Dhabi		3	*4.8*	*5.8*
Das Island 1	1977	2	2.3	2.8
Das Island 2	1994	1	2.5	3
Oman		2	*6.6*	*7.3*
Oman LNG	2000	2	6.6	7.3
Qatar		5	*13.8*	*14.9*
Ras Laffan (Qatargas)	1996/98	3	7.2	8.3
Ras Laffan LNG (RasGas)	1999	2	6.6	6.6
Asia-Oceania		27	54.3	63.7
Brunei		5	*5.3*	*7.2*
Lumut 1	1972	5	5.3	7.2
Indonesia		12	*25.8*	*29.4*
Bontang A-H	1977/99	8	16.8	22.6
Arun I-III [b]	1978/86	4	9	6.8
Malaysia		7	*17.2*	*19.6*
Bintulu MLNG 1	1983	3	6	7.5
Bintulu MLNG 2	1995	3	7.8	8.4
Bintulu MLNG 3 [c]	2003	1	3.4	3.7

Table 4.1. LNG liquefaction capacity at the end of January 2004 (continued)

	Start-up date	Number of trains	Nominal capacity (mtpa)	Present capacity (mtpa)
Australia		*3*	*6*	*7.5*
Burrup / Withnell Bay	1989/92	3	6	7.5
WORLD TOTAL		**66**	**124.3**	**133.5**

(a) Skikda: following the accident in January 2004, where 3 trains were completely destroyed, the plant was closed. The three remaining trains in Skikda are expected to be reopened between May and October 2004, after inspection works.
(b) Arun: 2 trains out of 6 are closed on Indonesia's Arun plant due to depletion of gas reserves. They were decommissioned in 2000.
(c) Bintulu 3: one train commissioned in March 2003 but shutdown in August because of fire. Train II commissioned in October 2003.
Source: Data from Cedigaz. updated to January 2004

Producers are envisaging more expansions and greenfield[27] plants over the coming decade (see Table 4.2). The number of possible LNG exporters is rapidly increasing, with new projects developed in Egypt, Norway and Angola. Russia, with Sakhalin, and Iran also have projects to enter the LNG business. Judging by the number of projects on the drawing board, overall production capacity could exceed 220 mtpa (300 bcm/a) by 2010. Even an estimate based solely on expansions under construction at existing plants, could still reach 170 mtpa (230 bcm/a) by 2006.

Competition among LNG suppliers is fierce. An illustration of this is the negotiation of the Guangdong contract. Chinese buyers issued a tender with their minimum requirements, leading to tough competition between suppliers to gain the contract to enter the promising Chinese gas market. Competition is also developing among Asian producers, as Australia and Indonesia together have more than 20 mtpa of LNG contracts coming up for renewal by 2010, more than half with Japanese utilities. Fierce competition is already lowering prices. New LNG projects, (Malaysia Tiga, Sakhalin and Bayu Undan) bringing a combined output of more than 15 mtpa, are due for completion in the next six years, all of them targeting the Asian market.

---

27 A greenfield project is defined as a new plant being built at a new site; a brownfield project involves adding trains to an existing project.

Table 4.2. Expansion of LNG capacity at existing plants and new greenfield projects

Country	Plant name	Operator	Start-up date	Number of trains	Annual capacity (mtpa)	Receiving countries
Extensions – Under construction						
Australia	North Western Shelf (4th train)	Woodside, Shell, BHP, BP, TexacoChevron, Mitsubishi, Mitsui	Mid-2004	1	4.2	Asia (China, Japan)
Indonesia	Bontang (debottlenecking to 24.6 mtpa)	PT Badak NTL Co. (Pertamina, 55%, Total,10%, Jilco, 15%, Vico, 20%)	2004	-	2	Asia
Malaysia	Malaysia LNG III Tiga - Train I	Petronas, Shell, Nippon Oil, Sarawak, Diamond Gas	Apr-04	1	3.4	Asia (Korea)
Nigeria	Bonny Island / NLNGPlus (trains 4 & 5)	NNPC (49%), Shell, 25.6%, Total,15%, ENI, 10.4%	Late 2005	2	4 x 2	Europe, US
Oman	Qalhat LNG	Oman Government, Shell, Total, KOLNG, Misubishi, Mitsui, Partex, Itochu, Union Fenosa	2005	1	3.4	Europe
Qatar	Qatargas I (debottlenecking to 9.5 mtpa)	QP 63%, ExxonMobil 25%, Kogas 5%, Itochu 4%, LNG Japan 3%	2005	-	1.4	Asia, Europe, US
	RasGas II (3rd & 4th train)	QP, 70% and ExxonMobil, 30%	2004-2005	2	4.7 x 2	India, Italy, Taiwan
Trinidad & Tobago	Atlantic LNG (4th train)	BP, BG, RepsolYPF, NGC	First half 2006	1	5.2	Europe, L. America, US
			TOTAL	8	37	

Table 4.2. Expansion of LNG capacity at existing plants and new greenfield projects (continued)

Country	Plant name	Operator	Start-up date	Number of trains	Annual capacity (mtpa)	Receiving countries
Extensions – Potential						
Algeria	Skikda (replacement of 3 destroyed trains)	Sonatrach	2008	1	4	Europe, US
	Arzew (Gassi Touil)	Sonatrach + international partners	2008	1	4	US, Europe
Australia	N.W.Shelf (5th train)	NWS venture	?	1	4.2	Asia
Brunei	Lumut (6th train)	Brunei LNG : Brunei Government (50%), Shell (25%), Mitsubishi (25%)	2010	1	4	Asia
Indonesia	Bontang - Train I	PT Badak NTL Co	2007?	1	3	Asia
Nigeria	Bonny Island / NLNGPlus (train 6)	NNPC (49%), Shell, 25.6%, Total,15% ENI, 10.4%	2006-2007	1	4	Europe, US, Mexico
Qatar	Qatargas (fourth train)	QP 65%, Total 10%, ExxonMobil 10%, Mitsui 7.5%, Marubeni 7.5%	2007/2009	1	4.8	Europe, US
	Qatargas II (ExxonMobil)	QP 70%, ExxonMobil 30%	2006/07	2	7 x 2	UK/Europe
	Qatargas III (ConocoPhillips)	QP 70%, ConocoPhillips 30%	2009	2	7.5 x 2	US
	RasGas III (5th & 6th trains)	QP 70%, ExxonMobil 30%	2008-2009	2	7.8 x 2	US
Trinidad & Tobago	Atlantic LNG (5th & 6th trains)	BP, BG, RepsolYPF, NGC	?	2	5 x 2	America, Europe
			TOTAL	**15**	**82.6**	

Table 4.2. Expansion of LNG capacity at existing plants and new greenfield projects (continued)

Country	Plant name	Operator	Start-up date	Number of trains	Annual capacity (mtpa)	Receiving countries
New projects						
Angola	Antelope	State oil company of Angola, Sonangol (20%), Chevron Texaco (32%), BP, ExxonMobil, Total and Norsk Hydro, 12% each	2010	1 (first phase)	4	Atlantic Basin
Australia	Darwin (Bayu-Undan)	Darwin LNG, ConocoPhillips, Santos, Impex, Kerr-McGee, AGIP, Tokyo Gas, Tokyo Electric	2006	1	3	Japan
	Under construction					
	Gorgon LNG Venture (plant on Barrow Island)	ChevronTexaco (operator, 4/7th), Shell (2/7th), ExxonMobil (1/7th)	2008-2009	1 (initially)	5	US West Coast, Asia (China)
	Browse Gas	Woodside				
	Scarborough	Esso Australia				
	Sunrise	Shell, Woodside, Osaka Gas and ConocoPhillips				Asia, US
Bolivia-Chile/Peru	Pacific LNG	Total, Repsol, BG	?	2	6.6	North America
Egypt	SEGAS (Diametta)	Union Fenosa (40%), ENI (40%), EGPC (10%), EGAS (10%)	End 2004	1	4.8	Spain
	Under construction					
	SEGAS (Diametta)			1	4.8	
	Egyptian LNG (Idku)	BG (35.5%), Petronas (35.5%), EGPC (12%), EGAS (12%), GdF (5%)	Q3 2005	1	3.6	France
	Under construction					
	Egyptian LNG (Idku)	BG (38%), Petronas (38%), EGPC (12%), EGAS (12%)	2006-2007	2	3.6 x 2	US, Italy
Equatorial Guinea	Bioko Island	Marathon, GEPetrol and BG Gas Marketing Ltd (BGML)	2007	1	3.4	US (Lake Charles)

Table 4.2. Expansion of LNG capacity at existing plants and new greenfield projects (continued)

Country	Plant name	Operator	Start-up date	Number of trains	Annual capacity (mtpa)	Receiving countries
New projects (continued)						
Indonesia	Tangguh	Japanese partners (50.3%), CNOOC (12.5%), BP (Operator 37.2%)	2007	2	3.5 X 2	Asia (China, Japan Korea), US West Coast, Philippines
	Dongghi/Matindok Massela	Pertamina	?	2	7	
Iran	Iran LNG	NIOC (40%), BP (36%)/India's Reliance (24%)	?	2	9 to 10	India, Europe
	Pars LNG	NIOC (50%), Total (30%)/Petronas (20%)	?	2	9 to 10	Far East
	Persian LNG	NIOC (50%), Repsol (25%)/Shell (25%)	?	2	9 to 10	Europe
	NIOC LNG	NIOC (100%),	?	2	9.6	Europe/Asia
Nigeria	Brass LNG	NNPC, ConocoPhillips, ENI, Chevron Texaco	2008	2	5 x 2	US for train 1/Europe
	Nnwa and Doro Fields (offshore LNG plant)	NNPC, Shell, Statoil	?			
	West Niger Delta	ExxonMobil, ChevronTexaco	?	1 to 2	9	
Norway	Melkoye / Snohvit LNG **Under construction**	Statoil (operator, 33.53%), Petoro (30%), Total (18.4 %), Gaz de France (12%), Amerada Hess (3.26%), RWE DEA (2.81%)	2006	1	4.1	US/Europe (Spain, France)
Peru	Camisea phase II	Hunt Oil, Partner SK Corp of Korea				North America

Table 4.2. Expansion of LNG capacity at existing plants and new greenfield projects (continued)

Country	Plant name	Operator	Start-up date	Number of trains	Annual capacity (mtpa)	Receiving countries
New projects (continued)						
Russia	Sakhalin 2 LNG (Prigorodnoye, Aniva Bay) **Under Construction**	Sakhalin Energy: Shell (55%), Mitsui (25%) and Mitsubishi (20%)	2007 for train 1 - 2008 for train 2	2	4.8 x 2	Japan
	Shtokman field Under consideration	Gazprom, ConocoPhillips				US
	Yamal Under consideration	Gazprom, ConocoPhillips				Europe
US	Alaska North Slope LNG (Port of Valdez)	Phillips, BP, Foothills Pipeline, Marubeni	2010	2	7	Asia, US West Coast
Venezuela	Mariscal Sucre	PDVSA (53%), Shell (30%), Mitsubishi (8%), Qatar Petroleum (9%)	?	1	4.7	US
Yemen	Yemen LNG	Total, Yemen General Gas Corporation, Yukong	?	2	6.2	

Source: Cedigaz, IEA

Africa

Current liquefaction capacity in the region amounts to 30.4 mtpa, mostly in Algeria and Nigeria. New countries, including Egypt, Angola and Equatorial Guinea, are planning to enter the LNG business for export to Europe and the US.

Sonatrach, the **Algerian** national oil company, has the world's largest equity share in LNG plants, and is expected to remain a leading LNG exporter. The first Algerian LNG plant at Arzew came on stream as early as 1964. Skikda was built in 1972. Both plants were renovated at the end of the 1990s. By 2003, Algerian LNG export capacity amounted to 30.3 bcm, 7.8 bcm at Skikda and 24.5 bcm at Arzew. The accident in January 2004 destroyed three out of six trains at Skikda, which is now completely closed. The remaining three trains will be reopened after inspection work. Algeria intends to re-build a world-class LNG plant at Skikda (1 train, 4 mtpa). It also has a project to build a new integrated LNG project at Gassi Touil (4 mtpa), with international partners.

The **Angola** LNG project, a joint project involving the state oil company of Angola, Sonangol (20%), Chevron Texaco (32%), BP, ExxonMobil, Total and Norsk Hydro (12% each), is planned as an integrated project encompassing offshore and onshore operations to monetise significant gas resources from fields located offshore Angola. The project is planned to facilitate offshore hydrocarbon developments while reducing gas flaring in Angola. The LNG plant, to be constructed near Soyo in northern Angola, will initially have one train with a 4 mtpa capacity. The project is expandable to four trains. Start-up date is towards the end of this decade. The final investment decision is expected in 2005.

Currently, there are two LNG projects in **Egypt** at an advanced stage: Idku (Egyptian LNG, ELNG) and Damietta (SEGAS LNG). Idku consists of two trains with a capacity of 3.6 mtpa each. The first train is expected to come into operation by third quarter 2005 with exports to Gaz de France under a 20-year contract signed in 2002, whereas the second train is expected to come on stream by 2006 to supply LNG to Lake Charles, Louisiana, US. The project is tied into natural gas reserves from BG's Simian/Sienna offshore fields. A third train may be built by

2007. The Malaysian company Petronas is partner in the project, after buying Edison's stake.

The other project, Damietta, is built by the Spanish power group, Union Fenosa. In 2002, Eni became involved in the project after it purchased a 50% stake in Union Fenosa's gas business. The $1.3 billion LNG plant is expected to be completed at end 2004. Initial capacity of the first train is 4.8 mtpa. Unlike other LNG projects, this one is not tied to upstream gas development. Instead, Union Fenosa has signed a 25-year gas supply contract with EGPC. Union Fenosa will take 60% (2.9 mtpa) of SEGAS LNG. A second train is under serious consideration.

With expansion planned at both plants, Egypt could potentially increase its LNG export capacity to 20 mtpa by 2007. Egypt has proven reserves of 58.5 tcf (1,650 bcm).

In **Equatorial Guinea**, Marathon Oil has a project to build a liquefaction plant at Bioko Island for supplies to the US. BG and Marathon have signed a MoU for the export by Marathon of 3.4 mtpa to BG for a 17-year period from 2007. Approval of the LNG plant by the Equato-Guinean government has been received. GEPetrol, the country's national oil company, is planning to take a 25% stake in the $1 billion LNG plant.

Nigeria started LNG exports in 1999 from its Bonny LNG plant (2 trains, 5.9 mtpa). A third train entered into operation in 2002. In 2002, Nigeria exported 11.41 bcm of natural gas of which almost 96% went to Europe. Bonny LNG is operated by the consortium Nigeria Liquefied Natural Gas Corporation (NLNG), comprising NNPC (49%), Shell (25.6%), Total (15%) and ENI (10.4%). The first two trains are supplied from natural gas fields but the input gas for the third train consists of associated (previously flared) natural gas. Two additional liquefaction trains are under construction (Nigeria Plus), expected to be in operation by the end of 2005 and providing an extra combined capacity of 8 mtpa. A sixth train is under consideration. Capacity would then rise to about 21.5 mtpa (29 bcm/a).

Nigeria's LNG activities are set to increase rapidly during the next decade. Plans for additional LNG facilities are being developed at the West Niger Delta and a front end engineering design (FEED) agreement has been signed by NNPC, US ConocoPhillips, ENI and ChevronTexaco to build a LNG plant (two 5 mtpa trains) in the Niger Delta (Brass LNG). The plant is scheduled to come on stream by 2008 and would be the world's first offshore LNG plant with a capacity of 24 mcm per day or 8.8 bcm/a. The main market for the first train would be the US market. A third LNG plant may be built by NNPC, Shell and Statoil near Escravos. And a fourth project is promoted by ExxonMobil and Chevron Texaco.

Asia

Asia is a major LNG exporting region, with half of world's exporting capacity, and liquefaction plants in Australia, Brunei, Indonesia and Malaysia. There are several projects to further expand the export capacity.

Australia has exported LNG since 1989 and has sold over 1,500 cargoes to Japan. The country, which has large undeveloped gas resources with reserves at 3,930 bcm (Cedigaz), has proved itself a reliable and stable LNG producer. The North West Shelf project has an LNG production of 7.5 mtpa. Train 4 (4.2 mtpa) is under construction with a start-up at mid-2004, and train 5 is under consideration. Australia is going to supply LNG to the first Chinese regasification terminal at Guangdong. A second LNG plant is under construction in Darwin (3 mtpa of LNG), with gas coming from Bayu-Undan in the joint area with East Timor. Deliveries to Japan are due to start in 2006. There are four other LNG projects under consideration: Gorgon (operator: Chevron Texaco), Sunrise (operator: Woodside), Browse Gas (operator: Woodside) and Scarborough (operator: Esso Australia).

Brunei started to export LNG to Japan in 1972 from its LNG plant at Lumut (7.2 mtpa of capacity). The plant includes 5 trains and Brunei LNG is considering the construction of a sixth train with a capacity of 4 mtpa by 2010. Brunei LNG is 50% owned by the Brunei Government, 25% by Shell and 25% by Mitsubishi.

Since production began in the early 1970s, **Indonesia** has become the largest producer and exporter in the world. It has two LNG plants, including 14 trains, Arun (12.3 mtpa, 6 trains) and Bontang (22.3 mtpa, 8 trains). Arun now has four operating trains as two trains were decommissioned because of declining reserves. Contracted sales to Japan,

Korea and Taiwan amount to 27 mtpa. Future LNG projects are being considered at Tangguh (in West Papua), at Donggi/Matindok (central Sulawesi) and Massela (Arafuru Sea). Indonesia's proven reserves are estimated at 3,825 bcm (Cedigaz).

The $2.2 billion Tangguh project (2 trains of 3.5 mtpa each) is expected to begin operation in 2007, dedicated to supplying China (the second LNG terminal at Fujian), Japan, South Korea, and the US west coast. Partners in Tangguh involve Japanese partners (50.3%), Chinese CNOOC (12.5%) and the operator BP (37.2%). Tangguh partners signed heads of agreement for the sale of 3.7 mtpa to Sempra Energy of the US, and 2.6 mtpa to China (Fujian). However, BP is still seeking more firm agreements in China, South Korea, Japan and US to underpin the development of the project.

BP Migas[28] is to take a prominent role in LNG marketing, but state-owned Pertamina continues as LNG seller for existing contracts. Indonesia is seeking to supply new markets and new customers, US west coast and Mexico, Fujian China and Kwangyang, the terminal under construction in Korea.

Malaysia LNG (MLNG) Sdn Bhd produces and exports LNG to various countries across Asia. Based in Bintulu, Sarawak, MLNG is one of the world's largest producers of LNG in a single location, producing 19.5 mtpa. The plant is being expanded with an additional two trains of 3.4 mtpa each. The first of these, scheduled to come on stream in 2003, was delayed to April 2004, after a fire in August 2003. The second train was commissioned in October 2003.

Europe

An international consortium headed by **Norway**'s Statoil has secured long-term LNG sales contracts to bolster the $6 billion Snøhvit LNG project in the Barents Sea. This is Europe' first major LNG development. Production of 4.1 mtpa is planned to start in 2006 and expected to continue until 2035. In January 2004, Statoil bought Norsk Hydro's 10%

---

28 "BP Migas" has no relationships to British Petroleum. It is the short name for the Implementing Body for Oil and Gas Upstream Activities.

share in the Snøhvit liquefaction plant, bringing its total stake to 32.39%. Recoverable reserves are estimated at 190 bcm. An onshore LNG plant is going to be built at Hammerfest, north-west Norway. Iberdrola will purchase 1.6 bcm/a, while Gaz de France and Total, will each take 1.7 bcm/a. El Paso will buy 2.4 bcm/a.

Middle East

The Middle East has recently emerged as a major LNG exporting region, with plants now operating in Abu Dhabi, Oman and Qatar. In 2002, the three countries accounted for 22% of world LNG trade. Several new LNG projects and expansions of existing projects are under construction or at the planning stage. By the end of the decade, Qatar is expected to become the leading LNG exporter producing 70 mtpa.

Abu Dhabi was the first Middle East country to start LNG exports in 1977. The LNG plant located at Das Island has two trains with a capacity of 5.8 mtpa. Production is sold to Japan and Spain. There are no current plans to increase capacity.

Iran, the holder of the world's second largest gas reserves, is developing an LNG export policy under NIGEC (National Iranian Gas Export Policy). Four LNG projects are planned, each with some 9-10 mtpa, although with no start-up date or investment decision taken so far. Several consortia have made bids for projects based on phases 11 to 15 of the South Pars development: Iran LNG (NIOC/BP and Reliance), Pars LNG (NIOC/Total and Petronas) and ENI for phases 11 and 12; Persian LNG (NIOC/Shell and Repsol) for phase 13; and NIOC LNG for phase 15. For the time being, only one project is likely to move ahead, possibly involving gas supplied from different phases. NIOC LNG looks to be the best placed at present. BG and ENEL, who are primarily interested in securing LNG at competitive prices, are negotiating to join the NIOC LNG project as downstream partners. The government has indicated that it may provide as much as 50% of the financing for the project out of its reserve funds. The $1.75 billion facility at Bandar Tombak in southern Iran is intended to produce 9.6 mtpa of LNG from two trains. Targeted markets are Europe and Asia. In May 2003, Iran and India agreed in principle for deliveries of 5 mtpa for 25 years of Iranian LNG. It is unclear which LNG scheme will provide LNG when and for which market.

Oman LNG has been in operation since April 2000. The plant includes 2 trains with a current capacity of 7.8 mtpa. Oman is currently building a third train, Qalhat LNG with 3.4 mtpa of capacity, which is due on stream in 2005. 1.6 mtpa are committed to the Spanish Union Fenosa, but the rest is not yet committed. Sales are on an ex-ship[29] basis. The ownership of Qalhat LNG includes the Government of Oman 52%, Oman LNG 40% and Union Fenosa 8%. Oman is also de-bottlenecking the first two trains, which should have a capacity of 7.5 mtpa by 2006.

Currently, **Qatar** has two LNG liquefaction plants: Qatar LNG Company (Qatargas) and Ras Laffan LNG Company (RasGas). The Qatargas I downstream consortium comprises Qatar Petroleum (QP) (65%), Total (10%), ExxonMobil (10%), Mitsui (7.5%) and Marubeni (7.5%). The first shipment of the Qatargas venture, extracting gas from the North Field, was to Japan in December 1996. The LNG plant consists of three 2.4 mtpa trains with the last one completed in 1999. Qatargas is currently undergoing de-bottlenecking to increase capacity to 9.5 mtpa by 2005. Qatargas aims to increase exports with additional exports targeted at Asian and European markets. The construction of a fourth train is also planned (4.8 mtpa). Qatargas II (QP, 70%, ExxonMobil, 30%) signed heads of agreement in June 2002 for the supply of 14 mtpa (2 trains) of LNG to UK and Europe. France's Total is likely to take a stake in the project. Moreover, two other trains (Qatargas III with Conoco Phillips) representing 15 mtpa are planned for 2008/9.

Rasgas is Qatar's second LNG project. The shareholders of Rasgas I are QP (63%), ExxonMobil (25%), Kogas, 5%, Itochu 4% and Japan LNG 3%. The plant consists of two 3.3 mtpa trains. The first train was completed in early 1999 and LNG was sent to Korea. The second train came on stream in April 2000. Rasgas is being expanded with two additional trains of 4.7 mtpa each (Rasgas II) for deliveries to India, Italy (Edison) and Taiwan. In January 2004, Rasgas started LNG export to the Indian company Petronet at the Dahej terminal. Two additional trains are planned for a total capacity of 15.6 mtpa (Rasgas III – QP 70%, ExxonMobil 30%). Deliveries of gas are targeted to reach the US in

---

29 Ex-ship: Under an ex-ship contract, the seller has to deliver LNG to the buyer at an agreed importing terminal. The seller remains responsible for the LNG until it is delivered.

2008-09 under a 25-year contract signed between QP and ExxonMobil in October 2003. Qatar's original markets for its LNG exports were Japan, South Korea and Taiwan. India is now possibly becoming another market for Qatari LNG. The first term-contracts with Europe were signed between Spain and Italy, and the next two biggest markets will be the US and UK. Reserves at Qatar's North Field are estimated at 23 tcm.

Yemen initiated a $5 billion LNG export venture in 1996 with Total, establishing the Yemen Liquefied Natural Gas Company (Yemen LNG). The company was formed by Total and the state-owned Yemen General Gas Corporation, and included Hunt Oil, ExxonMobil and Yukong. In May 2002, the entire Yemen LNG project looked in danger of collapse due to its inability to find export markets and the withdrawal of Hunt Oil and ExxonMobil from the project. However, the Government continues to hold out hope and has given the remaining group (led by Total) until 2006 to find an export market. The Government has set aside certified proven gas reserves of 290 bcm for the project.

North America

Alaska was one of the first LNG exporters to Japan back in 1969 from the Kenai plant (1.5 mtpa) by Phillips and Marathon. It may now develop natural gas from North Slope to be shipped from a new LNG project. A feasibility study is expected to be completed by June 2004. The project encompasses an 800-mile gas pipeline to Port Valdez, an LNG plant and LNG tankers to carry LNG to the US west coast and Asia.

Russia

Russia is developing its first LNG projects at Sakhalin. Estimated reserves of the projects Sakhalin 1 (pipeline) and Sakhalin II (LNG) amount to 550 bcm. Shell, which is leading the entirely foreign consortium, gave the green light for the LNG project to proceed in May 2003. The project involves upstream development of an offshore gas field and the construction of a two-train liquefaction plant with a capacity of 9.6 mtpa. Total investment will amount to around $9 billion. Exports are destined to Japan and possibly later to Korea, as well as to California.

Gazprom is in talks with Conoco Phillips about a possible venture to tap huge gas reserves at the Shtokmanov field in the Barents Sea off north-west Russia as a source of LNG for export across the Atlantic. The project includes an LNG plant (14 mtpa) near Murmansk. The overall project, which would cost some $10 billion, also includes the vessels required to transport LNG to the US. Shtokmanov holds 3,200 bcm of gas reserves and could produce up to 90 bcm/a and 31 million tonnes of condensate. Furthermore, some of this production could be directed into the 20 bcm/a, 1,100-km North European Gas pipeline that Gazprom is investigating.

Separately, Gazprom has proposed building a huge, 25 bcm/a LNG plant on the Yamal peninsula, even though exports would necessitate the construction of expensive ice-class LNG tankers. Gas from Yamal has been targeted as pipeline gas for Europe.

South America

Trinidad is the only LNG producer in South America so far, but there are several projects to build LNG plants in the region. Most of the LNG will go to the North American market and to importing countries in the region.

Bolivia, a land-locked country, is investigating sending some of its reserves to an LNG plant on the Pacific coast in Chile or in Peru, which would allow exports to the United States or Mexico. Bolivian natural gas reserves are estimated at 54.86 tcf (1,550 bcm) as of 1st January 2003. The consortium Pacific LNG is trying to develop an LNG export project of 6.6 mtpa through a Chilean or Peruvian port. However, general resistance to gas exports erupted in violent demonstrations in October 2003 and the downfall of President Gonzalo Sanchez de Lozado. The new administration elected in October 2003 has decided to hold a referendum in March 2004 on exporting LNG to North America or other markets. The future of any LNG project will then have to be decided through this mechanism.

Peru, which is developing the Camisea gas field (reserves of 11 tcf) is envisaging the export of LNG. Phase I of the Camisea project, for which Pluspetrol of Argentina is the upstream operator, will bring gas from the

Amazon region, across the Andes, for use in Lima. Phase II is the LNG project is being promoted by Hunt Oil and Partner SK Corp of Korea. A MoU was signed in October 2003 by Hunt Oil to sell 2.7 mtpa of LNG to Tractebel for 18 years for its LNG terminal to be built at Lazaro Cardenas in Mexico. Hunt and SK are still seeking financing and additional partners for the LNG phase. Sonatrach recently entered into the upstream portion of phase I. Total investments for the project, including a reception terminal and the LNG tankers, is estimated at $2 billion.

Trinidad and Tobago operates a three-train liquefaction plant (9.9 mtpa at the end of 2003). It exported 5.4 bcm of LNG in 2002, mainly to the United States. A fourth train (5.2 mtpa) is being built. The government has also indicated interest in constructing a fifth and sixth train. The plant is located at Point Fortin and operated by Atlantic LNG Company. Atlantic LNG has been supplying LNG to the US, Spain, Puerto Rico and the Dominican Republic. Partners in train 1 are: BP, 34%, BG, 26%, Repsol, 20%, Tractebel, 10% and National Gas Company of Trinidad, 10%. Trains 2 and 3 partners are: BP, 42.5%, BG, 32.5% and Repsol, 25%. Following the recent discovery of the Angostura field off Trinidad's east coast, proven reserves now stand at 589 bcm of gas.

Venezuela has enough gas reserves to become a major LNG exporter, but projects for liquefaction plants have been stalled so far by a combination of poor economics and lack of political support. Venezuela is now developing an LNG project in the Gulf of Paria, the Mariscal Sucre LNG project. The initial capacity of the plant with one train would be 4.7 mtpa. The project includes PDVSA (53%), Shell (30%), Mitsubishi, 8%, and 9% recently acquired by Qatar Petroleum. The LNG export project is integrated with the development of the estimated 10.4 tcf North Paria reserves and is aimed at the US market, which is only 2,000 nautical miles away. The cost of the overall project is estimated at $2.7 billion. Venezuela may also consider piping gas to Trinidad for liquefaction and export as LNG.

COST REDUCTIONS IN THE LNG CHAIN

LNG projects are very capital intensive, with most projects costing several billion dollars. However, economies of scale are significant. They can be achieved by building several trains at the same site, benefiting from joint site preparation costs and economies of scale in the size of the trains due to scale-up effects, especially in compressor size.

Liquefaction plants typically consist of one or two processing trains. The standard economic size of each train is now about 3 to 3.5 mtpa. Adding a second train once a plant is built can reduce the unit cost of a liquefaction train by 20-30%. A single-train plant normally costs around $1 billion, although actual costs vary geographically according to land costs, environmental and safety regulations, labour costs and other local market conditions.

Technological progress over the past four decades has led to a sharp decrease in investment and operating costs of liquefaction plants. The average unit investment for a liquefaction plant dropped from some $550 a ton a year of capacity in the 1960s, to approximately $350 in the 1970s and 1980s, and $250 in the late 1990s. For projects starting operation today, the price is slightly under $200 (all in current dollars).[30]

Transport costs are largely a function of the distance between the liquefaction and regasification terminals. Using a larger number of smaller carriers offers more flexibility and reduced storage requirements but raises unit shipping costs. The largest LNG carriers today have a maximum capacity of 135,000-140,000 cm. They cost around $160-170 million to build. Substantial reductions in cost have been achieved over recent decades thanks to economies of scale. Tanker sizes have increased from some 40,000 cm for the first generation to 140,000 cm nowadays. Costs for LNG tankers dropped significantly in the wake of the Asian crisis in 1998.

Regasification plant construction costs depend on throughput capacity, land development and labour costs (which vary considerably according to location), and storage capacity. Economies of scale are most significant for storage. Tanks with a storage capacity of about 200,000 cm – the largest feasible at present, are currently optimal size.

< The last five to ten years have seen some major reductions in LNG supply costs. These have come largely from increases in train size, improved fuel

---

30   Valais M., Chabrelie M.F., and Lefeuvre T. (2001).

efficiency in liquefaction and regasification (mainly from high-efficiency gas turbines in on-site co-generation facilities), improved equipment design, the elimination of gold-plating and better utilisation of available capacity, and more use of competitive bidding procedures. From 1990 to 2000, liquefaction costs have fallen typically by 25% to 35% and shipping costs by 20% to 30%. The cost of regasification has fallen less than costs for the other parts of the LNG chain since the 1960s. Technology and productivity gains have been largely offset by higher storage costs, the largest single cost component.

Table 4.3. Cost reduction in the LNG chain
(Middle East to Far East LNG project) ($/million Btu)

	Cost estimate Early 1990s	Cost estimate Early 2000s
Upstream development cost	0.5 - 0.8	0.5 - 0.8
Liquefaction	1.3 -1.4	1.0 - 1.1
Shipping (LNG tanker)	1.2 - 1.3	0.9 -1.0
Regasification	0.5 - 0 6	0.4 - 0.5
Total cost	**3.5 - 4.1**	**2.8 - 3.4**

Source: Valais M., Chabrelie M.F., and Lefeuvre T. (2001).

LNG costs vary considerably in practice, largely as a function of capacity, particularly the number of trains in liquefaction plants and shipping distance. >

GLOBALISATION OF LNG TRADE

The way in which LNG is contracted is changing:

- Spot/short-term trade is increasing. It represented 8% of the global LNG trade in 2002;
- Price indexation is moving from oil index to multiple index and spot gas indexation;
- Tender process was successfully tested in China and India;
- Contracts cover smaller volumes with increased flexibility.

Growing LNG spot market[31]

There is growing recognition on the part of both producers and consumers of the growing role of short-term and spot sales, and even more for a niche function to sell spare build-up capacity on the producing side, and to complement long-term purchases for buyers. While long-term contracts will remain dominant in the foreseeable future, spot sales (which mean short-term deals or the sale of one cargo) are expected to take a growing share. However, most experts agree that this development will not lead to large-scale trading as happens in the oil market, with an extensive paper as well as physical market. There is an overall consensus that LNG spot trade may amount to 15-30% of global LNG trade.

Spot LNG trade has developed since the middle of the 1990s, thanks to spare production capacity, the deregulation of the Korean and Spanish markets and purchases by new entrants, the re-emergence of the US LNG market, and available LNG transportation capacity. Spot sales rose to 11.44 bcm in 2002, an increase of 66% over 2000, but still represent minor volumes. Short-term LNG trading represented 8% of all LNG trade in 2002. First estimates for 2003 indicate that spot trading has increased sharply to an estimated 20 bcm, under the impetus of spot transactions and arbitrages, mainly involving the US market.

The evolution of the spot LNG market[32] is indicated in Table 4.4.

More and more players are buying and selling spot LNG. This phenomenon was triggered by the 1997-98 Asian financial crisis, which generated supply surpluses in the Middle East. Another driver of increased spot sales in recent years was the strategy adopted by Spain and Korea to meet peak winter demand, by relying on spot cargoes to cover their seasonal demand. Spain imported 4 bcm of LNG under spot basis in 2002. Kogas bought 43 spot cargoes (3 bcm) during the winter of 2002/03. The next driving force was the re-emergence of the US market due to the high level of prices in 2000-2001, which led to spot cargoes being redirected from Europe to the US, in addition to direct LNG spot

---

31 A distinction should be made between LNG spot deals, which currently constitute what is called "LNG spot market" and sales of LNG to a spot liquid market as LNG going to the US.
32 Spot transactions and short-term contracts of less than one year.

Table 4.4. LNG spot and swap transactions, 1992 to 2002
By exporting country (bcm)

	1992	1993	1994	1995	1996	1997	1998	1999	2000	2001	2002
Abu Dhabi	-	-	-	1.42	1.39	0.08	0.34	0.65	0.64	0.32	1.21
Algeria	0.53	0.49	0.59	0.35	-	0.6	0.45	1.33	1.38	2.36	2.66
Australia	-	0.34	0.58	0.66	0.26	0.3	0.38	0.3	0.45	0.23	0.3
Brunei	-	-	0.3	0.08	-	-	-	-	-	-	0.21
Indonesia	0.23	0.23	0.37	0.53	0.6	0.28	-	0.38	1.18	1.91	0.15
Libya	-	-	0.05	-	-	-	-	-	-	-	-
Malaysia	0.3	0.53	0.45	0.23	0.08	-	-	0.08	0.08	0.52	0.68
Nigeria	-	-	-	-	-	-	-	-	0.37	1.29	0.53
Oman	-	-	-	-	-	-	-	-	0.6	0.83	2.27
Qatar	-	-	-	-	-	0.38	0.95	1.59	1.98	2.71	2.08
Trinidad	-	-	-	-	-	-	-	0.39	0.92	0.58	1.35
Total	**1.06**	**1.59**	**2.34**	**3.27**	**2.33**	**1.64**	**2.12**	**4.72**	**7.6**	**10.75**	**11.44**

By importing country (bcm)

	1992	1993	1994	1995	1996	1997	1998	1999	2000	2001	2002
Belgium	-	0.23	0.08	0.15	-	-	-	-	-	0.15	0.26
France	-	-	-	0.86	0.22	-	-	0.08	0.08	0.52	1.17
Italy	0.53	0.26	0.19	-	-	-	0.12	0.54	0.48	0.37	0.28
Japan	0.38	0.39	0.08	0.08	0.15	0.28	-	0.15	0.32	2.23	0.32
South Korea	0.15	0.45	1.05	0.9	0.67	-	0.08	0.3	1.47	1.87	1.79
Portugal	-	-	-	-	-	-	-	-	0.08	-	-
Spain	-	0.26	0.94	1.05	0.98	0.99	0.82	1.69	1.43	2.29	4.15
Taiwan	-	-	-	-	-	-	-	-	-	0.08	-
Turkey	-	-	-	0.23	0.08	-	0.58	0.3	-	-	-
USA	-	-	-	-	0.23	0.37	0.52	1.66	3.72	3.24	3.42
Puerto Rico	-	-	-	-	-	-	-	-	-	-	0.05
Total	**1.06**	**1.59**	**2.34**	**3.27**	**2.33**	**1.64**	**2.12**	**4.72**	**7.58**	**10.75**	**11.44**

Share of spot in global LNG trade (%)

	1992	1993	1994	1995	1996	1997	1998	1999	2000	2001	2002
	1.3	1.9	2.7	3.5	2.3	1.5	1.9	3.8	5.5	7.5	7.6

The figures include spot and short-term LNG sales and swap transactions.
Source: PetroStrategies

purchases. About 4 bcm/a was imported to the US under spot or short-term contracts in 2000, 2001 and 2002. Again in 2003, sustained high level prices in the US led to a surge in spot purchases and re-routing of LNG cargoes initially destined for Europe to the US market. US LNG purchases on a spot basis are estimated at 12.6 bcm in 2003, a sharp increase compared with 2002.

Spot trading in the last three years was also influenced by exceptional circumstances. The increase in global spot sales in 2001 resulted partly from the temporary shutdown of the Arun liquefaction plant in Indonesia whose production was replaced by spot cargoes from Bontang and other Asian LNG sources.

In 2002, LNG shipments from Oman and Abu Dhabi, destined for India's Dabhol, were available for spot sales. Middle East and Nigeria cargoes destined for the US were diverted to Europe where prices were more attractive. In 2003, the situation was reversed as prices in the US were more attractive than in Europe.

Spot trading in 2003 was affected by the shut-down of 17 nuclear power plants in Japan which led Japanese utilities to resort to power generation by gas-fired power based on LNG, resulting in increased spot sales or swaps with other Asian buyers. Hence, Tepco bought around 30 cargoes in the six months ending 30 September 2003 and Tepco and Kogas swapped 12 LNG cargoes in 2003. Japanese LNG imports increased to 80 bcm in 2003 (+9.6% compared with 2002). The Tepco nuclear shut-down structurally added 3 mtpa of demand and caused a short-term spot supply squeeze.

Spare capacity in infrastructure (liquefaction, LNG tankers and regasification) and a multitude of players on the LNG market are key prerequisites for spot trading. On the liquefaction side, the building of new liquefaction plants in the Middle East and Africa (Nigeria) in the second half of the 1990s, and the slow build-up period of long-term contracts, offered the possibility to sell spare capacity on the spot market. The delay in opening the Dabhol plant in India meant that deliveries from Abu Dhabi and Oman were diverted to other places in Asia and Europe. Spot volumes in 2002 were produced mainly by Algeria with

23%; Oman, 20%; Qatar, 18%; Trinidad, 12%, and Abu Dhabi, 11%. Spare capacity is the result of the build-up[33] of long-term contracts and will therefore disappear when the contracts have reached their plateau level. However, new plants and extensions to existing ones are built around the world, regularly providing spare capacity available for spot trading. Three plants, Atlantic LNG in Trinidad and Tobago, Nigeria LNG and Malaysia MLNG Tiga, have been expanded recently, while several plants are currently being expanded, and many owners of liquefaction plants are discussing additional expansions.

Transportation has been a bottleneck for spot trading in the last 2-3 years. In June 2003, only 6% of the LNG fleet was allocated to spot trade. However, the recent increase in the LNG fleet (26 LNG tankers delivered in the past two years) has removed this bottleneck. Several ships were built without dedicated trade and are available to seize spot trading opportunities. Of the 16 ships delivered in 2003, 4 were not committed to any specific project, as well as another 2 among the 21 ordered for 2004. Some of them are part of the portfolio strategy of major companies, while others are more speculative.

Furthermore, several older tankers are going to be freed from their current trade. These tankers, which have been fully amortised, are more profitable in spot trading than newly-built tankers. After being refurbished, they can be exposed to the risk of only intermittent usage. As an example, the *Tenaga Empat*, has recently been chartered for three years by Cheniere Energy after its 20 years operation of trade between Malaysia and Japan. A recent report of the Institute of Energy Economics of Japan (IEEJ) calculates that 34 LNG ship charters will end by 2010, 19 of which have not yet been tied to specific projects.[34]

Now that the four LNG terminals are re-opened in the US there is always an outlet (within the comfortable regasification capacity of these terminals) to sell LNG, accepting the netback of the US spot market at the terminal, but without the need to look for an LNG buyer.

---

33 During the term of a contract, there are different stages. The build-up period will typically consist of several steps by which the contractual quantity is gradually increased up to the plateau or peak level.

34 World Gas Intelligence, 31 December 2003.

Spot LNG "trading" is likely to remain a comparatively small market with limited liquidity. Some structural factors make it unlikely that LNG will easily develop the liquidity that exists in the oil market: the cost of transporting (and producing) LNG, the capital intensity of projects, which requires long-term contracts and makes it difficult to justify permanent spare capacity on economic grounds. However, spot trade might grow further and will continue to be used to overcome short-term imbalances, helped by the growth of the business, the flexibility created by vertical integration and additional future terminal and transportation capacity.

Table 4.5. Spot LNG sales and purchases as a percentage of total LNG exports and imports in 2002 (%)

Exporters		Importers	
Abu Dhabi	17	Belgium	7
Algeria	10	France	10
Australia	3	Italy	5
Brunei	2	Japan	0
Indonesia	0.4	South Korea	7
Malaysia	3	Spain	33
Nigeria	7	USA	53
Oman	28	Puerto Rico	8
Qatar	11		
Trinidad	25		

Source: IEA, Petrostrategies

Pricing development

A more flexible approach to and a wider range of pricing is emerging in the LNG industry. Suppliers are adopting different pricing policies according to the buyers' market. For instance, Qatar, which sells on the three main LNG markets, has pegged its LNG sales to crude oil prices in Japan, to Henry Hub spot prices in the US, to NBP spot prices in the UK and to fuel oil prices in continental Europe.

In Japan, cif LNG prices are based on a basket of crude oils imported into the country, known as the Japanese Crude Cocktail (JCC), which are adjusted on a monthly basis. In the past, this "cocktail" was a convenient basis for gas pricing because the main competitor of gas was light crude oils, whose prices are reflected in the JCC. However, as gas in electricity generation – the major user of gas in Japan – is no longer competing with crude oil, Japanese buyers require more flexibility in volume and pricing. Moreover, the contract signed by Australian North West Shelf (NWS) with Chinese buyers has set a new benchmark for LNG pricing in Asia. The price formula is reported to be similar to that used for the NWS Japanese contracts, i.e. an S-curve formula based on the average price of a cocktail of imported crudes, designed to protect the parties against sharp swings in oil prices. However, based on a reference barrel of $18, NWS partners have lowered the cif price to China to around $3/mBtu, or about 15% below the current Japanese price. Moreover, the slope of the S-curve is not as steep as under the Japanese formula. This means that for a price of $25/b, China would pay 25% less than Japanese buyers.

This price cut will greatly affect renegotiation of the Asian contracts which come up for renewal before the end of the decade (about 25 mtpa including Japanese contracts with NWS partners). A decrease in prices is expected; ToP obligations are expected to be relaxed and more pricing flexibility should be introduced in renewed contracts.

European LNG contracts are still predominantly linked to the evolution of gasoil and heavy fuel oil prices, with a reference period usually of six months to one year. European LNG contracts are less rigid than those in Japan, as they include renegotiation clauses and opportunities to reopen price discussions. In some contracts, other indices, such as electricity pool prices, have now been included to reflect the new competitive situation of gas in power generation, for instance in the formula negotiated between Trinidad and Tobago and Spain's Gas Natural. As gas trading develops and new gas market indices appear, future LNG contracts could be pegged to them. This is the case for LNG imports to the UK, which will be pegged to NBP prices.

In the US market, LNG prices are generally linked to the Henry Hub prices. Ex-ship prices tend to represent 80% to 90% of the futures prices at Henry Hub, as they are adjusted for the location of the LNG terminal. LNG supply will seek highest differential compared with Henry Hub spot prices first: Everett; Cove Point; Elba Island and then Lake Charles. However, the arrival of sudden large LNG supplies flowing directly into the US gas grid has an impact on the basis to Henry Hub prices and sometimes completely annihilates it. Expanding pipeline connections from the terminals is an obvious tactic for operators striving to preserve the differentials to Henry Hub.

These pricing mechanisms result in three different regional price patterns, as indicated in the following figure:

Figure 4.3. Evolution of LNG prices in the United States, Europe and Japan

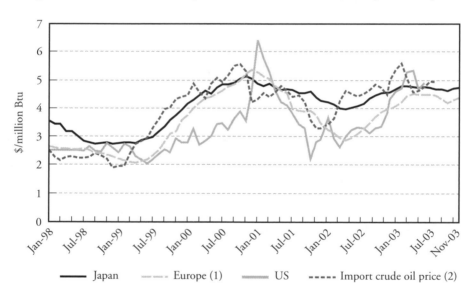

(1) Algerian LNG received in France
(2) Average import crude oil price in Japan
Source: US DOE/EIA, World Gas Intelligence, IEA

With increasing short-term trading and physical arbitrage in the Atlantic basin, inter-regional pricing links may evolve. To what extent will flexible LNG trading really link the hitherto-isolated markets of Europe and North America? Although some arbitrage exists, and more is anticipated, there is as yet little sign that movements from one area to another really have much effect on prices in the market left behind. Given the limited volume scale of price arbitrage so far, it is not surprising that LNG cargo diversions have had little effect on the markets from which they have been diverted.

In the Pacific basin, such arbitrage is not possible as long as no regasification capacity is available on the US west coast or Mexico. Even when such capacity becomes available, transportation distances may be a limiting factor for the development of arbitrage possibilities. Such a development would involve much larger differences in shipping distances than in the Atlantic basin. For example, it would take three times more ships to deliver an equivalent amount of LNG from Indonesia's Bontang to California as it now does to Japan. However, as the LNG market evolves, the Middle East is going to act as a swing supplier. The Atlantic basin market will be connected to the Pacific basin via Middle East producers, which may export to both markets.

A new paradigm

We are witnessing changes in the traditional seller/buyer relationship and the replacement of the classic LNG model by a more sophisticated flexible commercial approach. The classical LNG approach was based on a sellers' market where demand caused development of new supply capacity. Sales were based on long-term take-or-pay contracts with limited volume and destination flexibility. Most sales were primarily ex-ship. Prices were indexed to alternative fuels (oil products mainly) and to crude oil. Buyers' creditworthiness and capacity to market the volumes were extremely important.

This approach is under attack from a number of directions. The lower costs in liquefaction, transportation and regasification allow new LNG flows which would not have been economic 20 years ago. With the opening of electricity and gas markets and the increasing use of gas for power generation, new entrants (mainly electricity companies) are entering the LNG business and contracting their gas supplies directly. Their requirements are different from traditional buyers. They are requesting more volume flexibility and new pricing approaches. New long-term contracts have a shorter duration, 15 years instead of 20-25 years. Medium-term contracts, of 5 to 8 years, are also becoming more common. ToP obligations are being reduced. It seems that the need for secure supplies, which was eventually reflected in a price premium, is being replaced by a quest for more price and contract flexibility. Changes in the underlying economics of the LNG chain and the restructuring of the gas and electricity markets have implications for risk and reward arrangements. The vertical risk-sharing of long-term contracts – still widely used for greenfield projects – is increasingly complemented by vertical integration and risk taking in liquid markets.

There is an increased counter-party risk as off-take guarantees are less certain. In the past, the whole supply was dedicated to few markets where sales were guaranteed. Currently suppliers are able to negotiate multiple outlets for the same train. Selling to more than one market allows suppliers to spread the volume and price risks. Under these circumstances even buyers with less credit-standing are also entering the market (Indian electricity boards).

The new LNG commercial approach incorporates the very large competitive and liquid North American market. This market not only attracts large LNG imports but it can also take them at nearly any time (to the limit of import terminals). Whereas up to 2003, no LNG project had been developed on the back of a long-term sale into a liquid market, new contracts are signed to deliver LNG to the US and UK, based on spot gas prices on these markets. The major differences between new and traditional projects are the type of price risk and the possibility to sell the LNG anywhere in the world. The risk sharing in the ExxonMobil/Qatar Petroleum deal is more of a joint-venture risk-sharing than the vertical risk-sharing of a long-term contract.

Competition between suppliers is fierce as more and more countries are seeking to monetise their gas resources. Due to lower specific costs, project sponsors are absorbing greater risks but also have the potential for higher rewards. Greenfield projects and expansion trains are moving forward without all volumes sold on long-term contracts: MLNG Tiga (Malaysia), Sakhalin II (Russia) and Australia's NWS (expansion) are developed without all nameplate being sold, nor on a long-term basis. Major companies (such as Shell, Total, BP) are developing a portfolio approach, with "branded" LNG. Essentially, they are buying their own LNG and selling it into markets where they are already active. The liquefaction plants thus become "tolling" plants.

Producers have also hinted that they may be more willing to relax the rules governing the re-selling of LNG to third parties. Nigeria LNG has already removed any destination clauses on its LNG current and future contracts. Japan and South Korea have swapped LNG cargoes for the last three years.

To answer increased risks, producers are moving downstream and acquiring access to regasification terminals in Europe (UK, Spain, Italy) ahead of upstream development. They are also building non-dedicated ships to benefit from spot market opportunities.

Malaysian Petronas, for instance, is actively integrating downstream and becoming a more global player. It has bought 30% equity in the UK LNG import terminal being developed at Milford Haven by Petroplus. Petronas has also acquired significant assets upstream in Egypt. It has joined BG as equal 35.5% controlling partner in the Egypt LNG export scheme due to start in 2005.

Algerian state company Sonatrach (Spain's major supplier) took a 30% share in Spanish refiner Cepsa and French Total's joint gas sales business in Spain in September 2003. The deal represents Sonatrach's first downstream move in the EU gas market. The company is also present in the LNG regasification terminal built at El Ferrol. Sonatrach has also formed a joint venture with BP that will pool import capacity at the UK NGT LNG terminal at Isle of Grain.

Qatar is also integrating downstream in the US, UK and Italy. With ExxonMobil, Qatar Petroleum has a project to build a more than 20 bcm/a LNG import terminal at Milford Haven in Wales. The strategy of ExxonMobil and Qatar is based on an integrated supply chain from production, liquefaction, shipping and regasification, following the mode pioneered by BG but on a much larger scale. They are taking the market risk. The same model applies to the contract signed with Conoco Phillips. The partners in Qatar's two LNG projects Qatargas and Rasgas have advanced plans to build receiving terminals in the UK, France, Italy and the US. In the UK, the partners have arranged for the production venture to take the price risk, and ExxonMobil's marketing venture to take the volume risk. Qatargas (QP 70% and ExxonMobil 30%) will produce the LNG and ship it to a UK terminal owned by the same partners, where the buyer will be ExxonMobil. ExxonMobil and Qatar Petroleum have also taken a 90% stake (45% each) in Italy's Edison Gas North Adriatic LNG regasification terminal offshore Rovigo.

Statoil, which is developing an LNG project at Snøhvit, has acquired long-term rights in US Cove Point terminal.

Buyers, on the other hand, try to cover risks by securing a diversified portfolio of LNG supplies and carrier capacity. They are also moving upstream as they seek for additional value and risk-hedging all along the gas chain. Recent examples of integration upstream involve:

■ Gaz de France in Egypt LNG (5%);

■ Union Fenosa in Egypt Segas (40%);

■ CNOOC in Indonesia's Tangguh (17%), in Australia's NWS (25% stake in China LNG, the company created to handle the NWS-Guangdong LNG contract) and a possible 12.5% stake in Gorgon joint venture;

■ LNG Japan, a joint venture between Nissho Iwai Corp and Sumitomo Corp, with a stake of 6.3% in Indonesia's Tangguh.

IMPACT ON SECURITY OF GAS SUPPLY

The new paradigm creates more opportunities but also new challenges for security of supply. On the one hand, the flexibility created by competitive markets enables more LNG suppliers to access more markets and to mobilise gas resources – which were not previously available to OECD gas markets – more quickly. For buyers, it allows access to more and more flexible supplies. LNG may even play a critical role in the balancing of gas supply and demand within a country/region, but also between regions, allowing arbitrage and purchasing cost optimisation. On the other hand, the development of the LNG trade and industry raises several issues, linked with the location of LNG sources, the financing needs required to expand production/liquefaction and trade, and the safety of LNG in general.

The new balancing role of LNG

Since LNG trade and contracts have both become a lot more flexible in recent years, LNG can play a key role in controlling peak loads. The creation of procurement portfolio (including traditional long-term contracts, medium-term contracts and spot purchases) could considerably facilitate peak/seasonal load management.

This policy is illustrated by Spanish Gas Natural, which for many years bought spot cargoes (negotiated ahead of winter needs) to meet its seasonal winter requirements. Gas Natural has recently transformed its spot purchases into flexible medium-term contracts with most deliveries made in winter. South Korea Kogas has the same procurement policy and has negotiated spot and medium-term deals with its suppliers to cover seasonal needs.

Having LNG in their procurement portfolio will give power producers and gas retailers a competitive edge in markets with high volatility in prices, by providing flexibility in handling peaks of gas demand. LNG is a way to optimise gas procurement portfolios and reduce purchasing costs, with an additional diversification option. These objectives are a major driver of the strategy of companies developing LNG import projects in UK.

LNG presents even more advantages. As peak demand in different countries/regions may not necessarily coincide, consuming countries may balance their difference in seasonality. Current examples include the time-swapping of LNG cargoes between Japan and South Korea. Japan has its peak LNG demand in summer (boosted by air cooling requirements), whereas Korea's peak demand is for heating purposes in winter. Tepco and Kogas swapped 12 LNG cargoes in 2003. In the summer of 2003, the 12 cargoes were sent to Japan, and Japan sent the 12 swapped cargoes to Korea in the first three months of 2004. The exchange of cargoes allows both countries to manage their peak demand more efficiently.

On a larger scale, when LNG trade becomes more global, it could be possible to trade seasonality and the impacts of different precipitations on the power sector between different regions, for instance between the US and Europe, where periods of peak demand do not necessarily coincide.

Political risk associated with LNG

The risk associated with the rising LNG demand is not the lack of gas resources. Proven gas reserves are estimated at 181 tcm as of 1 January 2003, representing 70 years of current marketed gas production. Remaining gas resources are estimated at 450-530 tcm (Cedigaz). Driven by the wish to monetise gas reserves, gas producers are very active in developing new export projects. There are around 30 new greenfield LNG projects under consideration worldwide. If only the current expansions to existing plants are taken into account, an additional 37 mtpa of LNG capacity would be added to the 133 mtpa existing capacity. However, even if gas resources are more widely distributed than oil, the largest resources continue to be located in areas of possible regional instability.

Figure 4.4. Sourcing of LNG

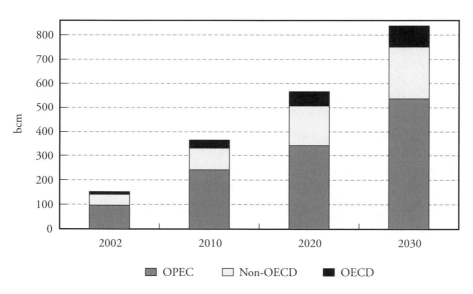

Source: *WEIO 2003*

By 2030, LNG trade is expected to account for about 50% of total trade, and 16% of global gas consumption. As shown in the following graph, most of the projects to be developed over the next 30 years are located in non-OECD countries, the exceptions being Australia, Norway and Alaska. OPEC countries – which hold half of global gas reserves (88,536 bcm as of 1 January 2003) – exported 96 bcm of LNG in 2002 (64% of global LNG trade). By 2030, they could export 565 bcm representing 64% of global LNG trade. By then, they will also produce 54% of global oil production. If exports from other non-OECD countries are added, that means that 90% of global LNG would come from non-OECD countries.

The geopolitical implications of this trade pattern are similar to that of the oil trade and give rise to the same concerns. The development of LNG trade could lead to similar geopolitical complications as were experienced for oil in the past. LNG suppliers from non-OECD countries could possibly try to influence LNG prices by trying to withhold capacity from the market, as is the case for OPEC and oil. >

<The current situation is comfortable, because importing countries have diversified their energy sources and supplies for gas, avoiding geopolitical risks from importing too much from a single region, and because oil and gas markets are different. So far, the LNG market is not global but characterised by the existence of three separate regional markets and by a predominance of bilateral long-term contracts. The cost of transportation makes LNG less "liquid" than oil. Gas transport costs easily exceed half of the gas market value. So far only 22% of global gas crosses borders compared to 57% of oil. >

Gas projects are also characterised by long lead times, as almost 10 years may elapse between the conception of a project and its first revenue, increasing the financial risks associated with it. Long-term contracts linking LNG suppliers to their customers therefore remain very important, allowing a balanced risk/reward and mitigating geopolitical risks. So far, LNG producers have maintained good relationships with their individual customers. Otherwise, they would risk not only losing their export revenues but also jeopardising their reputation in the case of a breach of delivery contract.

The current LNG business is also characterised as a buyers' market. There are many LNG projects and a number of gas fields waiting for development and for customers. Fields also tend to be developed on a joint venture basis, which creates considerable competition on the supply side and often commits government-owned companies. Finally, LNG has to face many competitors, starting with pipeline gas. As gas can always be substituted, it faces competition from other alternative fuels too. And finally, buyers are increasingly participating in the supply/liquefaction project, thus changing the dynamics of LNG supply and reducing the risk.

The trend is towards a more global market and increasing LNG supplies from only a few OPEC member countries: Qatar, Indonesia, Nigeria and Algeria. Therefore, although gas resources are abundant and LNG projects numerous, there is no room for complacency, and diversification policies should continue. The growing diversity of supply sources may help buyers to mitigate the political risks. Similarly, major companies with investments in affected countries can only spread the risks by investing in a portfolio of supply sources.

New security risks are also emerging stemming from political uncertainties, in Indonesia for instance. Indonesia is currently the world's largest LNG exporter. Unrest in the separatist Aceh region created a major supply cut in 2001 when ExxonMobil had to shutdown the Arun LNG plant for seven months. It resulted in changes in the way LNG is traded, with more flexibility requested by buyers and more cooperation developing between suppliers. After the disruption in 2001, Indonesia, Malaysia and Brunei pledged to work closely together to cover possible supply problems. There are still violent conflicts in Aceh and separatist sentiment is also growing in Irian Jaya (see below).

Territorial dispute between Australia and Indonesia delayed LNG projects from the joint shelf between East Timor and Australia, as East Timor entered into a treaty originally signed between Australia and Indonesia, before East Timor's independence. For the Bayu-Undan field, an agreement has been reached on sharing royalties from the project. The gas will be landed at Darwin in the Northern territory of Australia to be liquefied and delivered to Japan. The Sunrise project, which also lies on the shelf between East Timor and Australia, is still facing an agreement over the landing and liquefaction site and the split of royalties.

Indonesian supply problems

One challenge for the Indonesian government comes from the violent separatist movement in Aceh (where the Arun liquefaction plant is located) and growing separatist sentiment in Irian Jaya (where the Tangguh LNG plant will be built).

In March 2001, ExxonMobil decided to shut down three of the four fields supplying the Arun liquefaction plant, after repeated attacks on its workers from separatist rebels. This forced Pertamina, the state Indonesian oil and gas company, to declare a state of *force majeure* at the plant, which was closed for seven months. Indonesia made up most of the shortfall with spare capacity at Bontang; spot cargoes from Bontang to Japan and Korea amounted to 1.9 bcm in 2001. Arun's Japanese and Korean customers, Tohoku Electric and Tepco in Japan and Kogas in Korea, acquired the balance from other sources, mainly Qatar, Malaysia and Australia. Despite the squeeze in supplies, the closure had only a modest impact on LNG markets.

Recent disruptions at the Arun plant in 2003, after a fire in gas fields in August, have forced the Bontang plant to cover shipments to Korea, raising concerns over the country's future ability to meet scheduled deliveries. In December 2003, Pertamina had to buy four cargoes from the Middle East to supply its Asian customers and the company announced that it is going to acquire three cargoes in first quarter 2004 to meet its long-term contract commitments.

In addition to the political problems, Indonesian LNG prospects are currently undermined by continued demand uncertainty in Asia and increasing competition from Australia and the Middle East, as well as by the new oil and gas law adopted by the Indonesian Congress in 2002, which has created confusion among buyers. The economic implications are particularly worrying for the Indonesian Government, as LNG has become an increasingly important export revenue earner over the past six years as the country's crude oil exports started to decline: due to increasing domestic consumption against only slightly increasing production, Indonesia is becoming a net importer of oil.

Companies have adjusted to these types of political risk by requiring higher hurdle rates where such risks are a factor in development[35], and they have caused companies to delay projects that were otherwise deemed economic. During the 1990s following the Gulf war, the Qatargas project found it difficult to sign up Japanese customers because of the perceived political instability of the Middle East.

In the next few years Qatar is going to become the global leading LNG exporter. However, unless the political situation in the Middle East is settled, LNG coming from the region will not necessarily be considered as secure supplies. This is reflected in the rather low credit-rating of countries in the Gulf region. Nigeria also has very ambitious projects. However, the Nigerian oil workers strike in 2003 showed that energy supplies could be disrupted by local social actions. Venezuela, which is also developing an LNG project to supply the US market, had a major oil crisis in 2003, when unrest in the country took nearly 3 mbpd of oil off global markets. Such events would also affect potential LNG supplies.

A very important issue for security of LNG supply is the number of LNG tankers crossing the Strait of Hormuz or the Suez Canal. For example, the contract between Qatar and the US involving 15 mtpa would involve a fleet of 35 LNG tankers just to serve the trade between Qatar and the east coast of the US. The LNG tankers would cross both the Strait of Hormuz and the Suez Canal.[36] Here again, the security implications are important and difficult to manage. Much of the future LNG supply for the Atlantic basin – all of Qatar's supplies for instance – will come via the Suez Canal. The Canal has been a secure waterway since 1975. However LNG schedules are tighter than oil tanker schedules, and in addition half of the transit oil comes via the Sumed pipeline where oil is discharged in Suez to be transported by pipeline to the Mediterranean coast for shipping.

Another major source of political risk is the influence of changing tax regimes on supply projects. In an environment where tax regimes are often part of the negotiations with the host government, their outcome clearly influences the ultimate feasibility of the project. Host-government commitment is essential for LNG projects, which need broad political

---

35 Jensen J (2003b).
36 The use of the Suez Canal is subject to the payment of transit fees of around ¢18/mBtu.

acceptance of the national and local benefits. The export of natural resources is always a cause for concern to the host country. However, domestic use is limited by the size of the economy/population and their own gas demand; there are only a few gas-intensive products, mainly ammonia and methanol which might be the basis for an export industry based on cheap gas. The added value from potential LNG revenues must be recognised, along with the benefits from new employment, business opportunities and skills. But the basic issue remains access to gas at a competitive price, with a clear, transparent, predictable and practical regulatory and fiscal regime.

Timely investment in LNG projects[37]

Another key question is whether investment in LNG will meet the requirements over a given timeframe. Projected capital spending over the next three decades will total $250 billion – more than twice the amount spent over the past 30 years (*WEIO 2003*). Average annual investment in the LNG chain will double from $4 billion over the past decade to around $9 billion in the period 2021-2030, supporting a sixfold increase in LNG trade.

Table 4.6. Global LNG* investment, 2000-2030 (billion dollars)

Region	LNG investment
OECD	**102**
North America	44
Europe	28
Pacific	30
Non-OECD	**150**
Middle East	64
Africa	37
Latin America	21
Non-OECD Pacific	23
Transition economies	5

*Shipping is equally allocated between exporting and importing regions.
Source: *WEIO 2003*

---

37   This section is drawn on *WEIO 2003*.

LNG liquefaction capacity will need to expand almost fivefold from 133 mtpa at present to 720 mtpa in 2030 (Figure 4.5). This corresponds to about 100 new trains, assuming a steady increase in the average size of each train. The Middle East alone will account for 40% of this increase. Africa will account for another quarter, and Latin America and Asia for most of the rest. The portion of capex budget that is spent in the producing countries ranges from 50 to 70% of total investment, indicating the critical importance of host-country support in the development of the project.

Importing countries will need to add almost 900 bcm (660 mtpa) of new regasification capacity. Capacity currently stands at 358 bcm at 43 terminals, 25 of them in Japan. According to *WEIO 2003*, North America will account for almost half of the additional capacity and OECD Europe for another 30%. Korea, China and India will also need to significantly increase their number of regasification facilities. Importing countries, particularly Japan, are expected to maintain some spare capacity for energy-security reasons. Global average utilisation rate is nonetheless expected to increase substantially (from only 40% in 2001).

Figure 4.5. LNG liquefaction and regasification capacity, 2001-2030

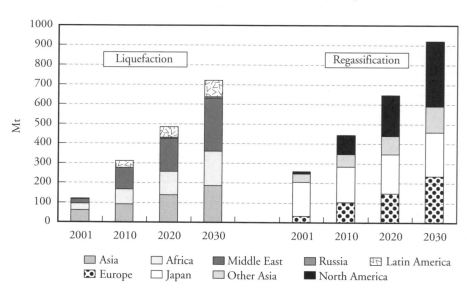

Source: *WEIO 2003*

The world's LNG shipping fleet, which currently numbers 154 ships (end 2003), will have to virtually quadruple by 2030 to sustain the projected growth in trade. The increase will be driven not only by the larger volumes traded but also by longer distances, as the Pacific basin market develops and also the Atlantic basin becomes supplied by LNG from the Middle East. For instance, the deal between ExxonMobil and Qatar for the export of 15.6 mtpa of LNG to the US will require the construction of up to 35 LNG carriers (at a total cost of about $5 billion).

Some 54 new tankers have been already ordered[38], for delivery between 2004 and end 2006 (Figure 4.6). Of these ships, 15 are not linked to long-term contracts. LNG liquefaction project developers control 60% of the existing fleet, but only 40% of the ships on order.[39] International oil and gas companies and LNG buyers account for over half of new orders.

Figure 4.6. A new building boom for LNG tankers

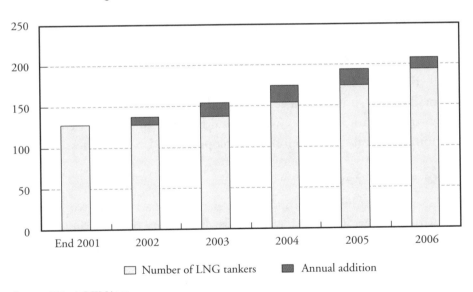

☐ Number of LNG tankers   ■ Annual addition

Source: Mitsui OSK Lines

---

38 Only eight shipyards in the world currently build LNG tankers: three in Japan, three in Korea; one in France and one in Norway. World LNG shipbuilding capacity is 28 LNG ships per year. The average new build delivery is 30 months.

39 CERA (2003a).

As stated in *WEIO 2003*, there is uncertainty about the financing and contractual arrangements and the structure of new LNG projects to supply North America, Europe and developing Asian countries. Market reforms and increased commercial and country risks are forcing players at different stages of the supply chain to change their ways of doing business. Deregulation, which is most advanced in Atlantic basin markets, is fundamentally changing the balance of investment risk and opportunities. These developments will shift most of the integrated project risk onto upstream producers and liquefaction project developers. Raising debt finance in the traditional manner may, therefore, become more difficult and costly. To accommodate this added risk, suppliers will continue to pursue downstream integration.

Different types of players are involved in different parts of the LNG chain. In 2001, more than 60% of the equity in global LNG liquefaction capacity was owned by state companies, in some cases in a joint venture with a major oil and gas international company. The large capital expenditures needed for a complete LNG chain mean that only super-majors have the balance sheet necessary to achieve a high degree of vertical integration and geographic diversification in the LNG business. Integrated global players, Shell, BP, Total, ExxonMobil, ChevronTexaco and Conoco Phillips, have adopted such a strategy and cover the full value chain of the upstream and downstream market and the Atlantic and Pacific basins. They benefit from economies of scale and economies of scope in the LNG business.

LNG safety record

LNG is and has been an important and reliable part of the world energy infrastructure for 40 years. Until the accident at the Algerian Skikda LNG plant (see below), it had enjoyed a virtually unblemished safety record since the beginning of international LNG trade. However, the LNG industry must now prove that LNG is safe and that the accident at Skikda was an exception.

Liquefaction

A recent study conducted by the International Gas Union on the safety record of the LNG industry[40] concluded that there have been no reports

---

40 IGU (2003).

worldwide of offsite damage resulting from an incident at an LNG facility. The blast at Skikda is the first serious accident ever at an LNG plant since the beginning of commercial LNG trade.[41]

LNG liquefaction terminals have gradually grown in number since the first plant to be operated on a commercial basis was established at Arzew in Algeria in 1964. Lessons are taken from past incidents, mainly through the evolution of the design of the plants, which have become safer and more reliable, and also in the accumulated experience of operating companies. The number of incidents in LNG plants is similar to, or lower than those in refineries. Obviously, as stated by the IGU report, LNG operating companies have a natural self-interest to avoid accidents at their own installations for the safety and security of their own personnel and equipment. For many years, the LNG industry has implemented Safety and Management Systems and Environmental Management Systems in the day-to-day operation of LNG plants, either in response to compulsory regulatory requirements, or on a voluntary basis.

LNG technology has evolved over the past 40 years. The early plants were built more or less according to refinery standards, and included robust steam-drive systems and water-cooling. Later generations of plants have benefited from the development of LNG's own standards and practices, similar to the lean designs that are now customary in the gas industry, i.e., the use of gas turbines and air-cooling.

Quite a number of LNG liquefaction and receiving terminals have been in operation for twenty years or more since their installation, and some of the facilities in these terminals have revealed problems of so-called aging. An important portion of the LNG production growth comes from the expansion of existing sites, with some copying their older designs, while others have introduced new concepts. Rejuvenation of the older facilities is becoming an important business, often linked with the renewal of supply contracts.

---

41 It followed a fire that happened in August 2003 at Malaysia LNG Tiga (train I), which damaged the new train and forced MLNG to shut down production until April 2004. At the time, MLNG invoked *force majeure*, as six cargoes due to be delivered to Korea in September 2003 were immediately affected by the temporary supply halt. The start-up of Train II in October 2003 allowed MLNG to compensate for the temporary delay in Train I. Train II is now running at 3.7 mtpa - well over the 3.4 mtpa nameplate capacity.

The IGU launched an investigation into LNG terminal facilities to avoid major repair and replacement work in the future and to minimise life-cycle costs of terminal facilities by taking proper steps now. In the course of this investigation, the IGU working group has carried out research all over the world to establish current deterioration states, maintenance states and repair/replacement states of the main facilities in LNG receiving/liquefaction terminals built up to and including 1990. The investigation revealed that the main facilities show no remarkable phenomena of time-related deterioration, and that any deterioration found so far could be dealt with by properly-conducted daily maintenance.

The challenge of the Skikda accident for the LNG industry

The accident at the Skikda complex on 19 January 2004 comes at a time when the international LNG industry is undergoing rapid expansion. The explosion and resultant fire at the Skikda LNG plant killed 27 people and injured over 70, and destroyed three of the six LNG trains (trains 20, 30 and 40). The plant is now closed. The three remaining trains will re-start operation after inspection works, which may last several months. An inquiry on the accident has been opened by the Algerian authorities. Skikda accounted for 7.8 bcm/a (or 26%) of Algeria's 30.3 bcm/a LNG export capacity.

Table 4.7. Algerian LNG output and capacity, 2002 (bcm)

Plants	Output	Capacity
Arzew GL1 Z	9.9	10.5
Arzew GL 2Z	9.4	10.5
Arzew GL4 Z	1.3	1.5
Skikda GL1K & GL2K	6.3	7.8
Total	**26.9**	**30.3**

Source: Cedigaz, IEA

The first three trains at Skikda came on stream in 1972 and the additional three trains were built in 1981. The plant was revamped in 1999. Skikda exported 246 cargoes in 2002 (6.3 bcm, including 2.8 bcm to Gaz de France, Fos-sur-Mer). Algeria exported 26.9 bcm in 2002 (about the same amount as in 2003).

Short-term impact on Algerian LNG buyers

Algeria's Sonatrach has not declared *force majeure* on any contracts. The company has been able to meet its contractual obligations by boosting exports by pipeline and from its other LNG export complex at Arzew. Likewise, LNG importing countries can use storage back-ups (France, Italy) or are able to boost LNG and pipeline shipments from other sources, or from Algeria itself.

■ Belgium is not affected as all its imports come from Arzew.

■ Italy imported only 8 cargoes from Skikda in 2002. Most Algerian imports come from the Enrico Mattei pipeline. The impact should be limited as Algerian deliveries through the pipeline can be boosted by 1 bcm to 24 bcm/a (exports in 2003 amounted to 23 bcm). Furthermore, the pipeline may be ready to take an extra 3 bcm/a after March 2004, when a new 300-km stretch of pipeline between Algeria's Hassi'R Mel and the Tunisian border is completed.

■ Spain, like Italy, only received small amounts from Skikda: 18 cargoes in 2002 (about 0.8 bcm). Most Algerian imports come from the Pedro Duran Farell pipeline. The capacity of the pipeline is going to be expanded from 8.5 bcm to 11 bcm/a, thanks to additional compression. This capacity should be available by the end of February/March 2004. With additional compression, the line is expected to reach a capacity of 13 bcm/a by 2005.

■ Turkey, an over-supplied market, was negotiating with Sonatrach to back out some of its 2-bcm/a-term LNG supply to US buyers. So Turkey should not suffer from the supply cut.

■ In Greece, DEPA was only lifting its minimum contractual volume of 0.5 bcm/a (all of which came from Skikda). Depa received two cargoes from Arzew in January 2004.

■ Gaz de France receives 8% of its needs (3.5 bcm/a) from Skikda, and 12% from Arzew. France imported less LNG from Algeria in 2003 as LNG cargoes were diverted to more profitable markets by Med LNG & Gas, the joint venture between GdF and Sonatrach. Overall,

France imports 11.5 bcm/a as LNG of its 40.5 bcm/a annual consumption. The country has a diversified portfolio, access to spot gas and large storage facilities. The impact of the accident will therefore be limited, as GdF may be able to use its storage facilities located in the south of France (Manosque).

■ On the other side of the Atlantic, in 2003, about 1 mt of spot Algerian LNG was shipped to the US, mainly to Lake Charles. It is unlikely that the same amount of spot cargoes will be released to the US buyers as long as long-term European customers are short. The recent three-year contract signed with Norway's Statoil to deliver Algerian LNG to Cove Point seems to be unaffected as LNG comes from Arzew.

For Algeria itself, the loss of 3 bcm/a of LNG capacity represents a threat to its ambition to build up its LNG market share, when established producers such as Qatar and Oman are looking for long-term European and US export opportunities. However, the upshot of this accident may also be to trigger new investment in upgrades and boost technical development of the Algerian LNG industry. The Algerian government has indicated that it would re-build a new 4 mtpa plant whose cost is estimated at $800 million-1 billion. At the same time, Sonatrach is speeding up preparations for the bidding round for the award of the Gassi Touil integrated project, which incorporates plans for the production of 4 mtpa of LNG. The contract is expected to be signed in November 2004. With these two projects, Algeria's LNG capacity could stand at around 38 bcm/a by 2007-08, compared with around 26.5 bcm/a after the Skikda accident (taking into account the capacity at the three remaining trains).

Repercussions for the industry

As the accident in Skikda is the first major accident in the global LNG industry, it could have a negative impact on the industry's image. The accident is likely to raise concerns about the risk levels that can be associated with LNG projects. It is likely to fuel public concerns about the safety of LNG in general. In particular, it may be more difficult to win crucial public support for the LNG plants and receiving terminals to be built all around the world, and in particular in the US.

It is likely that local opposition to new liquefaction plants and regasification terminals will be reinforced, and that more stringent regulations will be established for liquefaction plants and for receiving terminals. This will lead to higher costs for the industry, as well as higher insurance fees. Local political debate will centre around the creation of sensitive industrial sites much more than it did in the past.

It may also lead exporters in North Africa and the Middle East to devise solidarity mechanisms to cover possible shortfalls, as happened in Asia after the Arun shut down. This would increase security of supply of LNG.

The accident is also likely to provide political support for the proposed EC directive on security of supply, although the way it has been dealt with by the European gas companies and by their supplier, Sonatrach, suggests the industry is capable of meeting such a supply outage.

Transportation

Over the past 40 years, there have been 40,000 LNG ship voyages, covering 60 million miles, without any major incidents involving a major release of LNG in port or at sea. Unlike in oil transport vessels, double containment has been the standard in LNG vessels from the start.

The first commercial LNG transportation started in 1964 with deliveries of Algerian LNG to UK Canvey Island by the Methane Princess. The fleet now includes 154 LNG tankers (end 2003), and transportation is an integral part of the LNG chain. LNG tankers can only transport LNG and most of the ships are even dedicated to specific LNG projects. The fleet has an absolute safety and reliability record. The fleet is expected to quadruple over the period 2004-2030. The impressive number of new LNG tankers raises a major issue: although the transportation segment of the LNG business is very safe, what are the safety and security implications of 600 LNG tankers moving around the world?

Another safety issue is aging of the fleet.

- 14 tankers (or 9% of the fleet) are now more than 30 years old and will have to be replaced. This should not create any difficulties. Most ships to be replaced are small ships (which may be replaced by larger tankers, allowing transportation cost reduction). These ships are mostly dedicated to the Mediterranean LNG trade. The use of bigger tankers would require adaptation of jetties and harbour equipments at some regasification terminals which are not adapted to receive large tankers.

- 26 tankers are between 25 and 30 years old;
- 19 tankers are between 20 and 25 years old;
- 17 tankers are between 10 and 20 years old;
- 78 tankers are less than 10 years old.

Because of the high asset value and safety levels demanded, these ships tend to be very well maintained. Typically, the longevity of the ships is dictated by the condition of the ship's structure. Life extension studies are carried out as ships approach the age of 25 in order to check that, at the next refit, appropriate engineering systems and hull maintenance are carried out to ensure reliability and continued compliance with regulations. ⟩

However, risks stemming from new transportation regulations for LNG tankers cannot be excluded, as happened recently for oil tankers. What would happen, for instance, if a major importing country decided to refuse all LNG tankers of a certain age into its ports?

Regasification

Regasification LNG terminals also have an excellent security record. Not one accident has been reported since the beginning of commercial LNG trade. However, local opposition and environmental considerations have often delayed or even blocked the building of new terminals. The impact of the Skikda accident may well be increased public opposition to new LNG regasification terminals. The local population involved could be more demanding than in the past, insisting that industrial sites are based further away from residential areas. It may also result in more stringent regulations for onshore terminals which may lead to favouring offshore terminals. ⟩

Gas Quality

An additional issue at regasification terminals in the US and UK relate to the "interchangeability" of gas. Most LNG has a higher heating value and is richer in heavier hydrocarbons than required by typical North American or British natural gas pipeline specifications. Quality of LNG may be an obstacle to the growth of LNG trade in the US and UK and may limit spot trading.

Most of the existing world LNG markets (other than the US and UK) are accustomed to receiving and burning gas that has a gross calorific value (GCV) of 1,100-1,180 British thermal units per cubic foot (Btu/cf), and existing and new liquefaction facilities are generally designed and built to produce LNG within this GCV range (with the notable exceptions of export facilities located in Alaska and Trinidad).

In North America, many pipeline operators require very lean gas for transportation, and in some mid-west regions[42], natural gas gross calorific values range between 950-1,050 Btu/cf. In California, the acceptable gross calorific value is between 970-1,150 Btu/cf. The California Air Resources Board has also imposed tight constraints on gas composition, with the result that only LNG from Kenai, Alaska, currently has an acceptable composition for California. To solve that issue the exporting country would have to extract the ethane and other higher hydrocarbons from the gas. While the hydrocarbons higher than ethane have a market, ethane is more difficult to handle and has no market as such; however it can be transformed into polyethylene which has a market as a base material for modern plastic.

In the UK, a number of potential sources of LNG imports have a Wobbe Index (measure of the heat release when gas is burned at constant pressure) that exceeds the current upper limit in Health and Safety Executive (HSE) Gas Safety Management Regulations (SI 1996/550).

High Wobbe gas uses more oxygen to burn completely. And there is a risk that some of the British and US gas appliances or gas-fired burners may not be able to draw in sufficient oxygen to work safely. Problems include flame-lifting and backfiring, excessive carbon monoxide (CO) and nitrogen oxide (NOx) emissions, "yellow-tipping" and increased sooting. Backfiring is a dangerous condition that involves flashback of the flame through the burner venturi (mixing chamber), causing the gas to burn at the orifice of the mixing chamber instead of the burner tip. It is typically caused by an excess of primary air or too low velocity of the combustible

---

42 Mak J., Nielsen D., Schulte D. and Graham C. (2003).

Table 4.8. LNG characteristics

Origin	Nitrogen (N2) %	Methane (C1) %	Ethane (C2) %	Propane (C3) %	C4+ %	LNG density (kg/cubic meters)	Gas density (kg/Normal cubic meters)	Expansion ratio (Normal cubic meters/ Liquid cubic meters)	Gas GCV (MJ/Normal cubic meters)
Indonesia	0.1	90.6	7.0	2.0	0.3	454	0.800	567	43.9
Malaysia	0.3	89.8	5.2	3.3	1.4	463	0.822	563	44.7
Australia	0.1	89.3	7.1	2.5	1.0	459	0.813	565	44.4
Brunei	0.1	90.1	4.8	3.4	1.6	463	0.824	562	44.9
Algeria-Arzew	0.6	87.6	9.0	2.2	0.6	464	0.819	567	44.3
Algeria-GL1Z	1.0	87.9	8.5	2.0	0.6	464	0.814	570	43.9
Algeria-GL2Z	0.6	91.3	7.5	0.6	0.0	448	0.776	578	42.3
Algeria-Skikda	1.4	91.2	6.7	0.6	0.1	452	0.777	582	41.8
Abu Dhabi	0.4	85.2	13.2	1.0	0.2	463	0.820	565	44.6
Qatar	0.4	89.9	6.0	2.2	1.5	458	0.815	562	44.3
Libya	0.9	83.2	11.8	3.5	0.6	479	0.853	561	45.8
Nigeria	0.1	91.6	4.6	2.4	1.3	456	0.801	569	43.9
Oman	0.2	87.7	7.5	3.0	1.6	469	0.834	562	45.4
Alaska	0.1	99.3	0.3	0.2	0.1	425	0.725	586	40.2
Trinidad	0	96.9	2.7	0.3	0.1	430	0.763	582	40.9

This table gives the average characteristics of LNG at loading plants (typical, non-contractual values)
Source: GIIGNL

mixture through the burner tip. "Yellow-tipping" occurs when the normally blue flame becomes elongated and exhibits a yellow colour, and is often the result of incomplete hydrocarbon combustion. "Yellow-tipping" is often accompanied by excess carbon monoxide production, and over time can also result in excessive soot formation caused by the build-up of unburned hydrocarbons.

The typical methods of controlling the LNG heating value, or Wobbe Index ("Btu stabilisation") consist of such basic techniques as commodity blending (whether blending liquids in-tank or blending gas streams via pipelines) to Btu dilution by way of injection with inerts such as air or nitrogen, as well as Btu extraction techniques, such as stripping heavier Btu content hydrocarbon components from the gas system prior to send out.

Another option is to adapt the burners to higher calorific gas, as was done in continental Europe, as more and more higher calorific gas was imported. This, however, is not only a costly operation – which would have to be compared with the costs of a more central handling of the quality issue – but especially in view of the rapid change of quality in the UK, it would require a large workforce with special qualifications. In that regard the quality issue has some security of supply implications in the UK.

In the US, Lake Charles is the only US terminal that can handle the NGL-rich, high calorific value LNG from LNG suppliers such Nigeria and Qatar and from Algeria's Arzew, as it has an ethane-stripping plant adjacent to the terminal. Elba Island and Cove Point cannot because the downstream market cannot accept any quality. However, other terminals (planned projects) are being adapted to richer LNG in order to enhance flexibility in the LNG trade.

For new LNG terminals, alternative solutions include the use of an integrated LNG regasification and power generation facility which could improve the overall profitability of a regasification facility through co-production of LPG and an increase in electric power generation. This new technology would also allow LNG importers to accept LNG from a wide variety of sources.

Another issue which might impede the flexibility of LNG supply is different safety standards in various LNG harbours. Even if safety standards were absolutely equivalent, the certification may not be accepted by all port authorities, leading to problems when turning to LNG tankers, which have not yet entered a specific harbour. Such problems were experienced during the time TEPCO was buying extra LNG on the spot market. In Europe, in order to improve safe and effective interoperability between different European LNG terminals, GTE members undertook to examine the possibility of harmonising the procedural and operation rules attached to their respective terminal access contracts.[43]

Outlook on safety

Although the LNG industry has had an excellent safety and security record, it cannot be excluded that the recent accident at Skikda, at a time where several IEA markets are developing a pro-active LNG import policy, may result in some delays, more stringent regulations and higher insurance fees. Additional safety measures must be taken and brought to everybody's attention so that LNG wins back the trust of people in countries with liquefaction and regasification plants or projects around the world.

---

43 GTE (2003c).

PART B

REGIONAL ISSUES

5

GAS DEVELOPMENT IN OECD COUNTRIES

The three OECD regions have so far had a very good record as far as security of gas supply is concerned. Governments (through their policies), and market players (through their effective delivery) have ensured secure and reliable supplies to customers since the beginning of gas deliveries. The next 30 years bring new opportunities, such as relying on the market itself to balance supply and demand through the price mechanism, or balancing short-term imbalances at market hubs. It also brings additional challenges for security of supply in OECD countries.

While all IEA countries have embarked on gas market reform, the basic features of the gas industry vary strongly between IEA members, as do the starting conditions and the rate of progress in implementing reform. The existence of domestic gas resources, the development of supply and demand, the depth and liquiditiy of marketplaces, the role of gas in the power sector and the interlink between the gas and the power sector differ from one country to another. Similarly, what can be covered by the market mechanism in the short run as well as in the long run differs between the various IEA regions and has a corresponding impact in shaping the security of supply issue.

Chapters 1 to 4 look at generic/global security of gas supply issues. The following chapters address the current status of security of gas supply in detail for North America, Europe (with a separate Chapter on the UK), and the OECD countries of Asia Pacific.

North America has so far been one of the pioneers of gas market reform. One of the main issues in an open market is that of reliability of gas supply to the final customer and to what extent the market provides the signals and incentives to deliver that reliability. So far, gas market reform has resulted in a better use of existing capacities and the building of additional transportation capacity. Nevertheless, the situation requires monitoring as there are increasing signs of congestion in transportation and there have been two gas price hikes in the recent past. While high prices continue to trigger addtional drilling activity, the natural decline rate of producing wells is increasing and the overall replacement of production is not keeping pace with depletion. Until now, North America has imported only minor volumes of gas and has therefore not been exposed to any external security of supply issues. This is about to change, as the US will have to begin importing large volumes of LNG to satisfy increasing demand that can no longer be met by domestic production in the US and Canada from the areas open to exploration and production. However, the domestic production capacity and the size of the North American market would suggest that any conceivable disruption of external supplies could probably be handled by the liquid and deep North American gas market. The North American situation is reviewed in detail in Chapter 6.

The development of the **European** gas market was based on production from giant fields, beginning with the Groningen field in the Netherlands, followed by imports from outside the EU. These imports were also based on giant fields like the Algerian Hassi R'Mel, the Russian super-giant fields (Urengoi, Yamburg and Medvezhye) and the Norwegian Troll field. While imports are becoming more diversified and smaller fields are being tied into the import stream into the EU, the share of imported gas is rising. New suppliers – except for Libya and Azerbaijan – are LNG suppliers. The EU gas market is undergoing substantial changes: the increasing use of gas for power generation; the opening of the electricity and gas sectors; and the shift in the EU eastern border. The dependence from external suppliers is projected to grow substantially due to a rising share of gas in the energy mix, especially in the power generation sector. Short-term security of supply is not a problem given the spare capacity in transportation and supply, and the numerous tools developed by gas operators to cope with possible supply disruptions, such as an adequate level of gas storage. However, with growing reliance on gas supplies from non-OECD countries, the access to such supplies at competitive conditions becomes crucial, especially with respect to the investment environment in host countries to attract adequate and timely investments. The European situation is reviewed in Chapter 7, while UK-specific issues are reviewed in Chapter 8. The situation in the **United Kingdom** is different from that of continental Europe, and has more in common with

North America: the UK gas market has been opened for quite some time, and so far the UK has been self sufficient. As production from the UKCS is now decreasing and the UKCS is becoming a mature province, the UK's import share is bound to accelerate rapidly in the near future. The UK faces the same main challenge as the US, i.e., addressing the move from self-sufficiency to a large increase in imports which, on balance, will be used by the power sector.

The gas industries of the four **OECD** countries in the **Pacific** region differ very much from one another. As Australia and New Zealand are largely self-sufficient, Chapter 9 mainly focuses on security of gas supply issues in Japan and Korea, which are almost 100% dependent on LNG imports. Both countries are at the early stages of gas market reforms. Security of gas supply has always been a major concern in the region and the countries have developed a range of broad set of measures to ensure security of supply and deal with any disruptions (supply diversity, long-term contracts, power trade between companies, gas supply sharing, fuel switching, etc.). The flexibility coming from LNG has played a major role in their security of supply.

6

SECURITY OF GAS SUPPLY IN NORTH AMERICA

The North American gas industry is increasingly integrated and in particular, Canada and the US can be considered as one gas marketplace. However, it is difficult to make generalisations about the security of gas supply in North America, as the situation in Canada, a large producer and exporter of gas, greatly differs from the situation in the US, a big producer and importer, and from that of Mexico, an emergent gas market with limited linkage with the US market so far.

In this Chapter, we will mainly focus on security of gas supply issues in the United States. The gas market in Mexico is not reviewed as the Chapter focuses on open markets, while gas market reforms are still at the beginning in Mexico.

- Security of gas supply issues in the North American context include an *external* dimension, linked with the growing share of LNG imports in gas supply, and an *internal* dimension, linked with the proper functioning of the market.

- Security of gas supply means access to new domestic resources (in particular Arctic, Rocky Mountain, unconventional and offshore resources); access to external gas resources via LNG, which means building new LNG receiving terminals and signing long-term contracts with possible LNG suppliers, and managing increased import dependence and the possible impact a global LNG market could have on US and other importers. In particular, to the extent that the North American market will become dependent on a significant share of LNG imports, the question of external security of supply should be addressed.

- Other challenges include further investment in transmission and storage, to accommodate shifting supply sources. This raises the issues of whether regulations on infrastructure allow the market to work properly, whether customers could sign long-term contracts for capacity expansions and whether regulation barriers/rights of way problems may not impede the building of new pipelines. Additional significant capital investment will be needed in the future to inspect and refurbish ageing infrastructure, in order to maintain reliable service.

- Another issue has emerged more recently; although the failure of Enron did not result in any supply cut, it led to the downgrading of major US energy-trading companies. This has made access to capital more difficult – sometimes impossible – and has a major impact on the ability of companies to invest, the costs of financing, and consequently on future investments. Price reporting issues (and other market data, e.g., storage) must also be addressed.

- Another challenge is the increasing share of gas in power generation, especially in view of reduced capability to switch at short term to other fuels. A long-term issue is to what extent investment in other large-scale power production capacity (like coal or nuclear) is restricted due to regulations which make it very difficult, if not impossible, to choose a fuel other than gas. While wind and other "green power" may be promoted by some states, their contribution to the overall electricity mix is projected to remain low in the foreseeable future.

This Chapter briefly reviews gas market, regulation and industry structure in North America. It describes the current tight balance in US gas supply and the perceived gas shortage, which has led to sustained high prices on both the spot and futures markets. It then provides an analysis of North American supply and demand trends to 2030, which shows that expected demand growth is outpacing domestic gas supply at a rapid rate. This will lead to a structural change in US supply with more LNG imports, and therefore exposure to the international LNG market.

Adequate levels of investment in production, transmission and storage are essential to secure gas supply to the US market. This is elaborated further in this Chapter and it also includes a discussion on the current crisis of US trading companies as well as the difficulty of obtaining financing since the collapse of Enron. Price reporting issues are also reviewed as well as the relationship between gas and electricity markets and its implication for security of gas supply.

MARKET OVERVIEW

The North American[44] market gas market is the largest in the world with 717 bcm consumed in 2002. The region is self-sufficient in gas, the US imports 16% of its needs, 15% from Canada via cross-border pipelines and 1% from overseas in the form of LNG and exports about 7 bcm (2002) of pipeline gas to Mexico. However, the supply situation is structurally changing. Although the US is blessed with abundant gas reserves and a large unexplored potential, supply tightened in winter 2000/01 and again in winter 2002/03. The current tight balance has led to persistent high gas prices and a perceived shortage for the future (i.e., the difference between current domestic natural gas supply and expected demand). Natural gas prices have averaged close to or above $5 per million Btu (mBtu) for the past two years.

Figure 6.1. Evolution of North American gas consumption by major sector

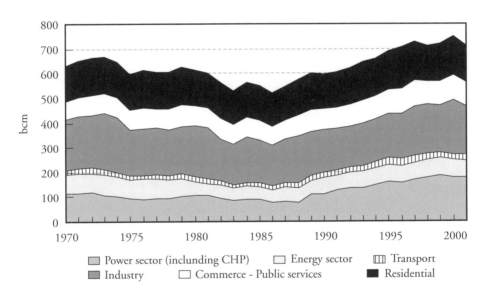

Power sector (inclunding CHP)   Energy sector   Transport
Industry   Commerce - Public services   Residential

Source: IEA

---

44 Defined in this Chapter as Canada and the United States.

The share of natural gas in the North American energy mix totals 24%. Gas consumption is diversified, the power sector accounts for 26% of North American gas consumption, industry 34% and the residential/ commercial sector 38% (the rest is consumed in the energy sector and transport – 2002 data, EIA). Gas demand by the power sector has rapidly increased in the past decade, from 112 bcm in 1990 to 178 bcm in 2001, and in the US only the share of gas-fired electricity generation, including CHP, reached 18% in 2002 compared with 12% in 1990.

Figure 6.2. Evolution of US gas production and consumption

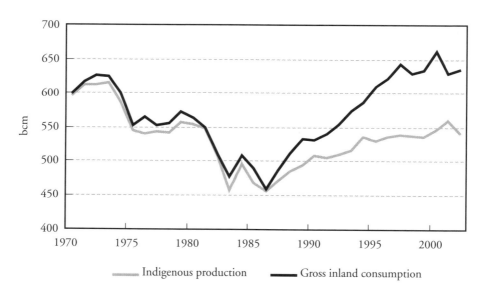

Source: IEA

The "gas bubble", defined as surplus gas deliverability at the wellhead, which characterised the US market during the 1980s and 1990s has disappeared with the erosion in supply capacity, and North America is moving from a period of low-cost domestic gas supplies to growing import dependence. US gas demand grew by about 40% since the mid-1980s, from 459 bcm in 1986 to 635 bcm in 2002. However, the rise was stopped in 1997 and since then, US consumption has been flat at around 630-640 bcm/a (except in 2000 when it reached 660 bcm). US production over the same period has increased slightly for most years, but not enough to cover the increased demand. Half of the increase in US demand over the period 1986-2002 has been met by an increase in Canadian imports. Since 1997, demand has been restrained as the US economy has generally become more efficient in its use of gas due to technological innovation, ongoing shifts to less energy-intensive industries, slower economic growth and government policies.

Natural gas consumption varies widely between seasons. This pattern is strongly driven by temperature-sensitive residential gas load. In the US, the average daily residential load during the peak winter month is more than seven times the level of the summer lows. Production and net imports exhibit fairly stable flows throughout the year. Storage, typically located close to consumption areas, is used to balance gas supply and demand throughout the year.[45]

Figure 6.3. Seasonality of US gas demand

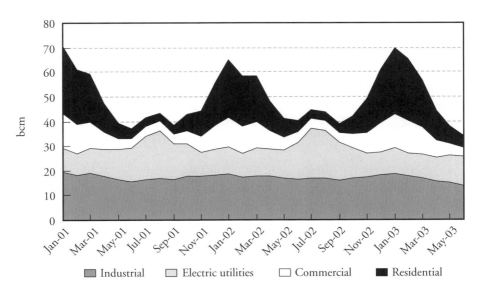

Source: EIA

---

45 Typically, gas is injected into underground storage during the non-heating season, and withdrawn from underground storage during the heating season. Storage is particularly critical in regions with significant heating load. Cold weather can lead to a surge in demand, requiring storage withdrawals to satisfy system requirements.

GAS MARKET REFORMS

The North American gas industry has undergone profound structural changes over the last three decades, largely due to regulatory reforms aimed at promoting competition and improving efficiency. In the United States, this process began with the phased partial lifting of controls on wellhead prices in 1978 (full decontrol occurred after the Wellhead Decontrol Act of 1989), followed by optional open access to the interstate pipeline and storage system in 1985 (Order 436). The Order authorised blanket certificates for interstate pipeline companies offering open access transportation and it encouraged the unbundling of sales and transportation. Order 636 in 1992 required pipeline companies to provide open access transportation and storage, and to separate sales from transportation services completely.

The Federal Energy Regulatory Commission (FERC) regulates interstate pipeline rates, construction of new and expanded pipelines and facilities, and certain environmental aspects, and ensures open, non-discriminatory access to gas transport for all competing suppliers.

The old price-controlled regime established price ceilings for different categories of natural gas and created distortions in the gas market. It caused supply shortages in 1976/77 as it did not provide any incentive to producers to replace reserves. This led to LNG import contracts with Algeria in the late 1970s, and the construction of the existing four US LNG receiving terminals. The cancellation of contracts in 1981 after Sonatrach tried to impose an increase in LNG contract price from less than $1/million Btu cif to more than $4/million Btu fob, led to the virtual stop of the LNG business in the US for about 15 years – until the Trinidad and Tobago project was launched.

In Canada, gas sales were unbundled at the end of 1985. The Governments of Canada and the three gas producing provinces of British Columbia, Alberta and Saskatchewan signed an Agreement on Natural Gas Prices and Markets in October 1985 which allowed gas buyers, for the first time, to directly contract for supplies with producers, marketers and other agents at negotiated prices.

These regulatory changes led to the competitive and more complex natural gas market that exists today. Producers now sell their gas to a variety of purchasers located across North America. Natural gas is bought and sold at many different locations, to numerous parties, and under different sales and transportation arrangements. Numerous entities, including utilities and marketers can buy, sell and re-sell gas in a variety of ways. Consumers can negotiate the best terms for supply and transportation to their site and simultaneously negotiate a price hedge in financial markets. The natural gas futures market is now the most active commodity market on the New York Mercantile Exchange (NYMEX).

The restructuring of the gas industry in North America has had a number of consequences on the way the industry operates. Cost reductions and increased efficiency in the industry led the operators to operate their infra-structure "just in time". Hence, spare capacities in infrastructure have decreased, as demonstrated by a number of key data which also indicate the efficiencies inherent in deregulation:

■ The ratio of reserves-to-production (R/P ratio) has long been in the 9 to 10 year range;

■ Production is flat over the year as producers tend to maximise the net present value of their gas and therefore produce at maximum capacity throughout the year. Storage facilities were developed in producing regions to reinject gas when demand is too low;

■ Production is close to production capacity. When there is a sudden increase in gas demand, prices spike as there is no available spare capacity to increase production on the spot;

■ Despite investment in transportation, peak day utilisation has increased over the last few years (to about over 90% and near 100% on some pipelines).

STRUCTURE OF THE GAS INDUSTRY

The North American natural gas market is composed primarily of producers, pipeline companies, storage companies, local distribution companies (LDCs), marketers (sometimes also referred to as "aggregators") and consumers.

In the US, there are over 8,000 natural gas producers, 500 of which account for 90% of natural gas reserves. Wellhead prices are now unregulated and producers may negotiate prices and delivery terms with customers or other firms, such as marketers and LDCs, for the sale of their products. In Canada, there are more than 3,000 producers. After production, gathering lines deliver the gas to processing plants and/or transmission lines. Pipeline companies connect to the production fields or after-treatment points and deliver the gas under either short-term or longer-term firm or interruptible contracts to their customers. There are more than 150 large natural gas pipeline systems in the US. These systems represent more than 212,000 miles of transmission lines with an estimated deliverability of approximately 133 bcf/d at end 2002 (3.8 bcm/d). About 85 pipeline systems make up the interstate network – about 50-55 are categorised as major by the FERC. Another 60+ pipelines operate strictly within the borders of individual states in the intrastate market. The intrastate portion of the grid (excluding gathering lines and local distribution gas distribution systems) accounts for at least another 73,000 miles of pipelines. In Canada, inter-provincial long-distance pipelines are regulated by the National Energy Board (NEB). TransCanada Pipelines Ltd (TCPL) is one of the largest carriers of natural gas in North America.

Hubs or market centres provide interconnections among pipelines. These hubs serve as major trading and transhipment points. They have allowed the development of spot markets for spot purchases of gas, and that of futures markets for price hedging.

Shippers purchase gas transportation services from pipeline companies. They separately purchase the gas they ship over pipelines. Marketers are unregulated firms that typically perform the "merchant" function for natural gas customers, usually packaging supply, storage, and pipeline delivery capacity on either a firm or interruptible basis. Many marketers are affiliated with pipeline companies, LDCs, or producers. There are more than 200 marketers in the US. In Canada, they are designed as "Agent/Broker/Marketers" and operate in accordance with a code of conduct and may be licensed. Storage firms are firms that have developed the facilities to store natural gas for later delivery. LDCs are companies that control local gas distribution facilities. They may be transporters of natural gas owned by their LDC customers, or they may be both suppliers and transporters. There are more than 1,500 LDCs in the US. LDCs are regulated by state Public Utility Commissions (PUCs) in the US and by provincial energy boards in Canada.

FRAMEWORK FOR SECURITY OF GAS SUPPLY

In North America, security of gas supply considerations differ greatly from those in continental Europe. The market plays a primary role through supply (and demand) response to price changes. In the short term, if the market is short of supply, prices will increase and producers will drill more wells, increasing gas supply with a certain time lag. Demand will also respond to price increases as some gas customers – for example, some power generators and industrial consumers – will switch to other fuels or stop their gas-based activity. The future markets provide price signals for domestic investment in new exploration and production (E&P) or for locking in new supply (including imports such as spot LNG cargoes).

Access to external supply in North America is not yet an issue. The North American market is fully integrated. External supplies provide only 2% of North American supply (2003), although this is expected to increase with time. The odds of a large supply interruption of domestic gas are low because of the diversity of supply (multiple producers) and the fact that there are many major pipelines, often each with several loops, so failure of one pipeline segment typically has limited and short-term effects on markets.

Although the market plays a primary role in securing gas supply, the Government and other stakeholders are also involved:

- *Federal Government.* The Government defines security of natural gas supply in the US energy policy through the Department of Energy (DOE), whose core mission is to support national and economic security by promoting a diverse supply of reliable, affordable, and environmentally sound energy. In May 2001, less than six months after taking office, the Bush Administration published its comprehensive National Energy Policy (NEP) plan. The NEP contained recommendations for increasing domestic and international production of natural gas, and for expanding the US gas and international transmission systems. Subsequently, further work has been initiated by the US administration to assess the current gas supply/demand situation and ways to improve it. In June 2003, US *Energy Secretary* Spencer Abraham and the *National Petroleum Council* (NPC) hosted a Natural Gas Summit with the natural gas industry to address risks over the next 24 months arising from a tight natural gas market, the resulting impact on the economy and consumers, and how to reduce the pressures. An LNG Summit gathering potential LNG suppliers was held in December 2003. The NPC released a report, requested by the Secretary of Energy, in September 2003, which includes a set of recommendations for Government and operators to: 1) solve the short-term natural gas crisis, and 2) work on a long-term vision of future supply/demand balance based on different policy measures.

■ Pipelines. In general, the service obligations of regulated entities are specified in tariffs that are approved by state or federal authorities (Public Service Commission or the *Federal Energy Regulatory Commission-FERC*). The FERC regulates interstate trade and transmission in energy, including natural gas. It also oversees environmental issues and administers accounting and financial reporting regulations and company audit. *Regulated entities* may be subject to prudency reviews by regulators, so they must stand ready to demonstrate that they have operated responsibly.

■ Local distribution companies. *LDCs* have an obligation to serve. That means that in exchange for a monopoly franchise, the utility must not fail to deliver natural gas to its core residential and critical needs customers such as hospitals and schools. The service must be provided on a non-discriminatory basis to all customers who desire it within the franchise area. In addition, some local distribution companies are required to provide information, annually, to state regulators about their supply plans for the upcoming peak winter season.

■ *State regulators* – Public Utility Commissions/Public Service Commissions have a role in security of supply as they have bestowed on LDCs the obligation to serve.

- Customers. *Customers* with interruptible service may be required to maintain stocks of alternative supplies for use if service is interrupted. For instance, the state of New York requires that customers with interruptible service have fifteen days of alternative supplies available at the start of the heating season. This requirement is a condition of service and the state regulatory agency monitors the stocks of alternative fuels prior to the start of each winter. There has been increased enforcement of this requirement since the winter of 2000/2001 when interruptions of gas service resulted in a significant spike in heating oil prices.

Emergency situations

In the event of an emergency or shortfall, the DOE monitors the situation and coordinates information with state and federal entities as well as industry. At the discretion of the Secretary of Energy and the President of the United States, the DOE has the following legal authority with respect to natural gas emergency response:

- Natural Gas Act, Section 3 – the DOE can authorise the import and export of natural gas;

- Natural Gas Policy Act, Title III, Sections 301-303 – the DOE can order any interstate pipeline or local distribution company served by an interstate pipeline to allocate gas in order to assist in the meeting of needs of high priority consumers during a natural gas emergency.

US ENERGY BILL

Security of natural gas supply could be affected in the future if the US enacts energy legislation that provides for access to additional supply sources. The US Congress has been giving serious consideration to comprehensive energy legislation over the past several years. Major legislation is now pending which would provide billions of dollars in tax incentives for oil, gas and coal producers and give a boost to corn farmers by requiring a significant increase of ethanol use in gasoline. It may also impose federal reliability rules on operators of high-voltage power lines for the first time, to reduce the likelihood of another cascading blackout like the one in August 2003. Further, the Energy Bill may include provisions for opening federal lands to production and for facilitating the construction of the Alaska Natural Gas Pipeline, a project that would bring additional gas supply to the US market. The pipeline may not be fully operational until 2018.

GAS SUPPLY AND DEMAND TRENDS

Current US gas crisis: a persistent tight balance?

The current US gas crisis is different from what would be considered a crisis in Europe. There is no interruption of gas supply but the available supply is more expensive. This is therefore a price crisis. Spot prices at Henry Hub, the most active spot market centre in the US, is high relative to historical levels. Spot prices continue to be volatile and have spiked in each of the last three winters. Forward prices also remain at a high level, suggesting supply is going to remain tight.

Figure 6.4. US spot prices – Henry Hub

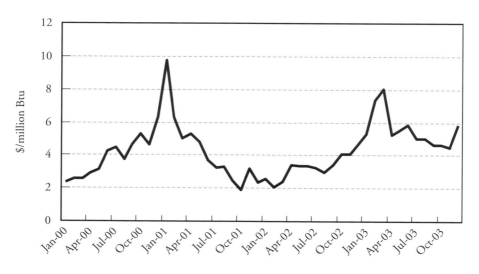

Source: Energy Intelligence

The current high prices are an indicator of the tight supply and demand balance in the US. They are not a failure of markets. They are rather the result of disappointing geological experience over the last few years plus restrictions on exploration areas, combined with a shift to new uses of gas that increased consumption. The result is a mismatch between supply and demand, and prices are performing their essential function: signalling market needs and changing conditions to both producers and consumers. While there was an increase in drilling activity in 2003, it is still low historically (see Figure 6.9, below). This is explained by three factors: *i)* limited available capital to invest in exploration and development; *ii)* maturing provinces and restrictions on available acreage for exploration; and *iii)* a lack of trust in the persistence of high prices.

i) While the largest companies own much of the acreage in the US, most exploration is done on a farm-out basis by independent companies. Most of the independents have a market capitalisation of less than $3 billion and they rely very heavily on the equity value of their stock and access to credit, primarily from banks. In the difficult financing environment, they do not have access to funds for drilling. Credit has also become an issue for utilities. Credit downgrading means that they are no longer able to contract long-term gas (5 years). Most transactions have duration of 1 to 2 years.

ii) The slow supply response, even at high price levels, is also due to geological factors: a) the natural basin exhaustion; b) accelerating decline rates per well: the annual decline rates are around 20%, which means that every year a fifth of the production has to be replaced just to keep production flat; c) regulatory hurdles act as a constraint. Large areas of federal lands are excluded from E&P.

iii) The lack of new investment in E&P also reflects industry distrust in the high prices. Companies are reluctant to invest in new production when prices are so volatile.

In the short-term, the market itself should solve the tight balance, by investment, technology and adjustments. But there are inevitable time lags. On the supply side, market response includes more drilling and production, new pipeline expansions, additional LNG terminal capacities and imports.

On the supply side, US natural gas rig count jumped 26% in 2003 (from an average of 691 in 2002 to 872 in 2003). Production should react, however, with a time lag of at least 6 months and as much as 18 months. In 2003, early estimates indicate that natural gas production increased approximately 2.1% over 2002. A major pipeline expansion, Kern River's "2003 Expansion Project" from Wyoming to California went into service in May 2003, opening an additional 906 mcf/d of supply capacity to California. The LNG import terminal in Massachusetts was expanded and terminals in Georgia and Maryland have been reopened and the fourth US LNG terminal, Lake Charles in Louisiana, was heavily utilised. Imports of LNG more than doubled in 2003 to 14.6 bcm.

On the demand side, in the short term, conservation and market reaction can play a key role in the tight balance in supply/demand. Gas demand is estimated to have declined 3.7% in 2003 largely due to high prices discouraging demand in the industrial and electric power sectors. Households have seen their gas bill rising in two of the last three winters. Average prices for households in the Midwest for instance averaged $8.39/thousand cubic feet in winter 2002/03 and 9.53/thousand cubic feet in winter 2000/2001. The price elasticity of household consumers is very low and they have very limited possibilities to react to fluctuations in prices. However, a conservation campaign has started and could help alleviate the tight supply/demand balance.

Prices are also boosting manufacturers' operating costs and hitting their profits. In particular, high gas prices have a negative impact on the chemical industry, the largest US industrial gas consumer. This industry needs gas prices between $2.5 and $3/mBtu to remain competitive on the world stage. One by one, fertiliser plants are closing. This situation has led some companies to move production overseas where gas is cheaper. The high cost of natural gas coupled with US low electricity prices are keeping most new gas-fired power plants idle because they are too expensive to operate. Gas demand by power generators decreased by 13% in 2003, while their demand for distillate fuel oil increased 40%.

The economic impact of the current price levels to households and gas-intensive manufacturers, like fertiliser and petrochemical producers, is significant and has focused policy-makers' attention on how to resolve it.

Gas supply trends[46]

In the longer term perspective, the prospects for adequate gas supplies depend on the ability of, and incentives for producers to: 1) discover and develop domestic conventional and unconventional reserves and connect them to the market; and 2) develop new infrastructure – mainly new pipelines from Canada and new LNG terminals – to import Canadian gas by pipeline and LNG from other suppliers. The global gas resource base is sufficient to satisfy North America's growing demand. Proven gas reserves are equivalent to more than 70 years of current production. However, North American regional gas production patterns will shift as production grows in the deep water Gulf of Mexico, Rocky Mountains, and Arctic, including Alaska and Canada. Changes in gas production patterns will shift pipeline flow patterns. A large increase in LNG imports is also expected. This will bring a structural change in supply, and the North American market will be exposed to international gas market turbulence.

North American resources and reserves

Proven gas reserves in North America amounted to 6,908 bcm at the beginning of 2003, or 4% of global gas reserves. Three-quarters of these reserves are in the United States. US proven gas reserves were estimated at 5,293 bcm (187 tcf) at the beginning of 2003, or 9 years of current production (EIA). About half of the nation's proven reserves are in Texas, in Louisiana and in offshore wells in the Gulf of Mexico. About a quarter are in the Rocky Mountain States of New Mexico, Wyoming and Colorado. The rest are spread out in small pockets from Alaska to Florida, and California to New York.

Current estimates of proven reserves in Canada are relatively modest, 1,615 bcm at the beginning of 2002 according to Natural Resources Canada. At current production rates, there is a 10-year supply.

However, the resource base is still very significant. Technically recoverable resources, including proved reserves, are estimated by the EIA at 1,279 tcf (36,217 bcm). At 2002 level of production, the US has about a 67-year supply of natural gas. 29% of the current resource base will be produced

---

46 This section deals with the Canadian and US markets.

by 2025. Canada's total gas resource base, including proved reserves, is 475 tcf (13,450 bcm). At 2002 level of production, Canada has about a 77-year supply of natural gas.[47]

However, restrictions on E&P in some areas have limited the development of resources. Almost 40% of the gas found on US federal lands is subject to production restrictions. Moreover, no acreage along the east and west coasts is available for E&P. According to the Independent Petroleum Association of America, there are opportunities for increased future production in the Rocky Mountain area. These regions could add 5.5 tcf per year (150+ bcm/a) to output over the next 15 years. However, federal restrictions on E&P in part of that area are preventing the development of 107 tcf. In addition, 80 tcf of offshore resources lie in leasing moratoria areas.

North American gas production

WEO 2002 foresees a 27% increase in North American gas production over the period 2000-2030. Aggregate production in the United States and Canada is projected to climb slowly to 823 bcm in 2010 (from 721 bcm in 2002) before beginning to decline around 2020, to 812 bcm in 2030. These prospects depend on producers discovering and developing conventional and unconventional reserves and connecting them to markets. Higher output will require increased drilling in established producing basins in the lower 48 US states and in Canada, as well as new greenfield basins. Resources to be found and developed over the next 25 years will be more challenging. These resources will come from reservoirs that are smaller, deeper, and/or lower in permeability. Technology will play a key role in commercialising these resources.

US DOE *Annual Energy Outlook 2004*[48] *(AEO 2004)* points out that most of the increase in US natural gas production will come from unconventional sources (tight sands, shale and coalbed methane). In the reference case, production is expected to increase from 19.1 tcf in 2002 to 24.1 tcf in 2025 (541 bcm to 682 bcm), which is 2.7 tcf less than the 2025 projection in *AEO 2003* (76 bcm). By 2025, *AEO 2004* projects

---

47 NRC (2003a).
48 EIA (2003a).

unconventional gas production to account for 43% of lower 48 natural gas production. US unconventional, undiscovered resources are estimated at 475 tcf (13,450 bcm).

In Canada, NEB[49] has revised its estimates of future production downward. In 1999, NEB estimated total production in Canada in a range of 8.1 to 9.0 tcf in 2015 and 7.7 to 9.9 tcf in 2025 (218 to 280 bcm). In contrast, NEB's 2003 estimates show 5.9 to 7.1 tcf in 2015 and 4.3 to 6.1 tcf in 2025 (123 to 173 bcm in 2025). The main reasons for the decline are falling natural gas production in the province of Alberta, which accounts for more than 75% of Canada's natural gas production, increasing use of natural gas for oil sands production, and recent disappointments in Canadian drilling results, including smaller discoveries with lower initial production rates and faster decline rates.

Gas demand trends

Demand scenarios

WEO 2002 projects an increase of 1.5% per year in North American gas demand between 2000 and 2030, from 752 bcm to 1,183 bcm.[50] The share of gas in total energy supply will increase from 24% in 2000 to 29% in 2030. The biggest increase in gas use is expected to come from power generation, especially in the current decade. The increase by the power sector accounts for three-quarters of the total increase (Figure 6.5).

There are similarities between the WEO and the EIA outlook through 2025. In the *AEO 2004*, the projections for US gas demand in 2025 range from 29.1 tcf in the low economic growth case to 34.2 tcf in the rapid technology case (854 to 968 bcm). In the reference case, natural gas consumption in the electric power sector is projected to increase from 5.6 tcf in 2002 to 6.7 tcf in 2010 and 8.4 tcf in 2025 (159 bcm, 190 bcm, 238 bcm, respectively). Demand by electricity generators is expected to account for 29% of total end-use natural gas consumption in 2025, as compared with 27% in 2002.

---

49 NEB (2003a).
50 In the Alternative Policy Scenario, total gas demand is 10.7%, or 123 bcm, lower in 2030.

Figure 6.5. Natural gas demand in Canada and the United States

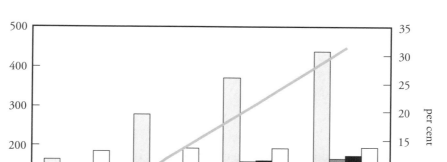

Source: *WEO 2002*

The National Petroleum Council (NPC) report published at the end of September 2003 offers a different perspective.[51] Unlike the *AEO 2004* and *WEO 2002* reference cases, which both assume the continuation of current energy policies, regulations and technology trends through 2025/2030 respectively, the two scenarios developed by NPC assume significant actions by policy-makers and industry stakeholders to change the fundamental trends of current supply and demand. The two contrasting scenarios represent plausible and feasible future trends in North American gas markets.

The "Reactive Path" scenario assumes continued conflict between natural gas supply and demand policies that support natural gas use, but tend to discourage supply development. This scenario results in continued tightness in supply and demand leading to higher natural gas prices and price volatility over the study period.

The "Balanced Future" scenario builds in the effects of supportive policies for supply development and allows greater flexibility in fuel switching and

---

51 NPC (2003).

fuel choice. This results in a more favourable balance between supply and demand, price projections more in line with alternative fuels, and lower prices for consumers than in the "Reactive Path" scenario.

Overall demand levels from both NPC scenarios are lower than other outlooks, resulting in less upward pressure on the supply/demand balance. In the Reactive Path scenario, demand increases by 23% in the period 2002-2025. Demand in the Balanced Future scenario is not greatly different as savings in gas demand through greater energy efficiency is offset by increased demand due to lower prices.

In Canada, NEB foresees an increase in gas demand in the two developed scenarios. The scenarios, called "Supply Push" (SP) and "Techno-Vert" (TV) consider the pace of technology and action on the environment as the two key uncertainties that will shape Canada's energy future. SP projections show natural gas demand growth across all sectors, led by increases for natural gas-fired electricity generation and development of massive oil sands projects. Average growth in demand is 1.1% to 1.5% on average over the period 2000-2025, when gas demand could reach 3 to 3.3 tcf (85 to 93 bcm). The report indicates that market adjustments will eventually be necessary. These adjustments would occur primarily in the industrial sector, probably in the form of fuel switching, perhaps with some non-energy industries relocating or discontinuing operations.

In the US, much of the demand growth has already been pre-built. 50 GW of new natural gas-fired capacity was added in the 1990s, and an additional 175 GW (representing 94% of new generating capacity) between 2000 and 2003, including 110 GW of efficient combined-cycle capacity and 65 GW of combustion turbine capacity, which is used mainly when demand for electricity is high. In the favourable financial environment of the end of the 1990s, power plant projects had been relatively easy to finance with 80:20 debt-to-equity ratios. This period of plentiful capital led to a generation capacity construction boom, in which CCGTs and gas turbines were going up at rapid speed nationwide.

Although recent capacity additions will meet near-term needs for electricity generation, more capacity will be needed eventually, as electricity use grows and older, inefficient plants are retired. From 2002 to 2025, 356 GW of new generating capacity is expected to be needed, most of it after 2010, when the current excess supply situation has subsided.[52] Of the new capacity, nearly 62% is projected to be natural-gas-fired combined-cycle, combustion turbine, or distributed generation technology. In the past, part of the existing gas-fired (boiler) capacity was replaced by more efficient CCGTs, so the increase in gas demand was lower. In the future, new CCGTs' capacity will fully translate into added demand.

Demand response

The outlooks presented above assumed a lower price than the price which has prevailed on the US market since the beginning of 2003. If prices remain at a level of $5-6/mBtu, it is questionable whether the expected increase in gas demand will be realised. The real growth might be slowed by higher prices that will principally affect energy-intensive customers in the industrial sector, that, unlike power generators, generally compete in world markets.

According to NPC, power and industrial price elasticity suggests that every $1 increase in gas prices (above a base of about $3.25/mBtu) reduces natural gas consumption by some 1.5 – 2 bcf/d (15 to 20 bcm/a). In 2003, gas demand decreased by 3.7% (about 24 bcm), whereas prices increased to $5/mBtu (+ $2 mBtu compared with 2002). Demand by power generators decreased by 13% in 2003 (21 bcm). Additionally, significant reductions in demand were found in the industrial sector, where permanent reductions (and relocation of some industries outside North America) are called "demand destruction".

The period of easy access to capital is now over, and in the current climate one of the only ways to secure project financing from the capital markets is with a long-term supply contract that guarantees a revenue stream. These long-term contracts are difficult to obtain in the short term. Since the end of 2001, many companies have shelved or cancelled CCGT projects because of overbuilding and no need for additional projects in the short term. There is therefore great uncertainty about the size of the increase in gas demand by the power sector. In particular, the next wave

---

52 EIA (2003a).

of CCGT building may be postponed if economics do not improve. Nevertheless, the new CCGTs built in the last five years will maintain a sustained level of gas demand.

Matching gas supply and demand

Even if lower than expected, US gas demand should nevertheless rise in the long term and the question is how to fill the expected supply gap. Traditional producing areas are expected to provide a large share (about 75%) of long-term US gas needs, but will be unable to meet projected demand.

Increased access to new frontier areas (Arctic gas) and wider access to world resources through LNG will be key to closing the long-term supply gap, albeit at a higher cost than experienced in North America in the 1990s. LNG imports will play a growing role in US gas supply, and could provide more than 20% of US gas supplies by 2030.

Until recently, Canada was expected to remain the primary source of natural gas imports for the United States through 2025, as projected in *AEO 2003*. However, the *AEO 2004* reference case projects that net imports of LNG will exceed net imports from Canada by 2015. The primary reason for the change in the *AEO 2004* forecast is the significant downward reassessment of expected natural gas production in Canada.

This may have a considerable impact on regional export patterns. For example, with declining production over time, Alberta natural gas may no longer reach the US north-east, requiring this market to increase imports from Atlantic Canada instead. Other US markets, such as California, may reduce their dependency on Canadian imports, relying instead on growing supplies from the US Rocky Mountains, Alaska or imported LNG.

The decrease in Canadian exports to the US has a number of market consequences. For some US regions, it means a complete shift in supply as Canadian exports would have to be replaced by LNG.

Figure 6.6 from the *AEO 2004* report illustrates the growing importance of unconventional gas, new frontier areas (Alaska) and imports of LNG.

Figure 6.6. Future US natural gas supply

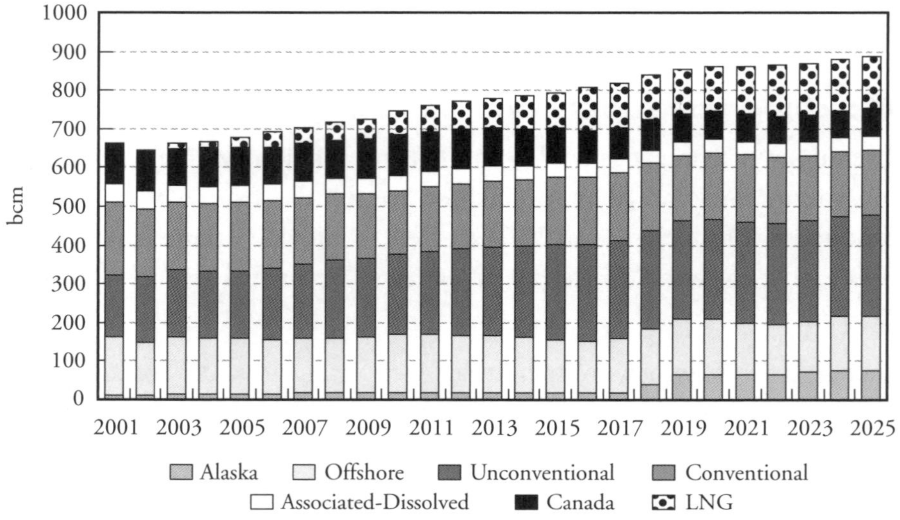

Source: EIA/*AEO 2004*

US LNG MARKET

This section looks at the role LNG can play on the US gas market for short- and long-term security of supply.[53] It analyses the recent changes in regulatory policy applied to LNG terminals, looks at the existing and planned LNG facilities and considers the possible impediments to the rapid development of the US LNG market.

Technical advances and cost reductions in the LNG chain and the widespread availability of gas supplies have led to a new environment for LNG in the United States. LNG is now competitive at $3-3.5/million Btu and is therefore expected to play an increasingly important role in the US in the next few years. LNG imports have political and regulatory support, resulting in concrete steps being taken to ease the process of constructing LNG terminals.

---

53   The US has long been an LNG exporter. An LNG liquefaction plant was built in Kenai, Alaska in 1969 and is still active. The terminal, owned by Phillips Petroleum and Marathon Oil, exports LNG to Japan (1.70 bcm in 2002).

An increasing LNG market has significant implications for US security of supply, as LNG is very flexible and can react quickly to market changes. It would also have an important impact on the global LNG market, due to the size of the potential US market. However, many uncertainties remain, among them the extent of future US LNG demand, the level of gas prices on the US market, the development of upstream gas resources and the building of new liquefaction plants. ⟩

US LNG trends

The US LNG industry experienced a period of growth in the 1970s followed by a prolonged downturn after 1980. LNG imports rose to a peak of 7.2 bcm in 1979. In 1980, after a price dispute with the Algerian exporting company Sonatrach, LNG trade with the US collapsed. It began to rise again in 1996 and has increased rapidly since 2000, although imported volumes are still low. In 2003, US LNG imports more than doubled compared with 2002, to 14.6 bcm, representing 2% of US consumption. Spot sales and sales under short-term contracts accounted for 12.6 bcm (86%), the rest being imported under long-term contracts. While Algerian supplies totalled just 1.5 bcm in 2003, for the fourth consecutive year Trinidad was the source country with the largest exports to the US, delivering 11.3 bcm. Other sources included Nigeria, Qatar, Oman and Malaysia.

An active Atlantic Basin arbitrage market has developed in recent years. It mainly involves supplies from Trinidad, Nigeria and Algeria trading off the US terminals against Spain and Belgium on the European side. LNG cargoes have also been swapped with European cargoes when prices were more favourable on the US market (see Chapter 4).

A number of factors contribute to the renewed interest in LNG. Technological advances over the past 20 years have led to a substantial decrease in costs for liquefaction and shipping. Additionally, higher US gas prices in recent years have improved the economics of LNG to the US market. Table 6.1 shows the calculated LNG exporter netbacks[54] at

---

54 The netback price here is calculated by deducting from the average LNG price the regasification cost and the cost for LNG transportation from the LNG liquefaction plant to the indicated LNG terminal.

Figure 6.7. Evolution of LNG imports in the US

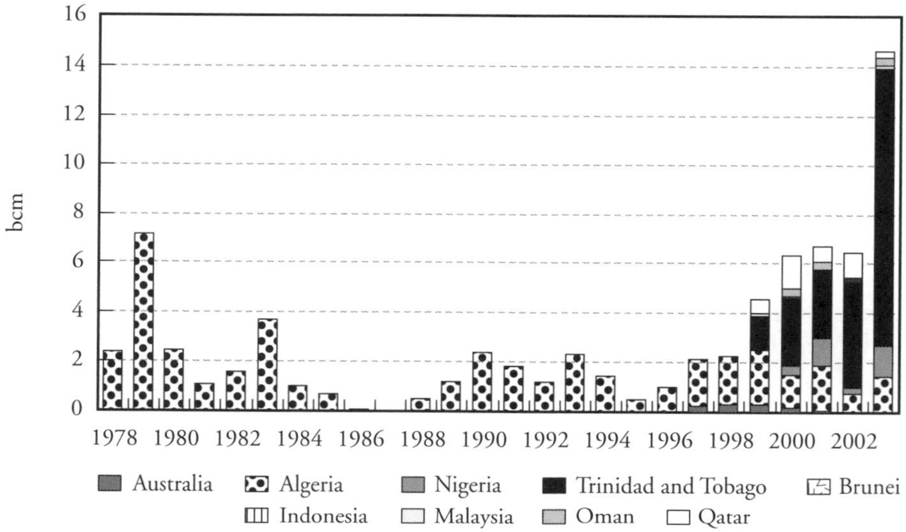

Australia   Algeria   Nigeria   Trinidad and Tobago   Brunei

Indonesia   Malaysia   Oman   Qatar

Source: EIA

receiving terminals in the US compared with netbacks at European and Japanese terminals on 23 February 2004. It shows that the US market is very attractive for Atlantic Basin producers, especially Trinidad, but also North and West African producers. Although the US is at a transportation disadvantage to Japan for Middle East supply sources, US prices also attract Middle East LNG supplies.

In the longer term, the wide range of LNG outlooks gives an illustration of how difficult it is to forecast the amount of LNG needed by the US market. Future LNG imports depend on the price of natural gas on the US market, the level of North American production and the availability of LNG supply.

WEO 2002 projects net imports of gas into the United States and Canada (and therefore as LNG) to reach 109 bcm in 2010 and 371 bcm in 2030 (reference case). New policies to promote switching to other fuels and to curb gas demand, not taken into account in the Reference Scenario, could reduce gas-import needs. In the *WEO 2002* Alternative Scenario, natural gas demand increase is reduced, leading to a reduction in the need for

Table 6.1. Comparison of LNG exporter netbacks at receiving terminals worldwide, as of 23 February 2004 ($/million Btu)

Exporters	US/Lake Charles	US/Elba Island	US/Cove Point	US/ Everett	Spain/ Huelva	Belgium/ Zeebrugge	Japan/ Sodegaura
Qatar	3.06	3.98	4.02	5.32	3.06	2.51	3.66
Oman	3.18	4.1	4.14	5.44	3.17	2.62	3.77
Abu Dhabi	3.12	4.06	4.08	5.43	3.11	2.56	3.7
Indonesia	2.83	3.69	3.7	4.97	2.66	1.74	4.21
Malaysia	2.8	3.66	3.67	4.94	2.67	1.76	4.16
Australia	2.92	3.8	3.79	5.06	2.63	2.14	4.08
Trinidad	4.28	5.14	5.13	6.36	3.57	3.06	2.68
Algeria	3.92	4.85	4.9	6.2	3.97	3.33	2.97
Nigeria	3.73	4.62	4.66	5.93	3.5	2.96	3.02

Source: World Gas Intelligence estimates[55]

LNG imports (246 bcm by 2030). In its *Annual Energy Outlook 2004*, the DOE forecasts a lower but still high growth rate for LNG imports. In the reference case, LNG imports are expected to increase to 2.16 tcf (61 bcm) in 2010 and to 4.8 tcf (136 bcm) in 2025, equal to 15% of total US gas supply.

Regulatory changes

Regulation applied to LNG, and in particular to new receiving terminals, will greatly influence the future of LNG in the US market. The US Government has moved quickly to encourage the construction of LNG terminals by adopting supporting regulation and streamlining the authorisation process.

---

55 The base price used in calculating US netbacks is the average of the Nymex Henry Hub closing price for the first or second month out for the three trading days before and including the date specified, with location adjustments based on *Natural Gas Week* spot price assessments for the prior month for Trunkline West Louisiana (Lake Charles); Transco Zone 6-Non-NY (Cove Point); Transco Zone 4 (Elba Island); and Boston City Gate (Everett). Instead of a flat 35 cents/mBtu regas rate for the US, World Gas Intelligence is now assuming 10% of the base price. For Zeebrugge, World Gas Intelligence uses a regas charge of 1 eurocent/cubic meter, applied to a base price that is the first or second month IPE price for the UK National Balancing Point, adjusted for earlier-year differentials in the succeeding month. Japanese prices are based on official average ex-ship prices for the most recent month available. Spanish prices are based on ex-ship price estimates from the most recent World Gas Intelligence European Border Price Table. *Source:* World Gas Intelligence.

Federal regulations

Major changes to the regulation of offshore and onshore terminals were adopted in 2002 to facilitate the construction of LNG facilities. Since the Amendment of the Deepwater Port Act in November 2002, the US Coast Guard is responsible for offshore terminals. Onshore, LNG receiving terminals are subject to FERC regulation. FERC is responsible for permitting new onshore terminals, for economic oversight of terminal services and for environmental and safety review of these terminals. The recent regulatory changes are described hereunder.

'Non-open access' to LNG terminals/market-based rates

Until the end of 2002, FERC considered LNG terminals as part of the interstate system and applied open access to them. The exception has been the Everett, Massachusetts terminal which has not been in open access. When its owner Distrigas filed its application to build the terminal, it took the position that the terminal would not be engaged in interstate commerce but in foreign commerce.

In December 2002, the FERC terminated open access requirements for new onshore LNG terminals, placing them on an equal footing with offshore terminals regulated under provisions of the Maritime Security Act of 2002. The FERC ruling, which granted preliminary approval to the proposed Dynegy/Sempra LNG terminal in Hackberry, Louisiana, is referred to as the **Hackberry Decision**. It authorised Hackberry LNG (now Cameron LNG) to provide services to its affiliates under rates and terms mutually agreed upon (i.e., market-based), rather than under regulated cost-of-service rates, and exempted the company from having to provide open access service. In essence, from a regulatory perspective, LNG import facilities will be treated as supply sources rather than as part of the transportation chain. This new policy allows owners of LNG terminals the exclusive use of the entire capacity of an LNG terminal, thus suppressing the uncertainty faced by LNG terminals developers.

Offshore terminals

In November 2002, the US Congress enacted the Maritime Security Act (S. 1214), which expands the Coast Guard's role in providing port security concerning a variety of maritime activities, including the transportation by tanker of oil, compressed natural gas and LNG. The legislation transferred jurisdiction for offshore natural gas facilities from the FERC to the Maritime Administration and the US Coast Guard. The amendments in the Maritime Security Act of 2002 lowered the regulatory hurdles faced by potential developers of offshore LNG receiving terminals. Placing them under Coast Guard jurisdiction both streamlined the permitting process and relaxed regulatory requirements. The Maritime Security Act of 2002 also exempts owners of offshore LNG facilities from open-access provisions, thereby granting owners the right to reserve for themselves all of the import and storage capacity at their facilities (proprietary access). Offshore terminals will benefit from this legislative change which speeds up the regulatory approval process.[56]

In February 2004, the FERC, Coast Guard and Department of Transportation announced an interagency agreement to provide for the comprehensive and coordinated review of land and marine safety and security issues at the US LNG import terminals.

State and local regulations

LNG receiving terminals must also meet state and local regulations which vary according to the proposed location. 'Not in my backyard' or 'NIMBY' issues frequently arise at the state and local level and may result in a difficult permitting process.

Existing and planned LNG terminals

Higher US prices in recent years and months and the new pro-active legislation stimulated plans for reopening and expansions of existing terminals and construction of new ones. Since the end of August 2003, all four existing terminals have been operational, with a capacity of of 29 bcm/year (2.8 bcf/d), to be expanded to 50 bcm (4.8 bcf/d) by 2008 (baseload capacity) – see Table 6.2.

In addition to the expansion of three of the four existing terminals, there are more than thirty proposals for new import facilities with a total

---

56 The streamlined application process under the new amendments promises a decision within 365 days of receipt of an application for construction of an offshore LNG terminal.

capacity in excess of 33 bcf/d (340 bcm/a), planned to come on stream from 2006 onwards. It is expected that only a few of these proposals will be built.

Two projects received Federal approvals recently. The Sempra LNG receiving terminal (Cameron LNG – formerly Hackberry) was the first to receive final approval from FERC in October 2003, only 16 months after the initial application was filed. It will be the first new LNG receiving terminal to be built in the US for 25 years. The second approved project is the offshore Port Pelican project, approved by the Maritime Administration in November 2003. It will be the first offshore terminal in the US and in the world. Both projects are located on the Gulf Coast. They have the advantage of being located at the heart of the pipeline grid system (close to Henry Hub), but it is more advantageous economically to locate in California or the northeast.

The next project scheduled for completion by the end of 2004-early 2005, the El Paso/Excelerate "Energy Bridge" project, offshore Louisiana, will add 0.5 bcf/d of gas import capacity. Energy Bridge is an innovative technology, in which a standard LNG shipping vessel is customised to convert LNG to vapour on board the ship.

Of the 36 projects listed in Table 6.2, 13 are located in the Gulf coast, 9 on the east coast, 11 on the west coast and Mexico and 3 in the Bahamas. It is not yet clear how many will be built. To meet expected US LNG demand by the end of the decade, it will be necessary to use the full expanded LNG import capacity at all four existing terminals and the capacity of two to three new LNG import facilities, with more facilities put into service over the following decade.

Because of "NIMBY' problems, new projects are located in three areas:

- The Gulf Coast where there is already a long tradition of industrial plants;

- Backdoor locations, such as Mexico or the Bahamas, where approvals may be easier to obtain;

- Offshore, where environmental approvals are less stringent.

On the west coast, efforts are under way to build California's first LNG facility near Los Angeles, and several more terminals are planned in neighbouring Mexico to receive Asian, Russian and South American LNG cargoes. Elsewhere, in Mexico, at least six plants have been proposed for the east and west coasts, some of which would supply gas to both Mexico – where gas demand is rapidly expanding – and the US.

Public opposition to LNG plants is likely to continue on environmental, security and aesthetic grounds. This "NIMBY" problem led El Paso, in July 2002, to withdraw its proposal to build a terminal at Radio Island, North Carolina. In February 2003, Shell and Bechtel shelved their plans to build a terminal on Mare Island, California. And more recently, in March 2004, Marathon had to cancel its plans to build an LNG terminal on the Pacific coast of Mexico, citing local and government opposition to the project.

Many proposals come from independent operators without upstream LNG assets which seek the opportunity to buy LNG surplus and sell it into the US market. However, the momentum for US terminal investment seems to be shifting in favour of the players with upstream assets, where the largest investments and risks are located. Among the major international oil companies aiming to become big LNG importers to the US market are ExxonMobil, ChevronTexaco, ConocoPhillips, Shell, BP and Marathon Oil Co, all of which have locked up import capacity at existing terminals or plan to build their own. Companies without upstream assets, such as Sempra Energy, Cheniere Energy and El Paso/Excelerate, will have to rely on contracts with third parties for supplies.

Conclusion on the US LNG market

The role of LNG on the US market is promising. There is no doubt that LNG imports are going to expand quickly and contribute to a growing share of US gas supply. In the longer term, increased LNG imports to the US would mark a major structural change in the global LNG business, and accelerate the move towards greater trading and possibly towards a closer price linkage between the US market and the European and Asian markets.

The new US Federal regulatory policy should help the building of new LNG terminals, onshore and offshore. Nevertheless, LNG terminals are only part of the LNG chain and there are still a number of impediments to the rapid development of the US LNG market. More details on LNG trade are given in Chapter 4.

Table 6.2. Proposed North American LNG import facilities at the beginning of 2004

Name	Location	Capacity (bcf/d)	Sponsor(s)	Companies target start-up date
Existing Terminals with Expansions				
A. Everett	Massachusetts	Current: 0.735 Planned: 1.035	Tractebel	
B. Cove Point	Maryland	Current: 1.0 Planned: 1.8	Dominion	Late 2008
C. Elba Island	Georgia	Current: 0.446 Planned: 0.806	El Paso	2006
D. Lake Charles	Louisiana	Current: 0.63 Planned: 1.2	Southern Union	2006
E. Guayanilla Bay	Puerto Rico	0.093	Eco Electrica	
Approved				
1. Cameron LNG	Hackberry, Louisiana	1.5	Sempra Energy	2007
2. Port Pelican	Offshore Louisiana, Gulf of Mexico	1.6	Chevron Texaco	2007
3. Ocean Express	Ocean Bay, Bahamas	0.84	AES Ocean Express	2006-2007
4. Energy Bridge	Floating Dock Offshore, Gulf of Mexico	0.5	El Paso Excelerate	late 2004
Proposed /Submitted terminals – FERC				
5. Calypso	Freeport Grand, Bahamas island	0.83	Calypso Tractebel	2007
6. Freeport LNG	Freeport, Texas	1.5	Cheniere / Freeport LNG Dev.	2007
7. Fall River	Massachusetts	0.8	Weaver's Cove Energy	late 2007
8. Long Beach	California	0.7	Sound Energy Solutions / Mitsubishi	late 2007-2008
9. Corpus Christi	Texas	2.6	Cheniere LNG Partners	Q1 2007
10. Sabine	Louisiana	2.6	Cheniere LNG	Q1 2007
11. Corpus Christi	Texas	1	Vista del Sol / ExxonMobil	2008-2009

Table 6.2. Proposed North American LNG import facilities at the beginning of 2004 (continued)

Name	Location	Capacity (bcf/d)	Sponsor(s)	Companies target start-up date
12. Sabine	Louisiana	1	Golden Pass / ExxonMobil	2008-2009
13. Logan Township	New Jersey	1.2	Crown Landing LNG – BP	2008
Proposed Terminals – Coast Guard				
14. Cabrillo Port Floating Plant	Offshore California	1.5	Cabrillo Port / BHP Billiton	2008
15. Gulf Landing (West Cameron Dock 213)	Offshore Louisiana	1	Gulf Landing – Shell	2008-2009
16. So. California	Offshore	0.5	Crystal Energy	2007
Planned				
17. Brownsville	Texas	n/a	Cheniere LNG Partners	
18. Humboldt Bay	California	0.5	Calpine	
19. Somerset	Massachusetts	0.65	Somerset LNG	
20. Louisiana Offshore	Louisiana Offshore	1	McMoRan Exp.	
21. Bahamas	Bahamas	0.5	El Paso/FPL / Seafarer	
22. California	Offshore	0.5	Chevron Texaco	
23. Harpswell	Maine	0.5	Fairwinds LNG – CP & TCPL	
24. Providence	Rhode Island	0.5	Keyspan & BG LNG	
25. Mobile Bay	Alabama	1	Cheniere LNG Partners	
26. Gulf of Mexico	Offshore	1	ExxonMobil	
27. Cherry Point	Washington	n/a	Cherry Point Energy	
28. Belmar	New Jersey Offshore	n/a	El Paso Global	
29. Altamira, Tamulipas	Mexico	1.12	Shell	
30. Baja California	Mexico	1	Sempra & Shell	
31. Baja California	Mexico	0.6	Conoco-Phillips	

Table 6.2. Proposed North American LNG import facilities at the beginning of 2004 (continued)

Name	Location	Capacity (bcf/d)	Sponsor(s)	Companies target start-up date
32. Baja California	Offshore	1.4	Chevron Texaco	
33. Lázaro Cárdenas	Mexico	0.5	Tractebel or Repsol YPF	
34. St. John	New Brunswick, Canada	0.75	Irving Oil & Chevron Canada	
35. Point Tupper	Nova Scotia, Canada	0.75	Access Northeast Energy	
36. St. Lawrence	Quebec, Canada	n/a	TCPL and/ or Gaz Met	

*The Everett terminal has an additional 0.09 to 0.10 bcf/d of sendout capacity by truck.
Source: EIA, FERC, Gas Matters, February 2004

Investment

Investment in receiving terminals is the smallest share of the total investment needed in an LNG chain (roughly 10%). If several of the proposed new LNG terminals are built, it remains uncertain whether the natural gas pricing structure prevailing in the US will be adequate to support the financial investments required upstream to develop the fields, and build the liquefaction facility and the LNG tankers. The development of LNG projects is capital-intensive and does not smoothly respond to short-term and volatile price signals when demand calls for new supply. Long-term contracts with LNG suppliers have been a prerequisite for investments in such projects in other parts of the world. On the US market, long-term access to firm regasification capacity will be essential to LNG suppliers.

Pricing

For the necessary investment decisions to be made, LNG-project sponsors need a price of around $3.5 to $4/mBtu on a long-term basis to make their project viable. Although most analysts project that US natural gas prices will remain high, periods of low prices cannot be excluded. LNG suppliers operate on the assumption that it is the US price level that will

Figure 6.8. Existing and proposed LNG receiving terminals in North America

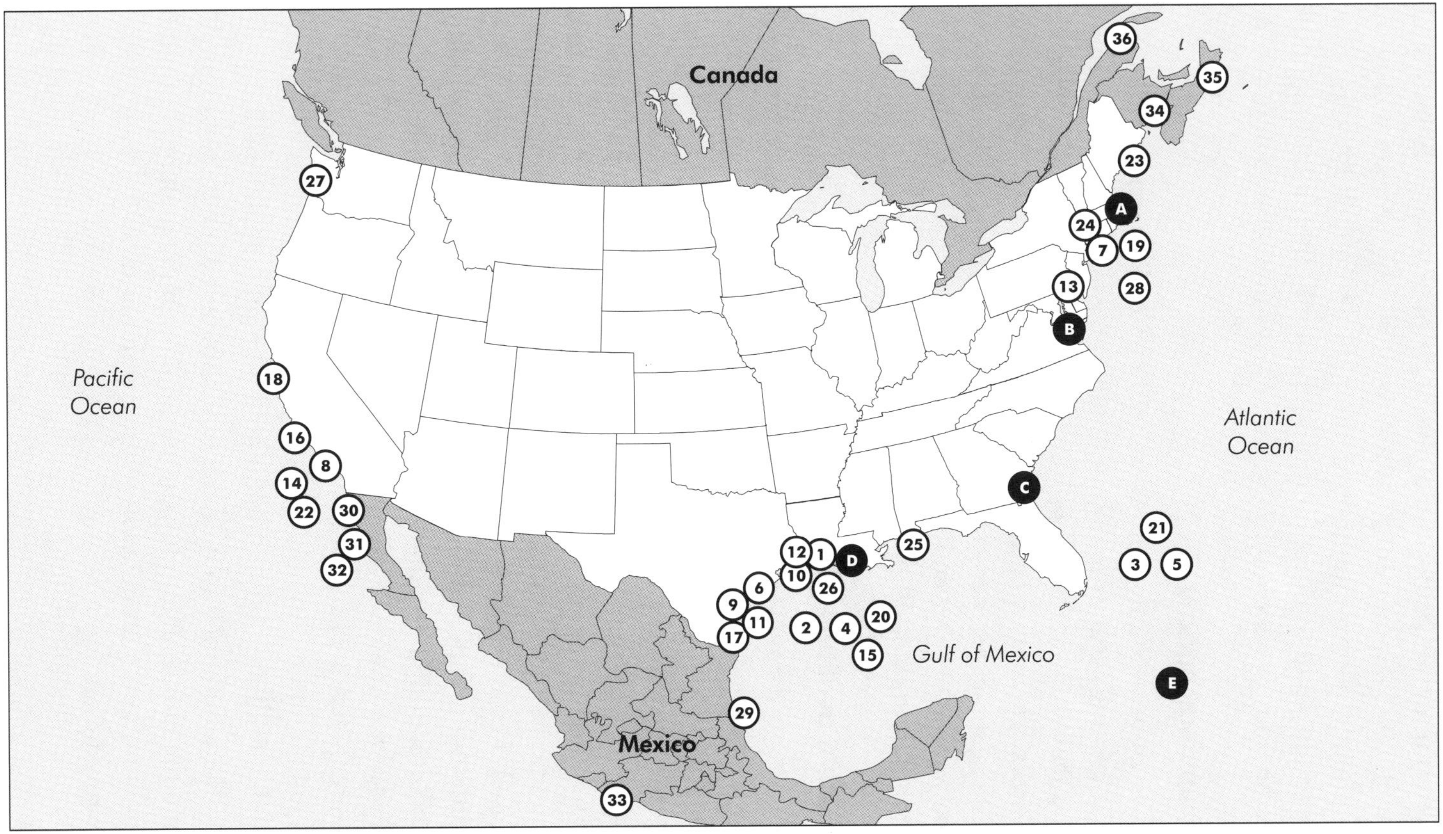

Source: FERC, Gas Matters, February 2004

determine their netbacks, not that their costs will determine the US price level. LNG imports will allow a decrease in US gas prices as they will bring additional supplies to the tight US market if enough LNG producers find it profitable to compete for the US market.[57] Several LNG suppliers seem to be ready to supply the US market and willing to accept the market risk.

Shipping capacity

The global LNG fleet includes 154 LNG tankers (end 2003) and most of the existing capacity is already booked on a long-term basis, offering little available capacity for exporting more LNG to the US. However, this bottleneck is disappearing. In addition to the 16 tankers delivered in 2003, some 54 new tankers have been already ordered for delivery between 2004 and end 2006. Of these ships, 15 are not linked to long-term contracts.

Global available LNG supply

Although the capacity of US LNG terminals now totals about 29 bcm/a (with planned expansion at 50 bcm/a by 2008), it is unlikely that it will be completely filled, even though current US gas prices make the market very attractive even for far-distant LNG suppliers. Current available LNG supply is limited. Most LNG volumes are already contracted long-term by Asian and European buyers. In the short-term, nevertheless, the coming on stream of the third train in Trinidad and Tobago in June 2003 has eased LNG trade to the US. In the medium/long-term, the supply situation is expected to improve. There are eight additional trains under construction at existing LNG plants and five new liquefaction plants are under construction. It is expected that global LNG supply capacity will reach 170 mtpa by 2006.

LNG quality

As the US imports LNG from more countries, the composition of LNG, and the interchangeability of LNG and other sources of gas, could become an important consideration, especially in places where the regasified LNG is not diluted by other supplies as it is on the Gulf Coast. Achieving "gas

---

57 Jensen J. (2003a).

interchangeability" means the ability to replace gas of a given quality with another gas source, such as LNG, without affecting the end use performance of the gas. The quality of LNG is determined by its composition, its heating value (Btu content) rising as the percentage of methane declines, and the presence of heavier hydrocarbons such as butane or propane increases. Btu content is one of the most important factors in determining interchangeability. Quality issues also include the presence of unacceptably high levels of impurities such as nitrogen and hydrogen sulphide.

The quality of natural gas – and LNG – varies throughout the world and there is currently a substantial range in quality of LNG, depending on its source. Some of the gas from these various sources may not meet the US standards for pipeline quality gas. In LNG markets outside the US, gas is received and burned at a greater Btu content (1,100 to 1,180 Btu per cubic foot) and the facilities are designed generally to produce LNG within this range. This tracts with the Btu content of gas being delivered into the US pipeline system that can be as low as 950 Btu per cubic foot, with a more typical range of 1,025 to 1,060 Btu per cubic foot. For example, any LDCs in the US do not have the ability to use natural gas with higher gross heating values, and this may restrain the potential LNG market. Quality and interchangeability issues are a concern of pipelines, LDCs and consumers. Pipelines are concerned about the impact of high-Btu gas on the integrity of their systems. LDCs are concerned about that high Btu content gas or gas with quality issues, such as a higher liquid content, will damage equipment and appliances or will require equipment modifications and retrofits that will be expensive. Pipelines are concerned with liquids in the gas stream affecting the operation of compressors and the increased possibility of pipe corrosion.

SECURITY OF GAS SUPPLY ISSUES

On the US market, the market itself plays a primary role in ensuring security of supply, through supply and demand response to price changes. There is a direct linkage of short-term investment to market signals. The question, however, is whether these market signals are sufficient to ensure secured and diversified domestic and external supplies, in both the short and long term, and whether regulation for pipelines will allow enough investments in expansions and new projects. An additional issue is the impact of credit downgrading of most US energy companies on access to and cost of capital.

Upstream investment

Domestic resources

Market signals are an important indicator for domestic upstream investment. North American drilling activity has historically responded quickly to market signals, increasing supplies from Canada and the US. It now appears, however, that natural gas productive capacity from accessible basins in the US and western Canada has reached a plateau. In addition, in mature provinces like those drilled in the US and Canada, more gas drilling may not translate into more overall gas production, but may just be necessary to maintain the level of production because of depletion.

Figure 6.9. Gas rigs tend to follow US spot prices with a 6-month time lag

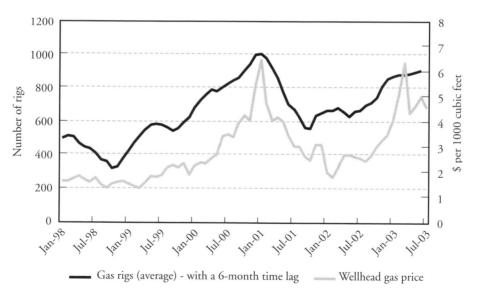

Gas rigs (average) - with a 6-month time lag   Wellhead gas price

Source: EIA, World Gas Intelligence

Drilling activity is linked to the level of gas prices. When prices are high, producers' cash flows are also high, inducing investment and drilling. Figure 6.9 shows the overall number of active rigs drilling for natural gas and natural gas prices. It shows that prices and drilling interact over time (with a time lag of 6 months). Hence, drilling rigs reached a historical record in July 2001 (1,062 rigs), soon after the price hikes observed in winter 2000-01. The number of rigs decreased in 2002, in line with price decreases, followed by the rise in prices observed since the beginning of 2003. However, gas drilling has not reacted as strongly as in 2000/01, and the record number reached in that period was not reached in 2003. Natural gas drilling activity, in turn, is directly related to the development of new productive capacity, with higher gas rig levels generally resulting in a higher level of natural gas discoveries. However, the response is not immediate. The delay between a price increase and a natural gas production increase may range between 6 and 18 months. The delay between changes in price and changes in new wellhead supplies increases the propensity of natural gas producers to over-invest in new productive capacity during periods of high wellhead prices and to under-invest in new productive capacity during periods of low wellhead prices.

Figure 6.10. Number of gas development wells and change in gas production

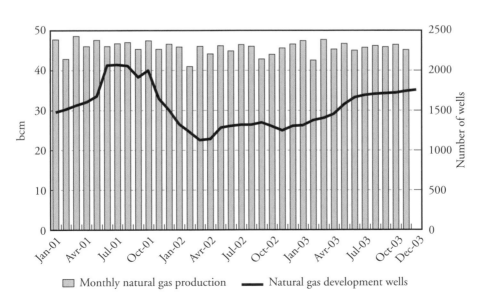

Source: EIA

Figure 6.10 illustrates the sensitivity of development wells to production. It shows that despite the surge in gas drilling in 2001, US production has not increased as fast as past trends would have suggested. Drilling activity increased 45% in 2000 and 30% in 2001, while overall production rose by 2 and 2.1% respectively. In 2002, drilling activity fell by 26%, while gas production fell by only 3.2%. In 2003, gas development activity increased 25%, whereas early estimates indicate that natural gas production will increase by only 2.1% in 2004.

In addition, in recent years, production from new natural gas wells has been declining more rapidly than in the past, partly due to technology advances that have increased initial flow rates, and partly due to the maturing of the accessible natural gas resource base. Moreover, because up to half of US current natural gas supply is coming from wells that have been drilled in the past three years, this decline trend is likely to continue. In addition to the needed growth in gas supply, US producers first have to replenish the stock that is produced each year. The US natural gas decline rate ranged from 26 to 28% in 2003. In practical terms, even with an increase in gas-directed drilling, US gas deliverability may not increase unless returns to drilling outpace production.

A more rapid extraction of resources is beneficial because it enhances the economics by increasing the present value of expected revenues. This allows the development and production from resources that otherwise might be sub-economic. Horizontal drilling techniques have helped this development. However, the associated rapid declines make aggregate production increasingly dependent on the level of gas drilling. The challenge therefore is to increase domestic production, and, in particular, replace older wells that are producing less and are becoming more expensive to maintain.

Consequently, because productive capacity is not price elastic in the short term, a relative scarcity in wellhead productive capacity could be expected to cause very high natural gas prices, and a relative surplus could be expected to cause very low prices. The natural gas industry embodies a set of dynamics that could cause periodic cycles in investment, drilling, supply and prices. The potential for unpredictable future price behaviour would result in an investment emphasis on projects that can be completed quickly during period of high prices, such as conventional onshore drilling investments in shallow reservoirs, at the expense of investments in highly risky rank wildcatting, which is necessary to test new plays.

Although upstream investment reacts to price signals sent by the market, the maturity of the provinces explored and constraints on restrictions in some areas mean that North America will have to rely more and more on unconventional resources and external supplies (LNG). Access to both domestic and external supplies will be key to future security of gas supply.

Access to external resources

Access to external resources is not a current problem. However, when the US market becomes more dependent on LNG supplies, the issue will be whether US market signals will be sufficient to encourage investment abroad in exploration and production, liquefaction and transport. In Europe, these investments have required long-term commitments from buyers. Is the liquid US market a sufficient guarantee for gas producers and LNG developers? Another issue linked to increased imports will be to diversify supply sources and promote flexibility of supply and markets.

The number of planned projects dedicated to the US market seems to be a good indicator that LNG suppliers are ready to accept the US market risk. Competition from suppliers indicates that diversification of supplies may come from the market itself as long as US prices are attractive.

In both the Atlantic and Pacific basins, the US market represents a very attractive option:

- Trinidad & Tobago's Atlantic LNG has made exports to the US a crucial part of its strategy;

- Egypt's ELNG and Nigeria NNPC are going to build new capacity dedicated to the US market;

- Algeria's Sonatrach is also considering the building of a new integrated LNG project with target sales on the US, while Norway has signed a contract with El Paso to deliver LNG to the US market;

- Middle East producers, Qatar, in particular, are also very keen to enter the US market. ExxonMobil signed an agreement with Qatar Petroleum to supply around 15 mtpa to the US for 25 years (Rasgas III). Deliveries are expected to start in 2008-09. Conoco Phillips has also signed a Memorandum of Understanding (MoU) with Qatar for long-term supply of 7.5 mtpa of LNG to the US market (Qatargas III);

- Another recent announcement is the MoU signed by Marathon with the Indonesian regulator BPMIGAS, which targets the US west coast, but is still far from a sales and purchase agreement. US Sempra has also signed a MoU with Indonesia to import between 6 and 10 mtpa to the US west coast;

- ChevronTexaco signed a MoU with Australia's Gorgon LNG to import 2 mtpa to the US market.

- The slow-moving projects in South America (Bolivia and Peru) would be targeted exclusively at the west coast.

- Elsewhere in eastern Russia, the Sakhalin II project has unsold capacity which could be exported to the US market and Gazprom is considering LNG projects dedicated to the US market.

The total above-mentioned contracted supplies already exceed 50 mtpa (about 70 bcm/a), although not all contracts are firm.

Investment in transmission and storage

While the US transmission network has expanded significantly to meet demand growth in the last 10 years, new gas demand by the power sector and a shift in gas demand and supply will result in the need for major expansion of natural gas transmission capacity.

Expansion of the North American network

The North American transmission grid is highly developed and well integrated. Supply reliability is ensured through diversification and flexibility. The system includes alternate transportation routes; transportation and storage are both substitute and complementary arrangements. Pipeline companies have so far been linked with their customers through long-term commercial arrangements for transportation.

Investment in transmission capacity is proceeding quite well and has increased rapidly in recent years. In the US, between 1991 and 2001, more than 60 bcf/d of capacity (through pipeline expansions and building of new pipelines) was incorporated into the lower 48 interstate gas transmission network, an average of 6 bcf/d per year. In 2002, more than 3,571 miles of pipeline and a record 12.8 bcf/d of capacity (+10%) were added to the network at an estimated cost of $4.4 billion. Pipeline capacity has also increased rapidly in Canada. Export capacity in particular increased significantly in the last three years. However, it should be pointed out that although capacity has increased by 20% in the last three years, the system is more and more constrained as peak day utilisation has also soared, despite investment in new lines.

While the US transmission network has expanded significantly to meet demand growth in the last 10 years, new gas demand by the power sector and a shift in gas demand and supply will result in the need for major expansion of natural gas transmission capacity. The lead times for developing new pipeline capacity are comparable to the construction time for new power plants, providing the opportunity to develop the infrastructure to support new gas-fired power plants coming on-line. Shift in gas demand and supply means that additional pipeline take-away capacity will be needed from the Rocky Mountains, the deep waters of the Gulf of Mexico, and western and eastern Canada.

In addition, the flexibility which was provided in the past by oversupply (the "gas bubble") has disappeared. Consequently, some other parts of the industry have to handle demand swings. Pipeline operations, storage, distribution and spot markets play a greater role in volume management than when production capacity has surpluses.[58] These new trends can be expected to place unusual demands upon the natural gas pipeline industry.

According to *WEIO 2003*, $119 billion in capital expenditures in the North American transportation sector are required between 2001 and 2030. At $4.4 billion per year, the rate of investment will be higher than in recent years. The capital cost of transmission projects alone commissioned in 2002 amounted to $4.4 billion, but the annual average for the period 2000-2002 was only $2.8 billion.

---

58 FERC (2003).

Figure 6.11. Main transmission pipelines in North America

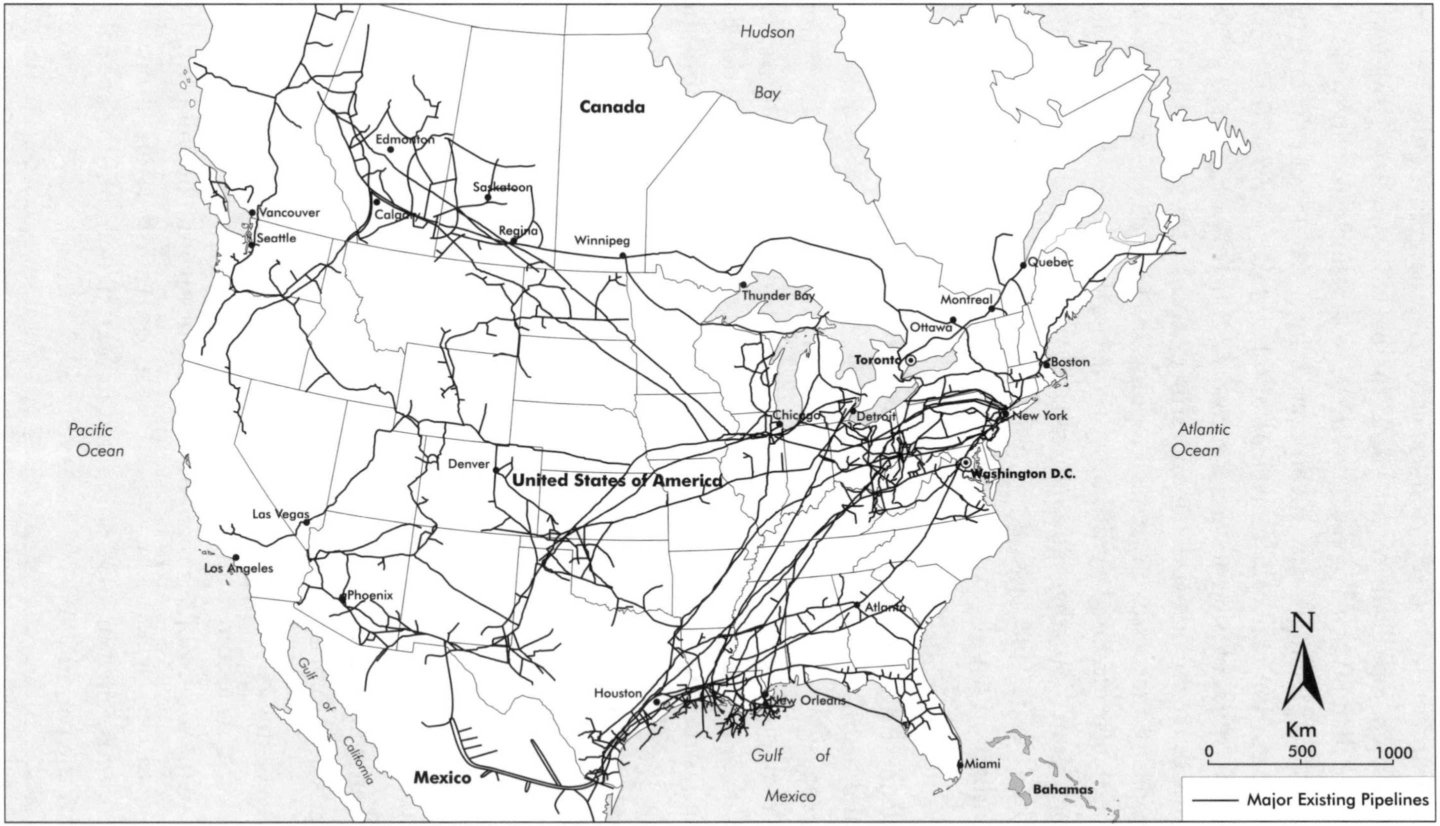

Source: IEA

As of March 2003, 112 natural gas pipeline expansion projects, in various stages of development, have been proposed for the lower 48 states for 2003 through 2005. It seems, however, that some projects will be either postponed or cancelled. Since late 2001, economic growth has slowed and many proposals to add new gas-fired electric generation capacity have been delayed or cancelled. As a result, the need for new natural gas capacity has also weakened.[59] The downgrading of credit ratings of a number of pipeline parent companies or sponsors (see below) may have been another contributing factor.

Until now, most transmission investments in North America have been relatively small scale. Most of these investments were carried out by a single operator and were typically financed out of cash earnings and corporate debt. For example, only 11 out of the 54 US natural gas pipeline construction projects completed in 2002 exceeded $100 million and only one cost more than $1 billion[60], although several long-distance pipelines completed in 1999 and 2000 involved investments of over $1 billion.

Open season and rate principles for gas transmission in North America

In North America, interstate capacity investment decisions are left to the market, subject to FERC and/or NEB approval. Construction and allocation of capacity of new interstate pipelines are made through open season procedures that ensure that capacity is allocated on a non-discriminatory basis. The contract and the tariff are the cornerstones of the firm transportation market. They provide the certainty investors require. The release of capacity is also regulated according to detailed rules defined in FERC Order 636 and 637. This secondary market of capacity provides a market-determined measure of the current value of rights to existing capacity. The secondary market in capacity rights also reveals values capacity differences at peak and off-peak times, which encourages efficient uses of existing capacity.[61]

---

59 For instance, ten major pipeline project proposals were cancelled during 2002, mostly because of changed market conditions. The most prominent of those cancelled was the Independence Pipeline Project (1 bcf/d – 400 miles) and the associated ANR Supply Link project (750 mcf/d – 73 miles) which would have created a new transportation corridor from the Chicago, Illinois area to eastern Pennsylvania.

60 EIA (2003b).

61 NERA (2002b).

Federal policy prevents the construction of unneeded pipeline capacity by requiring that a market exist for that capacity. Under the current rules, FERC does not grant approval for the construction of new pipeline capacity unless prospective shippers are willing to commit to long-term contracts for the new capacity.

The costs of new capacity can be allocated on either a rolled-in or an incremental basis. In the 1990s FERC adopted "rolled-in" tariff-setting principles, whereby costs of the expansion are rolled into existing rates. This practice lowers the tariffs that need to be charged for the incremental capacity and reduce the risk that throughput does not increase quickly enough in the early years of operation.[62] A major policy change was adopted in September 1999, when FERC adopted incremental pricing for new gas pipeline capacity, whereby the new shippers pay the costs of the new capacity, while existing shippers continue to pay the same rate. The FERC only supports roll-in pricing where obvious system-wide benefits, such as lower rates, will occur.

Following the open season, when all the shippers' needs are known, the cost of the pipeline/expansion is finally estimated and the application is made to FERC. The application process that includes a detailed economic review can take up to 18 months. However, FERC may be able to expedite the process on an emergency basis.

The FERC's role in this process is primarily the environmental review and the eminent domain consideration. FERC considers the market demand, impact on existing customers and ultimately decides if a project is incremental or not before issuing a Certificate of Public Convenience and Necessity. If a project is deemed incremental, shippers may have the option of dropping out and the project may be cancelled.[63]

From the early beginnings of the gas sector in the US, pipeline companies have used long-term contracts to secure financing for investment in new capacity. Long-term contracts therefore provided the assurance that investors needed to secure funds for investment in new capacity.

---

62 *WEO 2003.*
63 Office of Trade & Economic Development (2001).

The duration of gas transportation contracts varies greatly, depending upon the specifics of the particular contract. In the US, the average length of these contracts has been decreasing in the past ten years. The average term of a long-term transportation contract before Order 636 was approximately 15 years. After Order 636, the average term was 9.2 years, and currently 65% of contracts are shorter than 5 years, compared with 50% only five years ago. As the revenue stream by pipeline companies is viewed as more short term in nature, it is less likely to support long-term investments. FERC addressed this issue in Order 637 which allows pipelines to include a lower reservation rate for buyers who will agree to a contract term of more than 5 years.

Another important factor included in the contract is the creditworthiness of customers. In the US, pipelines are not obligated to serve shippers unless the shippers can demonstrate their creditworthiness. Contracts longer than one year also include "evergreen" or roll-over clauses, which give shippers additional security that their contracted capacity will not become unavailable at the end of the contract. Under these clauses the contracting shipper has a priority right to renew its contract with the pipeline.

The rate of return allowed by the regulatory agencies is essential in the investment decision. Recently, the FERC has allowed pipelines to earn return of equity in the area of 12-13%. In Canada, common regulated rates of return are in the area of 9-10%, but can also be negotiated. These rates are higher than what is common in Europe (7-8%). Allowed rates have also increased in the past few years. The return on investment (operating income divided by assets) for the 14 largest US pipeline companies over the period 1990-1997 averaged 7.6% for transportation activities.

Investment in storage

There were 417 underground natural gas storage facilities operating in the US at the end of 2002 and 39 in Canada. In the US, total underground working gas capacity is roughly 112 bcm, although volumes at the beginning of the heating season rarely get above 96 bcm (3.2 tcf). Withdrawal capacity amounts to 2,345 mcm/d. In addition, the US has 96 LNG peak-shaving units, which help to balance daily fluctuations in demand. These LNG peak shaving units represent a very small proportion of storage capacity (3 bcm). However, the high daily deliverability of these LNG facilities makes them an important source of fuel during winter cold snaps, in particular in the north-east consuming region where 82% of these facilities are concentrated. LNG peak-shaving facilities can deliver up to 311 mcm/d, or the equivalent of 12% of total storage deliverability (2002).

While the number of underground sites has increased from 392 in 1990 to 417 in 2002, the working inventory level at the beginning of the heating season has slightly decreased because of changes in inventory practices and new storage utilisation in the past 10 years. As storage facilities are cycled more frequently than in the past, the same level of capacity allows increased efficiency. Net withdrawal rates in peak winter months have risen by 50% compared with 1991. Many storage owners (marketers and third parties) are minimising inventories in an attempt to synchronise their buying and selling activities more effectively with market needs while minimising their costs. These changes have been reflected in the building of new storage facilities, which has favoured salt cavern facilities, characterised by their high daily withdrawal rates and multiple cycles. Although they account for only 4% of working capacity, they represent 17% of withdrawal capacity (2002).

Storage is usually integrated into or available to the system at the production and/or market end of the pipeline system as a means of balancing flow levels throughout the year. Producing regions hold 98 sites (24%, representing 31% of working capacity) and most of the salt caverns facilities. Consuming regions hold the largest number of storage facilities as well as almost all LNG peak-shaving facilities. There are different storage utilisation patterns in production and consuming regions. In production areas, storage is used for hedging purposes. Therefore, most new salt cavern facilities were added in producing regions over the past decade. In consuming regions, storage mostly fulfils its traditional role, i.e., meeting seasonal and daily variations in demand.

Reflecting these new needs, the contractual ownership of storage has evolved in the past ten years. Today, pipelines are still the principal owners of storage facilities (66% of storage facilities are owned by pipelines, 30%

by LDCs and 4% by independents). However, most contractual rights are held by LDCs: 73%, while 15% is held by marketers, 8% by pipelines, 3% by generators and less than 1% by other players. However, if Agency Agreements[64] are taken into account, the picture is different. LDCs and, to a lesser extent, pipelines, and electric generators, have transferred a significant share of the effective control of capacity to marketers. Marketers have increased the share of storage they have available for use from 15% to nearly 24% of all the working gas capacity, while LDCs control 66%, pipelines 7%, generators less than 3%.[65]

According to *WEIO 2003*, North American gas storage volume is projected to rise from 129 bcm in 2000 to 165 bcm in 2010 and 209 bcm in 2030, boosted by increasing demand, short-term trading and opportunities for arbitrage. $13 billion will need to be invested in the period 2001-2030.

Under FERC regulation, storage service is defined as a form of transportation service. Pipelines must offer (unbundled) access to their storage facilities on a firm and interruptible contract basis as a part of their non-discriminatory open-access transportation service.[66] In 1992, FERC allowed storage to charge market-based rates, i.e., whatever the market will bear, where the company could show that it lacked market power.[67] This new regulation has facilitated financing of new projects. Market-based rates allowed the investor to collect for project financing, which was not allowed with cost-based rates. This encouraged pipelines to pursue "at risk" projects that held greater returns and led to an increase in new pipeline projects, including storage. After this decision, more than 100 underground gas storage projects have been announced, although only 31 have been built so far. Most of the new projects are expansions of existing projects. Only a few are new greenfield projects.

---

64 Agency Agreements allow the partial commercialisation of storage assets by allowing gas marketers to use the storage and transportation assets held by a utility. So they allow for the gradual and limited transformation of access to storage capacity from utility use to commercial use. Individual storage facilities (in fact, storage contracts) can be split between the two different utilisations. These agreements allow a more efficient use of storage facilities and reduce the pressure to overbuild storage and transportation assets.

65 AGA (2001).

66 EIA (2002b).

67 In 1992, Richfield Gas Storage in Morton County, Kansas, became the first independent gas storage facility to receive FERC approval for market-based rates. Since then, most new storage projects have received approvals to charge market-based rates.

Figure 6.12. US underground gas storage facilities

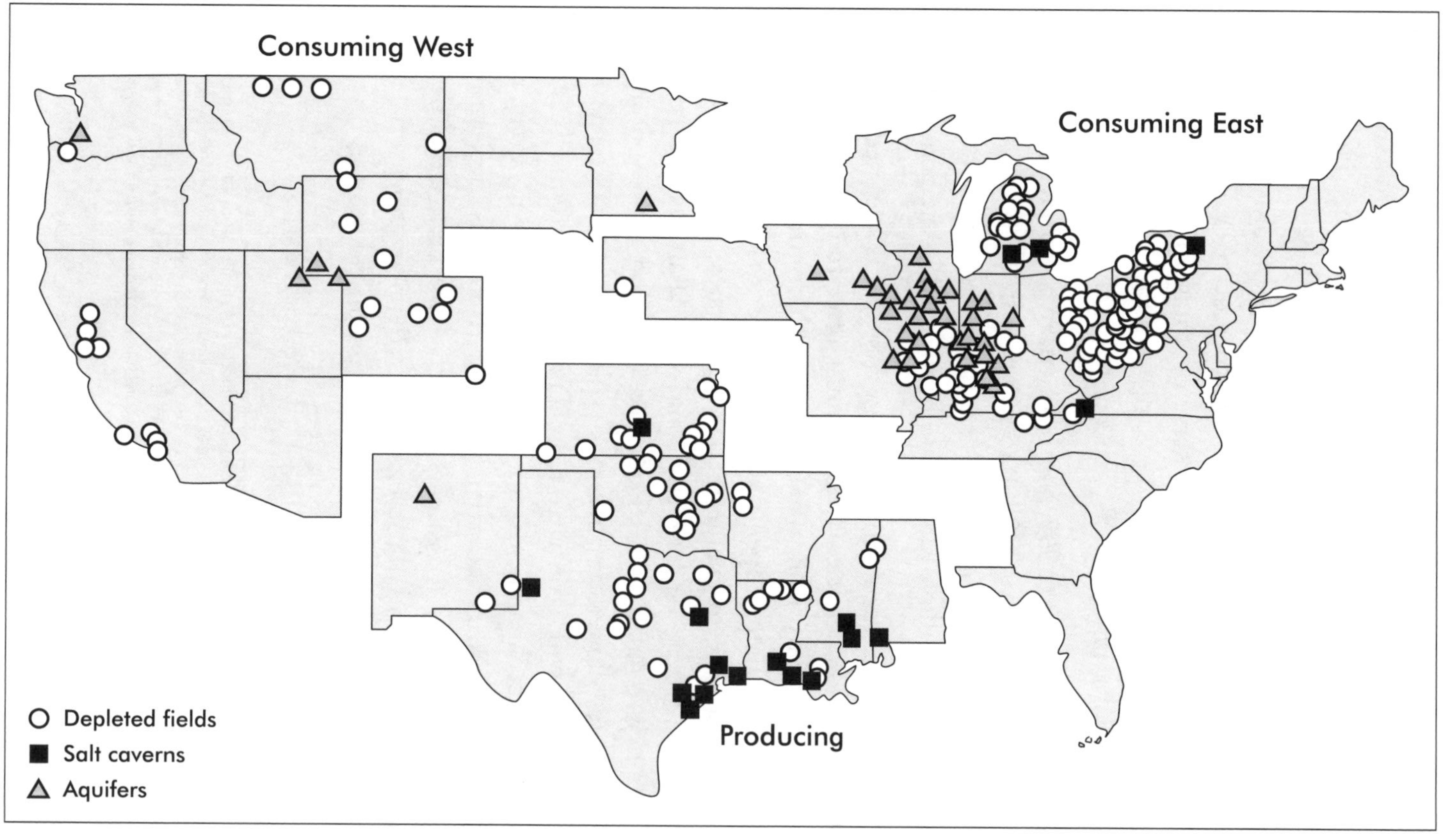

O Depleted fields
■ Salt caverns
△ Aquifers

Consuming East

Consuming West

Producing

Source: EIA

This segment of the gas industry is growing – with 62 storage sites planned for development or expansion between 2003 and 2005.

Investment issues and downgrading of US merchant companies

After the fall of Enron, almost all energy trading entities have encountered financial challenges. The collapse of Enron in December 2001, one of the largest bankruptcies in US history, has had a very negative effect on the $800 billion global energy-trading market. Financial stress has also spread to electric utilities, pipelines and distributors. US power and gas companies have been hard hit in 2002/03 by a series of credit downgrades and higher trading costs that have limited their ability to mitigate financial risks in the derivatives markets, and negatively affected their access to credit. Most energy trading companies, including Dynegy, Mirant, Calpine and Williams, saw their debt ratings downgraded from investment grade to "junk" status (see Table 6.3), making it tougher for them to obtain credit to sustain their operations. In some cases, their ratings are close to default – implying ratings of C or D in rating agency terms.

These companies have had to scale back ambitions and focus on core areas to survive. To improve their financial picture, some companies began selling assets. El Paso had to sell $3 billion in assets in 2003, on top of the 4 billion sold in 2002, to maintain its position as the US biggest pipeline company. In particular, El Paso had to leave the flourishing LNG business. The lack of confidence needed for a recovery in energy trading has led many companies, such as Dynegy, El Paso, and Williams, to abandon the activity, while others have scaled back participation. This eventually reduces liquidity and makes it more difficult for remaining counterparties to remain. The major oil companies have now become the largest traders and developers of LNG projects.

In the meantime, regulation authorities (SEC, FERC) and traders themselves are working to restore investors' trust in the energy trading industry. A coalition of major energy companies has prepared guidelines for disclosing risks of buying and selling electricity and gas. FERC and SEC have proposed a series of new rules to impede market manipulation by gas and power companies. The proposed measures include penalties in

Table 6.3. Credit ratings of major US trading companies

Company	Rating 6 August 2003	Last rating (date rated)	Previous rating (date rated)
Allegheny Energy Supply Co LLC	B/Negative/NR (local) B/Negative/-- (foreign)	BBB+/A-2 (local) (Apr 4, 2002) BBB+/-- (foreign) (Apr 4, 2002)	BBB+/A-2 (local) (Mar 9, 2001) BBB+/-- (foreign) (Mar 9, 2001)
American Electric Power Co Inc	BBB/Stable/A-2 (local) BBB/Stable/A-2 (foreign)	BBB+/A-2 (May 23, 2002)	A-/A-2 (June 15, 2000)
Calpine Corp	B/Negative/-- (local) B/Negative/-- (foreign)	BB/-- (Mar 25, 2002)	BB+/-- (local) (Dec 8, 1999) BB+/-- (foreign) (Dec 8, 1999)
CMS Energy Corp	BB/Negative/-- (local) BB/Negative/-- (foreign)	BB/-- (May 24, 2002)	BB/-- (Oct 15, 1997)
Constellation Energy Group Inc	A-/Stable/A-2 (local) A-/Stable/A-2 (foreign)	A-/A-2 (Mar 18, 2002)	A/A-1 (local) (July 9, 1999) A/A-1 (foreign) (July 9, 1999)
Duke Energy Corp	BBB+/Negative/A-2 (local) BBB+/Negative/A-2 (foreign)	A+/A-1 (May 31, 2001)	A+/A-1 (local) (Apr 19, 1999) A+/A-1 (foreign) (Apr 19, 1999)
Dynegy Inc	B/Negative/NR (local) B/Negative/NR (foreign)	BBB/A-3 (May 8, 2002)	BBB/A-3 (Apr 24, 2002)
El Paso Corp	B+/Negative/NR (local) B+/Negative/NR (foreign)	BBB+/A-2 (Apr 20, 2000)	BBB+/-- (local) (Sep 23, 1999) BBB+/-- (foreign) (Sep 23, 1999)
NRG Energy Inc	D/--/-- (local) D/--/-- (foreign)	BBB-/-- (Feb 11, 2002)	BBB-/-- (local) (Feb 16, 2000) BBB-/-- (foreign) (Feb 16, 2000)
PG&E National Energy Group Inc	D/--/-- (local) D/--/-- (foreign)	BBB/-- (Jan 18, 2001)	
Reliant Resources Inc	B/Negative/NR (local) B/Negative/NR (foreign)	BBB/A-2 (May 13, 2002)	BBB/A-2 (Apr 26, 2002)
Williams Cos. Inc. (The)	B+/Negative/NR (local) B+/Negative/NR (foreign)	BBB/A-3 (May 28, 2002)	BBB+/A-2 (Oct 16, 2001)

Source: Standard & Poor's RatingsDirect

case firms break the rules and new guidelines for reporting and developing price indices for gas and electricity.

⌐ Deterioration of financial conditions of energy companies has negative implications for natural gas markets. Credit downgrades mean higher interest rates and costlier projects as capital is more expensive, at least in the short term. This situation along with regional excess capacity has curtailed investments in new power plants, power lines and gas pipelines in the US. Although most regions are currently well supplied by the energy infrastructure, the US needs to continue to add to the energy infrastructure, on both the gas side and the power side. Gas-fired power plants typically take about three years to bring on line, including the time needed for financing, permits and construction. That time-frame is about two years for gas pipelines and five years for power lines. If no investment is made, the current infrastructure would be stressed to the maximum and parts of the US may be hit during exceptional weather conditions. ⌐

Price reporting issues

The North American natural gas market is the largest and most liquid gas market in the world. It includes 37 market centres (28 in the US and 9 in Canada), where transparent spot markets can expand. The largest market centre is Henry Hub located in Louisiana, which began operating in 1988. Volatility in prices is a natural development of these centres. To hedge against price risks, the NYMEX launched the world's first natural gas futures contract in April 1990.

Figure 6.4 of this Chapter shows Henry Hub prices for the last four years. After a long period of price stability during the 1990s at about \$2/mBtu, natural gas prices are now characterised by high volatility and a sustained higher level since the beginning of 2003. Prices have been very volatile in the recent period as supply tightened and neither supply nor demand are able to quickly adjust to unexpected changes in market conditions. Exposure to price volatility to a great extent is about choices that market participants make. Many customers and producers have access to a broad range of physical and risk management tools to help manage the risk of price volatility. Although these tools do not eliminate risk, they do allow creating price certainty.

There have been major changes in gas market participants over the past two years. Regional gas markets have suffered from a drop in liquidity, starting in late 2001 when Enron exited the market and the Enron on-line trading platform disappeared. The market liquidity issue continues to be one of the most critical in the industry as on-line trading operations have declined, along with the number of counterparts. With less liquidity on future markets, longer-term structured deals have suffered, as quotes in the market have become less representative, and long-term regulatory uncertainty has left many reluctant to value contracts beyond prompt month. Although forward markets on all futures markets are liquid, the liquidity falls when the term extends. For instance, open interest, i.e., the number of contracts that are still outstanding at a particular time for a particular NYMEX gas futures contract, decreases sharply when time elapses (Figure 2.3).

Another issue is the potential for price manipulation in certain natural gas marketplaces. The possible falsification of price information by some companies has led to an investigation into the price-gathering methodologies of companies reporting prices and into the validity of gas pricing information given to reporters by market players. This in turn has led some entities to stop reporting prices altogether to the trade press. However, without a wide and deep pool of market participants, prices become more opaque, less liquid and increasingly volatile, a vicious downward spiral. Transparency of gas prices – as well as reliability of fundamental data (production, demand and storage) – has also become a major issue in the gas industry.

Gas/electricity interface

Although the volume of future gas demand for power is uncertain, new gas-fired power plants will greatly increase the demand for gas even if only a portion of current planned projects are built. The gas/electricity interface should therefore be addressed. In North America, the main issue regarding the growing gas use of gas for power is not the over-dependence of the electricity mix on natural gas. Currently, natural gas represents 18% of the US electricity mix, compared with 50% for coal (although these percentages may differ at state level). By 2025, EIA expects this share to rise to 23% (52% for coal).

However, the growing use of gas in electricity means a growing use of imported gas for electricity generation. This means that gas supply problems would impact electricity too, unless some backstop measures are put in place, or unless the market is able to cope with a disruption in LNG supplies.

In addition, it is increasingly apparent that wholesale electricity and natural gas prices are subject to rising price volatility, and increasing convergence of electricity and natural gas markets means that extreme events are likely to affect both markets simultaneously. This has a number of important implications.

Plans to expand gas-fired electricity generation could lead to further strain on natural gas markets. Power generation improves load factors (summer peaking). However it also contributes to winter load. A key issue for some US states (in the north-east in particular) is the ability to meet simultaneous peak demands on the electricity and natural gas systems. In some states, peak demand for both systems tends to occur on the coldest days of the year. These are the times that are most expensive to serve, because of scarce commodity supplies and because it is expensive to size delivery networks to meet demands that occur infrequently. Backstop measures may include that new generators demonstrate sufficient pipeline or storage capacity to meet their peak needs, or allow generators to switch to distillates for a certain number of days per year. This may in turn have potential consequences for users of diesel and home heating oil, due to the size of power plants' demand. Burning distillate also results in significantly greater CO_2 emissions. Policy-makers need to monitor these developments and the costs and risks of each of these strategies. Coinciding peak demands for natural gas and electricity mean that extreme price events are likely to affect both markets simultaneously. This bears a number of implications for regional electricity and natural gas utility systems and for industrial customers purchasing their supplies directly.

There is also a possible impact on storage. Storage facilities are normally refilled in summer time when gas prices are lower. As demand for natural gas for electricity increases, there may be less gas available during off-peak periods for injection into storage facilities, and the gas that is available may be more costly. Peak electricity demand in the US occurs in summer.

If natural gas prices become more sensitive to the price of electricity, this may mean that natural gas will no longer be significantly cheaper during the summer months. The risk management strategies historically used by local gas distribution utilities may need to be revised in order to minimise the costs of gas service to traditional core-market customers as gas-fired electricity generation is added to regional natural gas demand. >

< Much of the power capacity built over the last few years paid limited attention to location or where a plant was situated in the transmission grid. As a result, many CCGTs were located close to the fuel source, i.e., the gas pipeline, but far from demand for power load, where congestion can limit unit dispatchability. This may have been a contributing factor to the power blackouts of 14 August 2003. 7

With the rapid growth of gas-fired generation over the past few years, volatility in the electricity market is having a greater influence on natural gas price volatility (and vice versa). When extreme cold or warm air moves into a region, demand for electric power can quickly escalate to meet the increased requirement for heat or air conditioning. In such circumstances, gas-fired "peaking units" will come on line to supplement the base load generation. Prices for this peaking generation will often be much higher than the prevailing price before the change in weather. Gas required for peaking generation is typically obtained from spot-market sales; hence, the price paid for gas by peaking generators will frequently follow the volatile electricity prices. Figure 6.13 shows the parallel and seasonal evolution of gas and electricity prices to US residential customers since the beginning of 2001.

Reliability and security may be improved by fuel diversity and dual-fuel capacity and the actual possibility to switch to oil products. A current key uncertainty is the actual level of multi-fuel switching capacity that exists on the US market.

A study[68] of the capability of electric generators to respond to high gas prices by switching to petroleum when market conditions dictate, found that about 29 GW of electricity-generating capacity actually switched between gas and petroleum during winter 2000/2001 when the level of

---

68 EMF (2003a).

Figure 6.13. US gas and electricity prices to residential customers

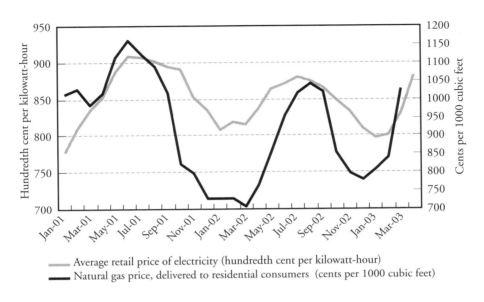

Average retail price of electricity (hundredth cent per kilowatt-hour)
Natural gas price, delivered to residential consumers (cents per 1000 cubic feet)

Source: EIA

gas prices dictated that all generators able to switch effectively switched. Approximately 40% of this capacity fired residual fuel oil/natural gas (old steam plants) with the remainder firing distillate/natural gas. This generating capacity when firing natural gas consumed on average 2.7 bcf/d (28 bcm/a). In addition, another 4 GW of capacity appears to switch seasonally between petroleum and gas. This seasonal switching occurs independently of price signals. Moreover, a segment of the electricity generation capacity exhibits indirect seasonal switching, which is defined as turning down one unit and replacing its generation with that from another unit. This segment switches away from natural gas to either coal, nuclear, or hydropower during the winter season. Indirect switching appears driven by the availability of low variable cost power production. The extent of this switching is significant: in the range of 20-60 GW of capacity. This indirect switching may have a larger impact on natural gas price volatility than direct switching between petroleum/natural gas.

The direct and indirect fuel-switching capability by generators, as well as fuel-switching capability by industrial consumers, seems to be largely sufficient to cover by market reaction a possible disruption in LNG supplies.

Conclusions on security of gas supply

If security of gas supply is defined as the possibility to bring supply and demand into balance at any time by the price mechanism, the US/North American gas industry does not currently have significant problems. Due to the large resource base and the possibility of a large, well-interconnected marketplace to react in the short term and long term to changing supply/demand conditions, it can be expected that prices will be able to balance supply and demand in North America, both in the short and the long term. In particular, it can be expected that the capacity of the US/North American market will be sufficient to meet the demand of sectors with inelastic demand.

However, the market outcome may not be satisfactory, due to high prices and high price volatility and their impact on gas-intensive industry and household customers' bills. Demand destruction (e.g., the relocation of gas-intensive industries to countries with low-cost gas resources) may be an unwelcome market outcome.

The North American market is at a turning point, from a self-sufficient market to a partly import-dependent market. Under this new environment, access to secure and diversified long-term supply both from domestic and external sources is essential for future security of gas supply. LNG can play an important role, bringing access to world gas resources and the ability to react quickly to changing market conditions. The Bush Administration supports development of oil and gas resources in areas that now are legally proscribed from exploration and development. Opposition in the Congress thus far has prevented such development. The US Federal Energy Regulatory Commission is moving on the regulatory side to facilitate the building of new LNG receiving terminals by removing regulatory and local barriers.

Demand-side response will also be an important component of future security of supply, which will allow curving peak gas demand and alleviating tight gas supply situations. Increasing fuel-switching capacity in power and industrial sectors in particular will serve to buffer short-term pressures on the supply/demand balance.

As the supply structure is changing, new investment will be needed in transportation and storage infrastructure to meet the future needs of the market. The possibility of relying on long-term contracts and the allowance of appropriate rates of return are two essential instruments to foster the building of new pipelines and storage.

Changing prices are a fact of life in commodity markets. However, the sustained high level of prices and its impact on the US economy and gas customers have opened a debate on how (and whether) policy-makers should intervene to prevent tight supply situations evolving further. Government measures are focusing on emergency plans and careful monitoring of the current situation. At state level, state commissions may oblige utilities to mitigate or hedge the exposure of small customers to the high volatility of spot markets.

7

SECURITY OF GAS SUPPLY IN OECD EUROPE [69]

The OECD European gas market is undergoing substantial changes. These changes are driven by major trends: the increase in the use of gas for power generation driven both by market reform and concerns about GHG emissions; the Gas Directive 2003/55/EC accelerating market opening and the unbundling of functions; new actors on the demand side; increasing imports from and through non-OECD countries; and the shift in the EU eastern border. Profound changes are taking place in the political structure of Europe with the enlargement from 15 to 25 member countries in May 2004 and discussions for further enlargement to the south east.

This Chapter reviews the impact of supply/demand trends and the effects that the increasing dependence on external suppliers might have on security of supply in OECD Europe. It also addresses the impact of market reforms on security, with a particular focus on the new challenges for security of supply coming from the transition from *de facto* monopolies to more competitive markets. In view of the importance for OECD Europe of gas imports from Algeria and Russia, a description of the present status and perspectives of gas exports from Algeria and Russia to OECD Europe, is given in Appendices at the end of the Chapter.

MARKET OVERVIEW

With 491 bcm of gas consumption in 2002, OECD Europe is the third largest regional gas market after North America and the Former Soviet Union. European gas demand grew at an average rate of 3.7% per year from 1973 to 2000. The residential sector is the single largest consuming sector, followed by the industrial, electricity and commercial sectors.

---

69 This Chapter reviews security of supply issues in OECD Europe. The Term "Europe" is used in the sense of OECD Europe. As major differences exist between the UK gas market and the rest of Europe, the UK market is reviewed in a separate Chapter. However, data and outlook included in this Chapter concern all countries in OECD Europe, including the UK. Comments on security of gas supply apply to continental Europe.

The use of gas in power generation is growing rapidly, especially in Italy, Spain, Turkey and the United Kingdom. Gas represented 17% of electricity generation in 2002. The largest gas markets are the UK, Germany, Italy, the Netherlands and France. Together, they accounted for three-quarters of OECD European gas consumption in 2002. Gas represented 23% of OECD European energy mix in 2002, compared to just 10% in 1973.

Figure 7.1. OECD European energy mix

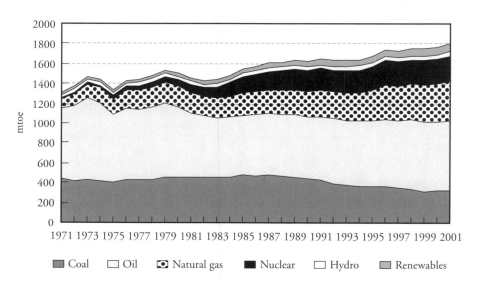

Source: IEA

Although indigenous production, concentrated in the UK, Norway and the Netherlands, has grown in recent years, it has not been fast enough to keep pace with demand. Imports from external suppliers have therefore increased, and now account for 37% of total European gas needs, compared to only 17% in 1980. Inside the region, Norway and the Netherlands provide the bulk of internal trade.

Russia is the largest external supplier to Europe, providing 110 bcm or just under two-thirds of total OECD European imports from external suppliers in 2002, and a quarter of total supply – entirely by pipeline.

Figure 7.2. OECD European gas consumption by sector, 2001

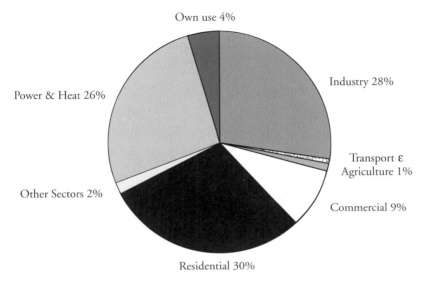

Own use 4%

Industry 28%

Power & Heat 26%

Transport ε
Agriculture 1%

Other Sectors 2%

Commercial 9%

Residential 30%

Source: IEA

Figure 7.3. OECD European natural gas production and net imports

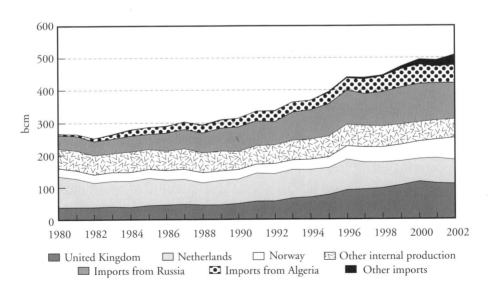

Source: IEA

Algeria, with 55 bcm, is the next biggest exporter of gas to OECD Europe, both via pipeline and as LNG. Imports of LNG play a small, but increasing role in Europe. 42 bcm were imported in 2002 (8.6% of total consumption). In addition to LNG from Algeria, Europe has been importing LNG from Nigeria since 1999, from Trinidad and Tobago since 2000, small volumes of LNG from Libya since the early 1970s and spot cargoes from the Middle East in recent years.

There is a marked difference between the supply situation in continental Europe, a large importer of gas from outside the region, and the UK, which so far has been self-sufficient.

European demand is very seasonal because consumption by the residential-commercial sector is dictated by outside temperatures. Power demand is also stronger in winter than in summer, thus amplifying the considerable seasonal swings.

GAS MARKET REFORMS

Reforms of the EU gas sector have progressed since the adoption of the Directive 98/30/EC in 1998 and its Amendment in 2003 (Directive 2003/55/EC). The main objectives are to bring choice to consumers and to promote competition and efficiency in the EU gas market.

In the first Directive, this was to be achieved via four main instruments:

- Accounting transparency of natural gas undertakings (Articles 12 and 13);

- Rights of access to gas networks on the part of third party operators (Articles 14,15, 16 and 17) on a negotiated or regulated basis;

- The legal right to TPA for "eligible" customers entering into contractual agreements with gas undertakings of their choice (Articles 18 and 19), and

- Objective, transparent and non-discriminatory criteria for the issue of authorisations for the activities of gas undertakings, including the construction of new pipelines.

The first Directive did not create a single European gas market, but rather 15 markets open to competition at different levels. By 2003, the degree of market opening in the different countries ranged from 28% to 100%. Even when open at 100%, there is a great discrepancy between theoretical and actual opening to competition among EU countries.

Table 7.1. Opening of the EU gas markets, 2003

Country	Declared market opening (% of total)	Large eligible customers switch (%, 1998-2001)	Unbundling transmission	Network access
Austria	100%	<2	Legal	Regulated
Belgium	67%	Unknown*	Legal	Regulated
Denmark	35%	2-5	Legal	Regulated
Finland	Exemption	-	-	-
France	28%	20-30	Accounting	Regulated
Germany	100%	<5	Accounting	Negotiated
Greece	Exemption	-	-	-
Ireland	85-88%	20-30	Management	Regulated
Italy	100%	10-20	Legal	Regulated
Luxembourg	72%	5-10	Accounting	Regulated
Netherlands	60%	30-50	Management	Hybrid
Portugal	Exemption	-	-	-
Spain	100%	20-30	Ownership	Regulated
Sweden	47%	<2	Accounting	Regulated
United Kingdom	100%	>50	Ownership	Regulated

* 1.6% of total gas consumption in 2002 (CREG annual report)
Source: European Commission, Government submissions.

The second Gas Directive (Directive 2003/55/EC) was approved in June 2003. Member States have one year, until July 2004, to transpose it into their national laws. The Directive includes quantitative proposals regarding progressively allowing all gas consumers to choose their supplier and qualitative issues designed to improve structural aspects of Community market and ensure equivalent access to the market throughout the European Union. It provides for a speeding-up of gas market opening, establishes provisions on the unbundling of transmission and distribution operators, public service obligations, regulatory tasks and third-party access to storage. The timetable for market opening follows a two-step approach, with deadlines on 1 July 2004 for non-household users and 1 July 2007 for household users. This process will take account of a report assessing the impact of liberalisation to be presented by the Commission in 2006. This means that from July 2004 the EU natural gas market will be fully opened to 530,000 industrial sites compared to the current 650 sites.

STRUCTURE OF THE GAS INDUSTRY

The European gas market was mainly organised around a very limited number of producer-exporter companies, usually with substantial state ownership and a limited number of importing companies based on exclusive concessions in their national markets. This institutional architecture allowed the development of stable and mature gas supply systems. Relations between producers and consumers were structured by long-term contracts of 20-25 years, allowing the risks to be shared between the two parties. In most countries, distribution was developed by regional and local authorities in the form of local distribution monopolies. But some countries, notably France and Spain, chose to integrate distribution with gas transport monopolies.

This structure is undergoing fundamental changes due to market reforms. The Directive 2003/55/EC involves a major structural re-organisation of the EU gas market, with the provisions on legal unbundling. This requirement is already translated in some countries which have legally separated their supply and transportation activities (see Table 7.1). In some cases, the separation includes ownership separation.

The European gas market nevertheless remains characterised by a small number of large gas companies, most of them with the state as a major shareholder, and with strong positions in their home market. Upstream, few producers inside and outside OECD Europe have a large market share (10 producers total 84% of European supplies, Gazprom alone accounts for 25%). Downstream, the concentration of the wholesale European market is very high. The first seven players account for 61% of European gas sales.

Figure 7.4. Downstream: major wholesale players in Europe, 2002
(Gas sales by major European companies)

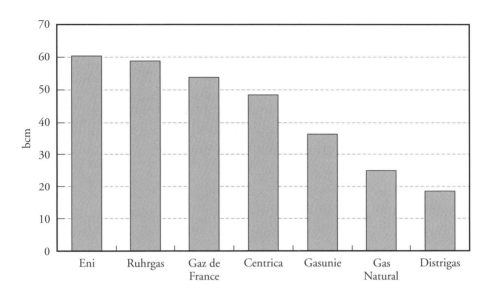

Source: Annual reports of companies

FRAMEWORK FOR SECURITY OF GAS SUPPLY

In the past, many governments delegated responsibility for security of supply to one single actor, either a monopoly (*de facto* or real) state-owned gas company, or a private company based on exclusive concession rights. In exchange, this entity would take responsibility for security of supply for the whole gas market. These companies successfully addressed issues of short- and long-term adequacy of supply, and adequacy of infrastructure for both normal and peak consumption rates. They also created assets designed to meet low-probability events, with low-capacity utilisation and passed on the costs to the final consumer.

Most OECD continental European countries are now moving from this traditional framework – which has successfully operated for 40 years without any major supply interruption, but with costs passed on to all customers – to a system where the instruments to provide security of gas supply are contracted with individual customers. Companies will not contract gas and build infrastructures above what is paid for by their customers. A new framework is currently being implemented in most continental European countries since gas market reforms are relatively new and are part of an ongoing process (see Part C, Annex 1).

The new framework for security of supply set up by the Directive 2003/55/EC

The Directive 2003/55/EC contains three major provisions related to security of supply: monitoring of security of supply, Public Service Obligations (PSO) and exemption from third-party access of major new gas infrastructures.

Monitoring of security of supply

According to Article 5, member states shall ensure the monitoring of security of supply issues. They may delegate this task to the regulatory authorities if deemed appropriate. This monitoring shall in particular cover the supply/demand balance on the national market, the level of expected future demand and available supplies, envisaged additional capacity being planned or under construction, and the quality and level of maintenance of the networks, as well as measures to cover peak demand and to deal with shortfalls of one or more suppliers. The competent authorities shall publish an annual report by 31 July including planned measures to guarantee security of supply.

Public Service Obligations

Article 3 relates to Public Service Obligations (PSO) and customer protection. In particular, member states may impose PSO which may relate to security of gas supply. These obligations shall be clearly defined, transparent, non-discriminatory, and verifiable, and shall guarantee quality of access for EU companies to national customers. Member states may introduce the implementation of long-term planning, and appoint a supplier of last resort for customers connected to the gas network.

They will also be responsible for implementing appropriate measures to achieve the objectives of social and economic cohesion, environmental protection (which may include means to combat climate change), and security of supply. Such measures should cover, in particular, the provision of adequate economic incentives, using, where appropriate, all existing national and Community tools, for the maintenance and construction of necessary network infrastructure, including interconnection capacity.

Article 26 regards safeguard measures. Although it does not define crisis as such, in the event of any sudden crisis in the energy market it allows member states to temporarily take the necessary safeguard measures and notify these measures to other member states and to the Commission.

Exemption from third-party access of major new gas infrastructures

Article 22 foresees possible exemptions from TPA for new major gas infrastructures, such as interconnectors between member states, LNG, and storage facilities. In particular, exemption may be granted when the investment enhances security of supply or where the level of risk attached to the investment is such that the investment would not take place unless an exemption was granted. These exemptions may also apply to significant increases of capacity in existing infrastructures and to modifications of such infrastructures which enable the development of new sources of supply.

New proposed Directive on security of gas supply

In addition to the new Gas Directive, the European Commission is considering a Directive to enhance natural gas supply security. The EC initiated the proposed Directive in September 2002 (COM(2002)488). The European Parliament revised the proposed Directive substantially during its first reading in September 2003. Energy Ministers unanimously approved the revised draft on 5 December 2003. Compared to the proposal by the Commission, the European Parliament revised draft switches responsibility to governments and lightens the Commission's role.

The proposed Directive establishes measures to ensure an adequate level for the security of gas supply. It sets a common framework for member states to define general, transparent and non-discriminatory security of supply policies compatible with the requirements of a competitive internal European market for gas; clarify the roles and responsibilities of the different market actors and implement specific non-discriminatory procedures to safeguard security of gas supply (Article 1).

According to Article 3, member states have to specify the minimum security of supply standards that must be complied with by the actors on the gas market of the member states in question. To that end, a combination of the following indicative instruments may be used: working gas in storage capacity; withdrawal capacity in gas storage; provision of pipeline capacity enabling diversion of gas supplies to affected areas; liquid tradable gas markets; system flexibility; development of interruptible demand; use of alternative back-up fuels in industrial and power generation plants; cross-border capacities; cooperation between transmission system operators of neighbouring member states for coordinated dispatching; coordinated dispatching activities between distribution and transmission system operators; domestic production of gas; production flexibility; import flexibility; diversification of sources of gas supply; long-term contracts; investments in infrastructure for gas imports via regasification terminals and pipelines. Member states are required to notify the Commission of the measures taken (Article 5).

Article 4 deals with the protection of specific customers and specifies that supplies for household customers inside their respective territory must be protected to an appropriate extent in some specific defined events (extreme weather conditions or partial gas disruption). Article 4 also allows member states to set or require the industry to set national indicative targets for a future contribution of storage, either located within or outside the territory of the member state, to security of supply. These targets must be published. No investment obligations would result from this provision, however.

Article 4 also states that if an adequate level of interconnection is available, member states may take the appropriate measures in cooperation with another member state, including via specific bilateral agreements, to achieve the security of supply standards using gas storage facilities located within that other member state.

The proposed Directive also includes the establishment of a *Gas Coordination Group* in order to facilitate the coordination of security of supply measures, in particular if an event occurs that is likely to develop into a major supply disruption for a significant period of time (Articles 7 and 9). A major supply disruption shall mean a situation where the Community would risk losing more than 20% of its gas supply from third countries for at least eight weeks and the situation at Community level is not likely to be adequately managed with national measures (Article 2 and preamble).

At the beginning of January 2004, the Energy Working Party fine-tuned the preamble to the proposal agreed by the Energy Ministers in December 2003. The preamble defines the length of a major supply interruption as one lasting at least eight weeks, suggests bilateral agreements between member states and assures that gas storage targets to be set by governments or industry would not create investment obligations. It also states that new market entrants and small players must not be loaded with disproportionate burdens of supply obligations.

The European Parliament will now be consulted on the changes.

Strategic storage

At present, there is a debate within the EU on whether or not countries should hold strategic gas stocks to respond to gas supply disruptions as they are already holding oil stocks for this purpose. IEA member countries are required to hold oil stocks equivalent to 90 days of the daily average of the previous year's net imports as the principal measure to respond to a severe oil crisis. EU member states have an obligation to hold oil stocks equivalent to 90 days of average daily consumption of the previous year. While a coordinated stock draw of emergency reserves was only implemented during the Gulf war in 1991, stocks have proven to be a valuable insurance policy, calming the reactions of market players when any shortfall occurs or is perceived to be about to happen. With the increasing use of natural gas as a share of energy, concerns about the negative effects of a severe shortage of gas have been raised.

IEA emergency oil stocks were developed in the wake of the severe supply disruption of 1973. Moreover, this disruption was a targeted boycott by OPEC countries against some consumer countries, notably, the United States and the Netherlands. So far gas has not been used as a political instrument against OECD countries, but there are increasing concerns about supply disruptions caused by technical or political events beyond the control of exporters, such as terrorist attacks against gas infrastructures as happened in Arun, Indonesia.

Markets are not always able to effectively handle such unpredictable but potentially damaging events. Therefore governments – as in the case of oil disruptions – see the need to protect their economies from such events and look to defining objectives and establishing measures to deal with such events. This requires governments to evaluate the degree of risk and economic damage vs. the overall costs to assuage the potential impact.

In the case of oil, IEA member countries have agreed on measures and procedures to assure decision-making and, when necessary, take action. The measures include demand restraint, fuel-switching out of oil, surge production in IEA oil producing countries, emergency reserve drawdown and, in extreme cases, allocation of oil amongst member governments. As studies have shown, there is now very little surge production capacity in IEA countries. With the increasing concentration of oil in the transportation sector, demand restraint is limited to this sector. For these reasons, the release of strategic oil stocks is recognised as the most rapid and effective response to mitigate the negative effects of supply disruptions. Furthermore, in a global oil market any stock release will have a global effect, which suggests an internationally coordinated approach to stock release. For oil, holding a minimum of strategic stocks, whether held by government or industry or a combination of both, seems to be the appropriate instrument to handle oil supply disruptions.

However, gas markets differ considerably from the oil market. While there is a large spot market for oil and oil products, exported gas is predominantly sold under bilateral commercial contracts. Any deliberate curtailment of gas supply would therefore be a breach of contract which would undermine the standing of the gas exporter. The exporter curtailing deliveries would suffer an immediate income loss, without any hope of being compensated by a higher price.

Also, natural gas in the energy mix varies substantially between IEA member countries. Indeed, some regions, such as North America and Australia, are self sufficient. Europe has some self sufficiency with the Netherlands,

Norway, Denmark and the United Kingdom as net exporters, while Japan and Korea are almost totally dependent on imports. At this time, there is still no real global market for gas, so the impacts of a disruption would only spread across a region, or, more likely, be contained within one country.

In countries where natural gas is used for heating, there are very large seasonal variations in demand (i.e., by a 3 or 4-fold increase in a winter month as compared to a summer month). Thus, the impact of a supply disruption for gas depends to a great extent on the season and on winter temperatures.

Depending on the share of gas in the energy mix, on whether there are issues of seasonality, and on import dependence, the impact of any gas supply disruption may or may not be compensated by *ad hoc* market reactions. In addition, response measures available to IEA member countries to cope with a potential gas supply disruption vary widely between them. They may comprise: *i)* a country's own spare production capacity, *ii)* spare import capacity from IEA countries and non disrupted non-IEA countries, *iii)* substantial demand-side reaction, e.g., in the industrial and power sector by fuel switching or switching input into the electric grid, or iv) more generally by a demand-side reaction on a deep and liquid marketplace for gas, or specific flexible instruments such as storage.

Due to its low energy density, strategic stocks of gas are much more expensive to hold than oil stocks. Gas storage is on the order of ten times more costly than oil per energy unit. Although LNG tanks can, in principle, be built everywhere, they are not only very expensive, but their unit capacity is only 100-200 thousand cm of LNG corresponding to 60-120 million cm of natural gas, just enough to cover a supply disruption of a few days. Natural gas in quantities adequate to respond to longer-term supply disruptions can only be stored in geological sites, like in salt domes, aquifers or depleted gas fields, whose feasibility obviously depends on individual country geology. Countries with no gas production seldom have the potential for geological storage sites.

Again, specific gas transportation costs are ten times higher than those for oil. The fact that gas transportation is pipeline-bound implies either restrictions on the use of strategic storage or potentially very high costs to bring the gas quickly from strategic storage to the place of consumption.

In cases where strategic storage is located along the supply chain of the supply source which is interrupted, then no extra transport capacity is needed. As spare transportation capacity cannot be guaranteed in the case of a disruption during an extreme winter peak when pipelines are being used at full capacity, substantial spare transport capacity is needed to make sure the gas from a stock release can always be delivered to the place of demand in case of a disruption.

While some of the arguments to ensure security of gas supply are similar to oil, the arguments for establishing stocks and a coordinated stock draw do not apply to gas. Strategic gas storage is much more expensive than oil storage and requires additional substantial investment into a spare transport infrastructure just in case of a disruption, giving a strong incentive to minimise the size of any strategic storage. Other instruments like interruptible contracts or fuel-switching may be less expensive instruments than strategic gas storage, if storage is possible at all. As the market is not yet global and disruptions only have a local impact, a global response is not possible.

Given that the impact of a disruption of gas supply varies strongly from country to country, a uniform response by all countries does not fit either. The design of a response is therefore best left to individual countries and their market players. Finally, where there is no deep and liquid marketplace for gas, a government-managed draw on strategic gas storage will necessarily have an interventionist character.

The preceding discussion is reflected in the draft Directive on security of gas supply promoted by the European Commission. The latest draft focuses on asking EU member states to set objectives for security of gas supply within some minimum standards, but leaving it to individual member governments to define what instruments should be applied and by whom. So while governments are defining the objectives to be covered by market players (for instance, covering the disruption of the largest external supplier for a defined timeframe), the means/instruments to be developed to achieve these minimum standards should be left to market players themselves. And finally, there is a clear recognition within the EU that the gas industry in the individual countries has so far been in a position to handle adequately any conceivable supply disruption.

GAS SUPPLY AND DEMAND TRENDS

Gas supply trends

European reserves/resources

OECD Europe's 7.1 tcm of proven gas reserves at the beginning of 2003 represents 4% of the world total (Cedigaz). About 90% of the region's reserves are in Norway, the Netherlands and the United Kingdom. For several years, the reserves-to-production ratio has been stable at about 20 years, despite rising production in the North Sea. Major reserves have been added mainly by new finds in the North Sea and Norwegian Sea and by higher recovery rates in existing fields, due to techniques to improve recovery, mainly horizontal drilling. However, the North Sea area is considered a mature area. Gas resources were estimated at 13,485 bcm in 2003 by the International Association of Oil & Gas Producers (see Part C, Annex 5).

Figure 7.5. Remaining proven natural gas reserves in OECD Europe at the beginning of 2003

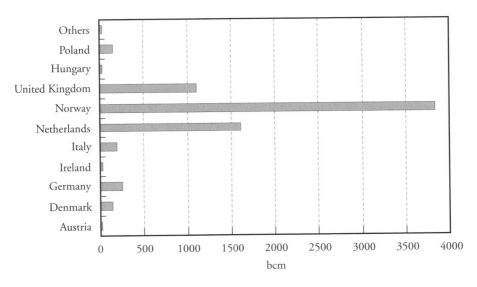

Source: Cedigaz

Production

OECD European gas production amounted to 311 bcm in 2002. Although indigenous production, concentrated in the United Kingdom, Norway and the Netherlands, has grown in recent years, output from the North Sea, which is a mature producing region, will dwindle over the coming decades. Only Norway is expected to increase its production. As OECD European gas demand is expected to grow considerably, increased imports from outside the region will therefore be needed to compensate for the decline in domestic production.

In most countries, production is flat over the year. However, this is not the case in the Netherlands (and to a certain extent the UK) where the Groningen field has a high production swing. The field is able to vary its production, and the short distance to its main customers in North West Europe allows it to serve as swing producer to them.

Figure 7.6. OECD European monthly gas production, 1995-2003

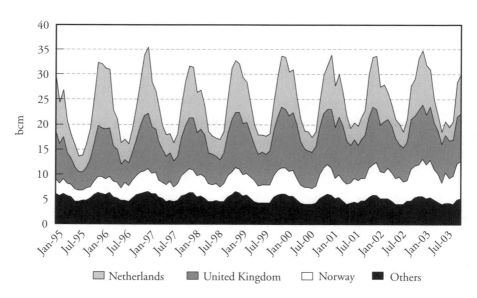

Source: IEA

OECD Europe includes four net gas exporters – the Netherlands, Norway, Denmark and (since 1997) the United Kingdom. Norway exports most of its volumes of gas to the Continent and small volumes to the United Kingdom. The Netherlands export half of their gas production to other European countries. The United Kingdom is still a net exporter through the Interconnector, but this situation is expected to reverse soon. Denmark is a small exporter to Germany and Sweden. The other OECD European countries depend heavily on gas imports from a limited number of producing countries, in several of which exports are exclusively handled by state monopolies.

Gas production in OECD Europe is expected to remain stable at approximately 300 bcm/a until 2020 and then decrease slightly to 276 bcm in 2030. The decline in UK production would be compensated by an increase in Norwegian production. Production could turn out to be higher depending on technological and price developments. Nevertheless, given the limited gas resources in most OECD European countries and the prospect of rising demand, imports from Norway and imports from outside the region are expected to continue to increase for the next two decades.

Gas demand trends

Gas consumption in OECD Europe reached 491 bcm in 2002, i.e., 23% of the energy mix. Over the last 30 years, OECD European gas consumption has quadrupled, and is predicted to continue to grow at a faster pace than any other fuel, at an average rate of 2.1% per year between 2000 and 2030, resulting in 87% growth to 901 bcm by 2030. Gas would then become Europe's second fuel after oil, with 33% of total primary energy supply in 2030.

Gas use is increasing in power generation and in all end-user sectors. A limited increase of 55 mtoe, or 66 bcm (+1% per year) is expected over the period 2000-2030 in the residential and commercial sectors, while consumption by industry is expected to increase on average by 0.8% per year during the period. The bulk of the increase in OECD European gas demand (72%) by 2030 is expected in the power generation sector, where gas will take up the predominant share in market growth. This is explained by the advantages of gas in combined cycle power plants: low capital costs, high performance, cleanliness of gas compared to other fossil fuels, modularity of construction and alternative use for gas, which make gas more compatible with expected environmental requirements and open markets. By 2030, the share of gas in the OECD European electricity mix is expected to reach 33% compared with 22% in 2000.

Figure 7.7. OECD European gas demand, 1971-2030

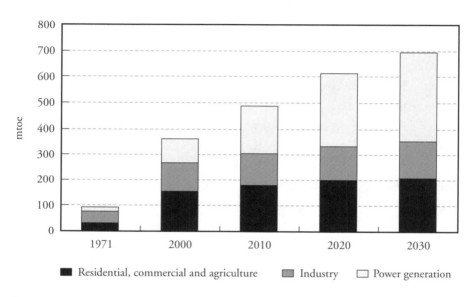

Source: *WEO 2002*

In the past decade, the increased use of gas in the OECD European power sector, from 47 bcm in 1990 to 121 bcm in 2001, was led by the "dash for gas" in the UK, where the share of gas in the electricity mix went from 2% in 1990 to 39% in 2002. In the UK, domestic gas has so far been used to fuel this increasing demand. Moreover, since gas prices at the beginning of the 1990s were low enough and electricity prices in the pool high enough to make new CCGTs commercially viable for base-load generation, gas soon displaced coal for base-load. This was a rather exceptional situation. In the rest of Europe, imported gas has to compete with nuclear, hydro and coal. The question arises as to whether importing countries are going to use gas extensively to generate electricity. So far, this seems to be limited to Italy, Ireland and Turkey, and emerging in Spain, none of which have any substantial domestic alternative and no nuclear power.

The reference scenario of *WEO 2002* projects a substantial increase of gas use in power generation in EU 15: 72% of additional gas consumption over the period 2000-2030 is used in power generation and 91% of additional power generation is based on gas. In the Alternative Scenario, which assumes a more stringent policy on energy saving and CO_2 emission reduction, the European energy demand is projected to increase at a lower rate and natural gas contributes to most of the reduction, around 100 mtoe (for EU 15) in 2030, with 87 mtoe savings in the power generation sector.

Nevertheless, both scenarios predict a large increase in gas to power. This trend raises two security issues (see Chapter 3). The first is that most gas used to produce electricity in Europe will be imported gas. OECD Europe will increase its imports by 399 mtoe between 2000 and 2030, and 243 mtoe will be consumed by the power sector. This situation is relatively new, as until now the extensive use of gas in the power sector has been limited to countries with gas reserves and based on domestic production.

The second issue is that as more electricity is produced from gas, security of gas supply will impact security of electricity supply. The parallel opening to competition of gas and electricity markets, combined with the increasing use of gas in the power sector, adds a further challenge to security of supply. Security of gas supply and security of electricity supply will become intertwined. Peak demand in both gas and electricity sectors may coincide, creating further stress on both systems, especially where both sectors are opened and arbitrage possibilities have developed.

Matching gas supply and demand

In the future, OECD Europe is going to rely increasingly on gas imports. Net gas imports are projected to rise from 198 bcm in 2002 to 625 bcm in 2030. Their share of total primary gas supply will increase from 37% to 69%. OECD Europe is geographically close to Russia's huge gas reserves, while those from the Middle East/North Africa, Latin America and West Africa are accessible via LNG tankers.

The bulk of OECD European imports are expected to come from its two main current suppliers, Russia and Algeria. Russia is projected to remain the largest single supplier in 2030, exporting about 200 bcm to OECD Europe. North and West Africa will also increase their exports to Europe (Algeria, Libya, mostly by pipeline, Egypt and Nigeria by LNG tankers). But the biggest increase in supplies is projected to be from the Middle East, mostly in the form of LNG, but also by pipeline from Iran and possibly Iraq towards the end of the projection period. Pipelines from Iraq, Iran and the Caspian region could play an increasingly important role in the longer term. Venezuela may also emerge in the longer term as a bulk supplier of LNG.

As both Norwegian and Algerian reserves are constrained, by 2020/2030, most of the incremental gas supply would have to come by pipeline from transition economies (mostly Russia and the Caspian Sea) and in the form of LNG from the Middle East, West Africa and Latin America (Figure 7.8). By that time, European supplies will be dominated by Russian/ FSU gas supplies and LNG imported from countries with an Atlantic coast or in the Mediterranean area.

Figure 7.8. OECD European gas balance, 1990-2030

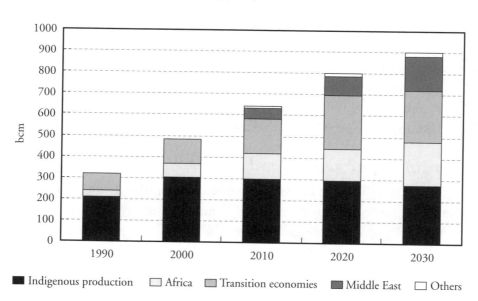

Source: *WEO 2002*

There is undoubtedly enough gas in these countries to meet OECD Europe's gas needs until 2030. But the unit costs of getting that gas to market is expected to rise as more remote and costly sources are tapped. Piped gas from North Africa and the Nadym-Pur-Taz region in Russia are the lowest cost options[70], but supplies from these sources will not be sufficient to meet projected demand after 2010. Pipeline projects based on fields in the Yamal Peninsula and the Shtokmanov field in the Barents Sea in Russia are among the most expensive longer-term options. So are pipelines from the Middle East and the Caspian region.

LNG, traded both under long-term contracts and on spot markets, could play a much more important role in supplying the European gas market if supply costs continue to fall. LNG would become especially important if Russian gas sector reforms lag and investment in Russian fields falls short of expectations. This could happen, if investment in new Russian fields is insufficient to compensate for the decline in production from existing fields. In any event, the distances over which LNG imports from new sources need to be shipped may well drive costs and prices up.

In practice, supplies are unlikely to be developed in strict cost-order since factors other than cost influence sponsors' choices of upstream projects:

- Political risk is a major consideration for many of the more distant supplies from non-OECD countries, particularly for pipeline gas which has to transit through several non-OECD countries. Country specific risks will add up along the pipeline and will negatively impact on availability and costs of financing;

- Competition for LNG is developing on a global scale. Import projects into the US, are creating increasing competition in the Atlantic basin with LNG projects for OECD Europe. Europe faces also competition from developing countries like China and India, although their impact will be more on the Pacific LNG market and gas imports into these countries will need some time to develop;

- Potential or actual government limitations on the proportion of imports from single suppliers may significantly influence supply patterns. In

---

70 For more details on cost of supply, see: *World Energy Outlook 2001, Insights: Assessing Today's Supplies to Secure Tomorrow's Growth*, http://library.iea.org/dbtw-wpd/bookshop/add.aspx?id=63

Spain, for example, imports from a single country are legally capped at 60% of total imports. This means that LNG is likely to be favoured over increased piped supplies from Algeria, which currently supplies most of Spain's gas;

■   Competition in downstream markets, on the other hand, will increase the emphasis on reducing costs of supply to stay competitive, to the extent that the constraints mentioned above allow;

■   LNG import options are going to compete with traditional pipeline suppliers. The choice between pipeline and LNG options will not be based on cost analysis only. LNG offers advantages in open markets that gas by long distance pipelines cannot challenge. LNG offers more flexibility. The economic optimal size of LNG projects is usually smaller than the economic optimal size of a long-distance pipeline, which facilitates the marketing of gas in smaller markets. There are no problems associated with the transit of gas, and competition between LNG suppliers means that a wide range of supplies is available. On the other hand, in many European markets LNG faces a cost disadvantage in comparison with pipeline gas because of the longer distance from production to market.

The role of LNG in Europe

OECD Europe imported 42 bcm of LNG in 2002. That amount represents 8.6% of European gas consumption. But the share is much higher for some Mediterranean countries. In Spain, for example, LNG accounts for 58% of gas supplies. The major suppliers have been Mediterranean countries: Algeria and, to a lesser extent, Libya. In 1999 and 2000, additional LNG supply started from further afield: Nigeria and Trinidad & Tobago. Middle East producers (Qatar, Oman, Abu Dhabi) are also exporting spot cargoes to Europe, and Qatar has started regular exports to Spain.

Despite strong competition from pipeline suppliers, LNG deliveries to OECD Europe are expected to rise steeply, reaching 107 bcm in 2010 and 241 bcm in 2030 (*WEIO 2003*). LNG makes an important contribution to the volume and diversity of Europe's gas supplies.

New LNG receiving terminals are planned in France, Italy, Spain and the United Kingdom (see Table 7.4). Competition among suppliers is likely to facilitate the development of new LNG projects in Europe. LNG clearly appears the best option for the oil majors to valorise their gas reserves (Shell, BP, Total, ExxonMobil and ENI) by developing integrated projects from field development to regasification plants. Access to regas is key for access to the marketplace as competition between suppliers heats up. Examples of oil majors and exporters investing further downstream into LNG regasification terminals are: BP in Spain (Bilbao); ExxonMobil with Qatar Petroleum in UK (Milford Haven) and in Italy (Rovigo); Sonatrach in Spain (El Ferrol).

The Mediterranean market is currently the fastest growing European market for LNG, which has been favoured by energy policies aimed at diversifying gas supplies, in particular in Spain, or at supplying new regions. Reforms of the gas and power markets in these countries have also favoured LNG. New receiving terminals are being built by new entrants to cater for additional supplies to the market (Spain and Italy). In Portugal, the Sines regasification terminal began operations in October 2003. Although Spain appears to be over-supplied, suppliers to Spain may divert contracted LNG to the Atlantic Coast of the US and swap supplies from Trinidad with the US market. The Southern Europe/Mediterranean market, which was the base of the LNG market in Europe, is now integrated into the Atlantic Basin market.

The UK market appears as the next high-profile target market for LNG suppliers, following developments in the Iberian Peninsula. Although LNG has to compete in a market supplied by domestic gas and lower-cost gas from Norway and the Netherlands, it adds diversification and flexibility to the UK market supply, which are important considerations for the future (see Chapter 8). In the other north-western continental European countries, LNG has to compete with established pipeline supply sources and in many cases is not likely to obtain a diversification premium.

The number of importers – mostly from the Iberian and Italian power industries (Endesa, Iberdrola, Union Fenosa, Enel, Edison) – is growing. Alongside the traditional LNG suppliers to Europe (Algeria, Libya,

Trinidad and Nigeria), new suppliers are developing greenfield projects or additional trains to supply the European market: Egypt, Norway, Qatar and Oman.

SECURITY OF GAS SUPPLY ISSUES

Gas security challenges in the continental OECD European[71] context include: *i)* an *external* dimension linked to increased dependence from external suppliers, i.e., availability of gas from exporting countries and timely investments all along the gas chain in export and transit countries where fiscal, legal and regulatory frameworks have not matured; *ii)* an *internal* dimension linked with market performance, i.e., timely investment all along the gas chain down to the final users, which includes a) the successful development of the internal EU market; b) the successful introduction of competition in each member country.

i) The external dimension of security of gas supply for continental OECD Europe covers:

■ Access to resources from resources-owning countries for export to OECD Europe on competitive conditions;

■ Ensuring timely investment into pipeline and LNG cross-border infrastructure and non-discriminatory access to existing infrastructure;

■ Securing transparent and non-discriminatory transit via pipelines;

■ Making sure a supply shortfall can be bridged by market means.

ii) For the 15 EU member states, and as of 1 May 2004, for the 25 EU member states, the internal dimensions of reliability of supply to the final customer raise the following points, triggered by the EU market reform:

a) Questions of creating a uniform market:

■ Interoperability issues;

■ Creating enough interconnections to trade gas between member countries.

---

71 It should be noted that most of these issues also apply to the UK gas market. However, as the UK market presents some particularities, it is dealt with in a separate Chapter and therefore in this section, we refer to "continental OECD Europe".

b) Issues about the success of market reform in member countries:

- Investment in national pipelines, storage and LNG receiving terminals in a new regulatory environment;

- Dealing with extreme weather conditions/interruption of supply;

- Uncertainty about the full implications of gas market reforms;

- Defining the responsibilities of the different market players;

- Growing use of gas in the energy and electricity mix and link between gas and electricity security.

The external dimension

Availability and access to external gas resources

As seen above, the availability of gas resources is not a problem. Gas reserves accessible to Europe are large enough to meet the growing demand for at least the next three decades. However, most of these reserves are located in non-OECD countries, and often in countries where conditions for facilitating investment, clear governance of the upstream sector, or effective depletion policies may be lacking.

In producing countries with mature provinces where the government depletion policy is defined in pure rent-taking/taxation terms, like the US and UK, price signals on the market will translate into more drilling activity and, with a certain time lag, more national production (although the production response may be limited). In continental OECD Europe, prices may not always translate into new investments in exploration, production and transport capacity in non-OECD supplying countries. A main reason is that the governance regimes for the upstream and export in non-OECD countries do not allow price signals to be transmitted and translated into investment, but also because gas provinces are often dominated by one or several super giant fields, like Hassi R'Mel in Algeria, or the three super giants in Russia which are handled under a depletion policy. In addition, whenever gas crosses a border, rent-sharing becomes an issue, even between OECD countries.

At present, OECD Europe is well supplied by domestic/OECD resources and by non-OECD gas imports under long-term contracts. Exporting countries (predominantly Russia and Algeria) have committed export capacity and a corresponding part of their reserves to long-term contracts, which are subject to international arbitration regarding the fulfilment of obligations. Long-term contracts also include a price mechanism which secures competitiveness of the gas delivered.

The use of gas in the residential/commercial and industrial sectors has reached a certain level of saturation, and growth in those sectors is limited. The main increase in consumption projected for OECD Europe over the next 30 years is in power generation. Figure 7.9 shows that, on balance, the part of demand which is inelastic (i.e., residential and commercial users, small industry and process gas for industry) could entirely be covered by domestic/OECD European supplies. Storage capacity in Europe and other flexibility instruments, as well as diversification of supply sources, ensure that an interruption from non-OECD sources can be bridged by market reaction at least for a defined period of time (see Tables 7.2, 7.5 and 7.7 below). Even in 2030, the coverage of the more inelastic part of demand will still be almost fully covered by OECD European gas production, whereas all of the gas requirements for power production will be based on gas imported from non-OECD countries.[72] The 40% of OECD European gas-based power generation would be based on gas imported from non-OECD countries (this is on average, as situations at country level may vary).

This dependence raises several questions:

- In the first instance, it raises the question of whether gas reserve-owning countries are prepared to monetise their reserves for use in power generation in importing countries. Not all gas resource-owning countries have clearly defined depletion policies or a clear policy regarding domestic use vs. exports. Using gas for domestic power production to export power-intensive products may be an attractive alternative to gas exports;

- Is gas-to-power adding to the security of supply by increasing the elasticity of demand or is it contributing to inelasticity of demand? This depends on dual-firing possibilities and/or the switching of generation units to coal, oil, etc.;

---

72 This is obviously on balance since gas supplies from domestic production/imports are not dedicated to a specific use.

Figure 7.9. OECD European gas demand vs. production/imports, 2000-2030

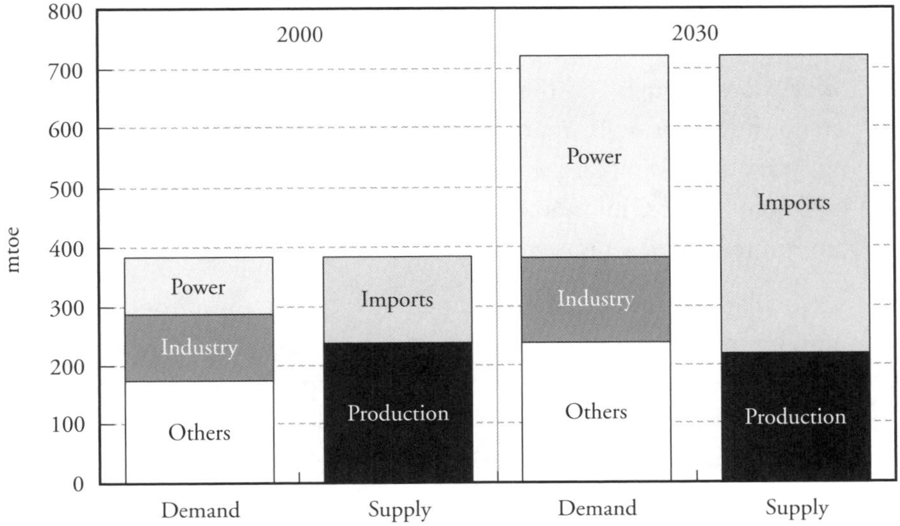

Source: *WEO 2002*

- In general, it raises the issue of how the interface between the gas and power sectors is commercially managed, which is difficult because of the inverse merit order between the long and the short-run marginal costs between coal and gas-fired power (see Chapter 3);

- The need to sell in competition with coal may be in the interest of newcomers to the OECD European gas market like Egypt, Libya (pipeline) and Qatar, given the balance in supply and demand for the years to come. The situation for Algeria, and to an even greater extent for Russia, looks much more complicated. The issue for them is whether they undermine the pricing for their existing contracts by selling into the power market of OECD Europe. While Algeria has only limited potential for domestic use, it can sell LNG to the US. For Russia, selling outside Europe has geographical limits in the near term. In the medium term Russia is looking at markets in the Asia-Pacific region (albeit from different gas provinces in Russia) and into selling as LNG;

- Are the present framework conditions for production and transit to the gas consuming countries in the EU a sufficient basis for private investors to undertake the necessary investment into the gas development and transport infrastructure? Imports from non-OECD into the EU are projected to increase substantially from 150 bcm in 2002 to 525 bcm in 2030. The question for Europe will be whether gas supplies will be diversified enough and the demand side flexible enough to cope with a major interruption by market mechanism. The importance of this issue will vary depending on the specific country. Over time European gas grids will become more integrated, and therefore better equipped to compensate within the EU for supply disruptions from outside the EU;

■ Particularly in European markets, there is need to monitor carefully the implications of uneven pace of reforms of gas markets along the gas chain. As the gas sector moves generally from the public sector to the private sector, different countries overcome the power of their gas monopolies to differing degrees – particularly outside the OECD. Greater convergence of practices toward open and transparent markets is essential to successful reform all along the gas chain.

Investment/transport infrastructure/transit issues

Growing gas imports need to be supported by timely investment in the Middle East, Africa and the CIS. The scale of investment required to meet the projected demand is massive. *WEIO 2003* projects that the total investment necessary to meet growing global gas demand up to 2030 would be $3.1 trillion. Investment needs in Russia, other transition economies, the Middle East and Africa, on which Europe will be increasingly dependent, would be $333 billion, $160 billion, $280 billion and $226 billion respectively.

Investment in production and transport outside of IEA countries will need to increase substantially if more remote and more difficult sources of gas are to be developed. For domestic and foreign investment to be attracted, competitive and predictable legal, fiscal and regulatory terms will be needed to ensure investments are undertaken in a timely and efficient manner.

The sovereign risks of investment are particularly high in politically unstable regions. Returns on investment, therefore, often need to be higher than other industries to compensate for the risk. However, investment returns in the energy sector in recent years have often been below the average for the rest of industry, as well as more volatile. Under such circumstances, mobilising energy investment in a timely fashion will require a very attractive investment climate in gas producing countries, particularly in non-OECD regions. In most of OECD Europe's potential suppliers, large monopoly companies (state-owned or with major state participation) are responsible for gas production and exports. Most projects are likely to be undertaken by Gazprom, Sonatrach or other national/State gas companies, eventually with the participation of major oil companies and that of buyers (for liquefaction, for instance). At the moment, the financing structure of new projects in those countries seems unclear; eventually it would need to be based on the sovereign credit of the country concerned – which is usually exhausted – or alternatively on the income from sales, assured by a credible long-term commitment of a gas buyer, with sound marketing. This is becoming more difficult, given the uncertainties of market reform in the EU itself. Another option would be to base the project on the prospect of selling the gas into a very liquid market with the banks discounting for price risks.

The main precondition for any gas export project remains a high degree of certainty that the gas can be marketed. Financing and risk mitigation are key ingredients to ensure that new supplies will be developed in time. So far, long-term contracts between exporters and importers have been a proven instrument for the development of upstream resources and transportation. They will remain a key element to maintain security of supply and reliability of income in the future. This is now recognised by the European Commission and reflected in the Directive 2003/55/EC and the proposed Directive on security of supply. It is, however, unclear how the concept of replacement value on which long-term contracts are based can be applied to selling gas to the power sector given the substantial difference between short-term and long-term replacement value for gas in power and the possibility of end users to arbitrage on the spot markets. One possibility would be to sell into an open and liquid market, with eventually a long-term contract for transportation/regasification as is the case in US. These conditions are not (yet) fulfilled in Europe. Another way might be vertical integration and risk mitigation, some examples of which are now emerging in Europe.

Joint-ventures/partnerships and integration along the gas chain, at both physical and financial levels, may be a way to ensure the development of new non-OECD resources for power generation. This is part of the corporate strategy of several companies, which seek to diversify their risks and integrate the whole value chain. Some suppliers to OECD Europe are moving downstream: the Algerian company, Sonatrach, for instance, has formed joint venture companies in Spain to market gas. Russian Gazprom is also present in importing countries, through several trading houses created in association with national companies to import and in some cases to market gas. Statoil, which is developing an LNG project at Snøhvit, has bought long-term capacity in the Cove Point LNG terminal in the US. Likewise, some importers are engaged upstream thereby diversifying their risks. Ruhrgas now has 6.5% of Gazprom' shares. Gaz de France is investing upstream in the North Sea. ENI, which has always been a big upstream player, currently has a gas portfolio almost equivalent to its oil assets.

A major issue for OECD Europe is to ensure that producing countries have sufficient incentive to develop and export the resources required for power generation rather than serving their domestic market. Long-term contracts play an important role guaranteeing stable revenue to exporting countries, while committing them to export. However, in the case of Russia, increases in domestic end-user prices may lead to competition between the Russian domestic market and the export market. To date, low revenues from the domestic market – which are even below recovering the costs of additional gas production - discourages major growth in non-Gazprom production. However, the Russian Government envisages increasing the price of gas to more cost reflective levels (outlook for $36/1,000 cm in 2006). In the long run, it is likely that the benefit of selling gas on the Russian market could equal or exceed that of exports to remote markets, consequently providing less incentive to increase exports. Given the high transportation costs for the export of gas and the challenges to attract investment for the substantial and lumpy export pipelines, Russia might prefer to produce final semi-finished products for export. There is nevertheless considerable potential for increasing the efficiency of gas production and consumption in Russia, which would free a substantial amount of gas. In other exporting countries, in particular in the Middle East, the R/P ratio is so high and the domestic market so limited, that this issue is of less relevance.

Investment in cross-border pipeline capacities into Europe

The volume of cross-border pipeline gas trade is set to increase, initially from existing suppliers. New pipeline supplies will come from the Mediterranean region, with direct links that have no transit issues (i.e., the Green Stream pipe from Libya, or the Medgaz and Galsi projects from Algeria direct to Spain and Italy). A major supply risk remains the transit through Ukraine and Belarus (see below). While Russia has sought to avoid transit routes, with the Blue Stream pipeline built to Turkey or the proposed North European Gas Pipeline, such pipelines may create surplus capacity which will ultimately result in higher costs than necessary. Besides transit issues in Ukraine and Belarus, transit through Russia for Turkmen and Kazak gas is another issue. With the expansion of the EU and other international frameworks, e.g., the WTO and the ECT, transit issues can be resolved more easily. A major question remains, if the substantial increase projected for gas demand in power generation, will be realised and if so to which extent it will be covered by LNG or pipeline gas.

Cross-border gas trade becomes increasingly important as gas imports to OECD Europe from external suppliers rise sharply. It is therefore essential that cross-border gas pipelines are built to deliver the required volumes to the market. However, cross-border gas trade carries risks because costs are substantial (billion of dollars) and can only be recouped over the long-term. The greater number of stakeholders, sometimes with conflicting interests, creates additional complexity. Matching long-term supply contracts and long-term transit and transportation contracts is vital to securing both supply and adequate mid-stream investments. A concern for several European countries is the risk of under-investment in interconnectors. This raises the issue of how to mitigate risks in cross-border gas pipelines.

The role of governments is still essential in spite of the growing part played by the private sector. Their major responsibility is to establish a clear, transparent and predictable framework for private (domestic and foreign) investments within their country, and in particular to establish and enhance legal regimes for cross-border gas transportation throughout the wider Europe. They have to harmonise technical regulation. Cross-border trade does not necessarily require identical market opening on each side of the border[73], but policy makers must remain alert to the implications of different practices. Of particular importance is that investors have confidence in the legal/contractual mechanisms to resolve conflicts pertaining to the economic viability of their investments.

The strategic importance of ensuring secure multilateral arrangements for transit and investment (such as the Energy Charter process) will only increase in future years, as OECD Europe's dependence on gas imports from distant production areas continues to grow. Very helpful instruments provided by the Energy Charter Treaty are the provisions of Article 26 for the settlements of disputes between an (energy) investor and a contracting party (i.e., the host Government where the investment is taking place). They provide first for an attempt of an amicable settlement. Failing a settlement within three months, Article 26 allows the investor to bring the dispute up to an international arbitration procedure by his unilateral choice according to either the rules of the International Centre for Settlement of Investment Disputes (ICSID), the United Nations Commission on International Trade Law (UNCITRAL) or the International Chamber of Commerce (ICC) in Stockholm. International arbitration is a strong protection for investors and helps to provide financing for international projects and protects international sales contracts. Given the consequences of a negative arbitration award against a country, which can be enforced under the New York convention of 1958, it is a strong protection against interference into any energy related contract by any host state which is a signatory of the Energy Charter Treaty (see Part C, Annex 5).

Dialogue between producing and consuming countries is also an important vehicle to foster cooperation between exporting and importing countries. Dialogue between the governments of gas producing countries and gas consuming countries, both through bilateral channels and multilateral mechanisms, such as the IEA, the recently-established International Energy

---

73 IEA Cross Border Gas Trade Issues Workshop, 26-27 March 2002, http://www.iea.org/Textbase/work/
   workshopdetail.asp?id=41

Forum, the Energy Charter process, the EU-Russia partnership and the Mediterranean partnership, is therefore more needed than ever.

The TEN European initiative is providing seed money to study further infrastructure development inside the EU and for the supply of the EU. The European Investment Bank (EIB) and the European Bank for Reconstruction and Development (EBRD) could also help to promote and finance gas-supply projects to Europe, although their role so far is limited, except for the involvement of the EIB in the Pedro Duran Farell (Maghreb) pipeline.

Additional cross-border transportation capacity is underway. Natural gas from North Africa will be boosted in the short-to-medium term as a result of Algeria's expansion plans on its existing Enrico Mattei line to Italy and on the Pedro Duran Farell to Spain (from the current 32.8 bcm/a to 43 bcm/a). In addition, two new lines (Medgaz and Galsi) would add a further 16 bcm+/a of capacity. Sonatrach's target is to boost its gas and LNG exports from 60 bcm/a to 85 bcm/a by 2010. Libya is also poised to consolidate its position on the European market with a 570-km pipeline due to start delivery of an 8 bcm/a contract to the Italian market in 2004. Russia aims to reinforce its export network, already designed to transport around 170 bcm/a. Major new Russian pipeline projects include the opening of a new export route, the Northern European Gas Pipeline via the Baltic Sea, and the project to convey gas from the Shtokmanov field in the Barents Sea to Europe (see below). Russia and Ukraine also intend to increase the capacity of the Ukrainian corridor by 29 bcm/a. Connections are also being considered between Iraq and Turkey and between Turkey and the Balkans, representing potential breakthroughs for Middle East and Central Asian gas to Europe. Construction of the South Caucasian pipeline is soon expected to start in Azerbaijian. A completely new supply route from Turkey to Austria Baumgarten and further to Western Europe, which is now being examined as a TEN Project, could bring between 25 and 30 bcm/a additional gas from the Caspian region and the Middle East.

DEPA of Greece and Edison Gas of Italy, with the participation of BOTAS of Turkey agreed to study the feasibility of a Turkey-Greece-Italy route beneath the Adriatic Sea as an extension of the interconnection between Greece and Turkey – with the support of the TEN Program. The planned capacity would initially be 10-12 bcm/a with a possibility to upgrade to 22 bcm/a.

Growing import dependence

Table 7.2 shows import and source dependence in OECD Europe. European countries have very different levels of natural gas import dependence. In 2002, out of the 22 OECD European countries, 12 were dependent on imports for more than 95% of their gas demand, while only four were self sufficient or net exporters.

Import dependence on natural gas is rapidly increasing in OECD Europe. In 2030, 69% of natural gas supply will have to be imported from non-OECD countries compared to 36% in 2000 (net imports). Net imports are projected to surge from 198 bcm in 2002 to almost 625 bcm in 2030. In the European Union (EU 15), net imports of natural gas will expand from 44% in 2002 to 81% of total EU gas supply in 2030. The enlargement of the European Union to twenty-five countries will increase the degree of gas-import dependence as eight of the new accession countries are net gas importers. Reliance on one supplier and a single supply route in most EU accession candidates will exacerbate security of supply risks.

These projected high levels of import dependence will mean that it is important to understand the possible risks to security of supply and whether the market itself is able to manage such risks. There are no criteria applicable across countries and circumstances for determining when a gas import dependence ratio becomes alarmingly high. A country may be comfortable importing 100% of its gas supply if the share of gas in total energy supply is moderate, the share of consumers that can switch to alternative fuels is high, and/or its location and infrastructure allows for imports from multiple sources. Nevertheless, it is important to maintain a portfolio of diversified supplies and diversified routes.

Source dependence

The net gas importers among the OECD European member countries vary considerably not only in terms of import dependence but also in terms of import diversification. Table 7.2 and the graph below show that

European importing countries always seek to diversify their portfolio of suppliers. They also show the diversity of situations inside OECD Europe:

■ Countries, like the Slovak Republic, are highly import-dependent and not diversified (its biggest supplier, Russia, represents almost 100% of total gas supply). In some countries, in particular in central Europe, the options available to reduce this dependence are limited;

■ Some countries, like Italy and Germany, still have significant domestic production (about 20% of their supply) and a diversified portfolio of suppliers;

■ Countries, like France and Belgium, are heavily dependent on diversified external suppliers;

■ Finally, Norway, the Netherlands, and to a lesser extent, the UK, are self-sufficient. The situation in the Netherlands is changing rapidly. Imports represented more than half of gas consumption in 2002, although the country has increased its exports and thus remains a large net exporter.

Figure 7.10. Indicators of import dependence and diversification of sources in OECD Europe, 2002

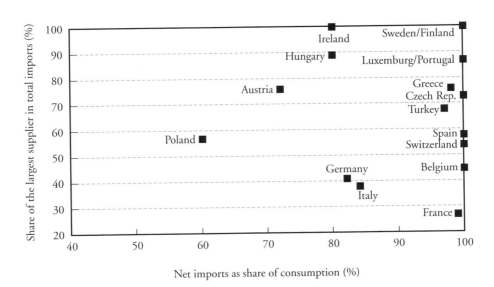

The graph only shows net importers of gas.
Source: IEA

Table 7.2. Natural gas import and source dependence in OECD Europe

Country	Share of gas in energy mix (%)	Gas imports (bcm)	Share of imported gas in total consumption (%)	Share of imported gas from IEA countries in total gas consumption (%)	Share of imported gas from non-IEA countries in total gas consumption (%)	Share of the largest supplying country in total imports (%)	Share of the largest supplying country in total consumption (%)	Number of external supplying countries
Austria	22.4	6.35 (2001)	77	17	60	60 (Russia)	60	3
Belgium	22.1	15.58	100	74	26	26 (Algeria)	46	4
Czech Republic	18.7	9.73	99	27	72	72 (Russia)	72	2
Denmark	23.7	0	0	0	0	0	0	0
Finland	10.6	4.53	100	0	100	100 (Russia)	100	1
France	13.9	45.27	98	43	55	27 (Norway)	27	7
Germany	22	81.34	84	49	35	35 (Russia)	35	4
Greece	6.1	2.13	98	0	98	76 (Russia)	74	2
Hungary	43.6	10.7	77	8	69	69 (Russia)	63	3
Ireland	23.5	3.43	80	80	0	80 (UK)	80	1
Italy	35	59.29	76	18	58	35 (Algeria)	32	5
Luxembourg	26.1	0.78 (2001)	100	100	0	88 (Belgium)	88	2
Netherlands	46.8	26.77	54	54	0	41 (UK)	20	3
Norway	20.6	0	0	0	0	0	0	0
Poland	11.5	8.2	60	7	53	88 (Russia)	53	3

Table 7.2. Natural gas import and source dependence in OECD Europe (continued)

Country	Share of gas in energy mix (%)	Gas imports (bcm)	Share of imported gas in total consumption (%)	Share of imported gas from IEA countries in total gas consumption (%)	Share of imported gas from non-IEA countries in total gas consumption (%)	Share of the largest supplying country in total imports (%)	Share of the largest supplying country in total consumption (%)	Number of external supplying countries
Portugal	10.7	3.1	100	0	100	87 (Algeria)	87	2
Slovak Republic	32.7	7.33	97	0	97	100 (Russia)	92	1
Spain	14.3	20.73	97	10	87	58 (Algeria)	53	8
Sweden	1.6	0.98	100	100	0	100 (Denmark)	100	1
Switzerland	9.2	3.03	100	88	12	54 (Germany)	50	5
Turkey	19.8	17.11	98	0	98	68 (Russia)	68	3
UK	37.3	5.47	5	5	0	62 (Norway)	1	2

Number of external supplying countries excludes spot cargoes
Data for 2002 (unless otherwise specified)
Source: IEA

One aspect of security that may be a weakness in competitive markets is gas supply diversification. Traditionally, this has been covered by incumbent companies. Although a competitive market may be expected to value diversity, it is not certain that this will be the case. However, governments can, if they wish, require suppliers to maintain an adequate portfolio, as illustrated by the measures taken by some IEA governments, such as Spain, which has established a quota for the largest supplier (no more than 60% can be imported from one single supplying country), while Italy has put financial incentives on companies to import from new supply countries.

Another issue is that contractual source diversity as shown in the previous figure and table may differ from actual physical flows.

Transit and facility dependence

Because 91% of OECD European imports are delivered by pipeline, gas is transported across several sovereign territories, creating a further layer of risk, especially of a commercial and political nature, and hence heightening security concerns.[74] These risks are difficult to manage because the balance of interests between exporter and importer (gas against revenue) may not necessarily exist for transit countries. 60% of gas imports into OECD Europe cross at least one border and 37% of gas supplies transit through one or several non-OECD countries. Gas transit is therefore an issue, especially when transit occurs outside OECD Europe. EU enlargement will decrease the number of transit countries as two major transit countries (the Czech and Slovak Republics, already OECD members) will join the EU in May 2004.

Except for LNG supplies, Algerian gas transits either Tunisia or Morocco before reaching Europe. No transit problems have been reported with these transit countries. This is unfortunately not the case for Russian exports through Ukraine, which transits 80% of Russian gas exports, or through Belarus. The sudden transformation in 1991 of the previously-unified Soviet pipeline system into an inter-state system crossing various national jurisdictions, has given rise to several problematic issues:[75] lack of transparency over the conditions on which access is granted to export

---

74 Stern J. (2002).
75 Kemper R. (2003).

capacity in gas pipelines; and a lack of clearly-established criteria for the setting of tariffs for gas flows in transit. Transit agreements with Ukraine were negotiated on an annual basis and payment was by delivery of gas in kind, but a long history of transit problems between Russia and Ukraine led Gazprom to favour the building of direct routes.

The limited number of pipelines and importing entry points in Europe raises the issue of facility dependence. Whereas OECD Europe imports only 25% of its imports from Russia, 90% of Russian gas production is transported through the Yamal-Nenets corridor and 80% of Russian exports transit Ukraine thorough Uzhgorod. The Transmed pipeline to Italy transports about 30% of Italian gas consumption and the Maghreb line transports between 25-30% of Spanish consumption. Troll and associated pipeline infrastructure account for more than half of Norwegian production and exports.

OECD European gas supplies are vulnerable to potential accidents at key transmission and import facilities, some of which are remote from European territory. As OECD European production decreases, future dependence from importing points or pipelines from more remote areas will increase. It will therefore be necessary to continue the diversification of routes and import points, and to enhance interconnection of the grid.

A broader application of the principle of freedom of transit will improve the security of the system. To the extent there is unregulated monopoly control over gas supply and transport infrastructure in producing, transit or consuming countries, there are important implications for the economies and security of supply of end-use customers all along the supply chain.

Because the economics of long-distance gas pipelines dictate that these infrastructures are designed to run at full capacity, flexibility may more easily come from LNG and short-haul gas pipelines. The new LNG receiving terminals being built or planned in Europe will add to the options for delivery routes into Europe. Although most LNG trades continue to rely on dedicated LNG liquefaction plant and dedicated receiving terminals, there is a growing spot market for LNG cargoes. As this trade develops, then its contribution to security may gradually increase (see Chapter 4).

The role of the EU internal market for security of gas supply

The above discussion has highlighted the elements of external security of supply to the EU integrated gas grid and the challenges to provide long-term gas at competitive prices as well as the risk in the infrastructure to the entry point and beyond into the European gas market.

The next important question for the EU is whether the internal market is liquid enough to react in case of a shortage and to allocate the available gas to its highest value use (within the physical tolerances), which raises the issue of interconnectivity and interoperability of the European gas grid. Interconnectivity may also be indirect, e.g., via the electricity grid which adds demand-side response for gas to power, or via the re-routing of LNG tankers. Building new interconnections between EU member states, not linked to the original imports, will make it possible to draw on spare capacity in other areas of the system, but will incur costs that private companies may be reluctant to invest. A clear assessment is needed of the costs and benefits of such extra investment and a clear idea of who (customers or tax payers) will have to pay and who will benefit.

Another question is whether the current market reform triggered by the EU Directives will result in adequate and timely investment and reliable deliveries, and the development of risk insurance assets in an open market. This raises the issue of the right framework, the right incentives for investment, and the division of roles and responsibility between the various stakeholders.

Within the EU, the Directive 2003/55/EC repeals the Transit Directive of 1991, while keeping the existing transit contracts. For new transit contracts, there will be no distinction between the TPA rules applied to transit and national transmission. This raises the following points:

- The main issue is whether the new regime will allow congruence of transportation capacity contracts and long-term supply contracts. In particular, are national rules established by the different countries appropriate to transit?

- Another major issue is whether new investment in capacity could be supported by long-term commitments for transportation capacity. Who will initiate investment in new transit lines? So far the building of European infrastructure was driven by large import projects.

- How to reconcile reforms of national tariffs and existing and future transit tariffs?
- What are the implications of interference on existing contracts with international partners? In particular, there is a trend at national level to move to entry/exit tariffs. Are entry/exit tariffs adapted to transit? If not, how to differentiate between transit and transportation?
- How to avoid any structural cross-subsidy between transit and domestic transport?
- Is it necessary to have a pan-European regulation for transmission?
- As there is increasing interdependence of networks, how to ensure that transportation capacity outside the country will be adequately developed (and can be long-term contracted and paid for) and who will pay for it outside the country?

Investment in European infrastructure

Although existing production and import capacity are sufficient to cover OECD European consumption until approximately 2007/08, the capacity to handle increased imports within Europe will need to be increased substantially during the period 2010-2020. Due to the long lead-time of gas investments, decisions on these investments must be taken now. *WEIO 2003* projects that the gas sector in OECD Europe would need $474 billion up to 2030 to satisfy its growing demand: $110 billion for transmission & storage; $29 billion for LNG; $108 billion for distribution; and $227 billion for exploration & production.

Pipelines

Current situation

The European gas transportation grid has developed rapidly since the 1970s and a grid of interconnections was built between western and central Europe. In 2003 it totalled 224,000 km in length (OECD Europe, includes high-pressure national networks) compared to 71,000 km in 1970. Today the east and west pipeline system is well integrated and extends from Siberia to Ireland.

Figure 7.11. Average annual gas investment in OECD Europe

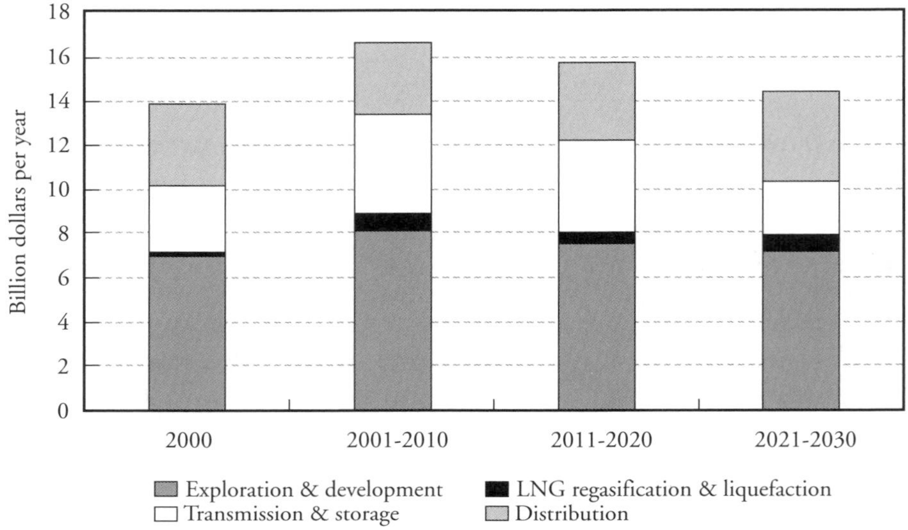

Exploration & development | LNG regasification & liquefaction
Transmission & storage | Distribution

Source: *WEIO 2003*

The cross-border European grid was based on single large pipeline projects which were driven by import projects and implemented jointly by the companies involved. Even the Interconnector between the UK and the Continent was economically driven by several export projects. In general, such pipelines were tailor-made to serve the import projects and their expansion, allowing spare capacity mainly during the build-up phase of the project, and with the option to adapt capacity by successively adding compression or looping the systems. The increasing interconnection of these pipelines meant that more trade and more optimisation of flows inside the European system became possible. However, the physical flow inside the European system is very much determined by the inflows of the main suppliers, Russia, Algeria, Norway and the Netherlands, which are characterised by different qualities of gas. In the past, the system was designed by the integrated companies to transport at a quality specs that was the economical optimal along the complete gas chain – from production at a given quality, blended in the grid and supplied at a certain quality at the lowest cost. As the gas grid was not designed for an open market, harmonisation will require additional investments, and increasing EU internal trade will therefore need reinforcement of capacity in several places.

Recent years have seen the completion of a string of new transmission pipeline projects inside Europe and several more are being implemented or planned. The new Balgzand Bacton Line (BBL) is expected to be built by 2006, linking the Netherlands to the UK, while the Danish and Dutch networks are being joined via a new offshore pipeline which will be operational in 2004. Norway will add 20 bcm/a capacity with the Langeled pipeline from Ormen Lange to Easington and a further 15 bcm/a by the end of the decade. The TAG pipeline to Italy is also going to be expanded.

However, parts of the European grid are congested, in particular at border entry points. Gas Transmission Europe (GTE)[76] indicates with traffic lights the spare capacities and bottlenecks of the European gas grid. Although the situation can change quickly, some parts on the grid may need to be expanded or reinforced, in particular entry points in Italy, and interconnection between Spain and France, to allow for more EU internal gas trade. Another issue is how much interconnection within the European system is necessary to share available supplies in the case of shortfalls in self-contained regions like the Iberian or Italian peninsula, and who should pay for that delivery back-up.

Investment in gas grid

Security of supply implies that the necessary gas transportation infrastructure is in place for gas to be deliverable in the case of low-probability events. As gas transportation is strictly capacity bound, and capacity strictly defined by the dimensions of the pipeline and compression capacity, it cannot be changed at short notice. Providing spare capacity in transportation is therefore important to allow a certain level of flexibility in gas supplies, in cases of unusually high demand or of re-routing gas flows due to the interruption of gas supplies. However, as gas transportation capacity is capital-intensive, there is a trade-off to be found between the flexibility offered by the grid and its overall utilisation, and other means to cover such shortfalls like storage, or a reaction on the demand side, e.g., by price mechanisms.

WEIO 2003 estimates cumulative investment in transmission within OECD Europe at $87 billion over the period 2001-2030. The length of

---

76 GTE website: http://www.gte2.be/

the transmission grid within Europe is expected to increase from 224,000 km to 378,000 km. There are stark contrasts between mature markets (Germany for instance) where investment is mostly directed towards increasing rehabilitation and reinforcement, and growing markets, like Spain, where the considerable increase in gas consumption, mainly for power generation, requires large infrastructure investments in the gas high-pressure system. Even in a mature market like the UK, large infrastructure decisions will be needed to cater for changing patterns of gas flows due to the surge in gas imports in the next few years (see Chapter 8).

As stated in *WEIO 2003*, financing will not be a major concern for domestic projects, particularly those that involve the extension or enhancement of existing pipeline networks, including the construction of new compressor or blending plants or looping of existing lines. This type of investment is usually considered to be relatively low-risk, particularly where returns are protected by the regulator through explicit tariff setting. Nevertheless they still require clear rules and regulations in the light of the reorganisation of the European gas industry by the EU Gas Directives. The absence of stable and predictable rules may lead to postponement of investments. Even more, if the regulatory framework does not give incentives competitive with similar types of investments, there will be no investments in the grid and this may reduce security of supply in the future.

Interoperability issues

Interoperability, or the harmonising of gas qualities, is a major issue in the context of market opening and market liquidity and increased cross-border trading. Interoperability problems are obviously an obstacle to achieving these objectives as well as a key issue to security of supply.

Main quality features are: the gross calorific value (GCV) (important for household metering which is on a volumetric basis), the Wobbe index which characterises the combustion and transportation properties of the gas, and in more recent times the methane number (which like the octane number describes combustion behaviour in engines). As described below, gas comes with a variety of compositions stemming from their *in situ* composition and from optimising the costs of quality treatment. In theory it would be possible to extract all other components but methane from any natural gas, although this would be extremely costly.

Although modern appliances across Europe are widely compatible with different gas qualities, many older appliances, are calibrated to use lower calorific gas and are consequently often unable to burn gas from a neighbouring market safely and efficiently. This may even become a security of supply issue, for example in the UK, where most households are still using burners calibrated for gas with a Wobbe index lower than that found in other parts of Europe (see Chapter 8).

Even if a large number of customers are actually equipped with appliances running with different gas qualities, the conversion of old appliances will be necessary in order to face the decrease in low calorific value gas supplies (L-gas). The related cost of these massive conversions will remain expensive – even in the future.

Another question is the range of GCV which can be managed by the customer, e.g., some laws stipulate that invoices to households can only be based on the average GCV (only in view of volumetric metering) if the variation of the GCV is within plus/minus 1%. In addition, some industrial users, such as glass producers, need to rely on very narrow quality parameters of the gas they use, thus setting restrictions on the delivery of gas from different sources to their supply region.

The issue of different measurement conditions (such as standards for pressure and temperatures) as well as different units of measurement can give rise to inaccuracies which complicate trading within the EU. At the Madrid Forum[77] VI held in October 2002, GTE presented a proposal on harmonisation of definitions and units of measurement to be considered by the whole European gas industry. At the Madrid Forum VII held in September 2003, EASEE-gas[78] endorsed GTE recommendations which were adopted by the Madrid Forum.

---

77 The European Gas Regulatory Forum, which meets twice yearly in Madrid, groups representatives of EU member states and Accession candidates, regulators, industry and consumers under the chairmanship of the European Commission.
78 The European Association for the Streamlining of Energy Exchange (EASEE-gas) was founded on 14 March 2002 to develop and promote common business practices to simplify and streamline business processes between shareholders leading to an efficient and effective European gas market (see www.easee-gas.org).

Quality issues

Gas from the Netherlands being predominantly L-gas (low calorific gas, due to its significant content of Nitrogen) is handled by a separate grid for gas in north-west Europe. Households using L-gas cannot be switched to H-Gas (high calorific gas) without health hazards, unless the burners are modified to handle the H-gas. H-gas from Russia, which for the time being is close to pure methane, and H-gas from Norway, the Netherlands and Algeria and LNG, have different shares of higher hydrocarbons and differ in composition.

As a result, the quality of gas (i.e., the composition of the gas mainly characterised by the GCV and the Wobbe index) will vary in zones which are within the reach of different suppliers. This either requires that customers have equipment to handle variations in Wobbe index and GCV or that the system operator blends the gas to deliver a gas quality within defined quality variations. Both systems are in use. The different qualities of gas which result from different compositions of the gas reservoirs (and the costs to extract the richer hydrocarbon components from the gas) thus impose restrictions on the interoperability of the pipeline systems. Apart from that, the main restrictions are due to pipeline diameter and the design of the compressors along the pipeline and the resulting pressure difference. While it is possible to reverse the flow in a pipeline, the reverse flow will not necessarily have the same capacity. An example of that is the UK/Belgium Interconnector, which so far has a capacity of 20 bcm/a from Bacton to Zeebrugge, but without adding compression in Zeebrugge, which is now underway, only has a capacity of 8.5 bcm/a in reverse flow. Having an integrated system will reduce the average flow distance of the gas in the system. However, it is not automatically given that in the case of a shortfall of one supplier, the remaining supplies could be evenly distributed to all customers.

The following units were recommended by EASEE-gas and supported by the Forum:

– Pressure: bar;

– Energy: kWh (with a combustion reference temperature of 25°C);

– Volume: cubic metres (at 0°C and 1.01325 bar) (normal cm);

– Gross Calorific Value: kWh/cm (Ncm), with a combustion reference temperature of 25°C.

By 1 October 2005, all European TSOs will have to use the recommended units in communications with other TSOs and shippers. However, some important issues still remain to be tackled. For instance, in October 2002, GTE also presented concrete proposals concerning Gas Specification, Operational Procedures and Business Rules. EASEE-gas has been asked to further consider GTE proposals and make formal recommendations to the next Madrid Forum to be held in 2004.

EC legislation on transmission

The provisions in the Directive 2003/55/EC on the organisation of access to the system have been divided into two sections, one on third-party access (Article 18), which mandates regulated third-party access for transportation and one on new infrastructure (Article 22), which allows a regulatory authority to exempt major new infrastructure from Article 18 under certain conditions. In addition, there are various new obligations for system operators, such as providing system users the information needed for efficient access to the system.

In December 2003, the European Commission proposed a new legislative package aimed at promoting investment in the European energy sector both to strengthen competition and help prevent the recurrence of the blackouts that took place in summer 2003. Although the legislative package is oriented towards the electricity market, it also includes a regulation on access to gas transmission networks that will make the Madrid Forum's Guidelines for Good Practices[79] legally binding and empower the national regulators to ensure their implementation. The regulation is expected to be applied as of 1 July 2005. It includes detailed measures on rules for network access and services; capacity allocation and congestion management, including "use it or lose it" and secondary trading mechanisms; management transparency requirements, and tariff structures (including balancing projected demand and actual supply). The main points are: [80]

---

79 The second version of the "Guidelines for Good Practices" was adopted by the Madrid Forum in September 2003.
80 CEC (2003b).

- Access charges must be transparent, take into account the need for network security and reflect efficiently incurred costs, including an appropriate return on investments;

- Third-party access services must be offered on the same contractual basis to all network users. Network operators must provide firm and interruptible access services, both long and short term;

- Capacity allocation and congestion management procedures must be non-discriminatory and published. Where contractual congestion exists, unused capacity must be offered on the primary market on an interruptible basis and the user will be permitted to sell unneeded contracted capacity on the secondary market. If physical congestion exists, market-based solutions are to applied. TSOs must allow capacity rights to be tradable between network users in a secondary market;

- Transparency requires TSOs to publish detailed information on services offered, with physical, booked and available capacities on a numerical basis for all relevant points on a regular and rolling basis;

- Tariff structures must reflect efficiently incurred costs, including appropriate return on investment; facilitate efficient trade and competition while at the same time avoiding cross-subsidies between network users; promote efficient use of the network and provide for appropriate incentives on new investments;

- Balancing charges must be broadly reflective of costs, providing an incentive for users to balance input and off-take. They must avoid cross-subsidisation between network users and permit the entry of new market players. Balancing regimes must be compatible in order to facilitate gas trade across borders of different TSOs systems.

GTE raised strong concerns about the Commission's proposal for the regulation on access to gas transmission networks. The main concerns[81] are:

- The need for such a regulation has not been analysed:
  - Subsidiarity principle to be taken into account;

---

81 GTE (2004).

– Unlike electricity, cross-border exchanges have always been common practice in the gas sector (65% of the gas consumed in the EU crosses at least one national border, compared to less than 10% for electricity);
– TSOs always were proactive to implement the Guidelines for Good Practices in good faith;

■ The regulation would undermine the Madrid process:
– The Comitology Procedure would allow the Commission to adopt and amend *Guidelines for Good Practices* without formal consultation with the gas industry;
– There would be a strong disincentive for the gas industry taking into account the time and energy put into the preparation of the Guidelines for Good Practices;

■ Risk of over regulation:
– TSOs have to comply with the Internal Gas Market Directive adopted in June 2003;
– Over regulation would jeopardise the investment climate.

Possible barriers to investments in transmission

Although considered as low-risk investments, investments in new domestic pipelines in OECD Europe may be jeopardised by regulatory barriers. Potential investors may be deterred, if they cannot make full use of their investment. This fact has been recognised in North America since the implementation of the system of open seasons where economies of scale in transmission pipelines are shared at the design phase and also by the Hackberry decision relating to new LNG terminals which are not an essential facility.

The major challenges in open markets are linked with the accuracy of signals for new investment and funding, in particular for capacity investment for extreme events[82], with regulatory uncertainty and with unbundling of transportation and supply businesses.

The key issue is whether investment into networks are attractive for investors. The returns that can be made on investment in transmission depend to a large

---

82 GTE (2003f).

extent on the regulatory framework established in each country and on the competitiveness of the return offered in an international competition for capital with a similar risk structure. Some incentives may come from the possibility to increase profit through efficiency improvements. Most EU countries have applied regulated TPA to their transmission grid (see Table 7.1). Tariffs and the regulated asset base on which they are based are essential instruments used by regulators to incentivise investment, including for new investment and extra capacity to provide security of supply. The rate of return allowed by national regulatory authorities is determined according to the country specific situation. However, overall they are lower than the rates allowed in North America. The Brattle study on tariff systems in the European sector[83] noted "we suspect that many regulators have under-estimated the cost of capital for network infrastructure. We are concerned that these estimates may threaten the incentives to expand existing infrastructure". TSOs need to be adequately rewarded for the investments they make in existing and new infrastructure (reflecting the level of risk involved). In view of the extreme importance of investments for security of supply and the crucial role of rate of return for investment, defining the yardstick for the rate of return is a policy issue, i.e., a responsibility of governments.

Another key issue is whether and how gas transporters receive the necessary signals for investing in capacity for low-probability events and how these investments are funded. A major challenge for TSOs is how to translate indicative planning and non-binding projections of shippers into the necessary investment in the gas infrastructure. The same potential problem applies regarding bookings of existing infrastructure.

Due to competitive pressure, some shippers may reduce their capacity booking on existing grids assuming a peak or supply interruption will not occur, thus endangering security of supply at the customer level.

Procedures for reserving capacity[84] are a key issue for security of supply. Very often part or all of the capacity of pipelines has been contracted on

---

83 Lapuerta C., Moselle B. (2002).
84 As with network tariffs, there are three main methodologies for capacity reservation based on postalised, entry-exit and point-to-point capacity reservation. As for tariffs, CEER recommends that TSOs move to entry-capacity booking in order to take full advantage of an entry-exit system. Entry-exit capacity booking means that capacity at entry and exit points can be bought, sold and traded independently from each other in order to maximise tradability and flexibility on the gas market.

a long-term basis whether or not the capacity is actually used. The *Guidelines for Good Practices* require TSOs to offer "short-term on-demand" services and have introduced "use it or lose it" provisions. However, the booking of capacity may refer to the peak demand and therefore not be used frequently. It is therefore important that the resale of rights is reversible so that suppliers can transport their peak gas demands when the need occurs.

Another challenge for security of supply is created by the unbundling of functions of the former integrated companies. Such a full-scale unbundling may cause risks on synchronising decision-making in production/supply and infrastructure, and could also increase administrative and technical expenses in the event of over-regulation.[85] Due to unbundling, an overview of planned investment has become essential.[86] TSOs play a major role, as well as regulators which have to authorise the investments. However, as already stated, TSOs have to rely on the information given by shippers, which often is only indicative.

Investors need a predictable, transparent and stable framework in order to judge more accurately the economics of a project. They need to be sure that governments/regulators will not decide to change the financial parameters (for instance by subsidising other investments) after the investment decision has been taken. The realisation of investment projects depends on private transport companies which are the owners and operators of the network. The problem remains as to how investment can be imposed on a regulated private business, if incentives are not sufficient. In the case of Belgium for instance, the Belgian regulatory regime mandates the federal natural gas market regulator to produce ten-year plans for future investment (see Part C, Annex 2). These plans are indicative; they are an instrument to monitor security of supply by assessing gas demand trends and infrastructure performance, and especially peak capacity needs under extreme circumstances. However, if the Belgian regulatory authority

---

85 UN/ECE (2003).
86 Coordinated planning by TSOs and regulatory authorities helps to diagnose where regulatory uncertainty or other factors may be interfering with the proper functioning of a market. Auctions and secondary markets also provide useful market signals. Regulation for the authorisation of new projects can usefully supplement investment planning with market signals. For example, if a regulator or TSO is uncertain that a certain pipeline expansion project is worthwhile, an "open season" can be conducted to confirm shippers' interest.

CREG anticipates a lack of investment, it has to react in an appropriate way according to the Belgian Gas Law. For instance, CREG can attract new investors by guaranteeing revenues of a project. If CREG does not succeed in attracting sufficient investment to guarantee security of supply, it will advise the Minister to mandate an investment as a last resort.

Another factor is the fact that liberalisation may lead to a larger proportion of short-term transportation contracts. This makes the planning of long-term strategic investment for private investors more difficult, especially given the long lead-times for the development of new infrastructure. Here again, the importance of long-term contracts for both suppliers and transporters must be recognised.

In addition, clear mechanisms must be developed in case of supplier bankruptcy. Several IEA countries have put in place a last resort supplier and defined clear responsibilities (see Part C, Annex 1). Finally, it is important for security of supply to put in place contingency arrangements to deal with supply disruptions under emergency conditions.

Transmission tariffs

There is currently no standard structure for tariffs, and different parameters are used when calculating transportation charges:

- In Belgium and Germany, transmission operators have tariff structures with significant distance-related components. This is true, to a lesser extent, in France where tariff structures have been modified to restrain the distance-related element and include eight zones (also distance related);

- In the UK, the Netherlands, Ireland and Italy, transmission network operators use a tariff system based on variable charges for different entry and exit points, usually on a zonal basis. In Denmark, transmission tariffs are entry-exit but all entry and exit tariffs are uniform (postage stamp);

- In Sweden, Luxembourg and Spain charges are postage-stamp type. This is also true of exit charges in Ireland.

Although tariffs still differ greatly from one country to another, a rising number of EU member states already have or are in the process of implementing entry-exit systems, which were recommended by the Council of European Energy Regulators (CEER) and the Commission at the Madrid Forum V in 2002. Five countries have adopted entry/exit tariffs (UK, the Netherlands, Italy, Ireland and Denmark). Germany is also moving to an entry/exit tariff system. Not all have independent entry/exit capacity booking systems.

As Europe is moving towards to an entry-exit system (tariff and capacity booking), it is necessary to understand the benefits and shortcomings of this methodology.

The Madrid Forum has been the centre of intense debate on the question.[87] In particular, as security of supply is concerned, GTE argues that under a regulated entry/exit system, TSOs could face a significant problem in determining how to plan and finance insurance investment, especially where there is uncertainty as to where the gas will be put into the system. To enable such investment, regulators may allow for insurance investment to be included in the regulatory asset.

Therefore, although an entry-exit system allows the creation of a virtual point from which a market can be organised and allows an average effect for the end-user consumer, it also has shortcomings that will need to be resolved according to each specific national situation. The trade-off between promoting competition and cost reflectivity and security of supply challenges which may arise from the application of entry-exit tariffs should also be addressed.

One key question is whether these tariffs give appropriate signals for new investment. Although they can be used to signal expected future congestion at specific entry and/or exit points, entry-exit tariffs *per se* are not a sufficient guarantee of efficient long-term signals, as shown by the example of St Fergus in UK. The absence of long-term capacity inhibited investment and led the UK regulator to allow long-term auctions on entry points to better inform NGT Transco on congestion problems.

GTE has been invited to prepare comments with regard to the CEER *Entry-exit system guidelines* presented at the Madrid Forum VII. The GTE position will be presented at the next Madrid Forum in 2004.

---

87 CEER (2003c), GTE (2003d).

LNG regasification terminals and the role of LNG

Europe has 11 LNG regasification terminals with a vaporisation capacity of 56 bcm/a. In 2003, two new terminals started operations: Bilbao in the north-west of Spain and Sines in Portugal (Table 7.3).

In addition, there are several projects for new terminals, some in competition with each other: two projects in France at Fos (Gaz de France and ExxonMobil); five projects in Italy, three at an advanced stage (Marina di Rovigo, Brindisi and offshore Livorno); two projects in Spain at El Ferrol and Valencia; three in the United Kingdom at Milford Haven and on the Isle of Grain. Expansion of existing terminals is also planned in Belgium, Portugal and Spain.

Table 7.3. LNG regasification terminals in operation in OECD European countries, 2003

	Number	Storage capacity (thousand cm of LNG)	Nominal regasification capacity (bcm)
Belgium	1	261	5.3
France	2	512	15.3
Greece	1	130	2.2
Italy	1	100	3.7
Portugal	1	240	2.6
Spain	4	560	20.6
Turkey	1	255	6.5
OECD Europe	**11**	**2,058**	**56.2**

Source: IEA

WEIO 2003 estimates that 29 billion dollars will have to be invested in regasification during the period 2001-2030 in OECD Europe. The legislation on access to LNG terminals will be the determining factor for the building of new terminals. The financing of the new terminals, however, remains an open issue. The Directive 2003/55/EC has mandated regulated third-party access to receiving terminals and possible exemption to the provision for new infrastructure under certain conditions.

Table 7.4. New regasification projects planned and under construction in OECD Europe

Country	Company	Site	Capacity (bcm/a)	Start-up (date)	Status
France	Gaz de France	Fos-sur-Mer 2	8.2	2007	Authorised ($350-502 million)
	ExxonMobil	Fos-sur-Mer			
Italy	Edison Gas	Rovigo (offshore Adriatic)	8	2005	Authorised ($800-1 300 million)
	British Gas/ Enel	Brindisi	8	2006	Authorised ($300 million – Phase 1)
	Cross Gas (Falk)	Livorno offshore	3.75		Under authorisation
	Edison Gas	Rosignano (Tuscany)	3		Under authorisation
	LNG Terminal	Corigliano Calabro (Calabria)	8		Under authorisation
Spain	Union Fenosa	Sagunto (Valencia)	6.6	2007	Under construction
	Reganosa group	El Ferrol (La Coruna)	2.8	2009	Under construction ($200 million)
Turkey	Egegas	Izmir	4	2004	Almost completed
United Kingdom	NGT	Isle of Grain	4.4	Jan. 2005	Under construction
	ExxonMobil/ Qatar Petroleum	Milford Haven	20	2007-2009	Authorised
	Petroplus/BG/ Petronas	Milford Haven	9	2006-2007	Authorised

Source: IEA

Although pipeline gas will continue to dominate the European gas market, LNG has an important role to play in meeting future growth in gas demand and enhancing diversity of supply, bringing more flexibility and security. More terminal capacity will be key in attracting more supplies. However, the LNG suppliers have other alternatives and the European market will be in competition with other dynamic LNG markets, the US but also Asia. The US gas market, in particular, with its growing need for gas imports, current sustained high level of prices and favourable legislation for new regasification terminals, could become a

Figure 7.12. Existing and planned regasification terminals in OECD Europe

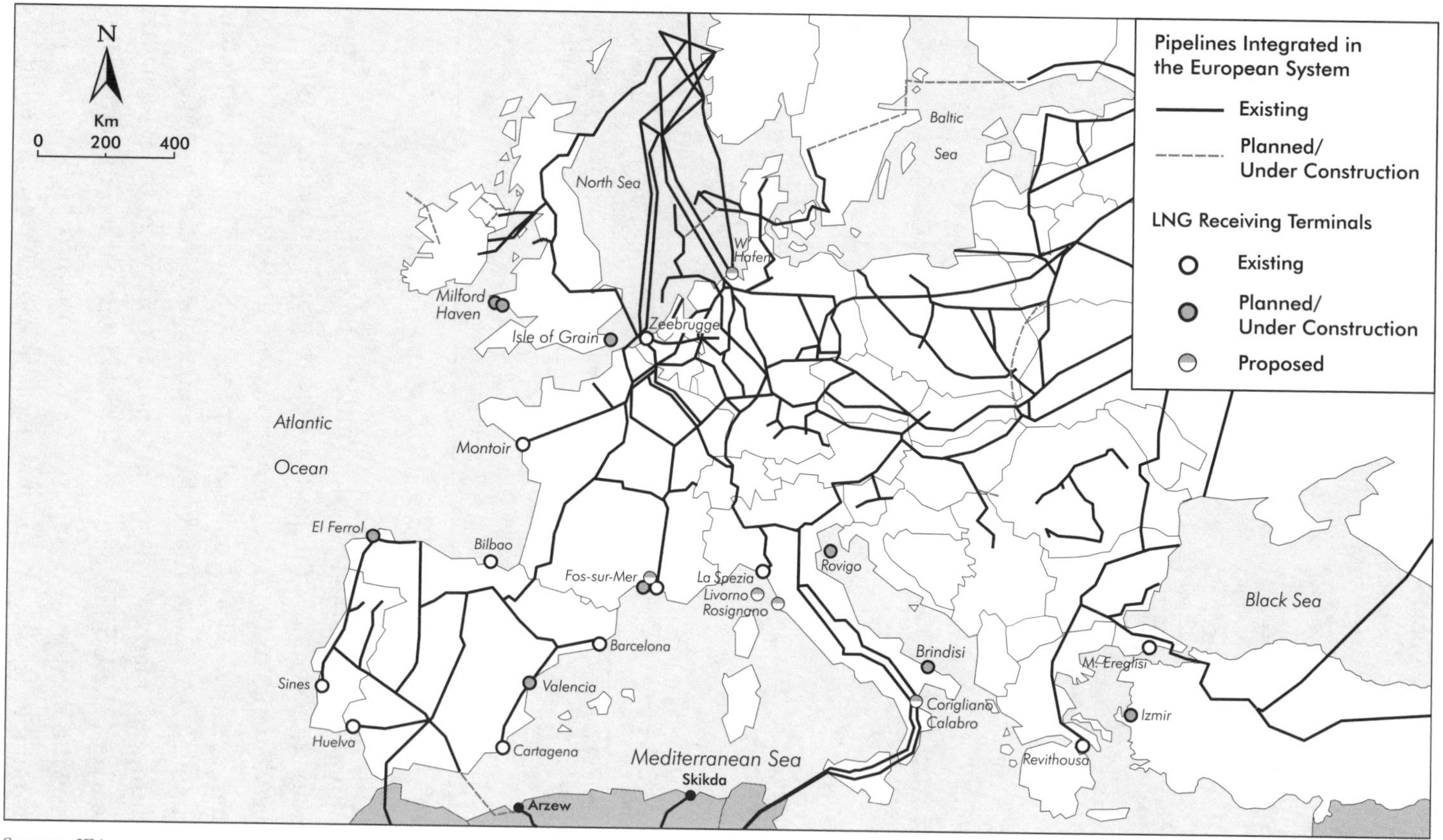

Pipelines Integrated in the European System

— Existing

--- Planned/ Under Construction

LNG Receiving Terminals

○ Existing

● Planned/ Under Construction

◑ Proposed

Source: IEA

major magnet for LNG. To make investment into LNG terminals attractive, regulatory policies for access to LNG terminals in Europe will need to be reviewed. Italy has been the first country to adopt specific legislation encouraging the financing of new LNG terminals. It allows priority of access to the sponsor of the new terminal[88] and a higher rate of return than is now applicable to the transmission network. The UK government has recognised the need to be flexible for new regasification terminals and decided that exemption[89] to TPA could be given to new plants on a case-by-case basis (NGT's Isle of Grain has obtained such an exemption, as well as ExxonMobil/Qatar Petroleum's South Hook LNG import terminal at Milford Haven, Wales). In the US the number of LNG projects soared after the Hackberry decision made it clear that no TPA is required for new LNG terminals.

Storage

Current situation

OECD Europe currently holds 103 underground gas storage facilities with a working volume of 64.7 bcm and a withdrawal capacity of 1.4 bcm/d. These capacities represent 13% of gas consumption, or 48 days of average consumption and 117 days of firm gas demand (Table 7.5). Three countries dominate the European storage scene: Germany (with 41 storage sites and 18.8 bcm of working capacity), Italy (with 10 sites and 12.7 bcm) and France (with 15 sites and 11 bcm). Storage capacity has grown rapidly in recent years. Since 1993, 15 new sites have been built, adding 25 bcm of capacity, most of them in Germany.

Storage at LNG import terminals also plays a role in countries such as Belgium and Spain, where geological options for underground gas storage are limited. There are 11 LNG regasification terminals in Europe with a capacity of 56 bcm/a and a storage capacity of 2.1 mcm of LNG corresponding to about 1.2 bcm. In addition, there are seven peak shaving units with a withdrawal capacity of 105 mcm/d.

---

88 TPA, however, will be raised from 20% to 30% according to the draft law on the restructuring of the energy sector in Italy passed recently by the House of Representatives and by the Industry Commission of the Senate.

89 Transco has sold the full capacity of the Isle of Grain terminal for 20 years to BP and Sonatrach, which makes regulations on TPA in fact unessential.

Table 7.5. Underground gas storage in OECD Europe, 2002

Country/region	Number of storage facilities	Working gas volumes (million cm)	Peak daily deliverability rate (mcm/day)	Per cent of gas consumption[a]	Number of days of largest external supplying country [b]	Number of days of firm demand [c]
Austria	5	3,020	34.7	37.7	222	478
Belgium	2	636	18.9	4.2	33	38
Czech Republic	7	2,147	42.5	22.5	110	167
Denmark	2	700	(13) / 24	13.7	-	249
France	15	11,000	214	24.6	342	167
Germany	41	18,830	444.9	20.8	209	153
Hungary	5	3,610	46.58	27	156	194
Italy	10	12,747	267	18.1	191	175
Netherlands	3	2,400	144	4.8	89	40
Poland	6	1,460	51.9	10.8	73	90
Slovak Republic	1	2,740	33.4	35.9	143	320
Spain	2	2,140	12.6	10.4	64	237
UK	4	3,271	64.4	3.3	(d)	27
OECD Europe	**103**	**64,701**	**1,388**	**13**	**203**	**117**

(a) Ratio of working gas to annual consumption
(b) Ratio of working gas to largest external supplying country multiplied by 365
(c) Ratio of working gas to residential and commercial consumption (2001) multiplied by 36
(d) not relevant, due to the small size of the largest external supplying country.
Figures do not include peak-shaving units (Belgium, the Netherlands and United Kingdom).
Source: IEA, *Natural Gas Information*, 2003 and Country Submissions

Investment

WEIO 2003 projects that OECD European storage working volume will increase from 64 bcm in 2003 to 138 bcm in 2030, an investment of around $23 billion, driven by the growth in gas demand. Europe has extensive geological potential for all types of storage facilities. Planned enlargements of existing facilities and 30 new underground storage projects are expected to meet OECD Europe's commercial storage requirements for the next 15 years. Furthermore, countries like the Slovak Republic and Latvia, which are close to the OECD European region, already have large gas storage capacities.

Storage, one of the flexibility tools

Flexibility is an essential component of gas supply.[90] In commodity markets, supply and demand are normally balanced by the price mechanism. Buyers and sellers react to price signals given by the market. The need for flexibility of volume – the ability to add to supply or reduce demand – reflects the nature of the commodity. In gas markets, demand, in particular by residential and commercial customers, is not particularly flexible. Residential and commercial gas demand is seasonal, temperature-dependent and inelastic. It must be covered as it arises. To respond to such variations requires flexibility. Flexibility here means the ability to adapt supply to foreseeable volume variations in demand (mainly seasonal) and to adjust for erratic fluctuations in demand (mainly short-term temperature variations), or to adapt demand (i.e., reduce it) when supply is insufficient. A variety of tools is available to balance supply and demand for gas at any time. These tools fall into three categories: those aimed at increasing supply flexibility, those that provide buffer stocks and those that reduce demand at times of peak gas use. Recently, balancing supply and demand by market-based mechanisms has become an important feature. Flexibility is achieved through physical instruments and contractual arrangements that anticipate likely variations in demand and balance the volume of gas supply and demand at any time. Physical instruments include variable supply in production and import contracts, gas from storage and line-pack. Contractual arrangements can take the form of contracts with "interruptible customers" that allow interruption of their supply at agreed times. Open markets bring a new market-driven approach to flexibility that supplements the traditional flexibility tools. Because of the availability of these alternatives, it cannot be assumed that storage is an essential facility.

Functions

As seen above, although storage is a vital part of the gas chain, it is only one of the tools available to balance supply and demand. In traditional markets, it performs three different functions for gas operators: flexibility, security

---

90   More details are available in the IEA publication *Flexibility in Natural Gas Supply and Demand*, (IEA 2002) (http://www.iea.org/dbtwwpd/bookshop/add.aspx?id=52).

and more efficient grid design. In the 1970s and 1980s, continental European companies built storage facilities to meet seasonal variations in demand under long-term long-haul supply contracts with a high minimum pay. Some companies also sought to bolster security of supply and developed strategic storage to protect customers in case of an interruption of gas supply. These functions are still relevant in open gas markets. In addition, however, storage is starting to play new roles, such as making use of price arbitrage and serving as a supporting tool to gas trade.

Load balancing requirements will emerge as a critical aspect of the new EU market. Seasonal and daily balancing imperatives, and the establishment of financial penalties for imbalances, will eventually lead to interruptibility and storage being contracted on a fully commercial basis.

In some countries storage plays a very important role for security of supply, as a top-up mechanism and to meet public service obligations:

- *Security of supply.* In some countries, there are flexibility requirements (mainly strategic storage of gas or back-up fuels) to anticipate interruption for technical, contractual or political reasons. The geopolitical risk mainly involves holding gas reserves to cover the possibility of a long-term disruption to supplies, since disruptions for technical reasons can normally be solved within a few days. Views about the need to hold strategic gas reserves vary widely across European countries, mostly depending on the role of gas in their energy supply, the sources from which their gas comes, and the state of market reforms (see above);

- *Top-up regime.* TSO can monitor levels at storage sites, as is the case in the UK. These monitor levels represent TSO's estimate of the volume of stored gas needed at different times of the year to ensure that security standards can be met. In countries with much cross-border trade and where storage is contracted cross-border, it is not always possible to allocate the use of storage facilities;

- *Public service obligations.* In some countries, public service obligations require gas utilities to keep storage or require consumers to finance storage costs, usually with the aim of securing safeguard measures and protecting specific categories of customers in case of need.

Legislation on storage

Regulations on storage differ among EU countries, reflecting the varying degrees of market development and the availability of different infrastructures and natural resources and therefore of alternative flexibility tools [see above and annexes of the publication *Flexibility in Natural Gas Supply and Demand*, IEA 2002a].

EU legislation applicable to storage[91]

Legislation on access to storage will play a key role in investment in new facilities. The Directive 2003/55/EC mandates access to storage and ancillary services (Article 19) but leaves the choice between negotiated or regulated access to member states. Gas undertakings have to keep separate accounts for their storage activities. New storage investments may also be exempted from TPA requirements under certain conditions – such as providing increased competition or increased security of supply – according to Article 22 of the Directive. The Directive also clarifies under what circumstances access can be denied, and underlines the important role of storage facilities to implement security of supply. Article 19 (1) restricts access to storage only "when technically and/or economically necessary [...] for the supply of customers". The Directive defines access to storage in such a way that priority use can be provided for exclusive TSOs' operational functions, gas production and public service obligations.

A note[92] on third-party access to storage facilities published by the Commission in January 2004 states that the Commission takes the view that if access to storage is related to a planned or existing supply contract it would always comply with the requirements of technical and economical necessity. The note also points out that the storage facilities to which access is requested and the customer who is supplied through TPA to this storage facility should not necessarily be situated in the same member state.

The note specifies that access to storage concerns those facilities that are not exclusively reserved for TSOs in carrying out their functions. In

---

91 The Madrid Forum VII in September 2003 stressed the need to ensure non-discriminatory and transparent access conditions to storage facilities in line with the provisions of the second Gas Directive and plans *Guidelines for Good TPA Practice for Storage Operators* to be presented at the next Madrid Forum in 2004.

92 CEC(2004).

addition, the portion of storage facilities used for production operations would also be excluded from the scope of the Directive. The note states that in the case of non-market-based balancing regimes, i.e., where TSOs want to exclusively reserve storage facilities or a portion of them for carrying out their functions, relevant authorities should make sure that there is a clear-cut delineation between which storage capacity is available to TPA and which is not, on the grounds of TSO needs. As for the latter, it should be made available to the market on an interruptible basis.

The note also makes it clear that security of supply requirements must be taken into account, but they have to be transparent and non-discriminatory. Regarding refusal of access on the grounds of PSO, the note states that it should be taken into account, whether the relevant PSO (e.g., for security of supply) could be achieved by using other instruments, such as supply flexibility, spot markets, interruptible contracts, etc., provided it can be economically justified.

In some countries, integrated gas companies operate storage as part of the gas system. Others have unbundled storage activities. Third-party access to storage is spread across the EU, with a few exceptions. Most countries with a high seasonality of gas demand have introduced direct third-party access to storage (as opposed to a bundled service). Most EU countries have opted for negotiated access (see Table 7.6). Some countries have opted for regulated access (UK for onshore facilities, Spain) or a mix of regulated and negotiated access (Italy, Netherlands). The priority of access to storage for public service obligations and security of supply purposes is quite common.

Storage[93] and other flexibility services or instruments offer a competitive advantage to a gas supplier. They lower costs, facilitate balancing and allow provision of greater flexibility and security of supply for customers. Storage is one of the several means to achieve flexibility and will eventually compete with other flexibility services, such as supply swing, interruptibles, spot and futures market. To the extent that competition develops between providers of flexibility services, there should be little

---

93 IEA (2002a).

Table 7.6. Access to storage and PSO linked with storage in EU

Country	TPA to storage	Negotiated or regulated	Access to Storage	Strategic storage/PSOs	Financing of PSOs
Austria	Yes	Neg.	Direct	Storage plays an important part in the emergency supply plan of the gas industry.	
Belgium	Yes	Neg.	Direct	PSOs: the network is designed to cover all firm clients' needs based on the winter of 1962/63. Daily delivery must be ensured down to minus 11°C. Obligation to store gas volume of 1-in-50 winter. Distrigaz must cover the sector's demand under PSOs.	PSOs are financed by the private sector with a special fund which is administered by the regulator.
Denmark	Yes	Neg.		PSOs: guaranteed supply to all non-interruptible customers, even in the case of a 3-day supply failure at minus 14°C and of a 60-day supply failure at normal temperatures.	PSOs are financed by the shippers as a security of supply charge in addition to the transmission payment. Shippers can choose between interruptible and firm security of supply services.
Finland	No storage			Stores back-up fuels.	Gasum
France	No		As part of the system	Storage has been sized to face the 1-in-50 winter (volume) and the 1-in-20 peak day.	
Germany	Yes	Neg.	As part of the system		
Greece	No storage				
Italy	Yes	Reg. (neg. for new storage)	Direct	Strategic storage equal to 10% of the volume annually imported from non-EU countries and to 50% of the average expected daily peak requirement at the end of the season.	Gas importers
Luxembourg	No storage				

Table 7.6. Access to storage and PSO linked with storage in EU (continued)

Country	TPA to storage	Negotiated or regulated	Access to Storage	Strategic storage/PSOs	Financing of PSOs
Netherlands	Yes	Reg/neg.	Direct	New decree of 23 October 2003: for households the TSO will serve as a supplier for the extra demand in case temperatures drop below -9°C.	
Portugal	One storage under development				
Rep. of Ireland	No storage			No - either source of supply could supply the non-interruptible gas market if there were a supply interruption in the other.	
Spain	Yes	Reg.	Direct	PSOs: shippers, retailers and customers have an obligation to store the equivalent of 35 days of their firm sales/consumption to distributors for the supply to non-eligible customers.	
Sweden	No traditional gas storage. A lined-rock cavern demonstration storage started operation in 2003.				
UK	Yes	Reg. (for onshore sites)	Direct	Through their contracts with shippers, suppliers are required to ensure sufficient capacity to meet the peak aggregate customers' demand, which, based on data from the previous 50 years, is only likely to be exceeded in 1 year out of 20, and taking into account interruptibility of customers. TSOs also have an obligation to ensure that the 1-in-20 obligation is met.	Suppliers/Shippers.

Source: Country and company submissions, CEER (2003b), and IEA (2002a).

need to regulate access to them. As indicated by Eurogas[94], "where alternative instruments are not available or cannot be expected to be made available then an appropriate un-intrusive level of regulatory oversight may be required until competition develops. The regulatory approach will not be applicable for all storage facilities, because in several areas storages are operating in competitive commercial national or cross-border markets with differing requirements and this should be recognised in the access system. Storage is in several respects comparable to a normal commercial business. Detailed interventions have the potential to distort the competitive market liberalisation is aiming at, as the flexibility market is closely connected with the (free) commodity market. Regulatory intervention will be counterproductive if it distorts the optimal allocation of investments in flexibility along the gas chain and could inhibit the construction of the many new storage facilities needed for security of supply in Europe's gas market."

Dealing with extreme events

To ensure security of supply, investments must also be made into assets for low-probability/high-impact events (extreme weather conditions, supply disruptions). In the past, the gas industry has had a very good record in covering such events. Companies developed assets with low return in case of extreme events, whose costs were passed on to customers. Under the new environment, commercial entities may not be expected to invest in such assets if this security is not contracted and paid for by their customers. Private companies are only responsible to their shareholders and their consumers (instead of the whole market).

Making end-users eligible to choose their supplier is also about giving end-users the responsibility for choosing and paying for their own level of security of gas supply. In the new market environment, security will probably become a separately priced commercial service, which eligible customers can purchase. For example, they can choose to purchase supplies from a diversity of sources, so as to enhance their security and pay more for their gas as a result, or to buy storage service or conversely, they can choose to be interruptible and pay less for their gas. This is a dramatic change, and

---

94 Eurogas (2004).

even large consumers may have problems assessing the value that they should attach to specific security services. When all customers in the EU market, including households, become eligible in 2007, the issue will be even more complicated because household customers are linked to networks which typically cannot discriminate between network users, i.e., deliver different security levels to different points of off-take. Furthermore, for safety reasons households should not be interrupted at all.

Hence the need for a framework that establishes minimum output standards and ensures that suppliers contract for sufficient supply for average and defined extreme events and reveal their real demand for capacity under both average and defined extreme conditions. In turn, TSOs receive the right signals and funding for capacity in extreme conditions.

The 1995 *IEA Study on Security of Supply* examined the impact of the largest conceivable disruptions to European gas supplies. The basis scenarios considered were a total interruption, starting on October 1st, in Russian supplies and independently, a total interruption in Algerian supplies. Under these two extreme assumptions, two scenarios were analysed:

- A best-case scenario, under which deliveries from non-disrupted sources can be increased to capacity and interruptible customers can be interrupted throughout the whole period of the supply shortage;

- A worst-case scenario, under which deliveries from non-disrupted sources remain at contractual levels and interruptible customers are cut only within general contractual provisions.

The analysis suggested that those countries with diversified supply options could, on the whole, maintain supplies to their firm customers for over a year if either Russian or Algerian supplies were disrupted; based on the 1992 situation, Spain and Turkey, whose gas markets were new and dependent on supplies from a single supplier were the most fragile;[95] Austria, on the eastern end of Europe, had the highest ratio of storage capacity to annual consumption in Europe; even without supply diversity this storage buffer could delay any serious impact on firm customers by

---

95 Their situation ten years later has dramatically changed. Spain now receives gas from eight suppliers and Turkey from four. Spain has four LNG receiving terminals with LNG storage tanks and is also developing its underground gas storage capacities. Turkey is currently over-supplied, following a slow-down of its gas demand increase at the beginning of the decade.

about four months. An interesting result was that under the Russian disruption case, 25% of the region's supplies were cut, but even under the worst-case set of assumptions the final shortfall of gas to end-users represented just 2.5% of total demand.

At the beginning of 2004, the European gas industry had to deal with two disruptions of gas supplies. The most recent was Gazprom's cut of transit flows for 1-day through Belarus on 19 February 2004 (see below). The supplier's flexibility portfolio, in this case withdrawal from the German Rehden underground gas storage (35% Gazprom/65% Wintershall), was used to supplement the ensuing shortfall of volumes for Germany and the Netherlands. Poland and more particularly Lithuania were affected by the cut, which led to some supply disruptions to industry, but not to households. Poland announced the same day its intentions to increase its Norwegian import volumes.

This whole incident highlights the security risks of the transit countries for both Russia and Europe, and thus raises for both the interest in building direct routes, e.g., through the North European Gas Pipeline. Although the cut was brief, Gazprom surprised European customers by showing a willingness to cut off supplies to its customers in order to force an issue in a transit country. The other disruption occurred in January 2004 when three trains at the Algerian Skikda LNG plant were destroyed in an accident. Here again, the supplier used its portfolio to make up for the disruption. The flexibility tools available in the importing countries could also have bridged the disruption, but were not needed. The impact of the Skikda accident is reviewed in Chapter 4.

Table 7.7 gives the ratio of working gas to largest external supplying country and volumes of working gas in storage compared with "captive demand". In the rapidly changing European market, these figures only give an indication of the security of supply situation in European countries. Furthermore, the current and future European gas market differs widely from the one prevailing in 1995, and opening the gas sector to more competition allows the price mechanism to balance supply and demand. New tools/instruments are available to cope with short-term supply disruptions, for instance backhaul flows, swaps, spot market purchases, and the flexibility brought by LNG.

Table 7.7. Security of gas supply in OECD Europe

Countries	Share of gas in TPES (%)	Share of domestic production in total consumption (%)	Diversification of supply	Import flexibility	Share of the largest external supplying country (% of total imports)	Storage: number / working capacity	Ratio working volumes/ "captive" customers (%)*	LNG capacity available	Interruptible sales	Share of gas for power (%)	Gas for power: % of multi-fired capacity	Spot markets / hubs
Austria	22.4	23.6	1 main supplier	Small	Russia (78.3%)	High - 5 UGS - 3 bcm	130	No	25% of total sales	21.8	77.4	Under development at Baumgarten
Belgium	22.4	0	3 main suppliers	High. from the Netherlands	Netherlands (45%)	Limited - 3 UGS - 0.6 bcm	10	Yes	30% of industrial demand is interruptible	15.5	85.9	Active hub at Zeebrugge
Czech Republic	18.3	1.5	1 main supplier	Small	Russia (73%)	Large - 7 UGS - 2.1 bcm	45	No	No	7.5	-	No
Denmark	23.5	100	-	-	-	Large - 2 UGS - 0.7 bcm	68	No	25% of gas sales	25.6	51.1	No
Finland	10.9	0	1 supplier	Medium	Russia (100%)	no	0	No	100% of gas demand can switch to alternatives	14.8	90.6	No

Table 7.7. Security of gas supply in OECD Europe (continued)

Countries	Share of gas in TPES (%)	Share of domestic production in total consumption (%)	Diversification of supply	Import flexibility	Share of the largest external supplying country (% of total imports)	Storage: number / working capacity	Ratio working volumes/ "captive" customers (%)*	LNG capacity available	Interruptible sales	Share of gas for power (%)	Gas for power: % of multi-fired capacity	Spot markets / hubs
France	13.6	3.8	5 main suppliers in 2004	Medium	Norway (27.5%)	High - 15 UGS - 11 bcm	46	Yes	1/3 of the industrial market	1.9	83.5	Under consideration (notional hub)
Germany	22	21.1	4 main suppliers	High. from the Netherlands	Russia (41%)	High - 40 UGS - 18.8 bcm	42	No	25% of industrial sales and 70% of sales to the power sector	10.5	54.6	Under development at Bunde
Greece	6.1	2.3	1 main supplier	Medium	Russia (76%)	No	0	Yes	No	10.5	0	No
Hungary	43.6	21.8	1 main supplier	Low	Russia (89.5%)	Large - 5 UGS - 3.6 bcm	53	No	Widely used for industrial customers that have fuel-switching capabilities	27	100	No

Table 7.7. Security of gas supply in OECD Europe (continued)

Countries	Share of gas in TPES (%)	Share of domestic production in total consumption (%)	Diversification of supply	Import flexibility	Share of the largest external supplying country (% of total imports)	Storage: number / working capacity	Ratio working volumes/ "captive" customers (%)*	LNG capacity available	Interruptible sales	Share of gas for power (%)	Gas for power: % of multi-fired capacity	Spot markets / hubs
Ireland	23.5	0.2	1 main supplier	Low	UK (100%)	No	0	No	Gas power plants are interruptible	35.2	82.3	Under consideration (notional hub)
Italy	35	20.7	4 main suppliers	Medium	Algeria (38.4%)	High - 10 UGS - 12.7 bcm	48	Yes	9% of sales	35.5	79.1	Under development (notional hub)
Luxembourg	28.1	0	3 main suppliers	High	Belgium (88%)	No	0	No	No	60	0	no
Netherlands	46.8	100	-	-	UK (41.1%)	Medium - 3 UGS - 2.4 bcm	11	No	Supplies to electricity generators can be interrupted.	55.4	39.2	TTF (notional hub) and Oude
Norway	20.6	100	-	-	-	-	-	-	-	0.4	0	-

Table 7.7. Security of gas supply in OECD Europe (continued)

Countries	Share of gas in TPES (%)	Share of domestic production in total consumption (%)	Diversification of supply	Import flexibility	Share of the largest external supplying country (% of total imports)	Storage: number / working capacity	Ratio working volumes/ "captive" customers (%)*	LNG capacity available	Interruptible sales	Share of gas for power (%)	Gas for power: % of multi-fired capacity	Spot markets / hubs
Poland	11.5	33.6	1 main supplier. 2 others	Medium	Russia (88%)	Small - 1.5 bcm	25	No	No	11.5	0	No
Portugal	10.8	0	1 main supplier	Low	Algeria (86.7%)	No	0	Yes	About 1/3	14.9	38.0	No
Slovak Republic	32.7	3	1 supplier	Low	Russia (100%)	Large. 2.7 bcm	86	No	No	32.2	75.6	No
Spain	14.3	2.5	8-10 suppliers	Medium	Algeria (58.5%)	Medium - 2 UGS - 2.1 bcm	64	Yes	6% of gas sales	6.2	45.9	No
Sweden	1.6	0	1 supplier	High	Denmark (100%)	Little - 1 UGS in Lined Rock Cavern	0	No	n/a	0.9	-	No
Switzerland	9.1	0	4 suppliers	High	Germany (53.7%)	No	0	No	42% of gas sales	1.6	0	No
Turkey	19.8	2.1	4 main suppliers	Medium	Russia (67.6%)	No	0	Yes	Used to reduce peak gas demand	35.6	32.2	Under consideration
United Kingdom	37.4	100	Not relevant so far	Yes (Interconnector)	Norway (62.6%)	Small - 4 UGS - 3.3 bcm	7	No	23% of total sales	30.4	3.3	NBP

* "captive" customers: commercial. residential customers.
Source: IEA, Country submissions.

Conclusion on security of gas supply

The current state of security of supply is high in OECD Europe, although the situation may vary from country to country (see Table 7.7).

The current oversupply in most continental OECD European markets helps to ensure a high level of security of supply for the near future. The European market also has some spare capacity in transportation systems providing a great deal of flexibility on the supply side, although some transmission pipelines are already operating near capacity. The OECD European situation is extremely diverse due to the specific situation of each gas market, as shown in the following examples:

- Austria, the Czech Republic, the Slovak Republic and Hungary have large storage capacities to ensure security of supply given their large reliance on Russian gas and are constrained in developing supply alternatives – only the Czech Republic among Central Europeans has been successful in sourcing 27% of its imports from Norway. Poland plans to import from the North Sea and expand its storage capacities;

- France has large storage capacities and diversified supplies. Storage and interruptible customers have a long-term role in security of supply and a short-term role for seasonal swing;

- Germany combines a high storage portfolio, production and import swing provided by the Netherlands, and diversified supplies;

- Belgium relies mainly on diversified supplies, import swing, its link with the Interconnector and the development of a gas hub at Zeebrugge;

- Italy relies on diversified supplies, storage (with a favourable geology) and some swing from its imported supply, in particular from Algeria;

- The Netherlands has a high production swing and is also developing storage facilities. The country is also promoting the development of virtual and physical hubs.

- Spain currently has little storage capacity and relies heavily on diversified supplies and entry points with a multiplication of LNG receiving terminals. It also has an ambitious programme to develop its storage capacity.

- The UK relies on beach swing, the Interconnector, interruptible customers and flexibility in the electricity system.

Most continental European countries are at the early stages of market reform. Many of them still rely predominantly on the classical flexibility instruments developed historically, like storage and a portfolio of diversified sources, as market reactions do not yet play an important role in balancing supply and demand. In order to improve gas trading between European countries, new interconnections will need to be built. This could be done by private investors in the context of a new import project, or to make use of arbitrage possibilities. If it is to create a larger marketplace, this may not necessarily be attractive for private investors.

Increasing demand will spur the need to build new pipelines and LNG terminals, and increase storage capacity and interconnectivity of the gas grids. Supply and transportation flexibility will decrease as imports have to come from more remote areas and exporters seek to make best use of their assets. This will be partly compensated by increased LNG supplies, which offer additional *ad-hoc* (spot) supplies if the price is competitive.

For continental Europe, it is important to ensure that the acceleration of market opening in EU countries will not result in ToP obligations problems. Long-term contracts were the backbone of the supply reliability and security and the expression of trust between the parties. It is now recognised that such long-term planning remains important for the gas industry, especially in countries that have to rely strongly on gas imports.

Challenges for security of supply in Europe come not only from a national dimension – which is key – but also from a regional and global dimension. For any EU European country, the European dimension is increasingly important for security of supply as cross-border gas trade develops. A clear understanding of the roles of governments, regulators and companies of the European countries and of the EU Commission is essential. With the development of a more flexible LNG market the global dimension is also becoming more relevant. For instance, it is important that European LNG importers can compete with other LNG importers.

The key external challenge on the OECD European market is how to reconcile the objective of competition with the need for many European countries to secure future supplies at competitive conditions in a timely manner from outside OECD Europe. The continental European gas industry is characterised by *i)* a capital-intensive supply infrastructure and customers who are bound by substantial investment to using gas, with most sources located outside OECD; and *ii)* a network-based infrastructure with remote production facilities, involving long lead times for investments and considerable reliance on producing countries, with only a few players involved. The European Commission's recognition of the importance of long-term contracts for gas supply acknowledges that situation. The same acceptance will be required for long-term transportation contracts – at least for transit. On the buying side, a credible commitment by the buyer is essential. The buyer has to be given sufficient room to develop the capabilities and the financial strength to aggregate demand, and purchase and deliver gas to the market in time.

A number of other issues arise from the earlier stage of market reform in Russia and the countries of the Former Soviet Union. These relate to the control of monopoly power, reform in gas transit markets and the interface with more rapidly reforming Western European customers (see Appendix II – Russian gas deliveries).

Two major internal aspects of market reforms for security of supply are the unbundling of activities, which in turn leads to the unbundling of responsibilities for security of supply; and the lack of clear market signals for investments in assets for low-probability/high-impact events.

Governments retain a key role and the overarching responsibility for security of supply, even if the management of security of supply shifts away from governments and incumbent companies to all market players. Governments are responsible for:

- Setting up a regulatory framework for market players that clearly allocates responsibilities for different aspects of security;

- Defining the role of market players and the responsibilities of regulators;

- The framework, at national (or European) level must be stable, predictable and transparent so that companies can rely on it when making investment decisions. Otherwise there is a risk that investors will adopt a "wait and see" attitude and investments will not be made in time. Its implementation should be transparent and accountable;

- Setting minimum standards for extreme events that must be covered for small customers. For instance, covering the most severe winter day or period on record; covering a certain time span of interruption of a major supplier – internal or external; a specific resilience against failure of a major element of the infrastructure. The means/instruments to be developed to achieve these minimum standards should be left to the market players themselves;

- Ensure monitoring of investment performance to ensure that companies provide an adequate level of security of gas supply. If the market fails to generate the necessary investment unaided, governments should act, i.e., provide additional market incentives, to ensure that timely investment in supplies and infrastructure is made to meet future demand;

- Defining the concept on which regulators determine the rate of return for investment in regulated infrastructure.

Governments should also play a role in encouraging cross-border trade by:

- Putting a stable market framework in place in their own country;

- Promoting international harmonisation of regulatory standards, e.g., within the framework of the ECT or the WTO;

- Helping to create a favourable political climate, e.g., by fostering more dialogue between gas producing, transiting and consuming countries;

- Encouraging and eventually backing FDI in production/transport/transit e.g., by the EIB, as was successfully done for the Maghreb Pipeline.

APPENDICES: MAJOR SUPPLIERS TO EUROPE: ALGERIA AND RUSSIA

Algeria and Russia play a significant role for current and future European supply. The development of their gas supply and export policy is described in these appendices.

Appendix 1: Algeria

The hydrocarbon industry plays an exceptionally large role in the Algerian economy, accounting for around 41% of GDP ($53.4 billion) and contributing 77% to the state budget through oil and gas tax revenues.

Supply

Total Algerian gas production in 2002 was 160 bcm, of which more than 70 bcm was reinjected, to improve oil and condensate recovery, and some 5 bcm auto-consumed in liquefaction plants. Marketed production amounted to 79 bcm, of which 59 bcm were exported by pipeline and LNG tanker, the rest being consumed domestically in power plants, as a raw material for the petrochemical industry and for industrial, residential and commercial use. Gas accounts for 67% of Algeria's energy mix and approximately 95% of the country's electricity is generated by natural gas.

Natural gas reserves amounted to 4,523 bcm at 1 January 2003 representing 56% of Algerian total hydrocarbon reserves and a reserve-to-production ratio of 55 years. The country's largest gas field is Hassi R'Mel, which initially held proven reserves of about 2,400 bcm and still accounts for about a quarter of Algeria's total dry gas production. The remainder of Algeria's gas reserves is located in associated and non-associated fields in the south-east and in non-associated reservoirs in the In Salah region of southern Algeria. The Rhourde Nouss region holds 370 bcm of proven reserves whereas smaller gas reserves are located in the In Salah region (280 bcm) as well as in the Tin Fouye Tabankort (145 bcm), Alrar (130 bcm), Ouan Dimeta (50 bcm) and Oued Noumer fields.

The government has embarked on a programme of reform in the energy sector. The new draft hydrocarbon law planned to open all upstream and downstream hydrocarbon activities to foreign and domestic competition and change the status of Sonatrach into a commercial company. Strong opposition from power trade unions forced the government to shelf the proposed law. This has not led to stagnation in the sector, however. The recently introduced transparent licensing rounds for new acreage led to an increase in the number of exploration contracts over the past few years. Under the current hydrocarbon law, foreign companies willing to invest in Algeria's energy sector have to do so in partnership with Sonatrach.

Total investment in oil and gas planned by Sonatrach and its partners amounts to over $25 billion for the period 2003-2007, with $10 billion of that amount coming from its foreign partners. The major part of this investment (75%) is earmarked for upstream activities, while Sonatrach is expected to invest $1 billion and foreign partners $2 billion downstream. There is an additional $4 billion to be invested in the gas and oil transportation system in Algeria.

The In Salah Project

BP and Sonatrach first signed a joint-venture agreement for In Salah in December 1995. The In Salah gas project was revived in August 2001 when Sonatrach and BP signed three construction contracts worth $2.7 billion, with the investment being split 65% BP, 35% Sonatrach.[96]

In June 2003, BP sold 49% of its share to Norwegian Statoil (along with 50% of its stake in In-Anemas gas and condensate project). The three companies will split the revenue from the project: 32% Statoil, 33% BP, and 35% Sonatrach. The In Salah project is the first full joint-venture deal between Sonatrach and a foreign company. In Salah's seven fields hold more than 198 bcm of gas, plus more in other adjacent reservoirs. The project includes 200 production wells, and a 520-km, 48-inch pipeline to Hassi R'Mel, where the gas will enter Sonatrach's export network linking to the export pipelines and LNG plants on the coast. The project aims to produce 9 bcm/a of gas, with the first delivery expected by mid-2004. The gas has been sold under long-term contracts to Spain and Italy.

---

96 The contracts were signed with Kellog, Brown & Root of the US and JGC of Japan for gas gathering and treatment plants; with Bechtel of the US for the 460-km pipeline to Hassi R'Mel; and with Enafor, a Sonatrach subsidiary, for drilling operations.

Gassi Touil project

The $2 billion Gassi Touil project aims at developing 9 bcm/a of gas production from six western Berkine Basin fields (in the south-west of Algeria) for export as LNG. The integrated joint venture, in which a foreign company (still to be chosen) is to join with Sonatrach, involves producing, processing and piping the gas to the coast, where some 5.5 bcm/a are to be exported from a planned new 4 mtpa LNG train at Arzew. LPG output of some 360,000 t/a is also planned. Reserves at the six fields are estimated at 255 bcm. Gassi Touil has attracted interest from 12 consortia[97] but has not yet been awarded. The project is now scheduled to be awarded in November 2004. The winner of the bid is expected to form a joint venture with Sonatrach and may also be involved in marketing the LNG targeted at the US and Europe.

Exports

Algeria exported some 60 bcm in 2002, 32 bcm via pipeline and 27 bcm as LNG. Exports to OECD Europe (55 bcm) represented 11% of European total consumption. Italy is the largest Algerian customer, with imports of 23 bcm in 2002, mostly through the Transmed pipeline. Spain imported 12.2 bcm in 2002 through the Maghreb-Europe pipeline and as LNG, and France is the third-largest customer with 10.2 bcm imported as LNG.

A price dispute with US and European customers in 1980 led to temporary disruption of LNG deliveries to Europe and to the collapse of LNG deliveries to the US market. Since, Algeria has consistently been a reliable supplier of gas, fulfilling its contractual obligations, in spite of the economic and social challenges in the country. The transit of Algerian gas through Tunisia and Morocco has never raised any problems.

The export capacity of Algeria amounted to 62.5 bcm at end 2003. The accident at Skikda, which destroyed three of the six LNG trains, decreased this capacity by 4 bcm (see Chapter 4). However, it is expected that Algeria's export commitments will be made up by other export facilities, so that there will be no delivery shortfall to Algeria's customers.

---

97 Bidders are Repsol YPF, Shell, Japan's Itochu with Teikoku, Statoil, Total, BHP Billiton with Woodside, Gaz de France with ConocoPhillips, Wintershall with Petronas, Anadarko with ENI and Maersk, Amarada Hess, Marathon with Petrofac and Occidental.

Table 7.8. Algerian gas exports in 2002 (bcm)

	Total exports	LNG exports
Belgium	3.2	3.2
France	10.2	10.2
Greece	0.5	0.5
Italy	22.76	2.2
Portugal	2.45	0
Spain	12.2	5.95
Turkey	4.08	4.08
US	0.76	0.76
Others (Tunisa. Morocco. Slovenia)	2.66	0
Total	**58.81**	**26.89**

Source: Cedigaz

Sonatrach intends to export 85 bcm/a by 2010. The increased gas exports will be generated by Ohnet (6 bcm/a), In Salah (9 bcm/a) and In Amenas (9 bcm/a).

Sonatrach's export strategies differ depending on the opening of the market and the customers. With its traditional buyers, Sonatrach insists on long-term contracts, but the company is now also adapting its contractual terms to market developments. For instance, recent formulae negotiated with LNG importers include Brent and oil products prices. This gives its clients the possibility of hedging on the UK marker crude future market. When selling to new entrants in traditional markets, Sonatrach is asking for access to the market. In open (and growing) markets (UK, US), Sonatrach is engaging all along the gas chain to spread the risk and in partnership with major players.

Sonatrach's strategy follows a very flexible commercial model, which couples volume insurance with price arbitrage in order to enable it to make the most of prevailing situations in the open market. Sonatrach's strategy is to transform its contractual guarantees (long-term take-or-pay contracts) into operational guarantees, by gaining access to several/multiple sources of gas outside Algeria and a portfolio of customers. The deal with BP for sales on the UK market is one illustration of this new strategy, because it allows drawing on either LNG supplies from Algeria or BP North Sea gas. The integrated Gassi Touil project may also include the possibility of marketing LNG in partnership and swapping it with other LNG sources to arbitrage and optimise transportation costs.

Sonatrach is aiming to establish itself as an international integrated gas player. Its sales strategy follows three major goals:

- Boosting the share of Algerian gas on its closest traditional markets in southern Europe, mainly through increasing exports by pipeline;
- Stabilising sales to markets already supplied with Algerian LNG and diversifying LNG sales as much as possible, entering new markets (UK, US). To achieve this goal, Sonatrach is raising its LNG capacity. It is also expanding its current LNG fleet of six LNG tankers. Sonatrach has ordered two new 140,000 cm tankers to be delivered in 2004, time-chartered two 130,000 cm methane tankers and launched a bid for a 70,000 cm vessel. The company will therefore have great commercial flexibility to deliver LNG to the US and Europe. Sonatrach is entering the UK market, in partnership with BP, and the US market, first with a three-year sales agreement to deliver 1 bcm/a to Statoil at Cove Point and later in cooperation with its partner in Gassi Touil;
- Establishing a commercial presence in northern Europe (on and around the UK market), with possible rights in the expansion of the Zeebrugge LNG terminal and a trading firm in London.

This development is supported through the participation in international upstream activities, commercial partnerships and downstream integration.

Export pipelines

Exports by pipeline are delivered through the Enrico Mattei (ex-Transmed) pipeline to Sicily in Italy, via Tunisia, and through the Pedro Duran Farell (ex-Maghreb Europe) pipeline to Spain and Portugal via Morocco. These pipelines have a current capacity of 24.3 bcm/a and 8.5 bcm/a respectively. The Enrico Mattei line will be expanded by 6 bcm/a by 2006, and the Pedro Duran Farell line, which is currently expanded to 11 bcm/a, will be increased to 13 bcm/a by 2005, with additional compression.

New pipelines are planned to increase exports. The MEDGAZ[98] project will create a new direct pipeline to Spain. It will be 747-km long, will have an initial capacity of 8 bcm/a and will go from Hassi R'Mel through the port of Arzew to Almeria, Spain. Medgaz is expected to be operational by 2006. Its full initial capacity has already been sold: 2 bcm/a to Gaz de France and 1 bcm/a to each of the following companies: Cepsa, Endesa, Iberdrola, Total, ENI and Distrigas. The capacity of the line could be raised to 16 bcm/a at a later stage. A further 900-km pipeline (GALSI[99]) will connect Algeria to Italy via Sardinia with an initial capacity of 8-10 bcm/a. It could be operational by 2008. A branch may also connect Corsica to the pipeline. The gasline export capacity is expected to be raised to nearly 60 bcm/a before the end of the decade.

Table 7.9. Algerian export capacity by pipeline

	Pipeline	Current capacity (bcm/a)	Expansion (bcm/a)	Capacity by 2010 (bcm/a)
Transmed	Algeria-Italy (via Tunisia)	24.3	+6 (2006)	30
GME	Algeria-Spain (via Morocco)	8.5-11 (2004)	+2 (2005)	13
Medgaz	Alegria-Spain (direct)	8 (2006)	Possible expansion to 16 bcm and extension to France	8
GALSI	Algeria-Italy (direct)	8-10 (2008)	Possible branch to Corsica. Possible expansion to 16 bcm	8-10
		32.8-35.3		59-61

Source: Observatoire Méditerranéen de l'Energie (OME), IEA

98   The partners in the MEDGAZ consortium comprise seven international energy companies: Sonatrach (Algeria), CEPSA (Spain), BP (UK), Total (France), Gaz de France (France), Endesa (Spain) and Iberdrola (Spain).
99   Shareholders of GALSI, created in November 2002, are: Sonatrach (40%), Edison (20%), Enel (15%), Wintershall (15%), and Eos Energia (10%).

LNG

The current liquefaction capacity amounts to 26.5 bcm (taking into account the loss of the three trains at Skikda). Sonatrach announced that it will rebuild a 4 mtpa world-class train at Skikda. The integrated Gassi Touil project also includes the construction of a 4 mtpa LNG train at Arzew. Algerian LNG capacity is therefore expected to reach around 38 bcm by 2007/08.

By the end of the decade, export capacity by pipeline and LNG is expected to reach around 100 bcm/a.

Table 7.10. Sonatrach LNG Facilities

Liquefaction plant	Location	Capacity (bcm/a)	Number of trains	Start-up
GL4Z	Arzew	1.5	1	1964
GL1Z	Arzew	10.5	6	1978
GL2Z	Arzew	10.5	6	1981
GL1K	Skikda	4[a]	3	1972/1981
Re-built	Skikda	5.5	1	2007
Gassi Touil	Arzew	5.5	1	2007/08
Total		**37.5**	**17**	

(a) The remaining three trains at Skikda should restart soon after inspection work is completed.
Source: IEA

Appendix 2: Russian gas deliveries

Since the break-up of the Soviet Union, the Russian economy has been fuelled by the energy sector, which accounted for almost 25% of GDP and 54% of Federal Budget revenues in 2002. The gas industry constitutes a key element of the Russian economy. It represents 8% of GDP and 25% of fiscal revenues, while more than 19% of the State's currency earnings originate from gas exports. The share of gas in the domestic energy mix is 50%, and gas represents 42% of the electricity generation mix (2000). Russia's state-controlled natural gas monopoly Gazprom[100] holds about 65% of the country's reserves, produces nearly 90% of Russian gas and operates the country's natural gas pipeline grid with a total length of about 400,000 km. The company manages gas exploration, production, transportation, export and wholesale supply.

Russia holds the world's largest gas reserves – 47 tcm. It is the largest gas producer, with 616 bcm produced in 2003, almost 70% of which goes to the domestic market. Russia's gas production is concentrated in the production of three super-giant fields which are now in their decline phase. While there is no lack of gas reserves to compensate for the decline and cover increased demand, a considerable range of challenges are linked to the development of these reserves, because many are located in even more difficult and remote areas, onshore and offshore. The development of the new production capacity requires a multitude of technical approaches and substantial financial resources, which need an appropriate framework to attract domestic and international investors.

Russia is also the world's largest gas exporting country (190 bcm in 2002). Russia exported 110 bcm to OECD Europe in 2002, i.e., 22% of European consumption. Gas exports account for 20-25% of total Russian export revenues. Russian supplies have a very high reliability record: no major curtailment of gas supplies to IEA countries has occurred since the beginning of Soviet gas exports in 1968, not even during the break-up of the Soviet Union. For geographical reasons central and western Europe are the obvious markets for Russian gas exports from the fields of west Siberia, while the eventual development of gas reserves in the east of Russia will

---

100 The state directly owns 38.4% in the company and controls indirectly another 16.3%.

look to Japan, Korea and China as obvious markets. As the west of Russia is almost landlocked, the export of LNG to the Atlantic basin is not an obvious solution and its economics remains to be proven.

Unlike Canada and the US, where gas exports are subject to competition and open gas markets on both sides of the border, the situation between Russia and OECD Europe is very different. First, both the OECD European and Russian gas industries are geologically different from those of North America. The gas industry in both OECD Europe and Russia is based on production from giant and super-giant fields whose development is much more driven by singular policy decisions taken by governments and by the operators of those fields, and do not react as much to short-term market signals. In addition, imports play a much more important role in OECD Europe than in North America. Market opening is still in its infancy in most countries of Europe, raising questions of regulatory stability for all players involved. The most striking difference compared to US/Canada is that Russia is a country in transition from a centrally planned economy to a market economy. For the gas industry in particular, the legacy of the Former Soviet Union (FSU) – on technical, economic and social grounds – will continue to play an important role in the future.

The further development of the gas industry in Russia and other FSU states will build on the extensive pipeline infrastructure inherited from the FSU, just as the challenge of creating a more competitive gas sector will have to take as its point of departure the existing structure of Gazprom. Increasing gas production from Russian oil companies and the emergence of independent gas producers argues for sector reform, and this reform will need to reflect the enormous investment challenges ahead. Another legacy of the Soviet system is the pricing structure where households (and other customers such as district heating plants and services) hardly pay cost-recovery prices. Changes here will have to be carefully implemented to mitigate the social implications of higher prices. Another problem inherent in the extreme distances from supplies to markets is the existence of large price differentials from the Russian borders with Central Asian suppliers on the way to the countries of the EU 25 where market-based pricing predominates. Finally, the reordering and reform of Soviet trading relationships and practices with former Warsaw Pact partners which include problems of non-payment, barter, vestigal preferential relations and other non-market practices make market reform all the more difficult and retard the development of an effective Eurasian gas market.

It is expected that gas exports to Europe will continue to rise. Russia is also considering targeting new markets in Asia (pipeline gas and LNG) as well as entering the Atlantic LNG business. Growing domestic and export sales will call for higher investment in all links in the gas supply chain over the next three decades.[101] Most of the capital will be needed for upstream developments to replace the maturing Western Siberian super-giant fields that have been the backbone of the Russian gas industry for decades. But a failure to implement much-needed market reforms, including raising domestic prices and giving independent producers fair access to Gazprom's monopoly national transmission system, could impede the financing of new projects and limit opportunities for independents to develop their own reserves.

It is therefore in the interests of European gas markets that investors succeed in mobilising the investment for additional Russian and ultimately Central Asian gas export projects. In the long run, the best basis for security of gas supply and revenue will be the successful transition to a market economy and a gas industry open to competition in Russia. This coupled with the successful opening of the gas and electricity markets in the EU will ensure that a growing number of decisions along the gas chain will be driven by competition and markets. The dialogue between the EU and Russia will be important in developing a joint appreciation for the investment challenges needed to maintain secure gas deliveries in the future. It can also reinforce proven instruments for gas investors, like long-term contracts and joint ventures, while adapting them to the new realities of open markets in the EU and other European gas customers. The resulting increased transparency in supply and transit will contribute to improving the investment climate and security of supply.

Reserves/production

Russian reserves in 2003 were estimated at 47 tcm with most of it in Western Siberia (in the Nadym-Pur-Taz region). Gazprom holds almost

---

101 From *WEIO 2003*.

two-thirds of Russian reserves. At the current rate of production, reserves are equivalent to another 76 years of production. In 2003, Russian production climbed to 616 bcm compared with 595 bcm produced in 2002. Gazprom produced 540 bcm of this amount, its second consecutive year of increased production, while independent gas producers and oil companies produced 76 bcm.

Resources are widespread across the country in six onshore basins (West Siberia, Timan-Pechora Basin, Volga-Ural Basin, North Caucasus, Yamal and East Siberian Basin) and three offshore (Barents Sea, Kara Sea and in the Sea of Okotsk). Some 20 giant fields were discovered, each with 500 bcm or more in reserves, accounting for some 75% of the total discovered reserves. Only seven of these, including Zapolyarnoye, which came on stream in 2001, are currently producing – accounting for the bulk of natural gas output.

The main producing area is in Western Siberia, which holds 70% of total gas reserves, and produces around 90% of the country's gas production. The three super-giant fields, **Urengoi, Yamburg and Medvezhye,** constitute the bulk of gas production. However, their production has started to decline: Medvezhye at 76%, Unrengoi at 65% and Yamburg at 54% of peak production rate.[102] Whereas they accounted for 80% of Gazprom's production in 1999, their production amounted to only about 62% in 2003. Further investment can slow the decline, but ultimately production from other fields will have to be developed. The super giant **Zapolyarnoye** gas field, with gas reserves of 3.4 tcm, came into production in late 2001. The field is expected to produce 100 bcm/a by 2008 and will help to compensate declining levels of production from the other three super giants over the next 5 years. Gazprom will need to develop other deposits, mainly in Western Siberia, over the next decade if it hopes to maintain production levels. It plans to give priority to the development of new, smaller fields in the Nadym-Pur-Taz region in order to make use of existing pipelines related to the super-giant gas fields. These include the Kammennomysskoye fields, which lie just 150 km from the Yamburg field, with the potential to produce over 50 bcm/a by 2010.

---

102 IEA (2003h).

Gazprom expects gas production from new giant fields (Bovanenkovsk and Kharasavei gas fields) on the **Yamal** Peninsula to begin soon, possibly as early as 2008 reaching 190 bcm/a by 2020 and a maximum production of 250 bcm/a by 2028. Yamal proven reserves amount to 10.5 tcm or 22% of total Russian reserves. Outside Siberia, Gazprom is investigating with its partners when and how to bring the giant Shtokmanov gas field in the Barents Sea into production. **Shtokmanov** (an offshore field in the Barents Sea containing 3,200 bcm of natural gas) was discovered in 1988, though development plans have been delayed since then. Total investment is estimated at $20 billion. Production on Shtokmanov is expected to start at 22 bcm/a, rising to 60-90 bcm/a thereafter. A first phase development of 20 bcm/a is expected for European markets between 2010 and 2015. Recent talks between Gazprom and Conoco also addressed the possibility of producing LNG from Shtokmanov for sale to the US.[103] However, in mid-March 2004, Gazprom management decided to designate the as-yet-untapped 600 bcm South-Russkoye field in the Yamalo-Nenetsk region as the main source for natural gas for the planned North European Gas Pipeline (NEGP). This news appears to imply a temporary freeze on the project to develop the giant Shtokmanov field which faces major technological challenges with expected costs of some $20 billion. This news may also imply delays for the NEGP, given peak production of 25 bcm/a at the South-Russkoye field is expected only in 2013.

Although the potential for developing new fields is huge, Gazprom is facing a steep rise in production costs for the development of new fields in deeper strata and/or in the Arctic and other difficult-to-develop regions. Zapolyarnoye is considered to be the last relatively cheap gas in Russia. Much of Gazprom's production is currently from Cenomanian reserves with production costs estimated at about $10/1,000 cm. Over 1992-2003, the share of "lower cost" gas in Gazprom's output dropped from over 90% to 75%. This could be as low as 50% by 2010. The Russian Energy Strategy's estimates for the development of the Yamal field are in the order of $30/1,000 cm not including investments needed for new transportation infrastructure.

---

103 World Gas Intelligence, Vol. 14, No.38, 17 September, 2003.

In the Irkutsk region of eastern Siberia, TNK-BP is exploring the **Kovykta** gas and condensate field, which has reserves estimated at 1,400 bcm. The field would be developed under a licence held by Rusia Petroleum, a joint venture in which TNK-BP is the largest shareholder. It is expected to start production in 2005. The partners are expected to construct a 4,900-km gas pipeline from Kovykta to China and Korea, with start-up planned for 2008. Under this plan, China's National Petroleum and Natural Gas Corporation (CNPC) would take 18 bcm/a and Korea's Kogas 10 bcm/a. Recently, the Russian Government appointed Gazprom to be the coordinator of gas developments in Eastern Siberia and Russia's Far East although it has no share in any of the licences. Earlier, Gazprom had been openly critical of the feasibility study released by Rusia Petroleum for development of the Kovytka field. Gazprom has now announced a 17-year plan to exploit gas and oil resources in Eastern Siberia and the Russian Far East, which envisages state-led infrastructure development, a monopoly transporter and guaranteed export prices. The Gazprom programme, worth $30.37 billion of investment, envisages a production increase from those areas to 58 bcm/a by 2010, and to 110 bcm/a by 2020.

In February 2001, Russia and China signed a preliminary agreement on developing the **Chayandinskoye** gas field in north-eastern Siberia. The field contains estimated reserves of 1,240 bcm of gas. The $6 billion deal between the Sakhaneftegaz gas company and China's CNPC includes the construction of a 3,000-km pipeline from the field to Xinyang in the north-west of China, where the demand for imported gas however is low. In this respect, the economics of this project are less attractive than those of Irkutsk (Kovykta field) pipeline.

The other major development in the east of Russia is the $10 billion **Sakhalin** II project, which will export LNG. Shell, which is leading a consortium composed exclusively of foreign companies, gave the green light for the project to proceed in May 2003. The less advanced Sakhalin I project, led by ExxonMobil, is considering laying a $900 million sub-sea pipeline for natural gas exports to Japan. Sakhalin (I and II) are developed under production-sharing agreements (PSA). PSAs were introduced in 1995 as an alternative to the existing licencing system.

Independent producers

Currently independent gas producers and Russian oil companies account for 13% of production (76 bcm in 2003), although they hold licences to develop nearly a third of the country's proven reserves. According to the Russian Energy Strategy, their production is expected to represent 20% of production by 2020 at 140-150 bcm/a. Independent producers themselves estimate that their contribution could reach 250 to 350 bcm/a by 2020 given fair third-party access to Gazprom pipelines and gas prices at more cost-reflective levels.[104] Clearly independent gas producers and Russian oil companies could provide breathing room for Gazprom to invest in much more expensive developments. Recently, Gazprom has signed long-term gas supply contracts for substantial volumes with Central Asian countries, namely Turkmenistan, which gives it breathing room for several years but may also delay third-party access to its network by Russia's independent oil and gas producers.

Figure 7.13. Natural gas production by Gazprom and independent producers in Russia

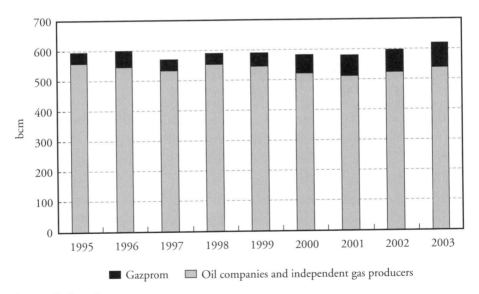

Source: Cedigaz, Gazprom

---

104 IEA (2003h).

Future production

WEO 2002 expects Russia to satisfy its growing domestic market *and* to remain the largest gas exporter in the world in 2030. Total Russian production or supplies are expected to increase continuously over the period 2001-2030 from 616 bcm in 2003 to 709 bcm in 2010 and 914 bcm in 2030. This is more than the expected production under the Russian Energy Strategy adopted in September 2003. The Strategy foresees an increase in Russian production to 680-730 bcm by 2020, of which 140-150 bcm produced by independent producers. Gazprom's business plan anticipates a production of 580-590 in 2020, by which time it aims to produce 180-190 bcm/a from the Yamal peninsula and 110 bcm/a from Eastern Siberia. Gazprom's target for 2030 is 610-630 bcm/a.

Foreign companies

Foreign companies interested in upstream gas investments can only do so in the form of joint ventures with the state-run company Gazprom or through participation in joint operating companies. Examples for possible joint ventures are developments at Zapolyarnoye, with Shell, Astrakhan in the north Caucasus with ENI, and Shtokmanov in the Barents Sea with Total, Fortrum and Conoco. Joint operating companies with little or no Gazprom equity stakes can be found in eastern Siberia, the Russian Far East (Sakhalin) and Kovykta with TNK-BP. However, as mentioned earlier, Gazprom is seeking involvement in this project and other developments in Eastern Siberia and the Far East. Only Wintershall has gained access to Russia's onshore gas fields through a joint venture with Gazprom and Achimgaz, to develop the 3,000 meter deep Achimovsk Suite at Urgenoi.

Deals with Central Asian countries

Gas in the new regions (Eastern Siberia, Far East and Arctic) will be more expensive to produce than existing fields in Western Siberia due to their great distance from existing pipelines and greater geological and geographic difficulties (great depths, deep water). Gazprom appears to have adopted a strategy to compensate for the decline of the three super-

Figure 7.14. Major gas fields in Russia

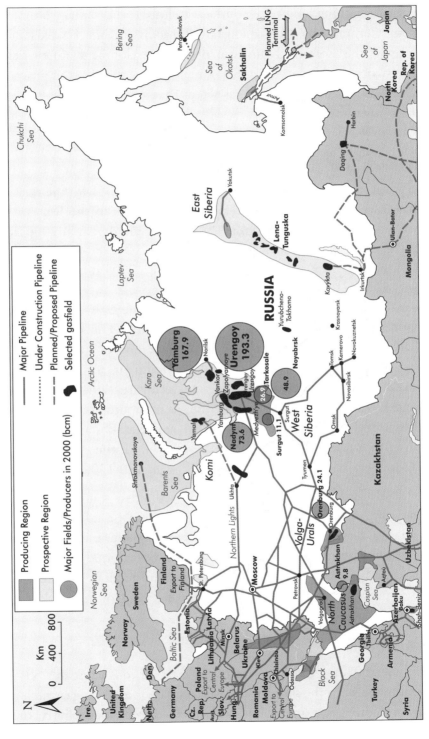

Source: IEA

373

giants by signing long-term contracts to import substantial volumes of gas from Central Asia (Turkmenistan, Kazakhstan and Uzbekistan), thus delaying the more costly investments into development of new fields and infrastructure. This strategy therefore may have the effect of postponing a restructuring of the Russian gas sector that would be necessary to attract these investments and, as a result, delay the increase in non-Gazprom Russian gas developments.

Turkmenistan

In April 2003, Gazprom signed a 25-year agreement with the state-owned firm Turkmeneftegas for delivery of Turkmen gas to the Russian border. Volumes will start at 5-6 bcm in 2004, rising to 10 bcm in 2006, to reach 60-70 bcm in 2007 and 63-73 bcm in 2008. From 2009 to 2028 Turkmenistan will supply 70-80 bcm/a. From 2004 until 2006, prices are agreed ($44/1,000 cm paid half in cash and half in gas equipment and services). After 2006, the delivery of large volumes is entirely dependent upon agreement on an acceptable price formula. For Turkmen gas to be delivered when the time for full implementation of the contract arrives, additional transport capacity will be required for which an inter-governmental agreement on pipeline reconstruction has already been signed. A study on how to increase the gas transportation network between Russia and Turkmenistan, Uzbekistan and Kazakhstan to 90 bcm/a is currently underway. Turkmen gas reserves are estimated at 2,860 bcm. Production of Turkmen gas is expected to hit 120-130 bcm/a by 2010.

In 2001, Turkmenistan and Ukraine signed a five-year contract to supply annually 36 bcm to Ukraine (almost two-thirds of total imports). This gas will flow to Ukraine through the Gazprom system, but under a contract with Eural Trans Gas kft. This is a unique, but opaque example of virtual third-party access to Gazprom infrastructure to flow Turkmen gas to a third party. Eural Trans Gas is re-exporting some of this Turkmen gas to Central Europe.

Kazakhstan

In June 2002, the Kazakh Government established Kazrosgaz, a 50/50 joint venture between the state oil and gas company Kazmunaigaz and Gazprom to promote gas exports. The agreement covers the delivery of up to

15 bcm/a by 2010, including Karachaganak, up to 7 bcm/a agreed up to 2006, and North Caspian (Kashagan) gas via existing pipelines.

Uzbekistan

In December 2002, Gazprom and the Uzbek oil and gas company, Uzbek-neftegaz, signed a cooperation agreement, which specifically envisages the delivery of Uzbek gas to Russia (5-10 bcm/a) for the period 2003-2012.

Table 7.11. Gazprom's expected imports of Central Asian natural gas (bcm)

Exporter	2004	2010
Turkmenistan	5	80
Kazakhstan	7	15
Uzbekistan	5	10
Total	**17**	**105**

Source: International Gas Report, N. 493, 13 February 2004.

Implications for security of gas supply

Gazprom's various arrangements with Central Asian gas suppliers raise the question of whether the deals have implications for security of gas supply to Europe. Of particular interest is the deal with Turkmenistan, under which Turkmenistan sells a substantial share of its present gas production to Gazprom which, in turn, uses the gas to supply its Western European customers under existing contractual arrangements.

According to Gazprom, the deals allow additional gas resources to be secured at relatively low cost using existing infrastructure. Gazprom argues that this gas backs up the delivery obligations of Russia and thus improves the security of gas supply of European customers. Compared to a direct sale of Turkmen gas to European customers, the reinforcement by Gazprom of Turkmen gas drawing on all the flexibility instruments available in Russia, ensures the reliability of Russian gas deliveries, that the European customers have come to expect of Gazprom.

As a matter of principle, mature market economies have agreed basic market rules that govern equitable and transparent market integration.

Transition economies including Russia and the Newly Independent States have made significant progress in moving towards the liberal standards they have set for themselves, but much more reform is needed. Within the framework of state sovereignty and sovereign rights over energy resources and in a spirit of political and economic cooperation, all states must promote an efficient energy market throughout Europe and Asia to contribute to a secure functioning of the global energy market on the principle of non-discrimination, market-oriented price formation and transparency. During this process, states must remain alert to the implications of uneven progress.

Caspian states collectively have substantial gas resources that can reach European markets in a number of ways. Various schemes are under study to bring Caspian Basin gas, e.g., across Turkey to European customers, whereas Gazprom logically seeks to encourage its flow through Russian systems retaining a predominant position in Eurasian gas markets. How these alternative sources of gas reach European customers will determine their ability to contribute to the diversity of European supplies, their influence on price developments as alternative gas sources compete for market position and the attractiveness of investment opportunities for upstream operators.

In the longer term, these same considerations will shape how or whether Middle Eastern gas reaches Europe through pipelines or as LNG.

Exports

In 2002, Russia supplied 34% (110 bcm) of OECD European imports of natural gas, making it OECD Europe's largest supplier. Gas for export to EU on average travels 3,400 km in the network. Gazexport, the subsidiary of Gazprom responsible for exports, supplies natural gas to 21 countries in western and central Europe, Ukraine and Belarus. The main market for Russian gas exports remain central and western Europe (133 bcm exported in 2003). Germany is the largest importer (35 bcm in 2003), followed by Italy (19.8 bcm), Turkey (12.8 bcm) and France (11.2 bcm). New importers are emerging, in particular the UK market, where Gazprom sold 2 bcm in 2003. Currency earnings grew to a record of $16.5 billion in 2003.

Figure 7.15. Russian gas exports to central and western Europe

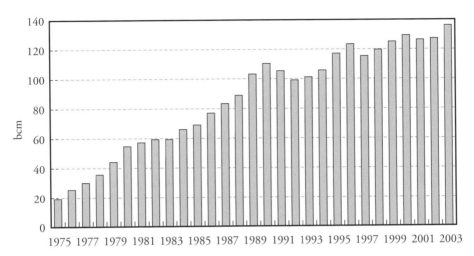

* From 1975 to 1989, exports from FSU.
Source: Cedigaz, IEA

WEO 2002 projects that net Russian exports will increase from 174 bcm in 2001 to 280 bcm 2030. As a result, Russia will remain the largest gas exporter in the world in 2030. OECD Europe will continue to attract the bulk of exports from Russia, but new markets, primarily in Asia, will also emerge. This is in line with the outlook of the Russian Energy Strategy (net exports of 230 bcm per year by 2020). Long-term export contracts amounting to a total remaining volume of 2,400 bcm have been signed so far. Long-term contracts are particularly important for Gazprom as their income acts as collateral for its foreign credits. Most of Gazprom's credit agreements stipulate re-payment from the proceeds of gas exports.

Transit

Russian gas exports to Western Europe transit either through Ukraine (around 80% of Russian exports in 2003) or through Belarus (20%). Russia's relationships with its two main transit countries have often been troubled, due to a legacy of unclear contractual arrangements about ownership, transit and payment problems from the Former Soviet Union. In several cases volumes declared for transit have not reached their destination. Transit problems through Ukraine convinced Gazprom to build the Yamal pipeline and recent transit issues with Belarus may be cited to underpin the construction of the North European Gas Pipeline.

Transit is an increasingly important element for security of gas supply to Europe. The most secure transit regime is typically one that is transparent and non-discriminatory. Such a regime allows an optimal allocation of gas flows and can attract the investment needed for maintenance and expansion. Existing transit routes, particularly those through Russia and Ukraine, are old and need investment to maintain their reliability. They are also controlled by state companies instead of market forces. Applying the principle of freedom of transit as recognised by all the signatories of the Energy Charter Treaty would improve the security of the system. Given the already dominant role of Gazprom, its attempt to extent its control over supply and transport infrastructure in economies in transition – however rational – has ramifications for countries dependent on FSU natural gas imports, and ultimately, for supply security in Western Europe.

Ukraine

Ukraine is a crucial issue for any Russian export strategy. The country transits about 80% of Russian gas exports (106 bcm in 2003) to Europe and has operated since the Soviet Union began exporting gas. After the dissolution of the Soviet Union, relations between Ukraine and Russia became tense over allegations of unauthorised siphoning, payments problems and other issues. Ukraine accumulated a large debt for gas use in the 1990s. The situation improved in 2000, when the two countries agreed on Ukraine's $1.4 billion arrears for previous supplies. In 2002, they further agreed on a long-term transit agreement. The long-lasting dispute between the two countries led Russia to actively seek alternative routes to European markets, such as the Yamal pipeline, via Belarus and Poland to Germany and more recently the Blue Stream pipeline to Turkey. This latter was a tremendous technical challenge but the route avoided any transit country.

In June 2002, a tri-lateral agreement between Ukraine, Russia and Germany was signed to create the framework for an international consortium to manage the gas transit system (GTS) including Gazprom, Naftogaz of Ukraine and foreign partners (Ruhrgas, in particular) to address its management. However, since that initial agreement, negotiations have been limited to Gazprom and Ukrainian interests. Western interests are said to be expected to participate at a later date. The main interest is that gas is reliably delivered to European customers. Western interests are aware that taking over a part responsibility for the Ukrainian transit system will not be without risk, but companies would do it, if it would offer a final reliable solution to the tiresome transit problem. In spite of the wish by Western companies to participate, they have so far not been invited to participate in the negotiations.

Gazprom and Naftogaz have started to negotiate the details, in particular, ownership rights of the consortium. The two sides have agreed in principal to build a new gas transit pipeline parallel to the existing one; the capacity would be up to 29 bcm/a. This agreement leaves several questions unanswered including how Ukraine will pay for maintaining the existing, larger pipeline responsible for the majority of gas flow. Under the agreement with Gazprom, the new pipeline will be financed through debt that would be repaid with gas transit fees rather than by companies that might invest, avoiding the need for debt financing.

GTS was built as part of the integrated Soviet gas pipeline system without regard to national borders, combining domestic supply and export functions. It has a theoretical transit capacity of 170 bcm/a, of which 135 bcm/a is dedicated to central and western European requirements (the system also delivers gas to FSU and Southern Russia). Most of the pipes are over 25 years old. Lack of reinvestment in maintenance and repair has raised questions about a gradual deterioration of the reliability of the system and its impact on security of supplies. Estimates of investment required in the system in the next 20 years range from $10 to 20 billion. As these sums would require the participation of international companies to provide the financing, an open, transparent regime would be a prerequisite. The consortium, if opened to other investors and structured to attract equity investment, could provide such a regime.

Belarus/Poland

Prior to the opening of the Yamal pipeline, virtually all Russian gas supplies to Europe transited Ukraine to Slovakia. At the end of the 1990s, to diversify its supply routes Gazprom decided to build a new pipeline through Belarus and Poland to Germany with delivery at Frankfurt/Oder at the German/Polish border. Now completed, the capacity of the pipeline is 19 bcm/a.

The Belarusian section is owned by Beltransgaz; the Polish section is operated and owned by EuRoPol Gaz, a joint venture between Gazprom (48%), POGC (48%) and Gas Trading (4%). It is scheduled to reach full capacity by 2005 (around 32 bcm/a). The original project foresaw another parallel line of 32 bcm/a. However, plans for a second pipeline through Poland have now been put on hold as Gazprom has favoured the option with the North European Gas Pipeline, bypassing any transit country.

On 19 February 2004, Gazprom cut all deliveries to Belarus including all transit volumes. While Gazprom has cut domestic supply in Belarus and other FSU countries in the past, this was the first time their actions have effected transit volumes to Europe. Deliveries were resumed the next day. The disputes between Gazprom and Belarus about valuation of the Belarus transit system, the transit fee, the price for gas deliveries the duration of contracts, payments etc. are very complicated and can only be resolved by the parties.

On the other hand, the dispute led to Gazprom interrupting the flow of gas to the transit system. Contractual deliveries by Gazprom to Germany and the Netherlands were fulfilled by delivering out of the storage in Rheden (North Germany), owned by Wingas (65% Wintershall, 35% Gazprom). Poland and Lithuania were affected by the cut, leading to some supply cuts to industry, although smaller customers continued to be supplied.

While the incident caused some rearrangement of gas flows in the EU gas system, its impact for the EU market was handled in the first instance out of the supply portfolio of the supplier (like for the Algerian Skikda accident). While the buyers in Germany and the Netherlands would have been able to cope with the problem if necessary, the incident was a reminder to public policy makers that assuring reliability of gas supply requires also looking through borders and beyond contractual arrangements to the practices of ultimate suppliers and other parties involved.

Slovakia/Czech transit

Further downstream, Gazprom has an option – not yet exercised – to take over either one third or one quarter of the joint share of Ruhrgas and Gaz de France in the transit system in Slovakia (SPP). Ruhrgas and GdF acquired each a share of 24.5% when 49% of the Slovak gas company SPP was privatised in 2002. The composition of SPP ownership is a priority matter for the Slovak authorities as they seek to promote competition, diversification of supply and incentives to enhance energy efficiency, as their regulatory authorities gain strength.

The Czech transit system is now owned by German RWE since the privatisation of the Czech gas company Transgas in 2002. As in the case of Slovakia, the former arrangement from the Comecon era – where Russia was delivering gas in compensation for transit – was replaced at the end of the 1990s by standard long-term transportation contracts and separate purchase contracts for the gas, both designed in line with the usual Continental European practice.

New export pipelines to OECD Europe

New Russian export capacity includes the Yamal pipeline which can carry about 20 bcm/a and the Blue Stream pipeline which started operations in December 2002. Eni and Gazprom have invested $3.2 billion in the line, which has a capacity of 16 bcm/a.[105] Both of these pipelines were built to circumvent the problems Gazprom was experiencing in transit states. Whether the incremental capacity would have been required by a well-functioning commercial market is an open question – but if the capacity is in excess of requirements, then ultimately more costs than necessary are incurred.

Gazprom now plans a new direct transit project through Ukraine and is promoting the construction of a new direct line to Germany through the Baltic Sea – the NEGP.

---

105 Shortly after its commissioning in December 2002, deliveries via the Blue Stream pipeline were stopped, following a dispute between Gazprom and Botas on prices and invoices and in view of difficulties in taking the volumes. The contract signed by the two companies foresees the delivery of 365 bcm over the period 2003-2025, with a peak of 16 bcm/a to be reached in 2007. The original plan was for 2 bcm to be taken in 2003 (1.2 bcm was taken). After the resolution of the conflict, flows have started again and Turkey is expected to take 4 bcm in 2004.

North European Gas Pipeline (NEGP)

Gazprom's plan for a North European Gas Pipeline aims largely at providing a direct route for Russian gas into the EU and then on to the UK. The pipeline would be 5,000-km long and run through the Baltic Sea from Vyborg to the German coast and across Dutch territory. The project includes the construction of branches of the line to supply gas to Finland, Sweden, the UK and Northern European countries. The initial source of gas for the pipeline would be the gas fields in the Nadym-Pur-Tazov Region and later the Yamal peninsular, Obsko-Tazovsky Bay and the Shtokmanov gas fields. According to Gazprom, the pipeline should begin transporting natural gas in 2007, and be running at full capacity by 2009, although these dates seem very optimistic. The pipeline's capacity would be 19 to 30 bcm/a. The total value of the project is $5.7 billion. Gazprom's own financial resources would be used to finance the project. The pipeline project, included in EC TEN projects, received an important boost as Russian and UK energy ministers signed a preliminary agreement in July 2003 pledging to cooperate to bring the pipeline on stream. Potential partners for the North European Gas Pipeline include UK Centrica, Anglo-Dutch Shell, Germany's E-on and Wintershall, Dutch Gasunie, French Total and Finland's Fortum. In January 2004, the Russian Government approved the proposal to build the pipeline. The test of this pipeline proposal will be whether commercial operators are prepared to provide the capital necessary.

Domestic market

Gas consumption in Russia totalled 415 bcm in 2003 (including fuel consumption by the gas industry). The largest consumer is the power sector (about 40%), followed by industry (30%), residential (20%) and other (10%). Gas represents 42% of the electricity generation mix.

WEO 2002 projects that natural gas, already the main fuel in Russia's energy mix, will become even more dominant over the next thirty years. The share of gas in total primary energy supply is projected to rise from 52% in 2000 to 56% in 2030. Its share of final energy consumption will increase from 27% to 32%. Most of the growth in primary demand for gas will come from the power sector. By 2030, gas will fuel almost 60% of total electricity generation, compared to 42% in 2000.

This is different from the Russian Energy Strategy in which a major priority is to reduce the use of gas by power stations and increase the share of households, the municipal sector and the petrochemical industry in total consumption. In the Russian Strategy, new power stations will be based on coal, apart from CHPs in large cities, which will burn gas. Therefore the share of gas in the Russian energy balance is projected to decrease from 50% to 45-46% in 2020. However, with the restructuring and liberalising of the electricity market, market players will decide based on the most cost competitive and efficient fuel what future power generation will be. It is therefore difficult to project the future fuel mix for power generation.

The Strategy sets out an objective for reducing by 50% the energy intensity of the national economy. The improvement in energy efficiency depends largely on the implementation of price reform but also on the effective implementation of an energy efficiency policy. The Russian Energy Strategy calls for an increase in domestic gas prices to $36-41/1,000 cm by 2006 and up to $59-$64/1,000 cm by 2010 (not including VAT or distribution charges). Besides the increase in domestic gas prices, the Strategy plans other steps to stimulate competition in the Russian market: encouraging independent gas producers; opening access to the gas transmission network; and granting subsidies to low-income consumers to mitigate the social effects of price increases.

Modernisation of the economy

The potential conflict between using gas for domestic use or export raises the question of whether there will be sufficient incentive for gas producers in Russia to export gas for power generation in OECD countries (see Chapter 3) rather than producing more gas or electricity-intensive products for export. The Russian Government is considering proposals for the re-distribution of investment resources between the raw material extraction and processing sectors of the economy.[106] The concern is that Russia is exporting too much of its natural gas resources when it could earn more revenue by processing them and exporting the products. In the

---

106 Russian Energy Monthly, January 2004.

long-term Strategy, the Ministry expressed the hope that the share of crude oil and gas exports would decline in favour of added value goods such as oil products and petrochemicals. However this process will depend on the overall development of economic activity. Another strategy is to raise taxation in the resource sector and redistribute the revenue to stimulate the manufacturing sectors.

Reforms and domestic pricing[107]

The attractiveness of the Russian gas sector to investors (foreign and domestic) depends on the economic conditions in Russia in general, and on the success of upstream and downstream gas market reforms in particular.

Upstream, until recently, the completion of the production-sharing agreements (PSAs) was regarded as a crucial step in providing the fiscal and legal certainty and long-term guarantees necessary for large-scale investments in the oil and gas industry. However, in 2003 the State Duma passed a law requiring new acreage to be offered by open tender. Only those plots that attract no initial interest (mega-projects or smaller developments in difficult-to-develop regions or offshore) would then be offered under PSA terms. This should be viewed in the light of what was always intended by PSAs in Russia; i.e., a mechanism to ensure investment flows during a time when the Tax Code and other necessary legal and regulatory frameworks were being formulated, put in place, tested and gained the trust of investors. The fate of legislative developments on PSAs is also a function of international oil prices. At current oil prices, many Russian oil companies consider current fiscal terms attractive enough to invest in short term projects, enhancing production at existing fields. This could change, however, if the tax regime were to change again or if oil prices were to fall.

In the future, Gazprom developments will need huge long-term investments – and foreigners, if invited in, will need the assurances provided by PSAs – or some other assurances of stable investment terms over the life of the project, in particular to develop more difficult fields.

Downstream, government plans for the possible restructuring of the Russian gas industry are another major uncertainty affecting investment

---

107 This section is drawn from *WEIO 2003*.

prospects. The Government had approved the principle of reform of the gas sector in 2000, and discussed the matter in 2002 and 2003. Clearly, the pace and nature of any restructuring would have a profound impact on the monopoly position of Gazprom and the role of independent gas companies, and on the opportunities for investment. Currently, reforms are focused on domestic pricing and access to gas pipelines, and not so much focused on unbundling of Gazprom. However, in mid-March 2004, Gazprom's CEO Alexei Miller stated that by the beginning of 2005, Gazprom would financially unbundle its accounts according to activities – production, transportation, gas processing, storage and distribution. Financial unbundling will allow for transparency in transportation tariff setting – key for third-party access – and will also clarify where efficiency and cost-cutting can be enhanced. The Russian Ministry of Economic Development and Trade is encouraged by this first step proposed by Gazprom, viewing financial unbundling a first step many companies in other countries have taken towards effective and efficient restructuring. The impact on security of gas supply now depends on a successful implementation of this positive move.

The outlook to raise domestic gas prices to cost-reflective levels over the next 5 years is also a key factor in the reform of the gas sector. This is a major issue in Russian negotiations to join the WTO. The Government has therefore embarked in a progressive reform of domestic market prices, in line with increase in power purchase and GDP. In particular, households will continue to benefit from discount prices (around 70% of wholesale price). Export profits have financed the maintenance of regulated gas prices in the domestic market and are used by the Government as a tool to subsidise the rest of the Russian economy.

The Energy Strategy assumes that prices will be gradually raised to full-cost levels of $59 to $64/1,000 cm by 2010, and completely deregulated thereafter. Wholesale prices for gas sold to Russian customers increased by 20% in the first quarter of 2004 (RR825.5/1,000 cm – $29.5) from their level in 2003 of RR690/1,000 cm ($24.6).[108] The increase proposed for

---

108 While domestic sales may look profitable for Gazprom on an accounting cost basis – the company is expected to make a profit of RR1.7 billion ($60 million) on domestic sales in 2004 – when the return on capital employed (economic cost) is considered, domestic sales are loss-making. The economic break-even point is estimated at $35/1,000 cm, a level soon to be reached. Gas Matters, April 2003 and IEA (2003h).

2006 is to $36/1,000 cm and for a lower increase thereafter. Although the Government recognises that prices must rise to allow investment in the gas industry (by Gazprom and other producers), it is concerned about the impact of price changes on the Russian economy. The Russian Ministry of Economic Development and Trade is also of the opinion that there are many efficiency gains to be made within the Gazprom management structure. Thus by limiting increases in gas tariffs, Gazprom will be forced to cut costs and improve efficiency. The Government also factors in the export prices on European markets and assesses the needed increase in domestic revenues based on Gazprom's export revenues. Thus high export prices reduce the incentive for meeting gas price reform targets set in the Strategy.

The establishment of an effective third-party access regime is likely to prove crucial to the outlook for investment by non-Gazprom companies. Although Gazprom is legally obliged to offer spare transportation capacity to third parties, few agreements have been reached, mainly because transit charges are considered prohibitive.[109] Gazprom also claims a shortage of capacity at gas-processing facilities and parts of its pipeline network. As all of these are owned by Gazprom, it is difficult for regulators or third parties wanting access to prove their point. As a result, independents often sell their gas, directly to Gazprom, or flare associated gas. Selling directly to Gazprom, however, provides limited incentive to independents to invest in developing gas fields, because they are faced with a monopsony buyer and have little leverage over price or reliable access to markets through Gazprom's infrastructure. Gazprom currently only pays independents around $20-25/1,000 cm. In some cases independents already sell directly to final customers and get prices in the range of $30-35/1,000 cm. Selling more gas directly to end-users and obtaining separate transportation contracts from Gazprom would allow independents to seek better pricing terms and give them stronger guarantees over future revenues. Concerns

---

109 Third-party access to transmission was introduced in 1997 with an independent regulator, the Federal Energy Commission (FEC), to oversee the design and implementation of tariffs for inter-regional transmission and of tariffs set by Gazprom (considered to be a natural monopoly) in transmission. It appears to be difficult for the FEC to verify whether spare capacity exists at all in Gazprom's transmission system. In November 2000 a Commission on access to oil and gas pipelines was created. Since 2000 there has been a single tariff for deliveries to domestic customers and to export customers from $0.60-1/1,000 cm /100 km improving incentives for independent producers to supply the Russian market.

over gas flaring may increase pressure on Gazprom to improve access conditions. So far Gazprom buys some of the associated gas, for instance in October 2003, Gazprom concluded a long-term agreement with Lukoil whereby it agreed to sell to Gazprom up to 0.75 bcm of natural gas in 2005 and in 2006 up to 8 bcm, of natural gas produced at a minimum price of \$22.5/1,000 cm. Lukoil foresees its gas production to grow to up to 40 bcm by 2013 and possibly doubling again by 2020.

In terms of Gazprom's export monopoly, both the Government and Gazprom remain clearly opposed to any move that would allow independents to sell their gas directly on export markets. Both argue that this would create competition between Gazprom and other Russian gas producers which would lead to lower export prices. When the objective of the Russian Government to increase domestic gas prices is achieved, parity between domestic prices and the netback from the European export markets might be achieved in view of the transportation cost differential. This would eliminate the economic disadvantage of natural gas producers selling into the Russian market.

EU/Russia energy dialogue[110]

Russia and the European Union are natural partners in the energy sector. The EU is Russia's largest trading partner, accounting for 25% of Russia's imports and some 35% of its export trade. Russian gas exports are a major part of EU gas supplies and are projected to take an even larger share. The relationships between Russia and the EU are therefore important in building mutual trust and alignment of interests. The energy sector in Russia represents a major opportunity both for foreign investment and for export revenues. The need for new capital in the sector has been estimated at between \$460 and \$600 billion to the year 2020. Moreover, the EU and Russia have a mutual interest in enhancing the overall energy security of the continent.

Recognising this growing interdependence, the EU and Russia launched the EU-Russia Energy Dialogue on the occasion of the sixth EU-Russia Summit (30th October 2000, Paris) to enable progress to be made in the definition and arrangements for an EU-Russia Energy Partnership.

---

110 See DGTREN website for more details on the EU/Russia partnership:
  http://www.europa.eu.int/comm/energy/russia/overview/index_en.htm.

The overall objective of the energy partnership is to improve energy relations, while ensuring that the policies of opening and integrating energy markets are pursued. The energy partnership, which covers oil, gas and electricity, is aimed at: *i)* improving investment opportunities in Russia's energy sector in order to upgrade the infrastructure; *ii)* promoting energy efficient and environmentally friendly technologies; and *iii)* enhancing energy conservation within Russia.

Since its launch in October 2000, the EU-Russia Energy Dialogue has become a major element in bilateral EU-Russia relations. After a preliminary analytical phase, in October 2001 the EU-Russia Summit established the future direction of the energy dialogue and highlighted that in the short term, progress could be obtained in the following areas:

- Improvement of the legal basis for energy production and transport in Russia;

- Legal security for long-term energy supplies;

- Ensuring the physical security of transport networks;

- The recognition of certain new transport infrastructures as being of "common interest" – such projects, and the choice of routes, clearly remain the responsibility of the states and companies concerned;

- The implementation of pilot projects in the Arkhangelsk and Astrakhan regions of Russia on rational energy use and savings.

In the gas field, one of the main objectives of the EU-Russia Energy Dialogue is the further integration of gas markets based on agreed regulatory principles of internal markets as well as on long-term supply contracts. In this context, the Commission has been in discussion for some time with Gazprom regarding territorial restriction clauses which exist in certain contracts. On 6 October 2003, the Commission announced that a settlement had been reached with the Italian company ENI and Gazprom on this subject (see Chapter 2).

A challenge for European negotiators over the next decade will be to identify and adhere to a critical reform path with Russia whereby the pace of reform and market liberalisation in Russia and the transit states is calibrated to reforms in Europe in such a way as to preserve the commercial and security interests of European gas operators and more importantly, European gas consumers. Russia has many challenges in advancing its own professed interest in reform. While these are being overcome, European public policy makers must remain alert to the evolution of gas markets and players along the entire path from gas reservoirs in Russia and beyond to end-use customers to ensure a systematic evolution towards open, competitive markets throughout Eurasia.

8

SECURITY OF GAS SUPPLY IN THE UNITED KINGDOM

The UK gas market is the largest in Europe. For the last twenty years or so, it has been self-sufficient, and even a net exporter through the Bacton-Zeebrugge Interconnector. Demand has grown rapidly over the past decade, driven by the increasing use of domestic associated gas in the power sector. The security of gas supply has therefore related only to the internal dimension of security, i.e., ensuring sufficient investment in gas infrastructure.

The UK market is the only fully liquid open gas market in Europe, which allows the UK to let the market balance supply and demand by itself. In addition, the power market has opened up and close links between the gas and power markets have developed in recent years.

The supply situation is now changing, with a rapid depletion of domestic resources after 30 years of intense exploitation resulting in the need for increasing imports. Several new projects to import gas by pipeline and LNG are being launched, attracted by the liquid UK market. It is clear that the switch from net exporter to large importer as well as the changes in the marketplace raise new issues for security of supply for the UK:

- Increasing import dependence to match a still growing demand;

- Availability of peak gas supply;

- Facility concentration;

- Quality of gas;

- Investments in transmission and insurance assets in an open gas market;

- Spot and future markets and adequacy of price signals for long-term investment;

- Gas and electricity interface.

After a brief overview of gas market development in the UK, the reforms since 1986 and the recent White Paper on energy, this Chapter looks at the UK framework for delivering security of gas supply and addresses the issues surrounding the external aspect of security of gas supply on the one hand and the internal aspect of reliability of gas supply to the final customer on the other.

MARKET OVERVIEW

The United Kingdom has the largest national gas market in Europe, and the third largest in the world (after the United States and the Russian Federation). Gas consumption (99.7 bcm in 2002) accounts for 37% of total primary energy supply. Gas demand increased rapidly in the 1990s, from 58 bcm in 1990 to 103 bcm in 2000, largely due to the growing use of gas in the power sector and the commissioning of several gas-fired CCGTs. The share of gas in electricity generation rose from 2% in 1990 to 39% in 2002. This trend was driven by the economic and environmental advantages of natural gas in CCGTs, and pushed by the availability of cheap gas from the UK North Sea. During the 1990s a shift occurred in production in the UK North Sea. Whereas at the beginning of exploitation of the UK Continental Shelf (UKCS), natural gas came from pure gas fields located in the southern basin of the UKCS, in the 1990s the percentage of associated gas rose sharply as wet gas fields located in the central and northern parts of the UKCS were developed. Natural gas from these fields had to be produced as a by-product of oil production. This gave a high incentive to use this gas in power plants, effectively competing with and ultimately displacing coal-fired power plants. At the same time, development of smaller gas fields was promoted by reductions in resource taxation.

Natural gas consumption decreased in 2001 and 2002 from its historic peak of 2000, due to relatively high gas prices compared with competing energy sources and a fall in manufacturing demand. The residential sector remains the largest single user of natural gas (34 bcm in 2001). Figures 8.1 and 8.2 show the importance of natural gas in the UK energy mix and the sectoral shares in gas consumption.

Figure 8.1. UK total primary energy supply by fuel, 1970-2002

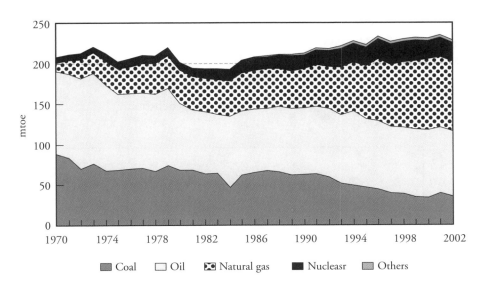

Source: IEA

Figure 8.2. UK gas consumption by sector, 2001

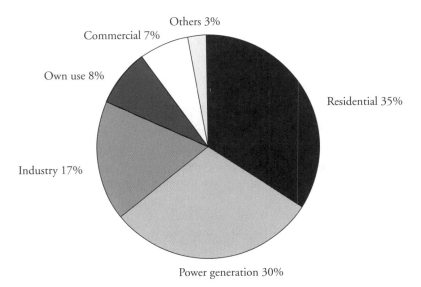

Source: IEA

Natural gas production in 2003 was 107 bcm, 0.7% lower than in 2002 and the third year of decline compared with the peak reached in 2000 (115 bcm). Figure 8.3 shows the share of associated gas in total UK production. Associated gas production accounted for 17% of total gas production in 1990. In 2001, this share was 51%.

Figure 8.3. UK natural gas production

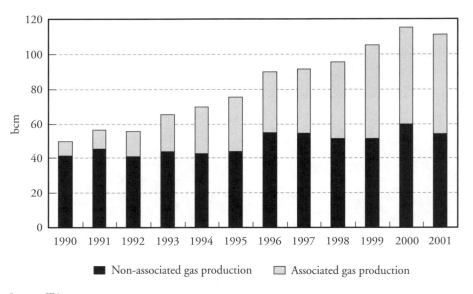

Source: IEA

The UK is still a net exporter of natural gas. Exports to continental Europe through the Interconnector and to Ireland through the Irish Interconnector amounted to 13.6 bcm in 2002, whereas gas imports doubled to 5.5 bcm. This was largely due to increased imports from the Norwegian sector of the North Sea though the Vesterled pipeline, which was commissioned in October 2001.

Although the UK has been self-sufficient so far, this is expected to change rapidly. It is predicted that domestic gas production will continue the downward trend that began in 2001 and will not suffice to cover the still growing gas demand, in particular for power generation.

GAS MARKET REFORMS

The liberalisation process of the UK gas market started in 1986 when the Natural Gas Act mandated the privatisation of British Gas, the state-owned monopoly in transportation, distribution and supply of gas, and required British Gas to open its transmission and distribution pipelines to all industrial large non-domestic customers. British Gas was privatised as an integrated business within the same year. The Natural Gas Act also created an independent regulator, Ofgas.

This was followed by a series of competition enquiries to stimulate competition on the UK market. In 1988, in order to enable new entrants to take a significant market share, the Monopolies and Mergers Commission (MMC) asked British Gas to publish information about its price schedules, which resulted in a rapid fall of British Gas' share on the non-domestic market. Two years later, British Gas was also restricted from buying more than 90% from any single field of the UK's North Sea gas resource.

In 1991/92, following a further review by the Competition Authority, the monopoly threshold for gas was reduced to 2,500 therms per annum, which allowed large households, shops or smaller industrial consumers to choose their own gas supplier. Over the same period, and in order to further open up the gas market to competition, British Gas was obliged to make gas available to the market by reducing its share to a maximum of 40%, and by releasing gas contracts to competing firms. Additional steps were taken in 1993, when, acting on the recommendation of the MMC, British Gas internally unbundled its gas production and marketing activities from its transportation and storage activities, making them separate business units.

The Gas Act of 1995 moved further to encourage competition by giving a stronger mandate to the regulatory agency and by revising the licensing framework to permit companies to acquire separate licences for transport, shipping and retail supply. A year later, the Network Code established a common set of rules for commercial arrangements for transportation. Consumer choice was progressively expanded over the next two years, with all consumers in the UK becoming eligible to choose their gas supplier by 1998.

Meanwhile, for commercial reasons, British Gas split into two independent companies in 1997: Centrica and BG plc. Centrica assumed the right to market gas in the UK under the branch name "British Gas", and acquired some gas production in the UK, including the Morecambe gas field. BG plc retained Transco and British Gas' exploration & production activities and the international downstream business. Transco was subsequently separated from BG plc in October 2000 and became a major part of the Lattice Group plc. LNG peak-shaving facilities within the transmission/distribution system were retained by Transco LNG, also part of the Lattice Group. The storage business (Rough and Hornsea facilities) was transferred to BG Group plc, which also kept exploration and production and the international downstream business. In October 2002, Lattice Group plc and National Grid plc merged to become one company: National Grid Transco plc (NGT).

In July 2001, US Dynegy purchased BG Storage (Rough and Hornsea facilities) from BG Group plc. In September 2002, Dynegy sold the Hornsea storage facility to Scottish & Southern Energy and in November 2002, Centrica purchased the Rough offshore storage facility.

The regulatory agency has also undergone structural changes. In 2000, Ofgas, the former gas regulator, and Offer, the former electricity regulator, merged in a single Office of Gas and Electricity Markets (Ofgem).

STRUCTURE OF THE GAS INDUSTRY

The British gas market is fully liberalised, with a highly competitive upstream sector. Most gas consumed in the UK is produced domestically, in offshore gas fields with diverse ownership. Natural gas enters the British pipeline network through beach terminals, which receive gas piped from offshore fields. There are six main terminals[111], of which two alone receive almost 60% of gas supplied to the country: St Fergus (NE Scotland) and Bacton (Norfolk). Beach terminals include gas processing plants and offer quality treatment. They then feed gas into the National Transmission

---

111 There are also a number of onshore connections including two smaller onshore fields and various storage facilities which also count as entry points.

System (NTS) at a pressure of around 75 bar (24 compressor stations are located around the network). National Grid Transco is owner, operator and developer of the primary gas transportation system in Great Britain, which represents 275,000 km of transmission and distribution pipelines within its National Transmission System and 8 Distribution Networks (the latter comprising the 12 former Local Distribution Zones).

In May 2003, NGT publicly announced that it would consider the sale of up to four Distribution Networks (DNs), which would represent a fundamental change to the structure of the gas industry. A decision should be taken in 2004 as to whether approval in principle should be given to this proposal.

Transco, a subsidiary of NGT, transports gas for approximately 100 gas shippers to more than 21 million industrial, commercial and domestic consumers. All gas customers – from households to large industrial – are free to choose their supplier. The network includes about 170 exit points, where gas is off-taken into either the Local Distribution Zones or to large loads such as power stations or interconnectors (to Belgium, Ireland and Northern Ireland). The interconnector linking the UK gas system to continental Europe (link at Bacton on the UK side, and Zeebrugge on the Belgian side) was put on stream at the end of 1998.

Spot trading is widely developed in the UK with NBP/Bacton as trading places with 80 counterparts. Gas has effectively become a commodity with its price set by supply and demand. About half of the gas consumed in the UK is traded on spot markets. The International Petroleum Exchange of London (IPE) launched a gas future contract in 1998.

ENERGY POLICY - WHITE PAPER

The UK's Energy White Paper published in February 2003 "Our energy future – creating a low carbon economy" places the environment at the heart of UK energy policy. It sets out four goals: cutting emissions of carbon dioxide by 60% by 2050; ensuring that every home is adequately and affordably heated; maintaining the reliability of energy supplies; and promoting competitive energy markets in the UK and beyond. It puts greater focus on international aspects of energy policy in addressing climate change, promoting liberalisation and producer/consumer relations, and innovation.

The White Paper recognises that the decline of gas reserves means that the country will once again be a net importer, potentially more vulnerable to price fluctuations and interruptions to supply caused by regulatory failures, political instability or conflicts in other parts of the world. This will require a different approach to gas policy, with more focus on external relations and substantial investment to build additional connections to the external sources of supply.

UK FRAMEWORK FOR SECURITY OF GAS SUPPLY

The UK framework for ensuring security of supply differs greatly from continental Europe's. There is an overall confidence that efficient and competitive traded markets can best deliver diversity and security of supply. Where the development of competitive markets is more limited (e.g., network owners and operators), effective regulation ensures diversity and security of supply. A major difference between the UK and continental Europe is the abundance of UK gas offshore fields – many of them associated gas fields – that so far have allowed the UK to meet annual and peak daily demands. The framework has not yet been tested in an import-dependent situation.

Both the market and the different stakeholders have a role to play in ensuring security of supply. The competitive *market* framework allows market participants to compete on price, service level, and choice of products, and allows prices to signal to investors the returns available from new investment.

The *Government* establishes legislation and is also responsible for offshore upstream regulation. It is the Secretary of State for Trade and Industry who sets the overall regulatory framework for the supply of electricity and gas. Under legislation, the duties of the Secretary of State relate to particular functions, in particular licensing. The Secretary of State lays down Standard Licence conditions which apply to all classes of licensees. Specific responsibilities are assigned through licences to gas transporters, suppliers and shippers. In addition, the Secretary of State has responsibility for offshore regulation of gas and strategic international issues, including European policy and hence for security of supply issues falling within these areas.

The Energy Act 1976 gives statutory powers to the Government to deal with emergencies in which supplies of oil, electricity and gas are disrupted. In the case of gas, Transco would act as the National Emergency Coordinator. If supply disruption were unavoidable, maintaining supply to households and other priority gas consumers (hospitals, etc.) would be prioritised.

The main roles of the regulatory authority, *Ofgem,* are to ensure that appropriate market rules are in place for the gas and electricity markets, to monitor behaviour within these rules, and to tackle any abuse of market power. Ofgem also has a key role in providing appropriate incentives through effective regulation of the "natural monopoly" electricity and gas network to ensure the timely expansion of capacity and efficient system operation.

Gas transmission planning and investment is currently undertaken by *Transco*. Under the Gas Act of 1986, Transco (as with other holders of gas transporter licences in respect of their authorised areas) has a duty to develop and maintain an efficient and economical pipeline system for the conveyance of gas. In addition, under the terms of its Gas Transporter's licence, Transco is required to develop and maintain the National Transmission System (NTS) to meet the peak aggregate daily demand which is likely to be exceeded once in 20 years taking into account data on weather derived from at least the previous 50 years. Transco is not responsible for the supply of gas.

Transco also has a Network Code requirement as Top-up Manager to ensure, subject to the availability of storage deliverability and space, that enough stored gas is available for the winter ahead to meet the demands caused by extreme weather. The top-up requirement ensures gas supply (deliverability) for a 1-in-20 peak day and volume (space) for a 1-in-50 severe winter. If insufficient supplies (including storage) are available, Transco declares a lower level of security.

As System Operator (SO), Transco is responsible for ensuring the physical balance of the network. Each shipper is financially responsible for the costs incurred to manage an imbalance in its supply and demand or a difference between its gas nominations and actual flows. Transco has a Network Code requirement to book Operating Margins to ensure the safe operation of its system. This is achieved by using storage (particularly LNG) to deal with operational incidents such as sudden losses of offshore supplies, compressor trips.

Each year, in accordance with its licence obligations, Transco is required to produce a Ten-Year Statement, outlining forecast system usage and network development over the next decade.

Shippers have a licence obligation to book sufficient capacity in the gas pipeline system to meet the peak aggregate demand of their domestic loads on a 1-in-20 peak day winter.

Suppliers have a licence obligation to meet the demands of their domestic loads on a 1-in-20 peak day and in a 1-in-50 winter.

Consumers, in particular large consumers (CCGTs and industrial customers), also play a role through demand response. Sales of gas on an interruptible basis accounts for more than 20% of total UK gas sales (23% in 2001).

Although obligations are put on each player, only Transco has mandatory obligations. Obligations put on shippers and suppliers are on a voluntary basis as soon as they are party to the Network Code.

GAS SUPPLY AND DEMAND TRENDS

Gas supply trends

Upstream legislation

In the UK, petroleum companies operate in the private sector on a commercial basis. The Government's role is restricted to technical regulation and taxation. The Oil and Gas Directorate of the Department of Trade and Industry (DTI) has the main responsibility for oil and gas regulation upstream. Its overall objective is to "maximise the economic benefit to the UK of its oil and gas resources, taking into account the environmental impact of hydrocarbon development and the need to ensure secure, diverse and sustainable supplies of energy at competitive prices".[112]

The Petroleum Act 1998, which came into force on 15 February 1999, consolidates and replaces the Petroleum (Production) Act 1934 and other legislation relating to petroleum, offshore installations and submarine pipelines.

The UK upstream fiscal regime has undergone numerous changes in the last three decades. A special royalty and tax system applied to petroleum exploitation from 1975, encompassing Royalty, Petroleum Revenue Tax (PRT), and Corporation Tax (CT). The system has been changed many times since then, generally increasing the tax burden when oil prices have risen. However, since 1983 the burden for new developments was reduced, and since April 2003, the burden for old fields was also reduced. Up to the beginning of 2003, two different systems applied to new and old fields. Government revenue from fields ranged from 30% (fields developed since March 1993) to nearly 70% (fields developed before). Mature fields were disadvantaged by a high burden of taxation and incremental projects were thereby discouraged. Taxation has been ring-fenced. Profits from one field cannot be offset against losses from another field.

In 2002 and 2003, the Government introduced two changes:

- As part of the 2002 budget, the government introduced a new supplementary corporation tax of 10% on profits from North Sea operations, counterbalanced by a 100% first-year capital allowance for capital expenditure, replacing the 25% allowance available previously;

- At the beginning of 2003, the government abolished the royalty payable by the 30 oldest North Sea fields which received development consent before 31 March 1982.

However, the remaining older fields are still subject to the Petroleum Revenue Tax and this burden is still very high. The marginal rate is now

---

112 IEA (2002c).

40% for new developments to 70% for the oldest fields, quite high compared with international standards. UKOOA (United Kingdom Offshore Operators Association) claims that this has the effect of reducing the life expectancy of the fields, causing premature cessation of production and early decommissioning. Once such fields are closed down, the possibility of producing small satellite reservoirs disappears.

The taxation regime and the declining size of fields have a negative impact on investment in drilling activity by major companies. Major companies, like BP, have been pulling out of the UKCS, in search of more profitable ventures. According to UKOOA, $5.1 billion of assets changed ownership in 2002 as majors disposed high-cost assets in order to free capital and boost spending in more promising and cheaper areas of the world. These assets are bought by smaller independent companies, often specialists in late-life fields.

The UK Government is encouraging the industry to continue to explore and develop oil and gas fields and to optimise the use of existing infrastructure.[113]

In his budget statement for 2003-2004, the Minister of Finance announced the abolition of the PRT for new projects as of 1 January 2004. This would simplify the fiscal regime for UKCS operations which would be charged a single corporate tax of 40%. According to industry statements, the abolition could potentially unblock a further 500-700 million boe from the development of currently uneconomic discoveries.

The Government's initiatives and the abolition of PRT may have a positive impact and help to maintain exploration and development in UKCS, which so far was rapidly declining.

---

113 Recent developments include:
  • The PILOT initiative, launched three years ago to bring together government departments and oil and gas industry representatives to secure improvements in the international competitiveness of the UK industry and continued E&D activity;
  • The Fallow initiative, designed to inject new life into areas of the North Sea by putting the holders of fallow assets under increasing pressure to use, divest or relinquish.
  • The Government actively encourages asset trading between licensees, better use of brownfield developments, and sharing of best practice;
  • The Promote licence, designed to encourage those with geoscience's capability to invest in generating UKCS prospects in exchange for an exclusive interest in a full production licence – with a rental fee for exploration/development cut by 90%.

Transportation regime offshore

Under the UK offshore regulatory regime, the use of infrastructure by third parties is not regulated, but has to be negotiated by the players within a legal and voluntary framework. A voluntary Code of Practice, which was introduced in 1996 and recently reviewed through a DTI consultation, provides guidance for infrastructure access negotiations.

Gas reserves/resources

According to the UK DTI, proven gas reserves[114] are estimated at 630 bcm, i.e., 6 years of current production. In addition, 370 bcm are classified as probable reserves, and an additional 330 bcm as possible. Gas condensate fields contribute 37% to the total remaining recoverable gas reserves (at proven plus probable level) and associated gas from oilfields contributes 17%, the rest being dry gas. Potential additional reserves[115] are estimated by DTI in a range of 70 to 265 bcm. Undiscovered recoverable reserves[116] are estimated to lie in the range of 235 to 1,390 bcm. With cumulative production to date of 1,726 bcm of gas, the total remaining UKCS reserves (including undiscovered) are estimated to lie in the range of some 934-2,984 bcm of gas.

Although far from negligible, UKCS potential has largely been explored and it seems that a decline in production may not be compensated by additional drilling efforts. After 30 years of sustained and ever-increasing production of gas, the North Sea is considered a mature province. Most discoveries in recent years have been small. Only two fields larger then 50 bcm have been put on stream in the past ten years. High costs are another deterrent. The region is located in deep water, is environmentally complex and tightly regulated.[117] Although the industry has managed to cut costs significantly over the period, unit costs remain high (15 p/therm on average for all fields in production at 2002 prices).

---

114 According to the UK DTI, proven reserves are those reserves which on the available evidence are virtually certain to be technically and economically producible (i.e. having a better than 90 per cent chance of being produced). Probable reserves are those which are not yet proven but which are estimated to have a better than 50 per cent chance of being technically and economically producible. Possible reserves are those which at present can not be regarded as probable but are estimated to have a significant but less than 50 per cent chance of being technically and economically producible.

115 Discoveries for which there are no current plans for development and are not currently technically or economically producible.

116 Statistical estimates of reserves in geological basin.

117 Petroleum Economist, April 2003.

Only a few frontier areas appear to have the potential for further discoveries of large oil and gas fields. The new provinces in the deep water west of the Hebrides have so far had little exploration success.[118] Table 8.1 shows drilling activity in the last ten years.

Table 8.1. Drilling activity in the UKCS

	1993	1994	1995	1996	1997	1998	1999	2000	2001	2002
Exploration wells	51	62	60	72	61	47	16	26	24	16
Appraisal wells	59	37	38	40	35	33	20	33	36	28
Development wells	162	202	244	261	257	276	230	216	282	249
Total drilling	**272**	**301**	**342**	**373**	**353**	**356**	**266**	**275**	**342**	**293**

Source: DTI

Development drilling for gas has continued at a sustained rate, despite a drop in 1999 and 2000, in reaction to low oil prices and reduced cash flow. However, exploration and appraisal activity have dropped over the period. One impact is that the industry is rapidly reducing its reserve-to-production (R/P) ratio, which is now less than 6 years. Indeed, it can be argued that this low ratio reflects market liberalisation and is a normal feature in competitive upstream industry and in mature provinces. The same trend has been observed in the US, where the R/P ratio has been below 10 years for more than 20 years now. However, in the case of the UK, the relatively limited size of gas resources negatively affects the prospects of gas production.

Gas production

UK production peaked in 2000, then started to decline. DTI expects gas production to remain flat for a short period then to decrease from around 2005. The timing and extent of the decline remain uncertain and are subject to a range of factors, including investment decisions and success in exploration. The decrease in production was accompanied by a decrease in peak production capacity in recent years.

---

118 IEA (2002c).

Gas demand trends

The largest increase in gas demand over the past 10 years was driven by the spectacular growth in gas demand by the power sector. The "dash for gas" was explained by low gas prices and large volumes of gas available from associated gas fields in the North Sea in the 1990s (at the beginning of 1990, gas was sold at about 12 p/therm), making gas a very attractive option compared to coal for base-load generation.

Under the electricity pool system, the power price was high enough to cover the full costs of CCGTs. This situation has evolved with NETA. The relative prices of power and gas in the UK under the NETA regime were such that gas-fired CCGT plants could not recover their full costs in 2001. Gas use was therefore reduced as generators sought to cut their fuel costs. In 2001, gas demand by electricity generators dropped by 3.8% compared with 2000, despite the fact that new gas-fired stations have come on stream. In 2001, electricity supply from gas-fired power plants fell by 2%, while supply from coal-fired power stations of major producers rose by 8%. In 2002, gas use for electricity generation rose again by 5.8% compared to 2001. Two gas-fired power stations completed their first full year of operation, but some of the larger established stations also increased their use of gas during the year.

In the longer term, it is expected that gas consumption will continue to increase slightly. According to the White Paper[119], gas demand is expected to reach 105 to 120 mtoe by 2020 (95 mtoe in 2001). The share of gas in primary energy demand would be 48% in 2020. Most of the increase is expected in the power generation sector. Natural gas is expected to generate 220 to 250 TWh in 2020, compared with 124 TWh in 2001 (about 70% of power generation, compared with 39% today). However, predictions of gas demand could be reviewed downward because of a downturn in manufacturing demand and delays to a number of new gas-fired electricity generating projects. The current prospect remains ambitious with at least 60% of electricity being produced from gas by 2020.

---

119 Data are based on the Energy Paper 68: Energy projections for the UK (scenario CH) adjusted for the full impact of the climate change programme measures not included in EP68.

Transco[120] forecasts an increase in annual demand from 1,162 GWh in 2002 to 1,370 GWh in 2012, i.e., a growth of 17.9% over the period, with peak demand growing at a similar rate. The share of gas in UK primary energy consumption is expected to grow to 46% by 2010. Projected growth in the early years continues to be depressed as a result of the slow-down in the manufacturing sector, higher forecast gas prices and slippage in the development of CHP plants. CCGT demand is forecast to grow throughout the period as gas generation progressively replaces coal and nuclear generation. Total annual demand is expected to grow by 1.7% per year over the forecast period to about 126 bcm by 2012/2013, well below the average of 5.7% per year seen between 1990 and 2002.

Matching gas supply and demand

Initially, a shortfall in gas supplies was expected by 2005. The Government now estimates that Britain should not face any shortfall in gas supplies until at least 2007/08, thanks especially to increased imports from Norway (Vesterled) and slowing demand growth. The import requirement is expected to grow rapidly after 2007/08 and may be as high as 80-90% of total consumption by 2020. The deficit between supply and demand could reach about 40 bcm/a by 2010 and 90 bcm/a by 2020.

Transco forecasts up to 2012/2013 predict the same trend (Figure 8.4). In general, the supply continues to be dominated by the declining level of gas production from the UKCS, which is expected to become particularly marked beyond 2005/06. The growing gas demand can only be covered by a high level of imports. Transco forecasts import requirements of 50% by 2010/11 and 67% by 2012/13.

Meeting peak gas demand

The challenge in the UK is not only meeting future increases in average gas demand, but even more meeting peak gas demand during winter cold days. DTI and Transco analyse the adequacy of gas supplies to meet peak gas demand during a severe winter, and particularly market reactions on both the supply and demand sides, during periods of potentially very high demand.[121]

---

120 NGT (2003a).
121 JESS (2002).

Figure 8.4. Forecast of annual gas demand and supplies

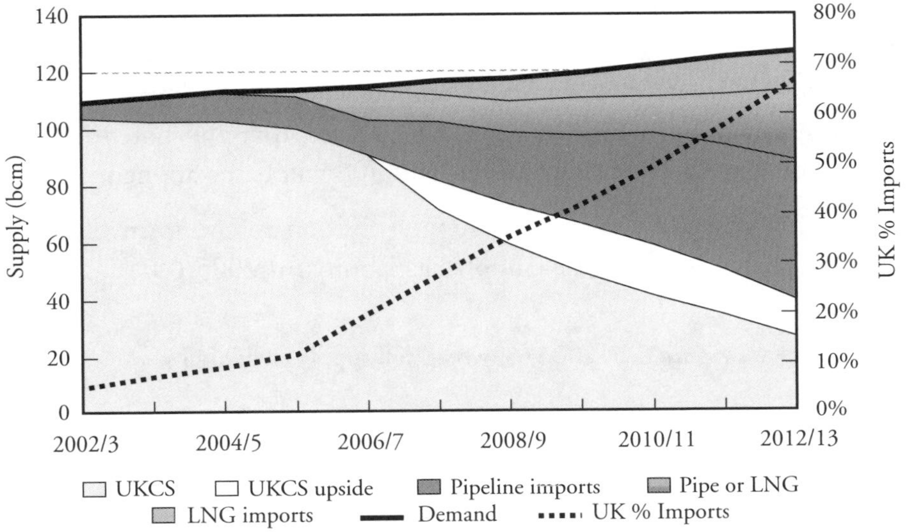

Source: Transco 10-Year Statement, December 2003

According to the Transco 10-Year Statement, peak gas demand is predicted to rise from 525 mcm/d (winter 2002/03) to 618 mcm/d over the next 10 years. The last time a 1-in-20 winter day was experienced was in 1986/87 and a 1-in-50 winter in 1962/63. To date, the highest gas demand that has been experienced on any single day is 452 mcm (4,490 GWh) on 8 January 2003. This represented 85% of the forecast 1-in-20 peak day. It should be noted that overall the 2002/2003 winter was 1-in-10 warm and was the seventh warmest winter on record. The System Average Price (SAP) reached 39 p/therm on 8 January 2003, whereas it was generally between 15 and 20 p/therm over the period October 2002-March 2003.

The rising trend in peak gas demand requires a similar rise in peak gas supply. This is challenging, as the trend in UK gas supply (average and peak) is decreasing. To meet Transco's peak gas demand forecast for the next 10 years, maximum deliverability is required from all supply sources: UKCS fields and Norwegian imports (collectively known as beach gas), imports through the UK Interconnector, and offshore and onshore storage facilities together with LNG peak shaving units. New sources of supply (pipeline and LNG) will also need to be developed.

The peak supply/demand picture suggests that 2005/06 is the first year in which peak demand can only be met (other than by demand management) by additional peak supply imports. These peak supplies are likely to be provided by the installation of compressor facilities for the UK-Belgium Interconnector and proposed new storage projects, most of them already under construction. This means that the potential peak supply deficit which was foreseen in 2005/06 will be postponed.

Figure 8.5 illustrates the winter supply position in the form of a load duration curve assuming full supply availability for 2005/06.

Figure 8.5. 2005/6 winter, full supply availability

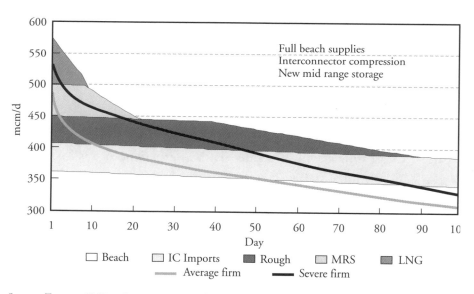

Source: Transco 10-Year Statement, December 2003

The realisation of this scenario depends, however, on the timing of investment (in supplies and transmission capacity), and gas market response to supply/demand imbalances. In its 10-Year Statement report, Transco stresses that undertaking investment on the NTS is becoming increasingly challenging as a result of changes to environmental legislation and mounting pressure from landowners for increased compensation payments. The planning system could also contribute to delays in the completion of new gas infrastructure projects.

The realisation of this scenario is also subject to some assumptions which may be questionable. In particular, the probability of 100% availability of beach gas is unlikely. Experience shows that an assumption of 95% is more reasonable (and even this level has not been achieved in the 2003/04 winter). Another key assumption is that the Interconnector would reverse the normal flow and import gas to the UK. This seems justifiable by expecting high gas prices on the UK market during periods of severely cold weather.[122] However, if severely cold weather is being experienced across the whole of Europe – or if there is a lack of supply on continental Europe – it is uncertain whether the Interconnector would flow in import or in export mode.

Market response on the demand side is not taken into account in this scenario. Although there are some short-term rigidities both in the supply and the demand side of the market, it is expected that if exposed to short-term price variations, gas consumers (i.e., power generators and large industrial customers with variable-price contracts) may react to the higher prices by reducing their consumption.

Figure 8.6 shows the trend in the margin of maximum UK supply over the 1-in-20 peak day as foreseen by Transco. This demonstrates that the peak day position has tightened significantly and will continue to do so until the completion of new import and/or storage projects. The High case assumes that the bulk of the reported import and storage projects proceed to their stated timescales and volumes, while the Low case discounts some of these projects and assumes a level of delay to others.

The figure shows that in most cases demand could be covered. However, if import projects are delayed, peak demand will not be covered as early as winter 2005/06.

As the UK becomes more dependent on imported gas, there will be an increasing need for new gas supply sources as well as investment in infrastructure projects to meet both annual demand and the seasonal and daily swings in demand. Different types of investment will be required:[123]

---

122 It is assumed that UK gas prices, which are market based, will react to any gas supply shortfall. In contrast, continental European prices are linked to crude oil prices and are lagged, so they cannot react quickly to market changes.
123 Wybrew J. (2002).

Figure 8.6. Peak day supply margin

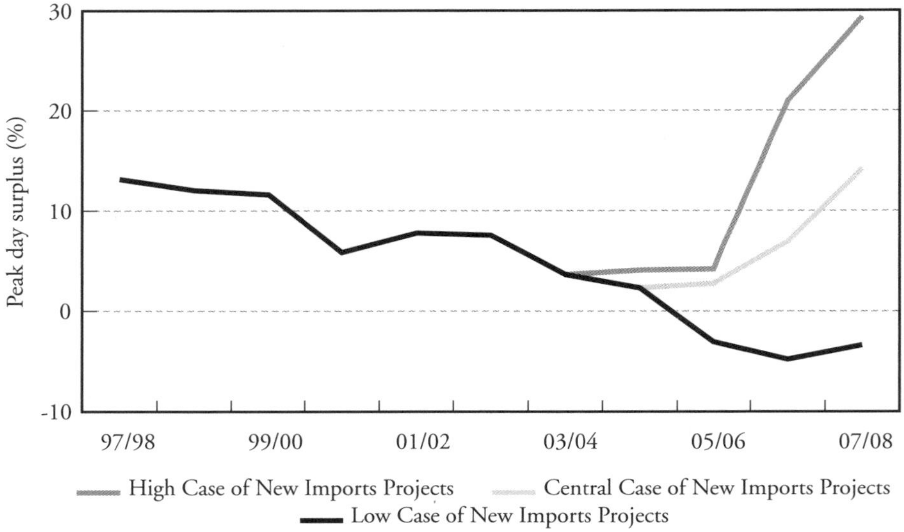

30
20
10
0
-10
Peak day surplus (%)
97/98
99/00
01/02
03/04
05/06
07/08
High Case of New Imports Projects
Central Case of New Imports Projects
Low Case of New Imports Projects

Source: Transco 10-Year Statement, December 2003

- Investments to meet the growth of annual demand under both summer – when UK fields export – and peak winter conditions. These would include:
  - Investments in new offshore infrastructure, for example to handle more Norwegian imports, a second European interconnector, and LNG import facilities;
  - Expansion of Transco's NTS infrastructure to handle the new supply patterns and provide sufficient flexibility for British suppliers to procure imports competitively.
- Additional 'insurance' investment to withstand possible supply shocks. This would require a combination of the following:
  - Additional investment in Continental transmission networks (in view of potential exports routes to UK);
  - Additional storage capabilities both onshore and offshore, to provide additional seasonal and daily swing capacity and to replace capacity which will be lost with the decline in UKCS swing capacity;
  - Resilience investment in the NTS to provide sufficient flexibility between entry terminals to accommodate the more extreme supply patterns.

NEW IMPORT PROJECTS

Players on the UK market have anticipated the change to a more import-dependent market and have signed contracts to increase their gas imports.

Imports by pipeline

In October 2003, the UK and Norwegian Governments reached agreement on the principles that will be incorporated into a new Framework Treaty, covering the tax, fiscal and safety regimes applying to cross-border operations. The agreement clears the way for the construction of the Langeled pipeline.

In 2002, Centrica signed two new long-term contracts with Statoil (5 bcm/a) and Gasunie (8 bcm/a) starting in 2005. These contracts demonstrate a new approach to long-term contracts since under both contracts gas is to be supplied from unspecified sources and delivered at the UK National Balancing Point (NBP). Gas will be priced relative to UK gas prices, probably the IPE front month quotation, i.e., the price at which gas is traded for delivery in the UK in the month immediately ahead.[124] According to Gas Matters, the core of the contracts could be a pre-determined pattern of daily nominations, rather than the more-traditional set of flexible, but linked, daily and annual obligations. This would mean that the contracts include no annual flexibility as is typically the case, but rather fixed annual volumes with a firm daily obligation to balance on each side. The Gasunie contract also includes a provision for summer/winter swing, with a summer rate of 0.75 of the annual average and a winter rate of 1.25.

These two contracts came in addition to a smaller contract signed by BP with Statoil in June 2001 for supplies of 1.6 bcm/a over fifteen years, starting on 1 October 2001, also for delivery at NBP. The gas is supplied by the Vesterled pipeline.

In October 2003, an additional contract was signed with Norway, this time using existing UK offshore infrastructure. Shell UK and Esso Exploration and Production UK (ExxonMobil) signed a deal with Statoil, Norske Shell

---

124 Gas Matters, July 2002.

and Esso Exploration and Production Norge for the exportation of Norwegian wet gas to the UK. The wet gas will be transported from the Statfjord reservoir through the FLAGs pipeline. It is scheduled to start in 2007 and will deliver 4 bcm/a of gas for 10 years. The gas will land at St Fergus terminal and will then be processed to extract natural gas liquids.

Table 8.2. Existing and possible UK gas imports by pipeline

Operators	Volumes (bcm/a)	Start-up date	Duration	Comments
Statoil/BP	1.6	Oct. 2001	15 years	Delivered at NBP
Statoil/Centrica	5	Oct. 2005	10 years	Delivered and priced at NBP
Statoil/Norske Shell/ Esso Exploration and Production Norge - Shell UK/ Esso Exploration and Production UK	4	2007	10 years	Delivered into FLAGS to St Fergus
Gasunie/Centrica	8	2005	10 years	Delivered and priced at NBP
Ormen Lange Partners	20	2007		Ormen Lange
Total	**38.6***			

* To which should be added volumes imported through the Interconnector.
Source: IEA

Infrastructure

To cope with new import needs, the UK is reinforcing its gas import capacity. The UK already has two import links: Vesterled and Interconnector. The Norwegian Frigg pipeline, recently renamed Vesterled, runs from the Norwegian part of the Anglo-Norwegian Frigg field to St Fergus, Scotland. Following the completion in October 2001 of a link between Vesterled and the Heimdal platform, gas from numerous Norwegian fields could be piped to the UK through Vesterled. The other import link is the Interconnector, with a capacity of 20 bcm/a in the Bacton-Zeebrugge direction and 8.5 bcm/a in the reverse direction. The capacity of the reverse flows is being expanded by adding compression. There are also interconnectors between Scotland and Ireland and Northern Ireland.

In addition, the UK has considerable scope for landing more gas through existing pipelines. In the northern North Sea, the FLAGS, UK Frigg, SAGE and Miller systems all deliver gas to St Fergus. Further south there are the Britannia and Fulmar pipelines, also delivering to St Fergus. The CATS pipeline delivers gas to Teesside and SEAL delivers to Bacton.

All of these pipelines extend from fields that lie reasonably close to the UK-Norwegian offshore border, with Norwegian gas infrastructure not too far away. Most have significant spare capacity already and most will see their unutilised capacity increase steadily after 2005 when the UK production decline is expected to start. Given the flexibility of Norway's landing infrastructure – gas from northern fields can be routed through the Heimdal, Sleipner and Draupner hubs – other possibilities for landing through UK pipelines are likely to emerge.

Furthermore, two plans for wholly new import pipelines are being pursued: Langeled (previously known as Britpipe) and the Balgzand (The Netherlands)-Bacton (UK) pipeline project (BBL).[125]

Ormen-Lange pipeline (Langeled)

The Langeled (ex-Britpipe) project will link the Ormen Lange field to Sleipner and to Easington and will bring 20 bcm/a from October 2007. This will account for around 20% of UK gas demand. On 4 December 2003, the plan for development and operation for the gas field was submitted to the Norwegian authorities. The Ormen Lange project has a cost frame of $9.5 billion, $2.8 billion of which has been allocated for the 1,200 km transportation infrastructure, including the Langeled pipeline.[126] This will be the longest underwater export pipeline in the world. Norsk Hydro (18%) is operator of Ormen Lange in the development phase, which includes the whole field development, a process plant at Nyhamna and the export pipeline project. Shell (17%) is the operator in the operational phase. The other partners are Petoro (36.5%), Statoil (10.8%), BP (10.3%), and ExxonMobil (7.2%).

---

125 In February 2001, Marathon announced plans for a multi-user pipeline, named Symphony, running from the Sleipner and Heimdal fields in Norwegian waters to the UK's Brae field and then south to Bacton. However, progress made on Ormen Lange may delay the need for a second new pipeline from Norway.
126 http://www.hydro.com/en/press_room/news/archive/2004_01/ol_progress_en.html.

BBL

The line proposed by the Dutch Gasunie will extend 230 km from Balgzand, near Den Helder, to Bacton, its route taking it across the coast at Callantsoog. A decision on the size has not yet been taken, but the basic design is for a 30-36-inch pipeline, able to deliver at least 12 bcm/a, increasing with additional compressors. The pipeline is expected to be operational in 2006. Gasunie's contract with Centrica is expected to take up the first 8 bcm/a of capacity in the pipeline.

North European Gas Pipeline (NEGP)

There are also plans for a North European Gas Pipeline aimed largely at providing a more direct route for Russian gas into the EU and then on to the UK (see Appendix on Russia). The pipeline project, included in EC TEN projects, received an important boost as Russian and UK energy ministers signed a preliminary agreement in July 2003 pledging to cooperate to bring the pipeline on stream.

LNG

To complement pipeline gas, LNG supplies are contemplated. BP/Sonatrach, BG/Petronas and ExxonMobil/Qatargas have plans to supply LNG to the UK market. There are also three projects to build new LNG receiving terminals. Regulation applied to new LNG terminals is an important factor for potential investors who need regulatory certainty. The DTI and Ofgem have informed potential investors in UK LNG import terminals[127] that they will be flexible and may grant exemptions to TPA under certain circumstances. They also indicated that they will request: 1) an initial offer of capacity to the market in a transparent manner, but with flexibility, if required; 2) rules and procedures that promote secondary trading of capacity rights and 'use-it-or-lose-it" mechanisms. The terminals at Isle of Grain and Milford Haven (ExxonMobil/Qatar Petroleum) have being exempted from TPA.

National Grid Transco (NGT) is converting its LNG storage facility at Isle of Grain, Kent, into an LNG receiving terminal. The terminal is scheduled for commissioning in 2005 and will be capable of processing

---

127 Petrostrategies, 7 July 2003 and DTI/Ofgem (2003).

3.3 mtpa of LNG (4.4 bcm/a). The project called Grain LNG requires the building of a new deep-water jetty to be constructed on the River Medway estuary. Contracts for the design and construction of the terminal were awarded in April 2003. Grain LNG has also applied for planning permission to triple the size of the available storage on site. In October 2003, NGT signed a 20-year contract with BP and Sonatrach for initial capacity at the terminal. The contract will enable BP and Sonatrach to supply 3.3 mtpa to the UK from 2005.

Petroplus has proposed an LNG receiving terminal at Waterston, near Milford Haven, South West Wales, where the company has operated an oil storage facility since 1998. The LNG receiving terminal will be able to supply about 9 bcm/a. In February 2003 planning permission was granted by the Pembrokeshire Authorities to construct the proposed LNG import terminal, consisting of a regasification plant and two storage tanks with a capacity of 165,000 cm each. In October 2003, Petroplus received planning permission to expand the capacity of the facility with the construction of a third tank with an identical capacity of 165,000 cm. In November 2003, BG acquired 50% stake in the terminal, with Petronas acquiring a 30% share the following month.

In partnership with Qatar Petroleum, ExxonMobil plans to build a considerably larger LNG receiving terminal near Milford Haven, South Wales, where the company has a refinery site. Planning permission was granted in November 2003. The terminal import capacity would be around 15 mtpa of LNG (20 bcm/a). The estimated cost is $1.9 billion. Construction of the first phase would begin in mid-2004 for completion in 2007, with the second phase to start in mid-2006, finishing in 2009. The terminal would receive LNG from the planned two-train facility at Ras Laffan (Qatargas-2 project) for which an outline agreement was signed in June 2003.

Although the UK is likely to become a substantial importer within a few years and the shortfall large enough for several suppliers, there will not be enough room for all the proposed projects. Some will have to be deferred or even cancelled. The key to building new projects will remain the willingness of suppliers to sign long-term contracts with gas or LNG producers, guaranteeing the timing of new infrastructure.

Table 8.3. UK gas import facilities

Facilities	Operator/Sponsor	Capacity (bcm/a)	Start-up date	Comments
Existing pipelines				
Vesterled (Frigg and Heimdal to St Fergus)	Gasco	11	1978/2001	
Interconnector (Bacton to Zeebrugge)	Interconnector UK	20 (8.5 reversed flow)	1998-2005	Can reverse flows. The capacity from Zeebrugge to Bacton is being increased from 8.5 bcm to 16.5 bcm/a by December 2005. An additional expansion has been announced. A third compressor station at Zeebrugge would bring total reversed capacity up to 23.5 bcm/a by 2006.
Planned pipelines				
Ormen Lange to Sleipner and on to Easington (Langeled)	Norsk Hydro (Shell after start-up)	> 22	Oct-07	Principles for pipeline agreed on 2 October 2003
Symphony (Sleipner and Heimdal to Bacton)	Marathon	> 18		Open season for expression of interest
BBL - Balgzand-Bacton pipeline, from Netherlands	Gasunie	> 12	2006	Open season for expression of interest
North European Gas Pipeline, from Russia	Gazprom and European companies	> 5-10*		
Planned LNG terminals				
Isle of Grain	NGT	4,4	2005	Contracts for design and construction awarded in April 2003 to Sweden's Skanska. Possible expansion under consideration.
Milford Haven	ExxonMobil/QP	20	2007-2009	Planning application granted in November 2003
Milford Haven	Petroplus/BG/Petronas	9	2007	Has received planning permission.
Total Import Capacity		> 100		

* For the UK market. The project involves a pipeline of 30 bcm/a dedicated to Europe.
Source: IEA

SECURITY OF GAS SUPPLY ISSUES

Import dependence and security of supply

A reversal from exporter to importer will have significant implications for the UK gas industry. Import dependence is not new for the British gas market. Prior to gas discoveries in the UK North Sea, the UK imported LNG from Algeria, and Norwegian gas by pipeline. The UK was in fact the first commercial LNG importer in the world. Algerian LNG deliveries to Canvey Island started in 1964. In the 1980s, the UK imported 30% of its gas consumption, mainly from Norway. Gas imports are set to increase rapidly, however, and may represent 80-90% of gas supplies by 2020. This underlines the importance of understanding the risks of high import dependence and whether markets will be able to manage these risks in a way that provides adequate levels of security.

The main risks involve:[128]

– Source dependence;

– Transit dependence;

– Non-UK facility dependence;

– Impact of neighbouring markets;

– Timing of investments;

– Investments to cover low-probability/high-impact events.

Source dependence

Initially, additional gas needs would come from Norway and the Netherlands and from the European market via the Interconnector. LNG supplies from Algeria and Qatar will also complement imports by pipeline. In the longer term, the UK – like continental Europe – will import from Russia and the Middle East, where most gas reserves are located, raising questions about source dependence. In continental Europe, dependence on external supplies has led countries to diversify their gas supplies and build strategic storage facilities. Diversification of gas supplies on the UK market seems to come from competition between

---

128 Partly drawn from *Security in Gas and Electricity Markets*, NERA (2002a).

different suppliers fighting to gain access to the competitive British gas market. It would therefore seem that there is no need for governmental intervention as diversification comes from a prudent approach by market players or reflects their strategy (LNG vs. pipeline). A concern of UK customers is that external suppliers would be less reliable than domestic suppliers. The history of imports in continental Europe shows that there is absolutely no evidence of this.

In continental Europe, one key point to secure long-term supplies has been the signing of long-term contracts with external suppliers. As the UK moves to a more import-dependent mode, long-term contracts between suppliers and importers are also becoming the standard of future supplies (Centrica/Statoil and Centrica/Gasunie).

Transit dependence

Transit can be a more difficult issue. However, in the case of the UK, short- to medium-term new gas supplies will come either from Norway or the Netherlands (pipelines) or by LNG tankers. In both cases, there are no transit countries involved. In the longer term, new supplies are expected to come from Russia, but here again, it seems that the preferred UK plan is for imports from the proposed North European Gas pipeline, which involves transit only through EU member states.

Furthermore, it is expected that in the medium to long term, liberalised gas markets in EU 30 will encourage cross-border and transit gas deals and that new instruments (for instance the ECT as such) will give some protection for the transit of gas.

Non-UK facility dependence

As stated in the 1995 IEA study on security of gas supply, "perhaps the greatest risk of prolonged interruption comes from the destruction of a major production or processing facility or a deep water pipeline whose replacement might take many months to build." Experience from the industry shows that the unavailability of one strategic production or processing plant can be a serious issue. In Australia, the explosion of the Longford processing plant caused a two-week interruption of supplies to all customers in Victoria state.

European and future UK supplies are also vulnerable to accidents at key transmission and import facilities. Uzghorod for instance, at the Ukrainian border, concentrates 80% of total Russian gas deliveries. This issue requires the continuation of policies to diversify not only supplies, but routes of imports.

Impact of neighbouring markets

Import dependence means that the UK gas market will be exposed to regional and global gas markets and their possible turbulences. The fact that the UK would import from Norway and the Netherlands does not isolate it from market changes and pressures in continental Europe. For instance, a supply failure from a large exporter to continental Europe would reduce gas supplies to Europe and put pressure on prices. This would also affect availability and prices on the UK market. This may reverse flow from the UK-Belgium Interconnector. Likewise, LNG is becoming more global. Events on the US market will impact all European LNG importers through the possibility for arbitrage between the US and European markets.

Timing of investments

Over the next 20 years, there will be an increasing need for new gas supply sources as well as investment in infrastructure projects to meet both the base annual load and the swing loads expected in winter.[129] Table 8.4 shows that about 100 bcm of import capacity projects are lining up to be built in the next five to ten years. However, so far, only two projects are under construction: the expansion of the Interconnector to 16.5 bcm from Zeebrugge to Bacton and the LNG plant on the Isle of Grain by NGT. Ormen Lange construction and engineering contracts are expected to be awarded in 2004.

The main challenge for security of supply is the timing of the new import and storage projects. Many importation projects required to fill the gap are technically challenging, have long lead times and very tight timescales. Similarly, the availability of imported LNG may depend on the relativity of market conditions on a global scale and competition from other LNG

---

129 JESS (2003b).

importers. In this context, it is worth noting that US and southern European demand for imported LNG is expected to increase significantly in the next few years.

Investments in insurance assets

The tightening supply-demand position and the rapidly growing import dependence also raise the issue of whether the present commercial and regulatory framework can facilitate the type of insurance investment that could help safeguard against a major supply shock, such as the prolonged loss of a key sub-terminal.[130] The possible mitigations to gas supply disruptions as a result of such shocks include strategic storage and onshore investment to provide greater network resilience. Flexibility and security brought by LNG imports is to be taken into account, as already demonstrated by experiences in Spain or Asia (see Chapter 4).

Gas processing plants and facility concentration

Offshore gas is landed in the UK to six main coastal terminals. These terminals include sub-terminals operated by different operators. Nevertheless, there is a high concentration of receiving capacities in the UK. Two terminals, St Fergus and Bacton, receive 60% of total supplies.

This raises serious questions about security of supply if an incident occurs at one of these terminals and affects the availability of a substantial proportion of their capacity for a significant period of time, particularly during the winter months.[131]

Recent summer interruptions on 17 and 18 June 2003 raise concerns about the impact of terminal failures in winter time. The contracted interruption to the UK/Belgium Interconnector and to a number of power plants was due to a combination of shortfalls at beach terminals (at both Bacton and Easington) following offshore fields outages and the absence of a market response to fill the gap. The interruption has also highlighted the importance of having robust arrangements for the provision of information about gas flows and the need for active cooperation and coordination between terminal operators and Transco.

---

130 NGT (2003b).
131 NERA (2002a).

Table 8.4. UK gas terminals, 2000

Gas terminals	Number of sub-terminals	1-in-20 peak entry capacity (GWh/d)	1-in-20 peak entry capacity as a % of 1-in-20 peak day demand
Bacton	3	1 237	23
Barrow	1	634	11
Easington	2	373	6
St Fergus	5	1 385	24
Teesside	1	432	7
Theddethorpe	1	439	7
Total supplies from beach			76
LNG			6
Storage			18
Total			**100**

Source: Ofgem

Besides a further diversification of entry points for gas – as will be the case for Norwegian Ormen Lange supplies, which will be landed at Easington – a reinforcement of the network and storage capabilities would mitigate this risk. Transco carried out a study to see which grid reinforcement would be needed to cope with interruption at each import terminal.

NERA modelled the impact of the loss of one of the six terminals and found that the offshore gas system and onshore seasonal storage facilities together provide sufficient flexibility to deal with any other eventualities except the cessation of inflows at Bacton. The loss of gas volumes delivered through Bacton would currently make it impossible to supply all firm gas demand. NERA's market analysis model did not consider the additional onshore infrastructure that would be required to mitigate the capacity requirements imposed by these events.

The issue of facility dependence highlights the issue of how low-probability/high-impact events are handled (or not) in the liberalised system. Although incremental investment in existing terminals is very cost-effective, from a security perspective it may be questionable to further concentrate supplies at either St Fergus or Bacton. This is recognised in a statement in the 2002 Energy review, that ..." the government should consider whether existing terminals are the right location for future developments".[132] However, it is rather difficult to judge between the considerable economic advantages of concentration (economic efficiency, development of trading hubs) and the negative externalities arising from the degree of facility concentration. The building of new LNG receiving terminals is a very welcome move to ease facility concentration.

Gas storage

Storage may provide a potential substitute gas source if supply from a terminal or elsewhere were interrupted. In addition, gas storage, both onshore and offshore, will be needed to provide additional swing load capacity and to replace capacity which will be lost with the decline in UKCS fields with high swing capability. The growth of gas demand for power generation will increase winter peak demand as well.

Storage is less developed in the UK than in other European countries. The UK has four underground gas storage and five LNG peak-shaving units with a working capacity of 3.8 bcm, representing 4% of gas consumption. In France, Italy, Germany and Austria, this ratio is between 20 and 30%. The storage capability in EU member states is roughly proportionate to each country's level of import dependence. Existing storage levels in the UK (or the Netherlands) simply reflect the fact that UK is not (yet) an importing country.

The current low level of storage capacity is explained by two main factors: UK production included a high level of swing, able to accommodate for variations in demand: and interruption of external supplies was not an issue on the UK self-sufficient gas market. However, the swing in production in the UK has decreased since the beginning of the 1990s, as shown in Figure 8.7.

This is partly explained by the availability of other flexibility tools. Interconnector acts as a particularly important source of flexibility. A decrease in demand seasonality can also be observed with more gas used in CGGTs for base load.

---

132 PIU (2002).

Figure 8.7. UK swing production

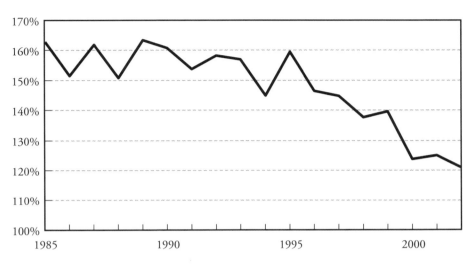

Source: IEA

With declining gas production, the UK will have to reinforce its flexibility to cover seasonal variations in demand and peak demand. New sources of supply such as Norway are likely to be delivered at a relatively low swing factor. The UK will therefore have to develop other source of peak gas.

There are a number of new storage projects on the UK market. Scottish & Southern, which has about a 10% to 12% share of the UK gas storage market through its acquisition of the Hornsea gas storage facility, is planning to spend an additional $280 million to develop storage at nearby Aldbrough, in a joint venture with Statoil. Other companies planning to develop gas storage sites in the UK include Star Energy, Scottish Power and British Salt.

All current storage projects are relatively small-scale onshore projects. Most of them are high deliverability projects (salt caverns).[133] They respond to the needs to cover peak gas demand (a matter of hours) and trading purposes. These projects will help to secure future peak gas supply. They come in addition to other possible options to provide the required amount of peak

---

133 Different storage facilities provide different withdrawal rates and hence different contributions to security.

Table 8.5. Existing and projected gas storage facilities in the UK

Storage facilities	Type	Owner	Capacity (mcm)	Deliverability (mcm/day)	TPA	Regulator	Comments
Operational							
Rough	Offshore depleted gasfield	Centrica	2,808	42	yes	DTI	Centrica bought Rough from Dynegy in November 2002. It has limited rights on the storage
Hornsea	Onshore salt cavern	SSE	324	18	yes	Ofgem	
Hatfield Moors	Onshore depleted gas field	Scottish Power	54	2	no	DTI	
Hole House Farm	Onshore salt cavern	EDF Trading	27	2.7	no	DTI	
Sub-total			**3,213**	**64.7**			
Avonmouth	LNG peak-shaving	Transco	81	14	yes	Ofgem	
Dynevor Arms	LNG peak-shaving	Transco	28	5	yes	Ofgem	
Glenmavis	LNG peak-shaving	Transco	47	9	yes	Ofgem	
Isle of Grain	LNG peak-shaving	Transco	52	17	yes	Ofgem	
Partingtom	LNG peak-shaving	Transco	103	20	yes	Ofgem	
LNG sub-total			311	65			
Total existing			**3,524**	**129.7**			

424

Table 8.5. Existing and projected gas storage facilities in the UK (continued)

Storage facilities	Type	Owner	Capacity (mcm)	Deliverability (mcm/day)	TPA	Regulator	Comments
Proposed storage facilities							
Aldborough	Onshore salt cavern	Scottish and Southern Energy and Statoil	420 (SSE: 280/ Statoil: 140)	18	n/a	Ofgem	Statoil and SSE formed a JV to develop the storage. Expected to be fully operational in 2009. Planning permission awarded in February 2000
Humbly Grove	Onshore oil field	Star Energy	100	3.3	no	DTI	
Byley	Onshore salt cavern	Scottish Power	170	16	n/a	Ofgem	2006/07. Public inquiry November 2002
Humbly Grove 1 + 2	Onshore oil field	Star Energy	290	7	yes	DTI	2004-Contract for 5 to 10 years
Welton 2	Onshore oil field	Star Energy	280	8	na	DTI	
Sub-total proposed			**1,260**	**52.3**			

Source: Updated from European Gas Markets, 29 November 2002 with JESS and Transco information.

gas: swing contracts; LNG terminals and import of spot cargoes; reinforced gas network and more integration with the European grid; access to liquid trading hubs; dual-fired capacity and interruptible customers.

However, these projects are not the solution to sustained seasonal variations in demand or any prolonged supply interruption. In the future, the UK will need new seasonal storage facilities to compensate for the decreasing swing in supplies. Depleted North Sea gas fields do offer a major potential storage resource. Investments will have to be made, which will be remunerated on the differential between winter/summer prices.

Under the current legislation, there are no specific regulatory requirements to provide storage to meet extended periods of delivery failure, though NGT is required to meet specific planning standards to deal with peak demands on particularly cold days and to meet severe winters. To maintain supplies in particular circumstances, Transco already books Operating Margins gas to cover short-term supply losses (up to 12 hours). However there is no strategic source of gas to cover a longer duration shock (unlike in continental Europe where storage facilities are also designed to cover a several-months interruption of the largest supplier). In the future, in the absence of any policy measure, it is very unlikely that market participants invest in assets with low return, such as strategic gas storage.

Transmission and balancing

Gas transmission planning and investment is undertaken by Transco. As Transmission system Owner (TO), Transco is required to ensure that the transmission system is physically capable of transporting sufficient gas to meet the 1-in-20 peak day demand.[134] As system operator (SO), Transco is responsible for ensuring the physical balance of the network.

In the period 1997-2002, Transco invested over £900 million in the NTS, making this the period of greatest expenditure ever on the NTS since the peak of initial construction in the early 1970s. It increased peak capacity by over 130 mcm/d, representing an increase of around one third. Additional investment in Transco's NTS and any new entry terminals will be needed to

---

134 Transco is not responsible for the supply of gas. Shippers and Suppliers have a licence obligation to meet the demands of their domestic loads on a 1-in-20 peak day and in a 1-in-50 winter.

accommodate the new supply patterns, and in particular the volume and location of new sources of imported gas. More investment in NTS flexibility would enable suppliers to procure gas competitively from the range of available sources, and facilitate trading. Expansion of the NTS depends to a great extent on the revenue allowed by Ofgem in the regulation of tariffs.[135] It also depends on the quality of information given by industry operators.

As a natural monopoly, Transco's gas transportation system is regulated and subject to price controls set by Ofgem. Transco's allowed revenues, which are linked to forecasts of the operating and capital costs associated with providing these services, are recovered via transportation charges and are subject to an RPI-X price cap, covering five-year periods. A new five-year regulatory contract took effect in April 2002 for the period 2002-2007. Ofgem retained the "un-focused" approach to valuing assets. Revenues are cut by 4% in 2002 followed by an annual 2% reduction. The revenue includes an assumed rate of return on its regulatory asset revenue of 6.25%. For the period 2002-2007, the level of additional investment required in the NTS is estimated by Ofgem at over £800 million.

The price review for the 2002-2007 period introduces a significant innovation in implementing separate price controls for the Transmission Owner (TO) and System Operator (SO) functions. The TO controls relate to the traditional transmission functions relating to costs of building and maintaining the transmission system according to agreed baseline capacity measures. For SO functions, Ofgem made proposals for new SO incentive arrangements that relate to the efficiency of the system operation function.

Transco investment programme

Every year Transco publishes a *Ten Year Statement* which explains Transco's volume forecasts, system reinforcement projects and investment plans. Transco collates the information required to assess future levels of 1-in-20 demand and the likely profile of supplies at their various entry points through a consultation process with the industry, known as "Transporting Britain's Energy". Transco receives non-binding information from gas

---

135 For the NTS, Transco operates an entry/exit tariff system. There are two types of charges for use of the NTS: capacity charges and commodity charges. Capacity charges are divided into entry capacity charges and exit capacity charges.

producers at field specific level, all shippers, major energy customers and relevant government departments. This information is used to derive the Base Plan Assumptions (BPA), which are used to assess the need for more capacity. In addition, Transco publishes an incremental entry capacity release statement, which sets how incremental capacity will be released to the market at entry points over and above the baseline plan. The actual amount of incremental capacity released is dependent on the bids received in the long-term entry capacity auctions.

The primary driver of infrastructure investment is the peak rather than the annual position. Transco's demand forecast indicates a 15.5% increase in annual demand by 2012/13, with peak demand growing by 20% over the same timeframe. As the exact source of future supplies is not known, there is major uncertainty on their NTS entry points. However, given the emerging clarity over the location of new imports, these supply scenarios are less extreme in terms of locational variation than the scenarios used a year ago. To encompass the range of investments that it may have to make, Transco has developed two principal supply scenarios. The first is a "pipeline" scenario, which gives greater emphasis to increased interconnectivity with Europe; the second is an LNG importation scenario, based on a more bullish assessment of the prospect for LNG imports. Both scenarios assume a mix of each import type; the differences relate to timing and scale. Investment requirement under these scenarios would be in the order of £1-1.2 billion over the next 10 years.

The new NTS price control has reflected the fact that NTS entry capacity is now sold through long-term auctions, allowing Transco to earn additional revenue for the provision of incremental capacity.

Investment in entry capacity

New investment will be needed at entry points, either to expand the capacity of existing points or create new ones (for LNG imports or storage, for instance). Up to 2003, entry capacity was sold through short-term auctions, which sell monthly and daily capacity rights.[136] These auctions

---

136 In October 1999, New Gas Trading Arrangements (NGTA) included provision for the sale of firm entry capacity rights to the NTS. NGTA provided for the sale of firm NTS entry rights via an auction mechanism, initially covering a period of six months from 1 October 1999, and appropriate commercial incentives for Transco to maximise the availability of capacity and to manage network constraints, Ofgem (2000b).

facilitated short-term availability and allocation issues. They did not, however, address the question of long-term signals and incentives for Transco to invest in a timely manner to ensure an efficient level of NTS entry capacity. To address these concerns, Ofgem approved the introduction of long-term auctions of entry capacity onto the gas network, supplemented by trading of entry capacity rights on secondary markets.

The first long-term auction took place in January 2003 and allowed gas shippers to purchase quarterly entry capacity for up to 15 years ahead (the period 2004-2017) at all entry points to the system.[137] There was active interest in the auctions until 2017, although the supply of capacity for later periods was not fully subscribed. Most of the activity at St Fergus was oversubscribed but only for the first few quarters. The January auctions therefore did not result in an allocation of obligated incremental entry capacity. However, Transco did release some non-obligated incremental capacity in certain winter quarters in response to this market demand.

The second round of long-term entry capacity auctions was held in September 2003 (covering the period October 2006 to March 2020). The major development of the auction was the sale of around 40 mcm/d for some quarters at Easington. Bids totalling this amount were placed in the winter quarters in each year from 2007/08 to 2018/19. A notable feature of the auction was the lack of a market signal to justify undertaking summer flexibility expenditure. The results of the auctions showed considerable seasonality with low levels of bookings in the summer. Consequently, levels of NTS investment to provide summer flexibility will be lower than those envisaged when the price control allowances were set in 2001.

So far auctions have not provided a sufficient signal to justify releasing capacity into the long-term over and above the levels that Transco is obliged to make available under its Gas Transporter's Licence. However, it provided useful, objective evidence about the future intentions of market participants to deliver gas to the UK. In addition, prospective suppliers of gas to the UK have been able to secure firm access rights to deliver gas to Transco's network for the next 17 years.

---

137 The TO output measures are based on an assessment of the maximum physical capacity at each NTS entry point. Transco is required to offer for sale 90% of these output measures (referred to as initial NTS SO baseline entry capacity) as firm entry capacity rights, with 80% currently via long-term auctions and the remaining 20 per cent (plus any previously unsold capacity) via shorter-term auctions, Ofgem (2003b).

It appears that Transco could not as yet rely totally upon auction signals as a basis for its investment planning, and that it should use these in conjunction with its existing planning processes. Eventually, Ofgem expects to see the long-term auctions signalling new investment in Transco's NTS, for new LNG import terminals at Milford Haven, new storage facilities and gas from new sources (such as Norway and the Netherlands). The first example of this came in February 2004 when Transco held a long-term auction specifically for new entry points. In this auction, bids were received for capacity at Garton, an entry point at the proposed Aldbrough storage facility. In August 2003, Ofgem approved a network code modification[138] which provides for Transco to conduct an extended auction for new entry terminals where there is agreement with a market participant(s) to fund Transco's costs of extending the auction. This will provide further flexibility in the auction framework for new entry terminals, such as Milford Haven.

Exit capacity

The licence modifications[139] that introduced Transco's price control and system operator incentives from April 2002 provided for the introduction of incentive arrangements for SO exit capacity, some of which of transitional nature, as well as proposals for longer-term reform of the NTS exit capacity regime to be implemented from 1 April 2004. However, Ofgem has postponed the reform and set up an exit reform advisory group to further consider how the system should be changed.

Balancing regime

As system operator (SO), Transco is responsible for ensuring the physical balance of the network. Each shipper is financially responsible for the costs incurred to manage an imbalance in its supply and demand or a difference between its gas nominations and actual flows. Transco has a Network Code requirement to book Operating Margins to ensure the safe operation of the system. This is achieved by using storage (particularly LNG) to deal with operational incidents, such as large changes in demand forecasts; sudden

---

138 Ofgem (2003d).
139 Reply by the UK Government to the IEA Questionnaire on security of gas supply (see Annex 1).

loses of offshore supplies; compressor breakdowns and breaks in the pipeline; orderly run-down of the system if supplies are exhausted.

The current balancing arrangements are daily. Shippers must provide accurate advance nomination information, and on the gas day stipulate their intended inputs and off-takes to the network. Commercial incentives on shippers to balance each day and on Transco to undertake its role as residual gas balancer in an efficient manner were recently revised. Transco can use a number of tools to balance the system:[140]

■ The On-the-Day commodity Market (OCM): this is a screen-based gas trading market in which shippers and Transco can post bids and offers to buy or sell gas either at the NBP or at specific locations on the gas network. Transco uses the OCM to signal the requirement of the system for more or less gas in order to achieve a physical balance.

■ Storage: Transco has access to some gas in storage, primarily LNG, to provide short-term cover against certain operational difficulties, such as offshore supply losses and onshore compressor breakdowns.

■ Top-up: Throughout the winter, in its role as Top-up manager, Transco monitors storage stock levels against a set of dynamic limits. If a shipper's nomination of gas out of storage would take the stock level below this limit, Transco is able to make a counter-nomination in order to secure an adequate level of storage for the remainder of the winter. Transco does not receive funding in respect of its Top-up obligations at present.

■ Constrained LNG: in respect of those LNG sites that provide transmission support to the NTS (effectively substituting for pipeline capacity) Transco procures the right to constrain shippers' storage gas onto the system when required. The rules surrounding this arrangement are set out in Transco's Network Code.

■ Interruption: In general, shippers use interruption rights in order to balance supply and demand, while Transco uses these rights to overcome transportation constraints.

---

140 Transco's reply to IEA Questionnaire on security of gas supply (see Annex 3).

Possible reform of the balancing regime

Balancing periods for electricity and gas are different. Whereas the electricity balancing regime is half an hour, the gas balancing regime is daily. Experience showed that generators, in particular, were significantly profiling their consumption within a balancing period, which could cause Transco to interrupt gas supply to power stations, affecting security of supply on the electricity network. Ofgem investigated reform of the gas balancing regime and the possibility of decreasing the gas balancing period. Ofgem's report on the balancing regime[141] highlights the current gas balancing debate in the UK. It concluded that fundamental reform of the gas balancing regime is not, at this time, necessary. In particular, the report concluded that current patterns of within-day gas flow profiling on the NTS do not pose an unacceptable threat to system security. However, it recommended an ongoing monitoring of within-day line-pack variation.

Quality issues[142]

Quality issues are a matter of concern for the UK market in view of growing imports. While appliances across most regions in continental Europe are calibrated to be compatible with H-gas and thereby can also burn gas with lower Wobbe Index[143] without safety hazards, appliances which are calibrated to burn lower Wobbe index gas are not equipped to burn gas with higher Wobbe index without health and safety hazards. The upper and lower limits for the specification of gas in respect of Wobbe Index are set out in the Health and Safety Executive's (HSE) Gas Safety Management Regulations (SI 1996/550). The Wobbe limit ranges between 46.50 MJ/cm and 52.85 MJ/cm. Appliances in the UK are tested against the current declared gas specification, but they are not tested against other gas specs. Some may be unable to handle wider Wobbe ranges.

A number of potential sources of gas imports for the UK market have a Wobbe Index that exceeds the current upper limit in HSE Gas Safety Management Regulations. High Wobbe gas uses more oxygen to burn completely. If the appliance cannot deliver sufficient oxygen, there is incomplete combustion, causing two problems:

---

141 Ofgem (2003a).
142 DTI website and European Gas Matters, 1 October 2003 and 16 January 2004.
143 Measure of the heat release when gas is burned at constant pressure.

- Production of carbon monoxide – a highly poisonous gas;

- Production of soot – an inconvenience which leads to higher maintenance costs.

DTI has started a comprehensive scoping study on the quality of imported gas. According to the result of the study, DTI with HSE and Ofgem may launch a consultation on the appropriate policy response. One option would be to increase the current Wobbe limit – with an advantage in terms of lower gas import costs but requiring the identification and removal of non-compliant gas appliances. This would mean examining appliances of the 21 million household customers and replacing certain appliances. The alternative option would be to retain the current Wobbe limit – avoiding the need to identify/remove certain gas appliances, but with a penalty in terms of gas import costs, and ease and reliability of access to an increasingly global and liquid international gas market. Producers looking to access the British market would be forced to process the gas to bring its spec into line with UK requirements. Alternatively, and currently appearing as the future solution, nitrogen should be injected into high-calorific gas and LNG imported into the UK. For instance, the Isle of Grain LNG terminal has spare room to build a nitrogen plant if required. According to a recent report by Ilex Energy Consulting, the quality specifications have not been finalised for any of the potential LNG import projects.

In all cases, there will be extra costs that will have to be reflected in the price of gas. Currently, it seems that the UK may import LNG from Trinidad, but not from Algeria, nor Nigeria, which have higher calorific values. Russian gas would be compatible with the UK system and Norwegian gas is usually compatible – though this is because the Norwegian producers process the gas before sending it to the UK. Dutch gas through BBL would be compatible for the same reason.

Forward prices and market signals

Forward prices are important indicators in competitive markets.[144] They are the only indicator of future prices (although by no means the exact

---

144 JESS (2003b).

level). These price signals help consumers, suppliers and producers alike to see when supplies are relatively plentiful or tight. If producers, traders and consumers anticipate that gas supply will – or may – run short within the next few weeks/months, their estimate of future value of gas will rise. This expectation would in principle drive up the current price of forward contracts, indicating the need for new supply (for instance, reverse flows from Interconnector). Forward prices for gas (and electricity) are now emerging several years ahead. The International Petroleum Exchange (IPE) is currently publishing price assessments for gas three years ahead. However, the volume of trade after one year is very low and the relevance of forward prices one year ahead or more should be viewed with caution.

Figure 8.8. UK spot and forward prices

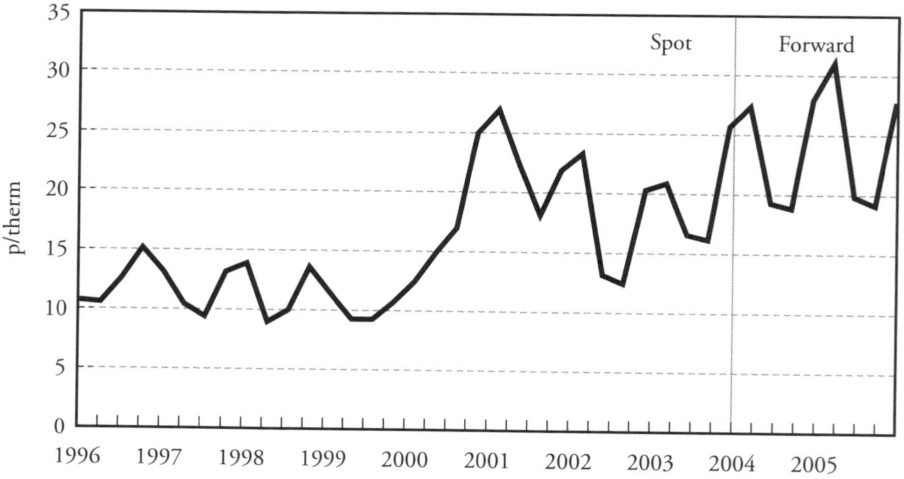

Source: Gas Strategies

Figure 8.8 shows the evolution of spot UK gas prices since 1996 and forward prices up to winter 2005. After a period of over-supply in the 1990s, which led to a fall in gas prices to around 12 p/therm, prices started to rise again at the end of the decade. The commissioning of the Interconnector in October 1998 linked UK gas prices to those of continental Europe and therefore to oil prices. In the future, beach gas prices are expected to rise due to the tightening supply situation. Forward prices are now in the range of 20-30 p/therm (around $3-5/million Btu). They recently peaked at 30-36 p/therm ($5-6/million Btu), and the Government is investigating whether the market has been manipulated or if this increase is a more structural change towards higher prices. Experience from other markets and commodities show that increased volatility may be expected in periods of high demand due to the tightening gas supply situation. Forward prices also show that the market is expecting a tightening of supply in winter periods. Prices for the first quarter of 2005 are 30.98 p/therm, they decline to 19.86 p/therm for the second quarter of 2005.

Gas/electricity interface

In the UK market, the gas/electricity interface involves major issues:

- The growing use of natural gas and eventually of imported gas for power generation;
- The impact of a tight gas supply on electricity supply;
- The possible coincidence between peak gas and electricity demand;
- Arbitrage possibilities between the two sectors linked to market liberalisation of both energy and development of energy markets in gas and electricity.

Growing use of natural gas in power generation

In 1990, only 0.8 bcm of natural gas was consumed by the power sector. This figure reached 26 bcm in 2001. In 2002, the share of gas in the electricity mix reached 39%. There is clearly an increasing level of interaction between the gas and the power sectors. 20 GW of CCGTs were built during the period 1991 to 2002. The moratorium on the use of gas in UK power stations decided by the Government at the end of 1997, marked a pause in the building of new CCGTs. Its demise by October 2000 allowed the building of new CCGTs which had been held back over the period.

However, it should be recognised that the "dash for gas" in the past 13 years has increased, rather than reduced, the diversity of the electricity market, by adding a substantial gas demand which – even in the short run – is highly price sensitive. In 1990, when natural gas contributed only 2% of the electricity mix, there was heavy dependence on coal which accounted for 65% of the electricity mix. By 2002, gas represented 39%, coal 33%, and nuclear 23%, a better diversified electricity mix than 10 years before.

Figure 8.9. New CCGTs built in the UK, 1991-2002 (year of commissioning)

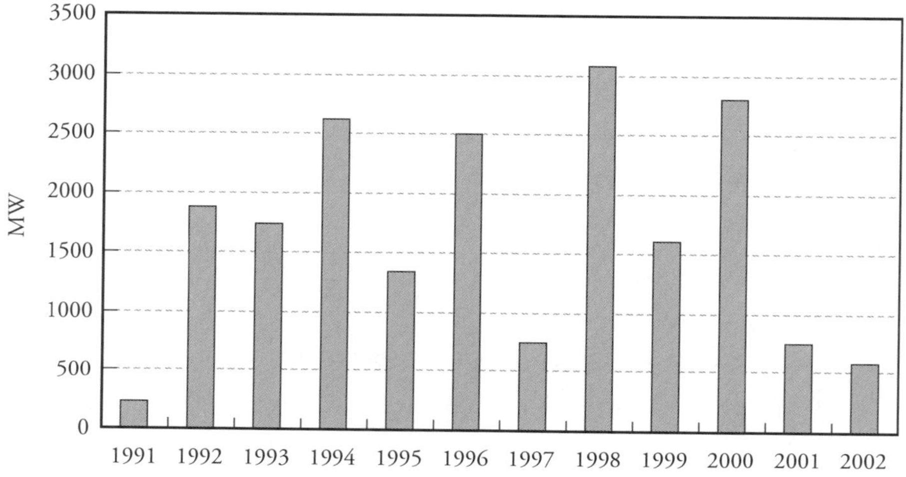

Source: DTI

In the future, DTI expects that generators will continue to favour gas-fired CCGTs. According to the Energy White Paper of February 2003, electricity produced from gas-fired stations (CCGTs and CHPs) could represent 60-70% of the electricity mix by 2020. Table 8.6 shows that most new power plants under construction or planned are CCGTs or gas-fired CHPs.

The eight CCGT projects and the gas-fired CHP projects represent an additional capacity of about 7 GW or 73% of total capacity under project. However, of these projects, only 1,560 MW are currently under construction and the future realisation of projects depends on their economics compared with alternative solutions. It is worthy of note that in the previous JESS report, there were 13 CCGT projects at the beginning of 2003 and CCGTs and CHP represented 92% of the additional capacity. In the last two years, investment in new gas plants has plummeted due to low electricity prices. The situation is not expected to be reversed before electricity prices reach a level which would make new

Table 8.6. Planned new electricity generation projects in the UK
(as of October 2003)

Station	Owner	Size	Type	Status	Under Construction
CCGTs:					
Partington, Greater Manchester	AES now TXU	380 MW	CCGT	Approved	no
Spalding, Lincolnshire	Intergen	800 MW	CCGT	Approved	yes
Fleetwood, North West Lancashire	Fleetwood Power (GE)	1,000 MW	CCGT	Approved	no
Raventhorpe	ABB	450 MW	CCGT	Approved	no
Isle of Grain, Thames Estuary	Enron (in administration)	1,200 MW	CCGT	Approved	no
Langage, South Devon	Wainstones (NRG)	1,010 MW	CCGT	Approved	no
Marchwood, Hampshire	Marchwood Power (Aquila)	800 MW	CCGT	Approved	no
Immingham, Humberside	Conoco	760 MW	CCGT/CHP	Approved	yes
Total CCGT's		**6,400 MW**			**1,560 MW**
ICGCC					
Hatfield Colliery	Coalpower	430 MW	Coal integrated gas - CCGT	Approved	no
Onllwyn, Port Talbot	Progressive Energy Ltd	480 MW	Coal integrated gas - CCGT	Being processed	..
Total ICGCC		**910 MW**			
Total CHPs		**691 MW**			**some**
Dual-Firing:					
Indian Queens	AES		Dual oil/gas Capability	Approved	no
Littlebrook	Innogy		Dual oil/gas Capability	Approved	no
Total Renewables and energy from waste:		**1,701 MW**			**90 MW**

Source: JESS, 2003a

CCGTs economical. On the positive side, having a bank of approved (consented) projects improves the ability of the market to respond to future requirements, by minimising the risk of potential sitting delays.

Impact of a gas supply crisis on electricity supply

The rapid increase in gas-fired power stations, both in absolute terms and as a percentage of electricity supply, has led to fears that gas supply bottlenecks could also trigger electricity supply problems.[145] Current concerns are that the past tendency to favour gas-fired CCGTs will continue unabated and that generators will make themselves dependent on gas, which within a few years will mean on imported gas. This raises the question of the link between security of gas supply and security of electricity. Today the risk is limited to the risk of gas supply restrictions due to field shutdown or pipeline/or compressor breakdown. In the future, the risk will include risks of a different nature, such as risks outside the country, under-investment in supplies in the non-OECD area, or lack of transportation capacity.

In a scenario where gas-fired power represents 60-70% of the electricity mix, these risks have to be seriously addressed. They can be reduced by a range of measures, such as gas supply diversification, long-term contracts for gas supplies and transportation, provision of flexibility in the LNG receiving terminals, gas storage, maintenance of mothballed coal-fired power plants, requirement for gas-fired plant to have alternative back-up fuel supplies. These measures are further detailed at the end of this Chapter.

Simultaneous peaks in demand for both commodities

The increasing share of gas in the electricity mix leads to concerns about simultaneous occurrence of peak demands in both commodities. Periods of peak demand for gas (due to colder than normal weather) will tend to occur at the same time for electricity.[146] However, although gas and electricity demand both increase in cold weather, peak demands for gas and electricity tend to occur at different times *during the day*. This gives certain gas-fired generating plant the potential to reduce production at times of peak gas

---

145 Stern J. (2002).
146 NERA (2002a).

demand and sell that gas back into the market, or decide not to buy high price spot market gas. Due to different balancing schemes for gas and electricity, operators of gas-fired power plants can use the grid buffer for free within the range of their nomination scheme. As concluded in an NGT report on winter operations for 2003/2004, under emergency conditions associated with a large-scale gas supply failure, arrangements could be put in place which maximise the security of supply for both gas and electricity consumers by using the variation in demand for both gas and electricity over a 24-hour period.[147] In particular, the winter load duration curve for electricity suggests that if gas supply interruptions to power stations could be restricted to 20 out of 24 hours (i.e., not interrupting gas-fired power stations over the few hours of the electricity demand peak) a significant proportion of risk could be removed. Line-pack would be used to deliver peak gas for peak power production, but indeed this will have some limits.

According to the report, NGT is able to provide adequate gas and electricity transportation capacity in its role as residual balancer of both networks. The system is able to cover a 1-in-50 severe winter if the UK experiences necessary combinations of high beach delivery levels with limited use of storage gas to support interruptible demand and for export to Europe. However, the report raises three major questions:

– The real level of beach gas availability;

– Switching capability by gas-fired CCGTs;

– Demand-side response.

The report underlines that the deliverability of beach gas is critical and will be dependent on both the extent of any offshore unreliability and commercial influences. In particular, the report notes that in recent years the forecast beach deliveries notified to NGT have not been achieved. NGT has therefore modelled the effects of a potential decrease in actual beach deliveries to 95%, together with the potential use of storage to supply interruptible demands (based on experience of earlier winters). The analyses suggest that with the top-up mechanism as currently applied, severe winter security could be significantly less than needed to cover a 1-in-50 winter.

---

147 NGT (2003c).

NGT states that under prolonged cold conditions it might also be expected that some or all CCGT generation will be interrupted. Based on registered capacities, taking into account commissioning and mothballed plant[148], total CCGT output capacity is 21.6 GW for winter 2003/04, of which 8.6 GW is interruptible by NGT or shippers. The total CCGT capacity that can be switched to distillates across all firm and interruptible gas-supplied power stations is 5.9 GW. If conditions in the gas market determined that all interruptible CCGTs were interrupted, this would reduce the available generation by 8.6 GW. However, given that a total of 5.9 GW of interruptible CCGTs can generate power on alternative fuels, a full interruption would result in a net loss of around 2.7 GW, if all power plants which can switch to distillates stop to take gas and those that can successfully switch fuels.

Regarding demand-side response, the report notes that aside from the CCGT sector, very few consumers are directly exposed to the spot gas price and therefore have no direct incentive to switch to alternative fuels or reduce their gas consumption.

To address these issues, NGT proposed a number of market changes; such as an increase of the level of Top-up; firmer shipper nominations (e.g., by a supplementary scheduling charge based upon the nomination prevailing at the start of the gas day); enabling trading of interruptible rights; relieving of interruption of gas to CCGTs (by both shippers and NGT) over the electricity peak demand hours; and establishing new trigger thresholds for interruptible gas supplies for winter security reserve purposes.[149] NGT implemented the former of these proposals, but the others were rejected.

NERA has developed a dynamic model for the electricity and gas markets to study the impact of a severe winter on the gas market for Transco. The model assesses the likely impact on gas and electricity prices of the optimal use of gas and electricity peak demands. NERA looks particularly at the likelihood of CCGT with firm gas contracts voluntarily self-interrupting in response to high prices. One of the findings is that power station

---

148 NGT states that out of 4,600 MW of generation that is currently mothballed, 2,600 MW can be quickly returned to the system during the winter months. However, generators have told NGT that they expect only 800 MW to be returned in a three-month period.
149 Under current arrangements, NGT can only interrupt when demands are above 85% of a 1-in-20 peak day other than to manage transmission constraints.

operators are potentially the most responsive group of customers to high prices, which is important as they account for 15% of demand at peak. Two important outcomes of the model are that generators are able to reduce their demand and sell gas into the market without jeopardising the electricity market, mainly because some stations are able to switch to alternative fuels (distillate). Therefore, it does not jeopardise the security of electricity supply.

Furthermore, at times of peak gas demand, gas generation is running on the margin within the electricity market cost merit order and is able to release gas during certain periods of the day (such as night-time or weekends) while still being available for the within day-time electricity system peak. Therefore, even at times of simultaneous peaks in both gas and electricity, gas-fired power generators can still potentially sell gas to other parts of the market and use line-pack for peak power production.

Transco has been consulting with the gas industry on the results of the research undertaken by NERA. Its consultation suggests that CCGTs with firm gas price contracts might respond to a differential between gas and electricity prices (the spark spread) if it was wide enough, but the response would be very dependent on market conditions and expected to be lower than the 50% of CCGT responding that NERA predicted. No allowance for this potential response is currently included in Transco's demand forecast, since it is highly uncertain whether the spark spread under such conditions (with interruptible CCGT's interrupted) would lead to this behaviour by the market.

The outcome of simultaneous peaks in demand for gas and electricity for security of supply largely depends on the capability of CCGTs to switch to alternative fuels (distillate) and therefore to maintain electricity supplies to the grid. This effectively means that alternative fuels must be available at peak times or for supply crisis, and that generators effectively switch. There is no data available on the amount of standby fuels held by power generators although it is estimated by NERA to be less than the 45 days that plants interruptible by NGT could be interrupted for. If switching lasts for more than a few hours or days, there may be an impact on the oil market. A report prepared by Merz and McLellan for the DTI concludes that a typical back-up fuel quantity would allow about 5 days generation at full output and many plants could face difficulties in back-up fuel replenishment during a prolonged spell of severe weather.[150] The report also concludes that although there is no technical problem associated with this high-level of gas-fired generation, many of the existing CCGTs generating plants have self-imposed limitations (i.e. inflexibility) on the gas supply arrangements which prevent the necessary flexibility for load following and frequency response.

NGT has been progressing a Grid Code Modification Proposal that would oblige generators to provide it with information relating to their capability for running on alternative fuels. Another outcome of the report is that under the current arrangements, incentives to locate power plants close to power demand are not strong enough to overcome the advantage of siting generation plants close to the source of fuel (gas pipeline).

Conclusions on security of gas supply

The UK framework includes an emergency plan for extreme situations, which would help to deal with a gas supply disruption in an orderly way. The present system of competitive markets and transportation regulation improves reliability of supply by allocating available volumes by the market. However this will not necessarily guarantee security of gas supply under low-probability/high-impact events. As long as the UK was completely supplied by many fields from the UKCS under the governance of the UK market, the probability and consequences of a longer-lasting loss of a source were low. This is set to change, as the UK will import gas under some large projects, also from non-OECD countries. The UK has installed comprehensive, transparent monitoring of key developments of the gas security of supply situation which should allow any upcoming concern to be addressed in a timely manner. This monitoring, however, does not yet address the implications of the new large import projects.

Emergency situations

The Government has in place contingency arrangements to help deal effectively with any sudden widespread supply disruptions that could occur

---

150 DTI (1998).

under emergency conditions. The Department of Trade and Industry has the primary responsibility in this area. The Government, Ofgem and industry have been working together to update the plans for handling energy emergencies. The Gas/Electricity Industry Emergency Committee (G/E IEC) has developed an Incident Response Plan to coordinate handling major or potentially major losses of supply to consumers.[151]

Relying on a large and liquid market

The UK gas market is in a rather unique situation being a liquid market and being linked to the liquid power market. The close linkage of the markets may provide security benefits in certain circumstances, particularly if a disruption in the gas supply were to occur at a time when electricity plant margins allowed some CCGT plants to stop generating. Conversely, it creates a potential issue under severe conditions when demands on both systems are high and the electricity market is dependent on gas. Some low-probability events, like low temperature, are dealt with by regulation. The handling of security of gas supply by market participants could be further improved by:

- Ensuring that generators have sufficient incentives to switch;
- Considering dual firing/standby fuels minimum standards;
- Mothballing coal-fired stations instead of demolishing them;
- Fostering interruptible contracts and demand-side response for gas;
- Giving incentives to cope with low-probability/high-impact events by:
  - Spare capacity in gas pipelines (including offshore and interconnectors);
  - Extra capacity in LNG terminals;
  - More gas storage.

Monitoring

In advance of each winter, Transco and the National Grid Company, now under the common ownership of NGT, review the interactions between the two networks to ensure their safe and secure operations under severe conditions.

---

151 JESS (2003a).

The UK Government carefully and transparently monitors the security of gas and electricity supplies. The Energy White Paper placed a commitment on Ofgem to produce a retrospective report on the performance of the electricity and gas industries in delivering security every six months. The first report was published in February 2004.[152] The report details issues which have given rise to security of supply concerns and recommends actions to address those issues in the future.

Some indicators have been developed by the Joint Energy Security of Supply working group (JESS). The JESS group, chaired jointly by DTI and Ofgem, brings together contributions from DTI, Ofgem, National Grid Transco and the Foreign and Commonwealth Office on energy security. The work that JESS undertakes on security of supply is focused on the medium to long term, rather than the short term. JESS has already published three reports. JESS monitors the progress of infrastructure projects and develops indicators, looking closely at electricity-generating capacity, the timing of crucial gas infrastructure projects, gas availability from the UK's North Sea gas fields and market developments such as forward prices and demand response. It does not yet address the impact of gas availability from import projects, which should be included as these projects take shape.

Not covered in the UK regulatory framework are obligations on shippers and suppliers or a framework to deal with low-probability/high-impact events (except for low temperatures), such as disruption of major imports, as well as avoidance of facility concentration.[153] The resilience of the gas market against substantial supply shocks is not known and it should be addressed if it has to be improved. Currently, obligations are put on Transco; however some events are completely outside its control, such as offshore supply losses due to production failure or offshore pipeline failure or failure of a sub-terminal/terminal or strategic component.

---

152 Ofgem (2004).
153 Stern J. (2003).

9

SECURITY OF GAS SUPPLY IN OECD PACIFIC

The gas industries of the four OECD countries in the Pacific region are extremely varied: Japan and South Korea are almost entirely dependent on LNG supplies, whereas Australia is becoming a large LNG exporter and New Zealand is so far self-sufficient. The level of market opening differs greatly too, with Japan and Korea in the relatively early stages of gas market reform, while Australia has been applying TPA to its grid since 1998. So far the issue has not been relevant in New Zealand, as most of the country's supply comes from one single field, transported and delivered under long-term contracts.

It is therefore not surprising that security of supply issues differ greatly from country to country. This Chapter focuses mainly on security of supply issues in the two import-dependent countries, Japan and South Korea. After a review of market trends in the OECD Pacific region, the Chapter discusses the two major issues related to security of supply in the region: high import dependence from external suppliers and investment performance in gas infrastructure.

MARKET OVERVIEW

The OECD Pacific region consumed 130 bcm of gas in 2002. Imports into Japan and Korea were 72 bcm and 24 bcm respectively, while Australia exported 10 bcm to Japan (from 35 bcm produced). New Zealand produced and consumed 6 bcm in the same period. Gas use has grown very rapidly in the region (+10% per year during the period 1971-2002) due to increasing demand for electricity. The power sector is the single largest consumer (more than half of gas use), followed by the industry, residential and commercial sectors. Gas represented 19.4% of electricity generation in 2002. The share of gas in the energy mix is limited: 12.9% for the region in 2002 (12.3% for Japan, 10.5% for Korea, 17.6% for Australia and 27.5% for New Zealand).

Figure 9.1. OECD Pacific energy mix

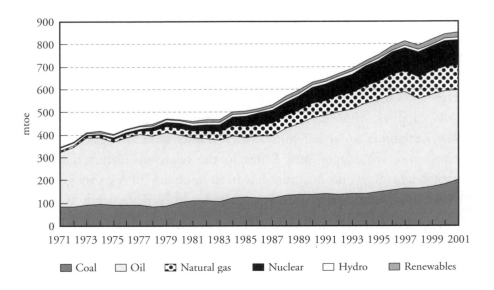

Source: IEA

Figure 9.2. Gas consumption by sector in OECD Pacific, 2001

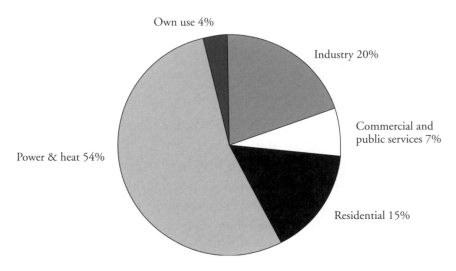

Source: IEA

Figure 9.3. Seasonality of gas consumption in Korea, 2000-2003

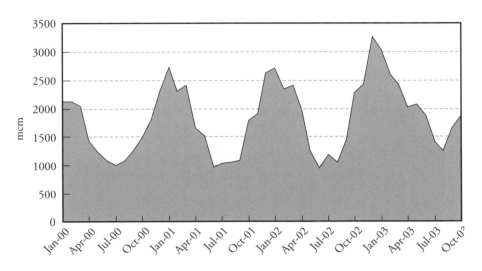

Source: IEA

Figure 9.4. Seasonality of gas consumption in Japan, 2000-2003

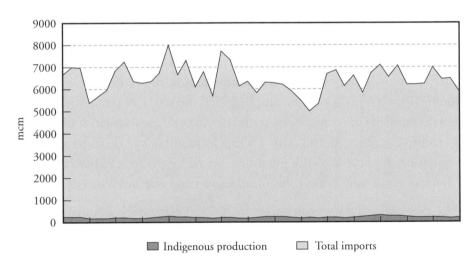

■ Indigenous production   □ Total imports

Source: IEA

Japan imports 96% of its gas consumption. It has eight suppliers, with Indonesia and Malaysia accounting for 50% of gas needs. Qatar started exporting in 1997 and already represents 13% of Japan LNG imports

(+27% per year between 1997 and 2002). Korea imports 100% of its gas consumption, with 57% of its needs coming from Indonesia and Qatar. Korea currently has six gas suppliers, with imports form Qatar and Oman growing rapidly.

Since heat is a large component of Korean gas use, gas consumption is subject to large seasonal fluctuations. The average monthly demand during peak winter months is two-and-a-half times higher than the monthly average in summer (Figure 9.3). In Japan, on the other hand, there is little swing in gas consumption as the winter residential-commercial demand is contra-seasonal to the summer power-generation demand (Figure 9.4).

GAS MARKET REFORMS

Downstream markets in OECD Pacific are in a state of transition, as governments introduce competition into the electricity and gas markets.

In **Japan**, the main legislation governing the gas sector is the Gas Utility Law. In 1995, the first regulatory reform introduced competition in the gas market, liberalising regulations on entry and rate-setting of gas supplies for large-scale consumers with an annual gas demand of 2 million cubic meters or higher. Eligible consumers were allowed to freely negotiate their gas rates with suppliers, and in 1999, the scope of retail liberalisation was expanded to consumers with an annual gas demand of at least 1 million cubic metres. In 1999, a mandatory third-party access regulation applicable to the pipelines owned by the four major companies (Tokyo Gas, Osaka Gas, Toho Gas, Saibu Gas) was introduced.

The Gas Utility Law was amended in 2003 to expand the mandatory third-party access regulation to all gas supply pipelines. The Government also promotes negotiated TPA to LNG terminals. In the area of retail liberalisation, the Government is trying to balance maintaining gas supply security with enhancing the competitiveness of the gas utilities. It intends to gradually expand the scope of retail liberalisation to consumers with an annual demand of at least 500,000 cubic metres in 2004, then to consumers with an annual demand of at least 100,000 cubic meters in 2007.

In **Korea**, the electricity and gas sectors are in the early stages of a long restructuring, deregulation and privatisation process. In 1999, the South Korean Government announced its intention to privatise the state-owned gas monopoly Kogas. Following an initial public offering of 33% of Kogas equity in December 1999, privatisation plans were stalled due to labour union opposition and to questions about the structure of the companies that would replace Kogas after privatisation. Although the legislation necessary to restart the process has not yet been passed by the South Korean legislature, certain deregulation policies may go ahead. The Government intends to open access to LNG receiving terminals and the transmission network, but the related legislation has yet to be passed. The Government requested Kogas to let Posco-SK, the private operator of the fourth terminal now under construction, to use the trunkline and Kogas agreed. Eventually, generation companies may import directly, whereas direct imports by city gas companies are likely to come later.

The **Australian** natural gas market has also changed considerably in the last few years. Competition has been introduced through non-discriminatory open access to pipelines, which cannot be contested, and intensified interstate trade through the removal of regulatory barriers and the interconnection of state infrastructure. Most states allow large and medium-sized customers to choose their own gas supplier. National legislation sets rules for interstate trade and competition and establishes the Australian Competition and Consumer Commission (ACCC) as the national regulator for the transportation pipeline grid. However, each state or territory has its own institutional arrangements, such as regulatory and appeal bodies, in applying the national Gas Pipeline Access Law in their jurisdictions, which is seen as a barrier by potential investors in new interstate pipelines.

The Government has therefore decided that Australia's gas and electricity markets are to be regulated by a single statutory body starting from July 2004. The Australian Energy Regulator (AER) will replace state-based regulators, thus eliminating unnecessary barriers for investors. The AER will come under the umbrella of the ACCC but will operate as a separate entity. It will progressively take responsibility for electricity and gas wholesale, network and retail regulation: gas transmission is to come under the AER in 2005, with distribution and retail responsibility following in 2006. AER will also have to compile an Annual National Transmission Statement to forecast possible interconnection and supply problems. Another body, the Australian Energy Market Commission (AEMC), is being established to develop markets.

Further reforms to the gas market are expected after the Government responds to the current Productivity Commission review of the national gas access regime (see below).

In New Zealand, the expected depletion of the Maui gas field, which produces 80% of the country's gas supply, signals the need for significant changes in gas supply arrangements in the New Zealand market. Production from an increasing number of smaller gas fields will require more sophisticated market arrangements. The Government has prepared a policy package designed to increase efficiency and reliability in gas production and transportation, and improve fairness for gas customers. The policy package invites the gas industry to set up a governing entity representing all stakeholders, to develop arrangements relating to production, wholesale markets, transmission and distribution networks, and retail markets. These industry arrangements should be in place by December 2004. Implementation will help promote efficient and secure energy markets for New Zealand. Open access to the Maui pipeline is also being considered, so that non-Maui gas can be transported on the Maui pipeline.

STRUCTURE OF THE GAS INDUSTRY

In **Japan**, the gas market is dominated by large electricity and gas utilities. About 70% of imported LNG is consumed by electricity utilities for power generation and the remaining 30% by gas utilities. The city gas market is dominated by the three largest companies, Tokyo Gas, Osaka Gas and Toho Gas, which account for 75% of the city gas market. Most gas utilities produce or import their own gas but some of the smaller companies buy gas from the larger ones. The city gas industry is fragmented into many vertically integrated regional companies. There is no interconnecting pipeline grid. As of March 2002, 234 utilities operated in city gas distribution, of which 172 were privately owned and 62 publicly owned. Following the partial reform of the gas market, some power companies, for example TEPCO, and other energy suppliers have entered the gas distribution market.

In **Korea**, the gas industry is broken down into two parts, wholesale and retail. Kogas, the state-owned company, is the world's largest LNG importing company and until recently was the only wholesale gas actor. Kogas manages LNG imports, storage, transmission and wholesale distribution to 29 city gas companies and 10 power generation companies. The 29 city gas companies supply gas to consumers (household, industry, commercial users). Apart from the major power company, Kepco, there are four major city gas consumers in Korea – LG, SK, Daesung and Samchurli. In addition to Kogas, Posco/SK is entering the LNG business with the construction of its own terminal at Kwangyang.

In **Australia**, there are about ten major gas producers, including foreign companies such as Esso in the Gippsland basin, Apache energy in the Carnavon basin, and Phoenix Energy in the Perth area. The majority of Western Australian gas is sourced from the North-West Shelf. The Goodwyn and South Rankin fields are operated by Woodside Energy as part of the North-West Shelf Gas project. The project has two components, one for domestic gas supply and the other for export in the form of LNG. The transmission grid in Western Australia (the largest gas consumer) is based around two very long pipelines – the Dampier to Bunbury Pipeline and the Goldfields Pipeline. Both are essentially point to point lines, although there are significant industrial/mining off-take points along the Goldfields Pipeline (which takes an inland route through the Pilbra region down to Kalgoorlie). Both pipelines are now privately owned. The principal gas sales are to large industrial users (almost entirely in the case of the Goldfields line). Gas is reticulated through a distribution network in and around Perth and to a small extent around Kalgoorlie. AlintaGas is the principal retail company. An industry-based regulator has been established and has authority to regulate all transmission and distribution pipelines in Western Australia.

Victoria (the second largest gas user) is primarily supplied from the Gippsland basin, supplemented by the Otway basin. Nearly all natural gas consumed in South Australia is supplied from the Cooper/Eromanga basin that extends from south-western Queensland to the northeast part of South Australia. The Moomba hub serves as a gathering point. Three market participants, BHP Billiton, ExxonMobil and Santos, account for more than 95% of gas reserves that have contractual commitments for consumption within the eastern Australian gas markets. A small number of end-users account for a significant amount of gas consumption. In the eastern states (including South Australia), seven firms account for 25% of gas consumption, and a further thirty-four account for 40% of consumption. There are only five major gas retailers in Australia: AGL, Australian largest energy provider, US TXU, Origin Energy, Alinta and Energex.

There is a project to build a 3,200-km pipeline from Papua New Guinea to northern Queensland (the Highlands project, led by ExxonMobil). The project has been on the drawing board for several years, and recently gained enough sales commitments to proceed.

In **New Zealand**, gas is produced by six companies. Natural Gas Corporation (NGC) operates the gas transmission network. NGC and Maui Development Limited own the pipeline network. There are five distributors and six retailers. Four of the retailers are also involved in distribution.

FRAMEWORK FOR SECURITY OF GAS SUPPLY

Japan's special market structure determines its approach to gas security. The policy on security of gas supply forms part of the comprehensive policy on energy security. With no domestic energy resources, Japan defines its policy on energy security as improving energy efficiency, reducing dependence on oil, diversification of energy supply sources, and developing domestic energy production, including nuclear power and renewable energies. Specific measures for ensuring gas supply security reflect such fundamental policies.

Japan is seeking diversification of gas supplies. Currently the country imports from eight suppliers and ten liquefaction plants and is going to further diversify its imports from Russia (Sakhalin project) and from the LNG plant at Darwin in North Australia. The variety of supply sources substantially contributes to security of energy supply.

Traditionally, in order to ensure a stable gas market, the Government grants gas utilities an exclusive service territory while imposing a gas supply obligation on the utilities. The gas utilities are ultimately responsible for supply reliability in their own areas. Regarding the protection of specific market segments, the general gas utilities are subject to a service obligation, which requires the utilities to supply gas to non-eligible consumers, including household consumers, within their own franchised service area (Gas Utility Industry Law). In principle, they should manage extreme weather conditions, market failure, or interruption of a large supply source. The Government does not impose any obligation for gas stockpiling to reserve spare supply capacity, but major gas utilities voluntarily have LNG stock for 20-30 days to fulfil their stable supply obligation. In addition, gas utilities could accommodate each other with LNG supplies in an emergency situation. Japanese utilities increasingly have more diversified energy supply sources that can help implement these measures.

The Japanese companies have developed a series of measures providing insurance against supply interruptions in the gas sector:

Supply security measures in Japan

Supply diversity. Eight countries supply LNG to Japan. Individual Japanese companies generally have more than one supplier. Osaka Gas, for example, has six suppliers, under nine separate contracts.

Long-term contracts. Suppliers and customers are interdependent and have a common interest in security of supply. They are linked by long-term contracts that have proved a stable basis for managing business in the past.

Modular supply systems. Production and liquefaction plants include a number of separate units; several tankers are involved in each contract; most importing companies have more than one terminal; terminals have more than one jetty.

Supply flexibility. Most supply contracts have from 5% to 10% flexibility either written into the contract or on a "best endeavours" basis.

Gas supply sharing. Although there are few pipeline connections, a number of terminals are shared between gas and electricity companies.

Furthermore, there is a high degree of standardisation of shipping capacity: extra supply available from a particular source can usually be transferred to another company that might be facing difficulties.

Fuel-switching. 40% of gas-fired power generating capacity is dual-fired, with crude or fuel oil as the main alternative. Fuel-switching would pose few logistical problems as the sites are all coastal and have storage and handling capacity. This flexibility will decline somewhat in the future as new gas-fired generation will be mainly single-fired combined cycle gas turbine plants. For city gas contracts there is less flexibility. There are no interruptible contracts as such. Only about 20% of larger city gas consumers – accounting for a small proportion of total demand – have dual-firing, and that proportion is declining.

SNG manufacture. The capacity for manufacturing synthesised natural gas (SNG) from naphtha is around 1.4 million tonnes annually for city gas companies as a whole.

Storage. Although Japan has little underground storage capacity, it has a large above-ground capacity designed to cope with fluctuations in supply (see Table 9.1). Total storage, at 2 bcm, amounts to 32 days of average consumption. Most companies try to maintain stocks at least this high.

In **Korea,** the Government (Ministry of Commerce, Industry and Energy - MOCIE) is the major actor in ensuring security of gas supply. MOCIE handles LNG demand and supply in Korea under the Act on City Gas Business. Efforts to enhance security of gas supplies have been focused on the stable supply of gas through gas stocks (construction of additional LNG storage tanks) and on the diversification of natural gas import sources.

Australia is addressing security of gas supply issues through market reform mechanisms to encourage competition, investment in infrastructure and management of risk. The Australian Government has in place a range of policies to manage both short-term and mid- to long-term issues relevant to Australia's energy security – both security of supply of energy and of energy-related critical infrastructure.

A Memorandum of Understanding exists between Federal and State/Territory governments regarding emergency policies to deal with extreme weather and interruption of supply. State/Territory governments possess emergency powers to impose gas rationing. Extreme weather is only a specific consideration in Victoria and is addressed by the Victorian Networks Corporation (VENcorp) under its market rules.

In **New Zealand**, the Government's overall energy policy specifies that a general objective is the reliable and secure supply of essential energy services. New Zealand's upstream gas industry is currently market driven and therefore security of supply is not regulated by the Government, although it is prepared to use regulatory solutions if necessary.

GAS SUPPLY AND DEMAND TRENDS

Gas supply trends

Natural gas resources and production in the OECD Pacific region are concentrated in Australia, which had 3,930 bcm of proven gas reserves at the beginning of 2003. New Zealand also holds some gas reserves (65 bcm). Gas production in the OECD Pacific region amounted to 43 bcm in 2002. Australia will provide the bulk of the future increase in OECD Pacific production, which is expected to grow to 63 bcm in 2010 and 122 bcm in 2030.

Australian production (35 bcm in 2002) occurs in eight basins of differing size. The Carnavon basin off the west coast of Western Australia is by far the biggest, with almost 60% of gas production. The next two biggest production areas are the Cooper/Eromanga basin in Queensland/South Australia and the Gippsland basin off the Victorian coast. Reserves in the Carnavon basin amount to roughly half of Australian proven reserves.

New Zealand produced 6 bcm in 2002. All gas is produced in the Taranaki region, mainly from the Maui field. However, the Maui gas field is being depleted and New Zealand will have to find new gas supplies in the very near term (2005). The Government favours the production of domestic smaller gas fields, but New Zealand could possibly become a net importer of gas in the coming decade. In **Japan**, domestic natural gas production amounts to

2.5 bcm and accounts for 3.3% of demand. Proven domestic reserves are 40 bcm and they will be depleted within 16 years at the current rate of use. **Korea** has very limited indigenous gas reserves. The country began producing a small amount of domestic natural gas from the offshore Donghae-1 field in November 2003 (reserves estimated at 7 bcm). The field is a relatively small development, which will only cover 2% of Korean demand.

Gas demand trends

Natural gas consumption in OECD Pacific reached 131 bcm in 2002. Between 2000 and 2003, it is expected to grow at an average annual rate of 2.3% to reach 243 bcm. This is far less than the 11% growth observed during the period 1971-2000.

In Japan and Korea, the gas market was shaken by the Asian financial crisis of 1997-1998, when LNG buyers found themselves vastly over-supplied. Growth has picked up again and is expected to continue. However, the pace of future growth in Japan remains uncertain. Future demand will depend on the strength of the economy and the power sector, which consumed approximately 70% of LNG imports. LNG demand for power generation is expected to increase steadily due to growing environmental awareness and the uncertainty of the future siting of nuclear power generation facilities. Demand for residential and commercial use is expected to increase rapidly. Tokyo Gas, the largest gas utility company in Japan, forecasts that LNG demand will increase to 63 mtpa in 2015 as a low case, and 80 mtpa as a high case (85-108 bcm, compared with 72 bcm imported in 2002). In 2003, Japan imported 80 bcm. The increase came predominantly as a result of outage of Tepco's 17 nuclear power plants due to data falsification problems and the consequent fuel substitution in the power sector. Tepco gas-fired generation surged to cover the nuclear shortfall, mainly through the purchase of LNG spot cargoes. In 2004, part of the gain in LNG consumption could be eliminated as more nuclear reactors are brought back on line.

Korean gas demand also promises to be strong in the future. It could almost triple in the next thirty years (from 24 bcm in 2002 to 70 bcm in 2030). Just less than two-thirds of the incremental gas demand will come from the power generation sector, and half of the rest from the residential sector. Korea continues to have the largest volume of uncovered gas demand in the Asian region. Contractual commitments are far from being large enough to meet the expected growth in demand.

In Australia, natural gas consumption could more than double in absolute terms in the next 15 years. This demand growth is expected essentially from the power generation and industrial sectors. The reserves/production of natural gas will be able to satisfy this demand, so it does not imply a security of supply challenge.

In New Zealand, future gas demand is uncertain. To maintain gas supplies to its captive market (petrochemical plants and residential users), the Government is promoting more exploration and production from smaller fields and the two largest energy suppliers, Contact Energy and Genesis Power, are considering importing LNG. A terminal could be built on the northern coasts, in order to take advantage of existing pipeline infrastructure.

Figure 9.5. Gas demand in OECD Pacific, 2000-2030

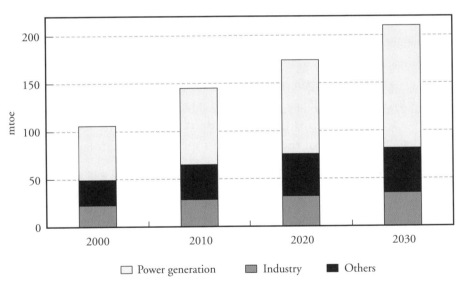

Source: *WEO 2002*

Gas demand in OECD Pacific is set to become more seasonal because of increased use of gas in the residential and commercial sectors and for upper and middle load in the power generation sector. Increasing seasonality in gas demand will require increased flexibility of supply.

Matching gas supply and demand

Australia delivered 10 bcm to Japan in 2002 and is expected to become a large LNG exporter. The dependence of OECD Pacific countries on gas imports from outside the OECD is therefore expected to fall, as Australia will partly provide the growing volumes of imported LNG in Japan and Korea. Import dependence from outside the OECD Pacific region was 67% in 2000. It is expected to be 50% in 2030. However, since the larger part of the region's gas needs will continue to be met by LNG imports from the rest of East Asia/Pacific and the Middle East, Japan's and Korea's energy security is very much affected by the energy security in the Asian region as a whole, and the Middle East.

Japan's main options to meet any future increase in natural gas demand include increased imports of LNG from Asia, the Middle East, Alaska and Sakhalin. LNG imports from Russia (Sakhalin II project) to Japan will begin in 2007, following the signature of supply and purchase agreements in June 2003. Japan is also starting to import LNG from the LNG plant under construction at Darwin in North Australia.

Another possibility is for Russian gas piped from Sakhalin or from Irkutsk via China and the Korean Peninsula. The Sakhalin I project would transport gas from Sakhalin to Japan by pipeline. In 2002, the Japan Sakhalin Pipeline Company, owned by Japex, Itochu and Marubeni, completed a feasibility study on the Sakhalin pipeline and announced the technical and commercial feasibility of the pipeline to supply 8 bcm/a to Japan.

Korea has completed a preliminary feasibility study of a gas pipeline from the Kovyktinskoye gas deposit in the Irkutsk region of Russia. The goal is to have a 4,100-km pipeline system supplying a total of 28 bcm/a to China and the Korean peninsula by 2008. The pipeline would bring 10 bcm/a to Korea. The Korean Government sees the project as a means of diversifying its gas imports and improving security of supply. However, the pipeline still has several barriers to overcome, one of the most important being that Irkutsk gas needs to go through China first, and it is unlikely that China will need the gas before 2010-15.

The most likely sources of additional LNG supplies to Korea are from existing major suppliers from the Pacific and the Middle East, and possibly Russia. One major issue for security of supply in Korea is that Kogas has not been allowed to sign long-term contracts since 1997, pending the restructuring of the gas sector, and is now short of gas (see below).

Another issue is the increasing seasonality of demand. The issue may be solved through a combination of swap agreements between LNG buyers in the region, spot LNG cargoes purchased during peak requirement periods and increased flexibility in new term contracts. The two recent medium-term contracts (7 years) signed by Kogas with Australia and Malaysia effectively include more flexibility: 0.5 mtpa with Australian LNG delivered in winter, and 1.5 mtpa (with 0.5 mtpa option) from Malaysia LNG Tiga on an 80% winter and 20% summer supply basis. The contracts also provide an option for supply to be redirected to Japan in special circumstances.

Although LNG demand is growing in both Japan and Korea, new LNG purchases will probably be with more competitive pricing formulae and more flexible contracts, with shorter terms, as reflected in the two above-mentioned Korean contracts and by the renewal of contracts by Japanese buyers with Malaysia. A growing proportion of any new demand is likely to be met by spot purchases. Long-term contracts, nevertheless, are expected to remain the basis of Japanese procurement when new greenfield projects are concerned. The supply and purchase agreements signed with Sakhalin partners have a duration of 21 years; those with Darwin LNG of 17 years.

SECURITY OF GAS SUPPLY ISSUES

In Japan and South Korea, security of supply issues are linked with import dependence, the possible conflict between the opening of the markets and the need to rely on long-term import contracts. The internal dimension of security of supply is linked with investment into new gas infrastructure, the issue of facility concentration, and investment in insurance assets for low-probability events. The interface between the electricity and gas sectors is not yet a relevant issue as the share of gas in the power sector is limited and the two sectors are not yet opened to competition.

External dimension

Import dependence

Japan and Korea are highly import-dependent. Japan imports 97% of its gas needs and Korea 100%. However, high dependence on fuel imports in itself does not need to pose insurmountable risks. The Pacific region shows that it can be addressed successfully with policies to diversify supplies, and cooperation with exporting countries and between LNG buyers.

Japan is an illustration of that policy. Japan, one of the largest economies in the world, has managed to cope well with its very high dependence on LNG (and oil) imports by adopting specific policy measures to address this situation. Japan has always maintained a highly diversified portfolio of supplies: LNG comes from eight countries and ten LNG plants. Suppliers include both Asia Pacific and Middle East producers. Over time, Japan has developed and maintained strong economic and political ties with the countries on which it depends, always with an eye open to the interests of the supplying countries. Japan has also developed financial links with its LNG suppliers, by investing in liquefaction plants dedicated to export to Japan. For instance, Japanese companies are involved in Indonesia's Arun, Australia North West Shelf, Brunei, Malaysia and Qatargas. More recently, Japanese companies have become partners in the development of the Russian Sakhalin LNG project. They also hold more than 50% in the Tangguh liquefaction plant being built in Indonesia and equity shares in the LNG project being built at Darwin in North Australia.

Korea has adopted the same policy regarding diversification of gas supplies. In 1998, Indonesia and Malaysia accounted for 94% of Korean supplies. Now its imports come from six suppliers, both from the Pacific and the Middle East. Korea currently gets most of its LNG from Qatar, Indonesia, Malaysia, and Oman, with smaller volumes coming from Brunei and spot cargoes from elsewhere. The supplies from Qatar, which is now the largest exporter of LNG to South Korea, began in August 1999 (Rasgas). First shipments from Oman were loaded in April 2000.

Another pillar of the security policy in the region is the strong cooperation developed between buyers, not only between Japanese LNG buyers, but also between Japanese buyers and Kogas. This allows the two countries to cover shortfalls in supply and also helps them to cover their peak gas demand. Cooperation with suppliers is also one of the pillars of the Japanese energy policy. The *Basic Energy Plan*, issued by the Ministry of Economy and Trade (METI) in October 2003, points out that a close relationship between Japanese gas buyers and suppliers is essential, particularly in preparation for an emergency. The Plan also points out that cooperation with producing nations on future gas exploration projects is one of the issues that need to be taken into consideration as Japan further promotes natural gas use.

This cooperation between suppliers and buyers and between buyers in the Pacific region, helped them to cope with the supply cut from Arun in 2001, without any major problems. ExxonMobil had to shut down the Arun LNG plant for seven months after repeated attacks against its workers in the separatist Aceh region. Indonesia was able to replace most of the missing supplies to its Japanese and Korean buyers with supplies from the Bontang LNG plant. The rest was imported from other LNG suppliers.

Cooperation again helped to bridge the supply cut coming from the shut down, due to a fire, of Malaysian Tiga III train 1 in August 2003. The new train was expected to deliver 1.5 mtpa to Kogas, starting with around 35 cargoes in winter 2003/04, mainly to cover seasonal peak needs. Most of the supply squeeze was replaced by additional supplies from Australia, Malaysia and by a time-swapping of LNG cargoes with Japan. Korea sent 12 cargoes to Japan in summer 2003 (when Japan has its peak gas demand), and Japan re-sent these 12 cargoes to Korea in winter 2003/04 (when Korea demand peaks, see Figures 9.3 and 9.4).

Ongoing reforms and their impact on long-term contracts

Japanese and Korean LNG buyers are seeking more flexible and somewhat shorter contracts. The share of spot purchases is expected to increase and to become part of the portfolio approach of the buyers. However, the two countries have adopted very different approaches for their future LNG supply.

Japan drastically increased LNG imports in the 1980s after the two oil price crises. Twenty years later, those LNG purchase contracts have reached or are reaching their renewal dates. However, gas and electricity utilities are finding it more difficult to enter into rigid long-term TOP contracts partly because of the uncertainty of future gas demand and partly because of increased competition between buyers.

Some of the expiring long-term contracts have already been renewed while others are in the process of renewal. New "traditional" long-term contracts were signed with Russia and Australia (Darwin). In the case of Russia, the deliveries are on a fob basis and the contractual terms were described by Tokyo Gas as "more competitive than any other LNG contracts the company signed in the past". The approach of Japanese buyers is different for the renewal of their existing contracts. With their existing suppliers, buyers are negotiating more flexibility (less ToP obligations), shorter contracts and a reduction in prices. Malaysia LNG Satu and Tiga, and Australia North West Shelf Train 4 contracts have given their Japanese buyers increased flexibility:[154]

- MLNG Satu: the renewed contracts with Tepco and Tokyo Gas for 7.4 mtpa include several periods (long-term for 15 years, short-term on a 4-year basis), flexibility in deliveries as part of the deliveries will be fob, the rest ex-ship, and a regular price review every four years. The contracts also allow the buyers to resell cargoes.

- MLNG Tiga: the contract signed in February 2002 by Osaka Gas, Toho Gas, and Tokyo Gas with MLNG Tiga includes a mixture of long-term (20 years) and short-term (1 year) volumes for a maximum volume of 1.6 mtpa. The optional quantities (0.4 mtpa) depend upon the buyers' needs and the sellers' availability.

- NWS Train 4: Japanese buyers, including Chubu Electric, Kyushu Electric, Osaka Gas, Shizuoka Gas, Toho Gas, Tohoku Electric, and Tokyo Gas, have negotiated independently for NWS train 4. This is in contrast to the buyers' approach taken with trains 1-3, where a consortium of buyers jointly negotiated and signed an ex-ship contract of 20 years for 7.33 mtpa.

- Tohoku Electric, which buys 3 mtpa from Arun's LNG plant, is expected to cut purchases by 1 mtpa once its contract expires in 2004.

---

154 FACTS (2003a).

- Kansai Electric, which has been the first company to renew its contract with NWS partners (trains 1 to 3) has renewed for reduced volumes of 0.5 mtpa in 2009-14, rising to 0.9 mtpa in 2015-23 (instead of the previous 1.13 mtpa for 20 years).

In **Korea**, only a small volume of contracts need to be renewed in this decade. However, the strong growth of gas demand means that new supplies must be added. The uncertainty over the future structure of the gas industry and of Kogas has impeded Kogas from concluding long-term agreements for new LNG supplies, even though additional volumes of LNG beyond current contracts were needed. Kogas had to rely on spot sales for its additional needs, but even so, Kogas was short of gas and had serious trouble accessing adequate volumes in winter 2002/03. The new Government allowed Kogas to sign two medium-term (7-year) LNG contracts with Australia and Malaysia. Both contracts are indexed to oil prices and similar to Kogas existing contracts. However, a major difference is the seasonal flexibility included in the contracts. Thanks to the new contracts, to time-swapping of LNG cargoes with Japan, and to favourable weather conditions, Kogas started the winter period 2003/04 with plentiful supplies and there was no repetition of the gas shortage scenario of winter 2002/03.

Nevertheless, Korea is short of firmly contracted volumes of gas. The gap is bound to widen every year as demand is rising fast. Existing long-term contracts no longer match total gas demand, and Kogas has to rely on spot purchases. The expiration of the Arun contract in 2007 (2.3 mtpa) and the increase in gas demand means that some 6 mtpa will need to be contracted for by 2010. Uncertainties about gas market reform have to be addressed promptly, to establish the rules based on which the market players can decide how to position themselves. Spot purchases are a good strategy in combination with long-term and medium-term contracts, in particular in a situation where many suppliers have spare capacity. However, as long as no deep and liquid LNG market exists, there is a danger of the market drying up, as illustrated by the problems Kogas encountered in finding spot supplies in winter 2002/03. A portfolio approach for additional LNG purchases may help to lock in required supplies to bridge the gap until the restructuring of the sector is completed.

Posco and SK Power are going to import their LNG supplies directly, partly alleviating the problem of supply. The two private companies signed a contract with Indonesia's BP-Tangguh LNG project to import 1.15 mtpa over 20 years from 2006 at their new terminal.

With around 6 mtpa of new uncovered demand by 2010, and new private companies, such as LG and SK coming to the fore, Korea will play an influential role on the global LNG scene.

Internal dimension

The internal dimension of security of supply involves the possible impact of ongoing market reforms on investment in gas infrastructure, and in particular in assets for low-probability/high-impact events.

The Government of **Japan**, based on the Gas Utility Industry Law, obliges gas utilities: 1) to have sufficient supply capacity to meet the projected demand (gas production facilities, pipelines and LNG storage facilities), and 2) to submit their annual supply plans, including demand outlook and investment plan. Also, the Government can place a change order in cases where it regards the submission to be inappropriate to perform the proper business of a utility.

Japan has 25 regasification terminals with a total capacity of 225 bcm per year. Two new terminals are under construction and another two are planned. Storage capacity of LNG terminals in Japan is about 11.6 mcm/d of LNG, i.e., 7 bcm. As shown in Table 9.1, the gas supply infrastructure has been developing gradually and steadily. It includes spare capacity which allows buyers to cope with extreme situations.

The situation is different for pipelines. Pipeline infrastructure has only been developed around LNG power plants close to import terminals and urban areas, thus limiting the use of gas. This is explained in part by the high costs of building pipelines due to geographical and safety considerations. An interconnected network would enhance security of supply by providing more flexibility. However, such an interconnection pipeline would come at substantial cost and face the difficulties of finding a suitable trace in a very densely populated country. LNG terminals already provide a back-up function.

Table 9.1. Regasification terminals in Japan and Korea

Terminals	Storage tanks (1,000 cm of LNG)	Nominal capacity (mcm/day)	Start-up date
Japan			
Negishi	1,180	40.8	1969
Senboku I	180	8.4	1972
Sodegaura	2,660	103.2	1973
Senboku II	1,585	43.8	1977
Tobata	480	24	1977
Chita I	300	26.5	1977
Himeji I	520	30.6	1979
Chita II	640	40.6	1983
Higashi-Niigata	720	31.8	1984
Himeji II	560	18	1984
Higashi-Ohgishima	540	62.9	1984
Futtsu	610	69.3	1985
Yokkaichi (Kawagoe)	320	29.2	1987
Yanai	480	8.2	1990
Shin-Oïta	320	17.2	1990
Yokkaichi	160	2.5	1991
Fukuoka	70	1.7	1993
Hatsukaichi	85	1.3	1996
Sodeshi	177	3.0	1996
Kagoshima	36	0.5	1996
Shin-Minato	80	0.9	1997
Kawagoe	480	18.4	1997
Ohgishima I	400	18	1998
Chita III	200	14.3	2002
Nagasaki	35		2003
Total Japan	**11,638**	**615. 1**	
Korea			
Pyeong Taek	1,000	60	1986
Incheon	1,280	90	1996
Tongyeong	420	29	2002
Total Korea	**2,700**	**179**	
Total	**14,338**	**794. 1**	

Source: IEA

Figure 9.6. Regasification terminals in Japan and Korea

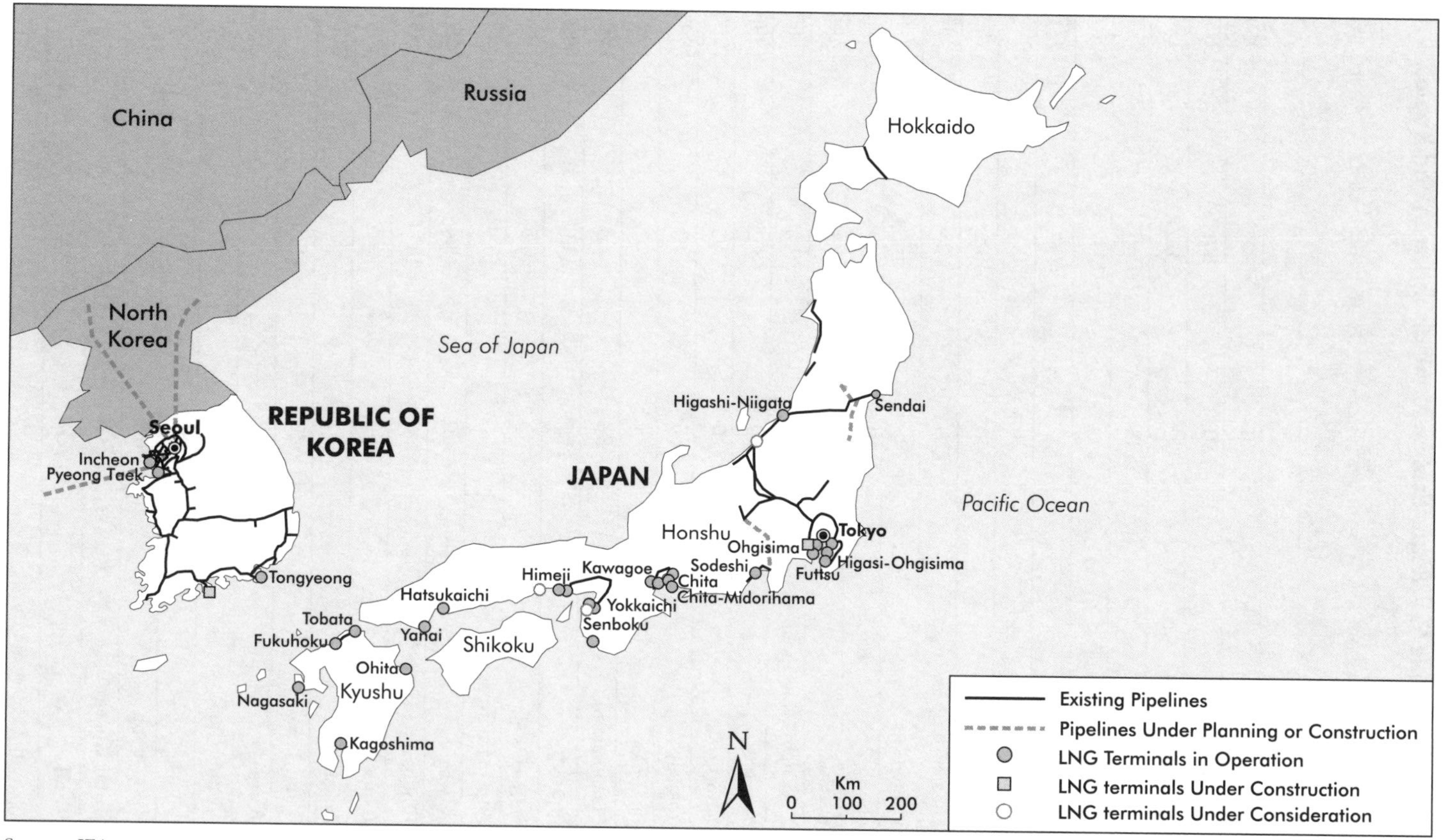

Source: IEA

While the construction and management of a natural gas pipeline is primarily the responsibility of the private sector, the Government would have to play a role to reduce business risks, *i.e.,* uncertain demand in the early stages of pipeline construction. In its *Basic Energy Plan*, the Government considers the lack of nationwide gas reticulation as an issue to be taken into consideration for the further promotion of natural gas use. The Government is considering measures to create incentives for the development of gas networks. The proposed measures, such as granting an exception for notification and publication of terms, rates and conditions for TPA or allowing higher rates of return for TPA for a certain period of time, can have a positive impact on the willingness to invest.

These measures and the ongoing market reforms create the possibility for new projects to venture outside their traditional markets or team up with other energy companies. Two recent examples include the Minami-Fuji Pipeline and the Osaka Gas-Chubu Electric pipeline network. Both are private initiatives to build natural gas pipelines to connect LNG terminals together.

The **Korean** Government also monitors investment performance. Every two years, MOCIE and related organisations jointly develop a *"Basic Plan"* for long-term supply and demand for the gas and electricity industry. Based on the result of the *Basic Plan*, MOCIE plans additional infrastructure and investment requirements for up to 15 years. Investment performance for gas production, transmission, storage and distribution is thoroughly reviewed and monitored by MOCIE, on the basis of its 15-year plan. The plan also includes the necessary investment to guarantee supply security.

Korea has three LNG regasification terminals with a capacity of 65 bcm/a, at Pyeong Taek, Incheon and Tongyeong. Storage capacity of LNG terminals in Korea is 2.7 mcm/d of LNG (1.6 bcm). A fourth terminal at Kwangyang, the Posco terminal, is expected to be completed by 2005. Its initial capacity will be approximately 2.3 bcm/a.

Security of supply is addressed by investment in spare capacity in LNG terminals (construction of additional LNG tanks) and pipelines. As shown by the above figures, the country has ample spare capacity and storage tanks. The Government is also conducting studies to convert the gas field found in the Sea of Japan off Korea into gas storage after its depletion.

In **Australia**, in addition to the growth in investment in LNG, there has also been significant investment, expansion and integration of the gas transmission and distribution network in recent years, particularly in south-eastern Australia, that has enabled competition and increased security of supply. Australia's gas transmission network has grown from 14,093 km in 1997/98 to 20,109 km in 2001/02.[155] The growth in the transmission network has facilitated the emergence of an interconnected pipeline system linking major gas supply basins and demand centres in south-eastern markets. New transmission pipeline investment enables gas to flow between the states of South Australia, New South Wales, Victoria and Tasmania. Most major consuming regions in Australia now have, or will soon have two pipelines providing gas from alternative sources of supply. With the establishment of the VicHub in February 2003 by Duke Energy International, the interchange of gas between Victoria and New South Wales can and does occur. The trading hub, located in Longford, Victoria, serves as the interconnector for the Eastern Gas Pipeline, Tasmanian Gas Pipeline and the GasNet transmission system. The recent completion of the hub and the opening at the beginning of 2004 of a gas pipeline from Victoria to South Australia enhance the interconnection of the network.

However, the Australian gas market continues to be fragmented. Although substantial pipeline development has occurred in recent years, the transmission network is best described as a 'point to point' network outside of Victoria. The location of Australia's natural gas reserves and the large distances between the consumption centres has created two main transmission networks not linked to each other, one in the eastern states and south Australia, and the other serving only Western Australia. The Queensland pipeline network is also a separate system, given that its only link to the rest of the eastern system is through a pipeline transporting wet gas from Queensland to the Cooper Basin processing plants in South Australia.

Further reforms of the gas access regime are expected, following the review by the Productivity Commission of the national gas access regime. The Commission's draft report, published in January 2004, indicated that the

---

155 Australian Gas Association, Gas Statistics Australia, various years.

Figure 9.7. Australian natural gas transmission grid

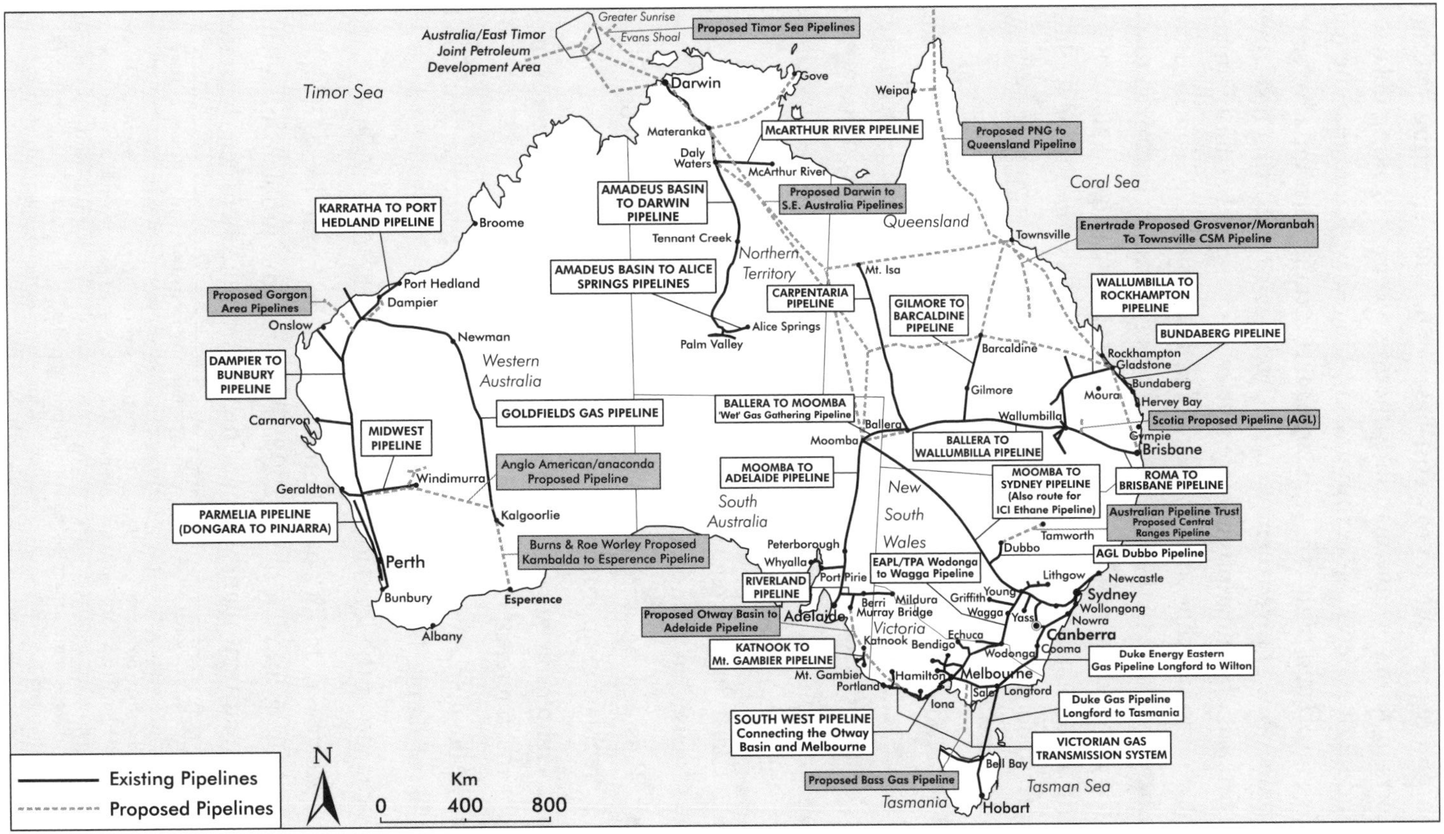

Existing Pipelines

Proposed Pipelines

Source: IEA

469

current regime, subject to a cost-based regulation structure, has significant costs in terms of information gathering, decision-making delays, appeals and merit reviews. More importantly, the review found that the regulatory risk associated with it is very large, and certainly has an adverse effect on some forms of investment – either deterring or distorting investment. The existence of regulations at state level was seen as a barrier by investors for new interstate pipelines. In particular, investors have identified core areas where they believe the regime could be significantly improved to avoid the risk of regulatory failure: improving access pricing, regulatory guidance and accountability; creating incentives for investment in new and existing infrastructure; and ensuring the appropriate scope, governance and administration of the regime.

The Productivity Commission has proposed improvements that would "reduce regulatory costs, while preserving the benefits from facilitating competition through third-party access to pipelines". The main proposals are:

- Including a "light-handed monitoring option for regulators as an alternative to cost-based price regulation";

- Clarifying the regime's objectives "by including an objects clause that focuses on economic efficiency";

- Raising the threshold for applying the existing cost-based price regulation approach;

- Tightening guidance to regulators for approvals of access arrangements and reference tariffs; and

- Allowing owners of proposed new pipelines to apply for 15-year regulatory holidays.

A change in the legislation is expected by the end of 2004.

In Australia, facility concentration has been an issue. The Longford accident[156] in Victoria in 1998 illustrated the problem of relying on a single treatment plant with no interconnections between the states.

---

156 On Friday 25 October 1998, there was an explosion at Esso's Longford gas plant in rural Victoria that jeopardised gas supply of the whole state. The Government of Victoria reacted swiftly and issued a Directive that protected gas supplies for essential services by giving the Victorian Energy Network Corporation (VENCorp) – the gas system security agency – the power to instruct households and business to stop using gas appliances. The powers had been provided to VENCorp under the Gas Industry Act that allows directions to be made on gas use to protect supplies. Within days, Victoria's entire gas supply was shut down and customers remained without gas for two weeks causing substantial damage to the Victorian economy and major inconveniences for smaller household consumers.

On 1 January 2004 a gas leak and fire caused damage to the Moomba Gas Processing Facility, resulting in its shut down. Gas from the plant supplied 100% of the South Australian gas market and 80% of the Sydney market. Despite a brief plant shut down, there were no curtailments of gas supplies as a result of the incident at Moomba as the consequences could be handled completely by market-based reactions both on the supply and on the demand side.

Moomba normal summer output is 400 terajoules per day. Since the incident, 150 TJ per day is being released from underground back-up storage at Moomba. Thanks to the new interconnections that opened at the beginning of the year, Western Victoria is currently providing 170 TJ per day to South Australia and an extra 100 TJ is being pumped into Sydney from Victoria's Gippsland Basin. In addition, a South Australia/New South Wales Task force was established to monitor day-to-day gas supply and demand issues.

The Moomba incident clearly highlights that a more integrated gas pipeline network is starting to take shape. Alternative sources of gas supply were available to both Adelaide and Sydney, due to the increased pipeline interconnection in South East Australia which greatly reduced the potential economic impact.

Gas/electricity interface

Most of the growth in gas demand in the region is expected to come from the power sector. Gas demand in OECD Pacific is expected to increase by 104 mtoe between 2000 and 2030, 68% of this coming from the power sector. However, natural gas is expected to account for only 21% of electricity generation in 2030, far behind nuclear (32%) and coal (27%). Overall, the interface between the electricity and gas sectors is not an issue in OECD Pacific. Nevertheless, the Japanese and Korean Governments are monitoring the situation.

In Japan, although 70% of gas is used for electricity generation, this accounts for only 23% of electricity generation. The electricity mix is well diversified. In addition, 40% of gas-fired plants can also accommodate other fuels, mainly oil. Electricity/gas demand, as well as peak load, is monitored by each utility. Regarding the measures to reduce electricity peak demand, electricity/gas utilities introduce various price options and the Government has taken the lead by introducing gas-powered air conditioners that contribute to cutting the peak power demand.

In Korea, gas accounts for 11% of electricity generation. The Korean Government maintains an appropriate portfolio of power energy sources which takes into account the economic and environmental particularities of each possible energy source. In addition, 53% of gas-fired plants can accommodate other fuels, mainly oil. MOCIE also monitors the daily gas supply/demand status.

UNITS OF MEASURES/ ABBREVIATIONS FOR UNITS

boe – Barrel of oil equivalent

bpd – Barrel per day

bcf – Billion cubic feet

bcf/d – Billion cubic feet per day

bcm – Billion cubic metres

bcm/a – Billion cubic metres per annum

Btu – British thermal unit

cm – Cubic meters

cf – Cubic foot

G – Giga – billion – 10^9

GJ – Gigajoule

GW – Gigawatt

GWh – Gigawatt hour

J – Joule

kWh – Kilowatt hour

m – mega – million – 10^6

mbpd – Million barrels per day

mBtu – Million British thermal units

mcf – Million cubic feet

mcf/d – Million cubic feet per day

mcm – Million cubic metres

mcm/a – Million cubic meters per annum

mcm/d – Million cubic metres per day

mtoe – Million tonnes of oil equivalent

mtpa – Million tonnes per annum (of LNG)

MW – Megawatt

MWh – Megawatt hour

PJ – Petajoule – 10^{15} joules

T – Tera – trillion – 10^{12}

tcf – Trillion cubic feet

tcm – Trillion cubic meters

Th – Therm – equivalent to 100,000 Btu

TJ – Terajoule – 10^{12} joules

TW – Terawatt – 10^{12} watts

GLOSSARY OF TERMS AND ABBREVIATIONS

Associated gas – Natural gas produced as a by-product of the crude oil or liquids.

At the beach – When gas has been brought ashore into a terminal by producers but is not yet in the national transmission system, the gas is called at the beach (UK).

Balancing mechanism – In a natural gas pipeline network, the means of ensuring that supply does not outstrip demand, or vice versa.

Base-load – The minimum amount of electric power delivered or required over a given period of time at a steady rate.

Basis – The difference in price for natural gas at two different geographical locations (e.g., hubs).

Bundled services – Two or more gas services provided jointly at a combined charge (e.g., gas transportation and storage).

Burner tip – A generic term used to refer to competitive situation at the final end-using equipment for natural gas (e.g., an industrial boiler).

Busbar – An electric connection point connecting a power station to the power network or connecting two power lines at a network substation, used to describe the competitive situation on the electric grid.

Calorific Value (CV) – A measure of the amount of energy released as heat when a fuel is burned. It may be measured gross or net, where gross includes the heat produced when the water vapour is condensed into a liquid and net does not.

CEER – Council of European Energy Regulators.

Churn – The ratio of traded volumes at a hub to actual physical volumes.

CO – Carbon monoxide.

CO_2 – Carbon dioxide.

Combined-cycle gas turbine (CCGT) – The combination of one or two gas turbines with a steam turbine: the hot exhaust gases from the gas turbine process pass through a heat exchanger to produce steam for the steam turbine.

Combined heat and power (CHP) – A power station system that uses the heat from the exhaust gases from the power generation part to produce heat or low temperature steam. Also known as cogeneration.

Compressor station – Gas transportation capacity in a pipeline is a function of the pressure drop along the pipeline. Therefore gas has to be recompressed at regular intervals, as it travels over longer distances. A compressor station, usually a gas turbine engine, is an installation which recompresses the gas to the required pressure.

Cost, Insurance and Freight (cif) – A cif price means that the cost of cargo, insurance and travel/freight to a given destination are all included in the price.

Counterparty – A participant in a financial contract.

City gate – Point at which a local distribution company takes delivery of gas; physical interface between transmission and local distribution systems.

Core market – Generally that part of the gas market that does not possess fuel-switching capability in the near term; typically residential, commercial and small industrial users.

Daily balancing – Balancing, on a day-by-day basis, the amount of gas a shipper puts into a pipeline system (UK).

Day-ahead gas – Gas for delivery on the day after the trade takes place.

Deliverability (from storage) – The rate at which gas can be supplied from a storage in a given period, usually one hour or one day. In a salt cavity storage facility for example, the rate would depend on a number of factors including reservoir pressure which is a function of depletion, reservoir rock characteristics and withdrawal facilities such as pipeline capacity. The term is also used for the volume of gas which a field, pipeline, well, storage or distribution system can supply in a single 24-hour period.

Derivative – Financial instrument derived from a cash market commodity, futures contract, or other financial instrument. Derivatives can be traded on regulated exchange markets or over-the-counter. For example, energy futures contracts are derivatives of physical commodities, options on futures are derivatives of futures contracts.

DOE – US Department of Energy.

DSO – Distribution System Operator.

DTI – UK Department of Trade and Industry.

Dual-firing – Where two different fuels – e.g., gas and oil – can be used alternatively to generate energy in a single piece of equipment.

E&P – Exploration and production.

EC – European Commission.

ECT – Energy Charter Treaty.

EIA – Energy Information Administration; part of US DOE.

Eligibility, eligible customers – gas users that have the right to choose their supplier or request third-party access to the grid. They have to meet criteria specified in the EU Gas Directive or in national legislation, such as a minimum volume of gas consumed per year.

EU – European Union.

Exchange – Any trading arena where commodities and/or securities are bought and sold – for example, the New York Mercantile Exchange.

Ex-ship – Under an ex-ship contract, the seller has to deliver LNG to the buyer at an agreed importing terminal. The seller remains responsible for the LNG until it is delivered.

FERC – Federal Energy Regulatory Commission (US); responsible for regulation of the US interstate oil and gas pipeline businesses.

Firm capacity – Amount of gas delivery in a buyer's contract that is guaranteed not to be interrupted.

Firm (uninterrupted) – Gas for which the full price has been paid on the understanding it will be delivered continually through the contract period.

Flat gas – Gas purchased with zero swing and 100% take-or-pay.

Forward contracts – Where products are traded individually on a bilateral basis ahead of their physical delivery.

Free-on-board (fob) – Under a fob contract, the seller provides the LNG at the exporting terminal and the buyer takes responsibility for shipping and freight insurance.

FSU – Former Soviet Union.

Fuel switching – Substituting one fuel for another.

Fuel-switching capability – The ability of an end-user to readily change fuel type consumed whenever a price or supply advantage develops for an alternative fuel.

Futures contract – An exchange-traded supply contract between a buyer and a seller whereby the buyer is obligated to take delivery and the seller is obligated to provide delivery of a fixed amount of a commodity at a predetermined price at a specified location. Futures contracts are traded exclusively on regulated exchanges and are settled daily based on their current value in the marketplace.

GCV – Gross calorific value.

GHG – Greenhouse gas – Gases covered by the Kyoto protocol under the United Nations Framework Convention on Climate Change, the most important greenhouse gas being CO_2; methane is another example of a greenhouse gas.

GTE – Gas Transmission Europe.

Henry Hub – A Hub located in Louisiana, which is the delivery point for the largest volumes of NYMEX natural gas contracts.

Hub – a transfer site or system where several pipelines interconnect and where shippers may obtain services to manage and facilitate their routing of supplies from production areas to markets.

IEA – International Energy Agency.

IGU – International Gas Union.

Interruptible customer – A customer that receives service only at those times and to the extent that firm customers do not demand all the available service.

Interruptible service – Gas sales that are subject to interruption for a specified number of days or hours during times of peak demand or in the event of system emergencies. In exchange for interruptibility, buyers pay lower prices.

IPE – International Petroleum Exchange, located in London.

IPP – independent power producer.

LDC (local distribution company) – A company that operates or controls the retail distribution system for the delivery of natural gas or electricity (US).

Line-pack – Increasing the amount of gas in the system or pipeline segment by temporarily raising the pressure to meet high demand for a short period of time. Often exercised overnight as a temporary storage medium to meet anticipated next-day peaking demands.

LNG (liquefied natural gas) – Natural gas (mainly methane) which has been liquefied by reducing its temperature to minus 162 degrees Celcius at atmospheric pressure.

Load balancing – To balance demand and supply (at any given point) in a grid/pipeline/supply chain.

Load factor – The ratio of average to peak usage for gas customers for a time period i.e. one day, one hour, etc. The higher the load factor, the smaller the difference between average and peak demand.

Long-run marginal cost (LRMC) – The long-run marginal cost represents the full cost of the last power plant to enter the market (includes construction and operating costs).

Merit order – Ranking in order of which generation plant should be used, based on ascending order of operating cost inclusive fuel costs.

MoU – Memorandum of understanding.

Mothballing – The closure of a power plant but maintaining the option to put it back into operation at a later time, usually requiring new technical approval.

NBP – National Balancing Point; a notional point on UK Transco's national gas transmission system, which is the reference point for gas traded in the UK.

NEB – National Energy Board (Canada); responsible agency for the regulation of provincial oil and gas pipelines.

NETA – New Electricity Trading Arrangements, in force in UK since 2001.

Netback pricing – Delivered price of cheapest alternative fuel to gas to the customer (including any taxes) adjusted for any efficiency differences in the energy conversion process and reduced by all costs to deliver it to the customer.

NGL – Natural gas liquids.

NGTA – New Gas Trading Arrangements (in UK).

NIMBY – Not in my back yard.

Nomination – The notification to how to make use of rights under an existing contract; e.g,. a gas flow nomination from a shipper to advise the pipeline owner of the amount of gas it wishes to transport or hold in storage on a given day.

NOx – Nitrogen oxides.

NTS – National Transmission System (UK).

NYMEX – New York Mercantile Exchange, where futures contracts for gas and other commodities are traded.

OCM – On-the-day commodity market (UK).

OECD – Organisation for Economic Cooperation and Development.

Off-take – Actual amount of gas withdrawn.

One-in-twenty (1-in-20) – The highest gas demand expected on any given <u>day</u> over a 20 year period.

One-in-fifty (1-in-50) – The highest gas demand expected in one single <u>year</u> out of 50 years.

Open interest – The number of futures or options natural gas contracts outstanding in the market.

Open season – A process during which shippers of natural gas can contract with pipeline companies for firm delivery capacity.

OTC – Over-the-counter – An over-the-counter deal is a customised derivative bilateral contract usually arranged with an intermediary such as a major bank or the trading arm of an energy major, as opposed to a standardised derivative contract traded on an exchange. Swaps are typical form of an OTC instrument.

Peak day – The day during which the greatest gas demand occurs in a one year period.

Peak load – Periods during the day when energy consumption is highest. The introduction of additional gas to cover this demand is known as peak shaving.

Peak-shaving – During times of peak demand, supplies from sources other than normal suppliers are used to supply peak demand on the system – e.g., from LNG peak shaving facilities or from storage with a high send-out rate like salt caverns.

PSO – Public service obligation.

Reserves-to-production ratio – Remaining recoverable reserves divided by annual production.

Seasonal supplies – Supplies of gas used for winter demand. This often includes gas from storage facilities.

Seasonality – All energy futures markets are affected to some extent by an annual seasonal cycle or "seasonality." This seasonal cycle or pattern refers to the tendency of market prices or demand to move in a given direction at certain times of the year.

SEC – Securities and Exchange Commission (US).

Shipper – A company which transports gas along a pipeline system. Shippers need to be registered with the local regulatory body.

Short-run marginal cost (SRMC) – The short-run marginal cost is the change in total cost resulting from a one-unit increase (or decrease) in the output of an existing production facility.

SOx – sulphur oxides.

Spark spread – The spark spread is defined as the difference, at a particular location and at a particular point in time, between the fuel cost of generating a MWh of electricity and the price of a MWh of electricity.

Spot market – The spot market is the physical/cash market for crude, refined product, gas or electricity. The market is for immediate delivery rather than for future delivery.

Spot price – The price of a commodity in the cash market.

Storage capacity – The amount of gas which can be stored to cover peak and seasonal demand.

Swing – Variations in gas supply or demand. A contractual commitment allowing a buyer to vary up to specified limits the amount of gas it can take at the wellhead, beach or border; the maximum daily contract quantity is usually expressed as a percentage of the annual contract quantity (100% equates to zero swing).

Swing factor – In gas purchasing agreements the swing factor is a measure of the flexibility to vary nominations and is expressed as a ratio of peak to average supplies.

Swing producer/supplier – A company or country which changes its gas output to meet fluctuations in market demand.

Take-or-Pay (ToP) – In a buyer's contract take-or-pay is the obligation to pay for a specified amount of gas whether this amount is taken or not. Depending on the contract terms under-takes or over-takes may be balanced as make-up or carry forward into the next contract period.

Tolling – Under a tolling agreement a power marketer or commercial electricity customer provides the fuel, say natural gas, to produce electricity for the marketer or customer at an agreed spark spread, and receives the rights to electricity output.

TPA – Third-party access; the right or possibility for a third party to make use of the transportation or distribution services of a pipeline company to move his own gas, while paying a set or negotiated charge.

TPES – Total primary energy supply.

TSO – Transmission System Operator.

UKCS – United Kingdom Continental Shelf.

Unbundling – The (organisational or legal) separation of the various components of gas businesses in order to introduce greater competition to these segments of the industry.

Volatility – A measure of the variability of a market factor, most often the price of the underlying instrument. Volatility is defined mathematically as the annualised standard deviation of the natural log of the ratio of two successive prices; the actual volatility realised over a period of time (the historical volatility) can be calculated from recorded data.

WCSB – Western Canadian Sedimentary Basin

Wholesale market – Sales of energy for resale.

Within-day gas – Gas for delivery within the day on which the trade takes place.

Working gas – The amount of gas in a storage facility above the amount needed to maintain a constant reservoir pressure (the latter is known as cushion gas).

WTO – World Trade Organisation.

REFERENCES

American Gas Association (AGA) (2001), *The Evolution of Underground Natural Gas Storage: Changes in Utilisation Patterns*, Washington, DC: AGA.

American Gas Foundation (AGF) (2002a), *Meeting the Gas Supply Challenge of the Next 20 Years, Non-Traditional Gas Sources*, Washington, DC.

AGF (2002b), *Meeting the Gas Supply Challenge of the Next 20 Years, Lower 48 and Canada*, Washington, DC.

Aissaoui A. (2002), *Gas-Exporting Countries: Towards Cartelisation?*, Oxford Energy Forum, Issue No. 50, August 2002.

Ait-Laoussine N. (2003), *Europe's Security of Gas Supply: A Producer's Perspective, Presentation at Flame 2003*, European Gas Conference, March 20, 2003, Amsterdam.

Bergmann B. (2003), *The Gas Agenda in Europe – From Regulation to Growth*, International Gas Union, 22nd World Gas Conference, June 1-5, 2003, Tokyo.

Bourdaire J-M. (2003), *The Growth of Natural Gas in Electricity: A New LNG Role for Supply and Flexibility*, International Gas Union, 22nd World Gas Conference, June 1-5, 2003, Tokyo.

BTU Weekly, Red Bank, various issues.

Cambridge Energy Research Associates (CERA) (2003a), *LNG Shipping: Boom or Bust?*, Decision Brief, April 2003.

CERA (2003b), *Pre-empting a Natural Gas Crisis*, special report, Dr. Daniel Yergin, June 26, 2003.

Cedigaz (2004), *LNG Trade and Infrastructures*, Rueil Malmaison: Institut Français du Pétrole.

Cedigaz (2003a), *Towards the Creation of a Single European Gas Market*, Rueil Malmaison: Institut Français du Pétrole.

Cedigaz (2003b), *Trends and Figures in 2002 from Natural Gas in the World*, Rueil Malmaison: Institut Français du Pétrole.

Cedigaz (2001), *Natural Gas in the World: 2001 Survey*, Rueil Malmaison: Institut Français du Pétrole.

Cedigaz News Report (weekly), Rueil Malmaison, various issues.

Center for European Policy Study (CEPS) (2001), *Security of Energy Supply: A question for Policy of the Markets?*, Report of a CEPS Working Party, Brussels.

Clingendael International Energy Programme (CIEP) (2003a), *The Case for Gas is Not Self-Fulfilling*, The Hague.

CIEP (2003b), *The Role of Liquefied Natural Gas (LNG) in the European Gas Market*, The Hague.

Commission of the European Communities (CEC) (2004), *Third-party access to Storage Facilities*, Note on Directives 2003/54/EC and 2003/55/EC on the Internal Market in Electricity and Natural Gas, Brussels: CEC.

CEC (2003a), *Directive 2003/55/EC of the European Parliament and of the Council of 26 June 2003 Concerning Common Rules for the Internal Market in Natural Gas and Repealing Directive 98/30/EC*, Official Journal of the European Union, http://europa.eu.int/eur-lex/en/, Brussels: CEC.

CEC (2003b), *Guidelines for Good TPA Practice*, revised version, Brussels: CEC.

CEC (2003c), *Long Term gas Supply Security in an Enlarged Europe*, October 2003, Brussels: CEC.

CEC (2001), *Green Paper: Towards a European Strategy for the Security of Energy Supply*, COM (2000) 769 Final plus Technical Document, November 29, 2000, Brussels: CEC.

CEC (2000), *Trading Opportunities and Promotion of Transparency in the Internal Gas Market*, study prepared by Energy Markets Limited, United Kingdom; Ramboll, Denmark, Brussels: CEC.

Council of European Energy Regulators (CEER) (2003a), *The Development of Gas Hubs and Trading Centres in Europe*, http://www.ceer-eu.org.

CEER (2003b), *Recommendations on Implementation of Third-party access to Storage and Linepack*, December 15, 2003, http://www.ceer-eu.org.

CEER (2003c), *Entry-Exit System Guidelines*, Report to the 7th European Gas Regulatory Forum meeting, Madrid, September 24-25, 2003.

CEER (2002), *Establishing the Preferred Tariff Methodology for Intrastate, Cross-Border and Transit Flows in European Gas Markets*, CEER Paper to the Madrid Forum, October 2002.

Department of Energy (DOE) (2003), *LNG Ministerial Summit*, Washington, December 17-18, 2003, various presentations, Washington, DC: US DOE.

Department of Trade and Industry (DTI) (2003a), *Energy White Paper: Our Energy Future – Creating a Low Carbon Economy*, London: DTI, www.dti.gov.uk.

DTI (2003b), *UK Energy Sector Indicators 2003, A Supplement to the Energy White Paper*, London: DTI.

DTI (2001), *Steering Group on Security and Stability Issues*, URN 01/674, March 29, 2001, London: DTI.

DTI (1998), *Conclusions of The Review of Energy Sources for Power Generation and Government Response to Fourth and Fifth Reports of Trade and Industry Committee*, Annex D, Summary of report of Merz and McLellan on *Security and Stability of the England and Wales Electricity Grid System*, London: DTI.

DTI, *Energy Trends*, London: DTI, various issues.

DTI/Office of Gas and Electricity Markets (Ofgem) (2003), *LNG Facilities and Interconnectors: EU Legislation and Regulatory Regime*, DTI/OFGEM Final Views, London: DTI/Ofgem.

Deutsche Bank (2003a), *European Gas: Playing on the Short Side*, London.

Deutsche Bank (2003b), *Picking the Winners from the Liquid Gas Boom*, London.

Energy Information Administration (EIA) (2004a), *Natural Gas Annual 2002*, Washington, DC: US DOE.

EIA (2004b), *Natural Gas Industry and Markets in 2002*, Washington, DC: US DOE.

EIA (2003a), *Annual Energy Outlook 2004*, Washington, DC: US DOE.

EIA (2003b), *Expansion and Change on the US Natural Gas Pipeline Network – 2002*, James Tobin, Washington, DC: US DOE.

EIA (2003c), *Natural Gas Market Centres and Hubs: a 2003 Update*, Washington, DC: US DOE.

EIA (2003d), *US LNG Markets and Uses*, Washington, DC: US DOE.

EIA (2002a), *Derivatives and Risk Management in the Petroleum, Natural Gas, and Electricity Industries*, Washington, DC: US DOE.

EIA (2002b), *The Basics of Underground Natural Gas Storage*, Washington, DC: US DOE.

EIA (2001a), *Impact of Interruptible Natural Gas Services on Northeast Heating Oil Demand*, Washington, DC: US DOE.

EIA (2001b), *Natural Gas Conveyance and Rates*, Barbara Mariner-Volpe, Washington, DC: US DOE.

EIA (2001c), *Natural Gas Conveyance and Restructuring*, Barbara Mariner-Volpe, Washington, DC: US DOE.

EIA (2001d), *Natural Gas Storage in the United States in 2001: A Current Assessment and Near-Term Outlook*, James Tobin and James Thompson, Washington, DC: US DOE.

EIA (2001e), *Natural Gas Transportation – Infrastructure Issues and Operational Trends*, James Tobin, Washington, DC: US DOE.

EIA (2001f), *US Natural Gas Markets: Mid-Term Prospects for Natural Gas Supply*, Washington, DC: US DOE.

EIA (2001g), *US Natural Gas Markets: Recent Trends and Prospects for the Future*, Washington, DC: US DOE.

EIA (1998), *Natural Gas 1998: Issues and Trends*, Washington, DC: US DOE.

EIA (1997), *Restructuring Energy Industries: Lessons from Natural Gas*, Natural Gas Monthly, Washington, DC: US DOE.

EIA (1995), *Energy Policy Act Transportation Study: Interim Report on Natural Gas Flows and Rates*, Washington, DC: US DOE.

EIA, *Electric Power Monthly*, Washington, DC: US DOE, various issues.

EIA, *Natural Gas Monthly*, Washington, DC: US DOE, various issues.

EIA, *Natural Gas Weekly Update*, Washington, DC: US DOE, various issues.

EIA, *Short-Term Energy Outlook*, Washington, DC: US DOE, various issues.

Energy Modeling Forum (EMF) (2003a), *Fuel Switching Potential of Electricity Generators*, a case study, John Pyrdol and Bob Baron, EMF working paper 20.3, Stanford University, Stanford.

EMF (2003b), *Natural Gas, Fuel Diversity and North American Energy Markets*, EMF Report 20, Stanford University, Stanford.

Energy Sector Management Assistance Programme (ESMAP) (1993), *Long-Term Contracts – Principles and Applications*, Washington, DC: World Bank.

Eurelectric (2003), *Security of Supply – A Key Issue for the European Electricity Industry*, Brussels.

Eurogas (2004), *Eurogas Views on Third-party access to Storage*, Brussels.

Eurogas (2003), *Eurogas Response to Proposed Security of Natural Gas Supply Directive*, Brussels.

Eurogas (2002), *Security of Gas Supplies, Markets, Principles and Actors*, Brussels.

Eurohub website, http://www.eurohubservices.nl.

European Gas Matters (fortnightly), London, various issues.

European Gas Regulatory Forum (2002), *A Long-Term Vision of a Fully Operational Single Market for Gas in Europe: A Strategy Paper* (draft), prepared by the Joint Working Group of the European Gas Regulatory Forum, January 28, 2002, http://europa.eu.int/comm/energy/gas/madrid/doc-5/strategy-paper-draft-28-01-2002.pdf.

European Parliament, Committee on Industry, External Trade, Research and Energy, *Report on Proposal for a Directive of the European Parliament and the Council Concerning Measures to Safeguard Security of Natural Gas Supply*, COM (2002) 488, Strasbourg.

FACTS (2004a), *Iran Gas Exports: Status in 2004?*, Gas Insights No. 29, January 2004, Honolulu: Fesharaki Associates Commercial and Technical Services, Inc.

FACTS (2004b), *Korea Gas Business: Update on Recent Developments and Deregulation*, Gas Insights No. 27, January 2004, Honolulu: Fesharaki Associates Commercial and Technical Services, Inc.

FACTS (2003a), *Changing LNG Market Structure in Asia: the Role of the Japanese Buyers*, Gas Insights No. 16, February 2003, Honolulu: Fesharaki Associates Commercial and Technical Services, Inc.

FACTS (2003b), *Future Scenarios for Korean Business*, Gas Insights No. 20, May 2003, Honolulu: Fesharaki Associates Commercial and Technical Services, Inc.

FACTS (2003c), *Indonesian LNG: A Case of Multiple Personalities?*, Gas Insights No. 14, February 2003, Honolulu: Fesharaki Associates Commercial and Technical Services, Inc.

FACTS (2003d), *Indonesian Oil and Gas Industry: Some Progress, but Much More Needs to be Done!*, Gas Insights No. 24, July 2003, Honolulu: Fesharaki Associates Commercial and Technical Services, Inc.

FACTS (2003e), *Japan's Long-Term Plans for Power Generation*, Gas Insights No. 21, June 2003, Honolulu: Fesharaki Associates Commercial and Technical Services, Inc.

FACTS (2003f), *Japan's Natural Gas Fundamentals and Forecasts,* Gas Advisory No. 16, February 2003, Honolulu: Fesharaki Associates Commercial and Technical Services, Inc.

FACTS (2003g), *A Year-end review of Japan's Natural Gas Situation,* Energy Advisory, No. 285, December 2003, Honolulu: Fesharaki Associates Commercial and Technical Services, Inc.

FACTS (2003h), *Korea's Gas Business under the New Administration,* Gas Insights No. 13, February 2003, Honolulu: Fesharaki Associates Commercial and Technical Services, Inc.

FACTS (2002), *Japan Gas Update,* Gas Insights No. 3, March 6, 2002, Honolulu: Fesharaki Associates Commercial and Technical Services, Inc.

Federal Energy Regulatory Commission (FERC) (2003), *2003 Natural Gas Market Assessment,* January 2003, Washington.

Frich M. (2003), *The Forced Removal of Destination Clauses: European Gas Security of Supply Implications,* Presentation at the Conference on Eurasian Natural Gas: Opportunities and Risks, November 13, 2003, Brussels.

Gas Connections (fortnightly), various issues.

Gas Matters (monthly), London, various issues.

Gas Matters Today (daily), London, various issues.

Gas Transmission Europe (GTE) (2003a), *Definition of Available Capacities at Cross-Border Points in Liberalised Markets,* Brussels.

GTE (2003b), *European TPA Transmission Tariff Comparison 2003,* Brussels.

GTE (2003c), *LNG Ship Approval Procedure,* Brussels.

GTE (2003d), *Potential Shortcomings of the Entry-Exit System,* Brussels.

GTE (2003e), *Proposals for a Directive Concerning Measures to Safeguard Security of Natural Gas Supply,* Brussels.

GTE (2003f), *Security of Natural Gas Supply,* Brussels.

Hartley N. (2003), *How Should We Assess the Risks of Increased Reliance on Gas?,* a background note written for the Joint IEA/NEA Workshop on Power Generation Investment in Liberalised Electricity Markets, March 25-26, 2003, Paris.

Hubco website, http://www.nwehub.com.

Institute of Energy Economics of Japan (IEEJ) (2003a), *Current Issues in the Japanese LNG Market – Relation with Gas Producers and Consumers*, Suzuki T., Ueda T., Sano S., Nagasaka S., Tokyo.

IEEJ (2003b), *Natural Gas Demand Supply Trends in the Asia Pacific Region*, Suzuki T., Morikawa T., Tokyo.

IEEJ (2002), *Japan's Long-Term Energy Demand and Supply Outlook, a Projection up to 2020 Assuming Environmental Constraints and Market Liberalisation*, Ito K., Tokyo.

International Energy Agency (IEA) (2003a), *World Energy Investment Outlook 2003*, Paris: OECD.

IEA (2003b), *Energy Policies of IEA Countries*, Paris: OECD.

IEA (2003c), *Energy Policies of IEA Countries, Japan*, Paris: OECD.

IEA (2003d), *Power Generation Investment in Electricity Markets*, Paris: OECD.

IEA (2003e), *Natural Gas Information 2003*, Paris: OECD.

IEA (2003f), *Electricity Information 2003*, Paris: OECD.

IEA (2003g), *Emissions Trading and its Possible Impacts on Investment Decisions in the Power Sector*, IEA information paper, http://www.iea.org/dbtw-wpd/textbase/papers/2003/cop9invdec.pdf.

IEA (2003h), International Conference on Energy Security: *The Role of Russian Gas Companies*, Paris, 25 November 2003, http://www.iea.org/Textbase/work/workshopdetail.asp?id=161.

IEA (2002a), *Flexibility in Natural Gas Supply and Demand*, Paris: OECD.

IEA (2002b), *Energy Policies of IEA Countries, Korea*, Paris: OECD.

IEA (2002c), *Energy Policies of IEA Countries, The United Kingdom*, Paris: OECD.

IEA (2002d), *Energy Policies of IEA Countries, The United States*, Paris: OECD.

IEA (2002e), *Energy Prices and Taxes*, Paris: OECD.

IEA (2002f), *Russia Energy Survey 2002*, Paris: OECD.

IEA (2002g), *Security of Supply in Electricity Markets – Evidence and Policy Issues*, Paris: OECD.

IEA (2002h), *World Energy Outlook 2002*, Paris: OECD.

IEA (2002i), *Developing China's Natural Gas Market: Policy Framework and Investment Conditions,* Paris: OECD.

IEA (2001a), *World Energy Outlook 2001 Insights – Assessing Today's Supplies to Fuel Tomorrow's Growth,* Paris: OECD.

IEA (2001b), *Energy Policies of IEA Countries, Australia,* Paris: OECD.

IEA (1995), *The IEA Natural Gas Security Study,* Paris: OECD.

International Gas Union (2003), *Working Committee 3 Report "Liquefied Gases",* 22nd World Gas Conference, June 1-5, 2003, Tokyo.

International Group of Liquefied Natural Gas Importers (GIIGNL) (2003), *The LNG Industry – 2002,* Paris.

Jensen J. (2003a), *LNG Comes of Age in North America,* a presentation to the National Association of Petroleum Investment Analysts, and the Petroleum Investor Relations Association, Miami, Florida, October 3, 2003 (unpublished).

Jensen J. (2003b), *The LNG Revolution,* Energy Journal of the International Association for Energy Economics, Volume 24, No. 2, 2003.

Jensen J. (2003c), *The North American LNG Revival,* a presentation to the Energy Modelling Forum – EMF 20, College Park, Maryland, July 1, 2003 (unpublished).

Jensen J. (2002), *The Outlook for US Natural Gas Supply and Demand and the Potential Role of Liquefied Natural Gas,* a presentation to the National Association of Petroleum Investment Analysts, and the Petroleum Investor Relations Association, La Quinta, California, October 10, 2002, (unpublished).

Joint Energy Security of Supply Working Group (JESS) (2003a), Department of Trade and Industry (DTI), Office of Gas and Electricity Markets (Ofgem), *Third Report,* November 2003, http://www.dti.gov.uk/energy/jess/jessreport3.pdf.

JESS (2003b), *Second Report,* February 2003, http://www.dti.gov.uk/energy/domestic_markets/security_of_supply/jessreport2.pdf.

JESS (2002), *First Report,* June 2002, http://www.dti.gov.uk/energy/domestic_markets/security_of_supply/jessreport1.pdf.

Jones Day Publication (2003), *Proprietary LNG Import Terminals: Salvation for the US Gas Market,* Washington, DC.

Keller F.J. (2000), *US Rockies: Non-Conventional Supply is Growing,* Barrett Resources Corporation, June 2000.

Kemper R. (2003), Presentation to the Gas Transmission Europe Autumn Conference, Organised by GTE, October 22-23, 2003, Paris.

Lapuerta C., Moselle B. (2002), *Convergence of Non-Discriminatory Tariff and Congestion Management Systems in the European Gas Sector*, The Brattle Group, London.

Lewis W., Lewis J., Outtrim P., Project Technical Liaison Associates, Inc., *LNG Facilities, the Real Risks*, LNG Journal, January/February 2003.

LNG Express, Houston Texas, various issues.

Madrid Forum VII (2003), *Conclusions of the 7th Meeting of the European Gas Regulatory Forum*, September 24-25, 2003, Madrid.

Mak J., Nielsen D., Schulte D. and Graham C., Fluor Enterprises Inc., USA, *LNG Flexibility*, Hydrocarbon Engineering, October 2003.

National Association for Regulatory Utility Commissioners (NARUC) (2003), *Gas and Electricity Interdependence – the Current Situations and Intermediate and Long-Term Solutions*, http://www.naruc.org/associations/1773/files/interdependence.pdf.

National Commission on Energy Policy (2003), *Increasing US Natural Gas Supplies*, Washington, DC.

National Economic Research Associates (NERA) (2003a), *Demand Response Measures: Using Market Forces to Fix Electricity Market Failures*, Energy Regulation Brief, March 2003, London: NERA.

NERA (2003b), *UK Energy Policy: Objectives, Means and Costs*, London: NERA.

NERA (2002a), *Security in Gas and Electricity Markets*, London: NERA.

NERA (2002b), *Network Access Conditions and Gas Markets in North America*, London: NERA.

NERA (2002c), *Study to Investigate the Likelihood of Firm Load Self-Interruption in a Severe Winter*, London: NERA.

National Energy Board (NEB) (2003a), *Canada's Energy Future – Scenarios for Supply and Demand to 2025*, Calgary: NEB.

NEB (2003b), *The Maritimes Natural Gas Market - An Overview and Assessment*, Calgary: NEB.

NEB (2002a), *Short-Term Natural Gas Deliverability from the Western Canada Sedimentary Basin 2002-2004*, Calgary: NEB.

NEB (2002b), *Canadian Natural Gas Market – Dynamics and Pricing, an Update*, Calgary: NEB.

NEB (1996), *Canadian Natural Gas Ten Years after Deregulation*, Calgary: NEB.

National Grid Transco (NGT) (2003a), *Transportation Ten Year Statement 2002*, http://www.transco.uk.com.

NGT (2003b), *Transporting Britain's Energy 2003: Development of NTS Investment Scenarios*,

http://www.transco.uk.com/publish/00base/TBE2003DevelopmentofInvestmentScenarios.pdf.

NGT (2003c), *Winter Operations Report 2003/2004*, http://www.ofgem.gov.uk/temp/ofgem/cache/cmsattach/4787_NGT_Winter_Operations_Report_Oct03.pdf.

National Petroleum Council (NPC) (2003), *Balancing Natural Gas Policy – Fuelling the Demands of a Growing Economy*, Washington, DC.

Natural Resources Canada (NRC) (2003), *Impacts of Canadian Electricity and Gas Exports in the United States*, 01GC-2021-03, Ziff Energy, Calgary.

Observatoire Méditerranéen de l'Energie (OME) (2003), *Medsupply – Development of Energy Supplies to Europe from Southern and Eastern Mediterranean Countries*, report prepared in cooperation with Sonatrach, June 2003, Sophia-Antipolis.

Office of Gas and Electricity Markets (Ofgem) (2004), *Security of Supply, April to September 2003*, Six Month Retrospective Report, London: Ofgem.

Ofgem (2003a), *The Gas Trading Arrangements: Reform of the Gas Balancing Regime, Next Steps*, London: Ofgem.

Ofgem (2003b), *The January 2003 Long-Term System Entry Capacity Auctions*, a review document, London: Ofgem.

Ofgem (2003c), *Summer Interruptions 17 and 18 June 2003, Conclusions,* London: Ofgem.

Ofgem (2003d), *Extended Long-term System Entry Capacity Auctions at New Entry Points*, London: Ofgem.

Ofgem (2002), *Ofgem's Response to the Government's Consultation on Energy Policy*, London: Ofgem.

Ofgem (2001a), *Dynegy Inc.'s Proposed Acquisition of BG Storage Ltd.* – a consultation document, London: Ofgem.

Ofgem (2001b), *The New Gas Trading Arrangments: Review of Transco's Exit Capacity, Interruption and Liquefied Natural Gas Arrangements*, a consultation document, London: Ofgem.

Ofgem (2001c), *Review of Transco's Price Control from 2002*, final proposals, London: Ofgem.

Ofgem (2000a), *A Review of the Development of Competition in the Gas Storage Market*, London: Ofgem.

Ofgem (2000b), *Long-Term Signals and Incentives for Investment in Transmission Capacity on Transco's National Transmission System, Conclusions on the Framework*, London: Ofgem.

Office of Trade & Economic Development, Washington State (2001*), Convergence: Natural Gas and Electricity in Washington, a Survey of the Pacific Northwest Natural Gas Industry on the Eve of a New Era in Electric Generation*, http://www.cted.wa.gov/energy/archive/Papers/Convergence.doc.

Oil and Gas Journal (weekly), Tulsa, Oklahoma, various issues.

Oil and Gas Producers International Association (OGP) (2003), *OGP Note on the Discussion on "Production Flexibility" in the Context of Third-party access Provisions*, August 21, 2003, http://www.ogp.org.uk/.

Overview Conferences, Various presentations at the European Autumn Gas Conference, November 17-19, 2003, Prague.

Performance and Innovation Unit (PIU) (2002), *The Energy Review*, Cabinet Office, London.

Petroleum Economist (monthly), London, various issues.

Petrostrategies (weekly), Paris, various issues.

Platts International Gas Report (fortnightly), Wimbledon, various issues.

Rogers D.R., *Gas Interchangeability and its Effects on US Import Plans*, Pipeline & Gas Journal, August 2003.

Stern J. (2003), *UK Gas Security: Time to Get Serious*, Oxford Institute for Energy Studies, Oxford.

Stern J. (2002), *Security of European Natural Gas Supplies: The Impact of Import Dependence and Liberalisation*, Royal Institute of International Affairs, July 2002, London.

Ter-Sarkissov R. (2004), *The Current State and Perspectives of Russian Gas Industry*, a presentation at the UN/ECE Working Party on gas, January 20-21, 2004, Geneva.

United Nations Economic Commission for Europe (UN/ECE) (2003), *Report on Security of Natural Gas Supply in the European Part of the UN/ECE Area*, UN/ECE Gas Centre, September 2003, Geneva.

United States General Accounting Office (2002), *Natural Gas – Analysis of Changes in Market Price*, GAO-03-46, report to Congressional Committees and Members of Congress, Washington.

Valais M., TotalFinaElf, Chabrelie M.F., Cedigaz, Lefeuvre T., Gaz de France (2001), *World LNG Prospects: Favourable Parameters for a New Growth Era,* presentation to the 18th World Energy Congress, October 21-25, 2001, Buenos Aires.

Weems P., Tonery L., Keenan K., King & Spalding LLP (2003), *US LNG Terminals: Taking Advantage of a More Friendly Regulatory Environment,* LNG Journal, July/August 2003.

World Gas Intelligence (weekly), New York, various issues.

World Markets Research Centre (Daily News), various issues.

Wybrew J (2002), presentation at the IEA high-level conference on security of gas supply, Paris, 23 October 2002 (unpublished).

The Online Bookshop

IEA PUBLICATIONS, 9, rue de la Fédération, 75739 PARIS CEDEX 15
Pre-press LINÉALE PRODUCTION
Printed in France by CHIRAT
(61 2004 24 1P1) ISBN 92-64-10806-8 – June 2004